Collins

Maths Matters 6

Series Editor
Mona Jhunjhunwala

Published by Collins India
A division of HarperCollins*Publishers* India Limited
HarperCollins *Publishers*
A-75, Sector 57, Noida, Uttar Pradesh 201301, India
1 London Bridge Street, London SE1 9GF, United Kingdom
Hazelton Lanes, 55 Avenue Road, Suite 2900, Toronto, Ontario M5R 3L2
and 1995 Markham Road, Scarborough, Ontario M1B 5M8, Canada
25 Ryde Road, Pymble, Sydney, NSW 2073, Australia
195 Broadway, New York, NY 10007, USA

Browse the complete Collins catalogue at **www.collins.in**

First published in 2016

ISBN: 978-93-5136-890-8

Content developed by **ExcelSoft Technologies Pvt. Ltd.**

Artwork and layout by **Mukesh Technologies Pvt. Ltd.**

Printed and bound by **Gopsons Papers Ltd.**

Acknowledgements

Cover: VictoriaBar, iStockphoto

Title Page: VictoriaBar, iStockphoto

Preface

Maths Matters is a series of eight books for Classes 1 to 8. The primary school series follows a universal approach whereas the middle school series is based on the syllabus prescribed by the Inter-State Board for Anglo-Indian Education.

Maths Matters focuses on developing thinking and reasoning skills in students. It enables students to comprehend the application of mathematics in real life. In addition, the coherent and structured approach is valuable for teachers as it helps the lesson flow from one level to the next. Sufficient number of solved examples, exercises and mental maths questions are provided to ensure a holistic grasp of the mathematical thought processes.

Some Key Features

Let's Get Started to revise the concepts learnt earlier

Mental Maths to sharpen the calculation skills and logical reasoning

Hints and Tips for better conceptual understanding

Try These to test student's understanding of the topic covered

Note brings the focus to certain important points

Remember to highlight key points of the concept discussed

Exercise to revise the topics just learnt

Revision Exercise for a well-integrated review of the concepts covered in a chapter

For the Curious Mind to encourage students to think beyond the textual knowledge

Worksheet to reinforce practice with fun exercise

Project to extend the concept learnt to real–life applications

We would like to take this opportunity to thank all the teachers who reviewed the books and provided their valuable feedback which helped in improving the quality of the content.

Any suggestions or constructive criticism from the users are welcome. We shall try to incorporate those in the future editions.

Authors

Key Features

Let's Get Started

To revise the concepts learnt earlier

Let's Get Started

What comes to your mind when you hear
How often do you come across numbers

Numbers are not only used to count, b
measure and label. For example, num

Mental Maths

Brings the focus to certain important points
To hone the calculation skills and logical reasoning.

Mental Maths

1. If you multiply a number by 3 and subtract 5 from it, you will get 10. Find the number.
2. If you multiply a number by 6 and add 13 to it, you will get 85. Find the number.

Try These!

To test student's understanding of the concept

Try These!

3 × 2 = ____
5 × 2 = ____
7 × 2 = ____
9 × 2 = ____

Note

To bring the focus to certain important points

Note

Bigger objects may not necessarily be heavier than smaller objects.
A lock is heavier than a pencil box

Hints and Tips

To provide hints and tips for better understanding of the concept

Hints and Tips

Distinguish between the terms Cost Price and Actual Cost. Always remember that if overhead expenses are mentioned in the question, then Actual cost = CP + Overhead expenses.

Remember

To highlight key points of the concept discussed

Remember

When we subtract 0 from a number, the value of the number remains the same; it does not decrease.

12345 – 0 = 12345
56789 – 0 = 56789

Exercises

To revise the concepts just learnt

Exercise 9.2

1. A lamp costs ₹835 and a book costs ₹ cost?

	H	T	O
Lamp costs			
Book costs			

   Thus, both the things cost ₹ ______.
2. Ram has ₹750. Shyam has ₹525. How have than Shyam?
   Ram has ₹ ______.
   Shyam has ₹ ______.
   Thus, Ram has ₹ ______ mo

Revision Exercise

At the end of each chapter for a comprehensive review of the concepts

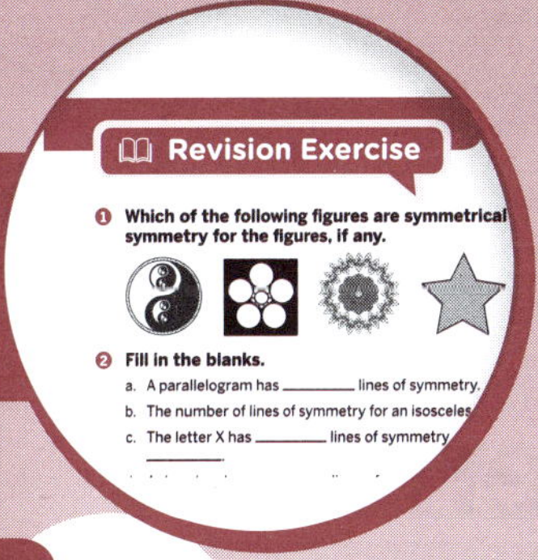

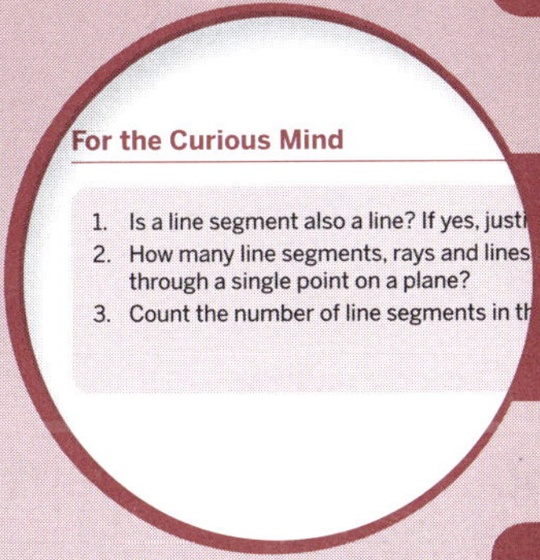

For the Curious Mind

To encourage students to think beyond the textual knowledge

Worksheet

To reinforce practice with fun exercise

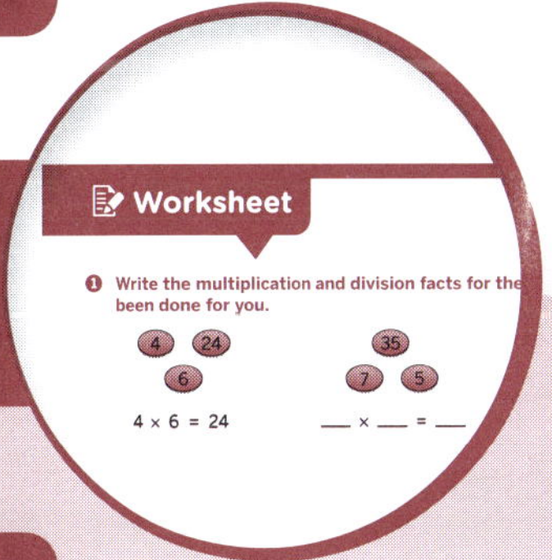

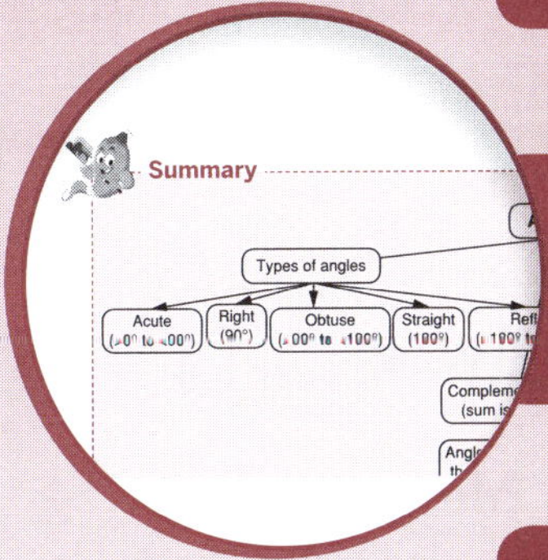

Summary

To provide the gist of the chapter for quick revision

Project

To extend the concept learnt to real-life applications

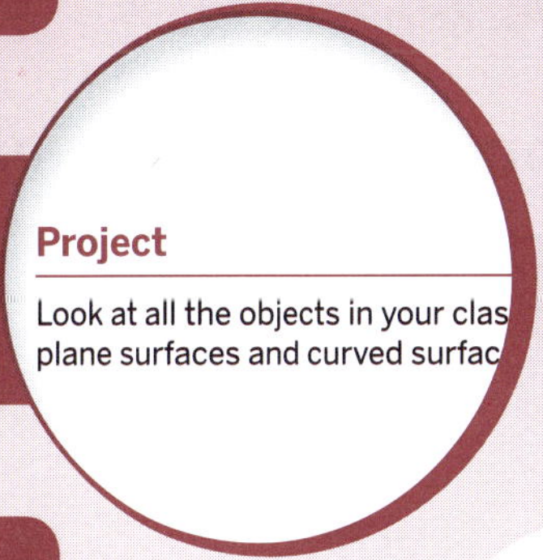

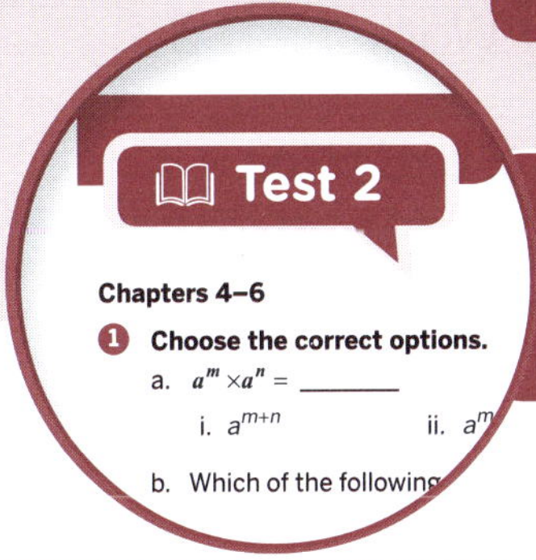

Test Paper

To provide more practice after every few chapters

Collins DigiSuite is an innovative digital solution for teachers. It contains four modules delivering classroom content that can be used to effectively integrate the teaching and evaluation tools with the coursebooks.

The **E-book** includes animations, interactive exercises and worksheets. The E-book reader also includes interactive teaching tools like pen tool, text highlighter, page zoom, search and bookmark.

The **Test Generator** is a question bank with a variety of questions for effective evaluation. It is an easy-to-use assessment tool for the teachers to create test papers and worksheets.

The **Teacher's Resource** consists of lesson plans, answer keys and teaching techniques for the teachers.

This module has a PDF of the **Collins dictionary** appropriate for each level with all the words and definitions one needs.

Contents

UNIT 1

Introduction to Number System 1

Let's Get Started

What I shall learn

- To understand natural numbers, whole numbers and representation of whole numbers on the number line
- To study about the Indian place value system and the international place value system

The contribution of Indian mathematicians to the world of numbers is noteworthy. Some of the notable mathematicians of India are Aryabhata, who introduced the number 0 (zero), Brahmagupta and Ramanujan.

Let us recall some of the basic terminologies related to numbers.

Aryabhata

Ramanujan

Unit

A 'unit' or 'unity' means a single quantity. When a number is written with unit, it means that the unit quantity is taken that many times. Thus, a book, a toffee, a table—all of these represent unit quantities.

In 2 kilometres, kilometre represents unit distance (1 kilometre) and 2 implies that the unit distance is taken 2 times (i.e. 2×1 kilometre).

Digits

The ten basic symbols, 0, 1, 2, 3, 4, 5, 6, 7, 8 and 9, used to represent numbers are known as digits. They are similar to the letters of the English alphabets or the basic letters of your mother tongue.

Note

All numbers are formed using digits just as all words are formed using letters.

Number

A number is a value in mathematics used for measuring or counting a certain quantity. Numbers are represented using the combination of digits from 0 to 9.

A number written in figures is called a numeral.

Numeration

It refers to the numbers being written in words.

> **Note**
>
> A set is a collection of well-defined objects. You will learn more about sets later in this book.

Natural Numbers

The numbers that we use in counting, that is, 1, 2, 3, ... are called natural numbers. The smallest natural number is 1. There are infinite natural numbers, that is, we cannot find the greatest natural number. We denote the set of natural numbers by N.

N = {1, 2, 3, 4, 5, 6, ...}

> **Note**
>
> The words 'nought', 'nil', 'nothing' and 'cipher' denote the same meaning as zero.

The Number Zero (0)

Aryabhata was the first mathematician to use the concept of zero. Zero refers to the absence of a quantity. For example, in a cricket match, if a batsman is out without scoring any runs, then we say that the batsman has made zero runs.

Whole Numbers

The set of natural numbers along with zero forms the set of whole numbers. The smallest whole number is 0. There are infinite whole numbers. We represent the set of whole numbers by W.

W = {0, 1, 2, 3, 4, 5, ...}

Representing Whole Numbers on the Number Line

Number line: It is a line marked with numbers. The numbers are marked with equal distances between them. The arrow heads indicate that the numbers continue up to infinity in that direction.

To represent whole numbers on a number line, we follow the given steps.

1. Draw a straight line and mark a point O on it as shown in the figure below.
2. Mark another point A to the right of O. The distance between O and A denotes one unit.
3. Now mark more points to the right of A at every unit distance. Label these points as B, C, D, E, ...
4. Write 0 below point O. Similarly, write 1, 2, 3, 4, ... below the points A, B, C, D, ... respectively.

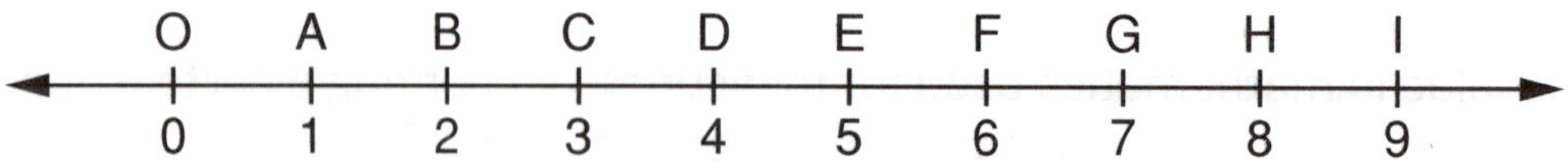

Even and Odd Numbers

Even numbers are numbers that are exactly divisible by 2. Even numbers end with the digits 0, 2, 4, 6 and 8. The number 0 is not an even number. The smallest even number is 2. The difference between two consecutive (immediately one after the other) even numbers is 2.

Examples: 2, 4, 6, 8, 10, 12, 14, ...

Odd numbers are numbers that are not exactly divisible by 2. 1 is the smallest odd number. The difference between 2 consecutive odd numbers is 2.

Examples: 1, 3, 5, 7, 9, 11, 13, ...

Integers

There are numbers less than zero, which are called **negative numbers**.

Examples: −1, −2, −3, −4, −5, ...

Negative numbers are the opposite of positive numbers (1, 2, 3, ...).

Whole numbers and a negative numbers are together known as **integers**. We represent the set of integers by Z or I.

Z or I = {..., −3, −2, −1, 0, 1, 2, 3, ...}

You will learn more about integers in the next chapter.

Note

Zero is neither a negative nor a positive integer.

Remember

The distance between any two consecutive points on the number line (for whole numbers) is equal to one unit.

The Hindu-Arabic System of Numeration

This is the most widely used system of numeration in the world. This system is also known as the base-10 system. The main features of this system are given below.

1. A combination of the 10 digits 0, 1, 2, 3, 4, 5, 6, 7, 8 and 9 is used to represent a number.
2. Numbers are grouped into ones (units), tens, hundreds, thousands and so on.
3. The concept of place value is used to represent a number. The digits of a number are grouped into periods. We use commas to separate periods. The value of each digit depends on its place in the period. Thus, we have the ones, thousands, lakhs, crores and arabs periods.

Successors and Predecessors

The successor of a number is the number that is 1 more than the given number.

For example, the successor of 5 is 5 + 1 = 6 and the successor of 12452 is 12452 + 1 = 12453.

The predecessor of a number is the number that is 1 less than the given number.

For example, the predecessor of 9 is 9 − 1 = 8 and the predecessor of 98563 is 98563 − 1 = 98562.

Try These!

Write the successor and predecessor of each of the following numbers.

a. 53,201 b. 24,389 c. 9999

Place Value and Face Value

The face value of a digit in a number is the digit itself irrespective of its position.

Place value of a digit = Face value of the digit × Value of its place

Note

The place value and the face value of the digit 0 is always 0 irrespective of its position.

Example 1: Find the place value and face value of 7 in the number 97,40,177.

Try These!

Find the face value and the place value of all the other digits in 637 and 80,509.

97,40,177		
Place	**Face Value**	**Place Value**
Ones	7	7
Tens	7	70
Lakh	7	7,00,000

Indian Place Value System

In the Indian place value system, the places are ones, tens, hundreds, thousands, ten thousands, lakhs, ten lakhs, etc.

The first three places from the right (ones, tens and hundreds) are grouped into one category called 'Ones period'. Then, as we move to the left from the ones period, every two places are grouped to form different periods. The following table gives the details of the periods and their place values.

Indian Place Value Chart									
Periods	**Crores**		**Lakhs**		**Thousands**		**Ones**		
Places	Ten Crores	Crores	Ten Lakhs	Lakhs	Ten Thousands	Thousands	Hundreds	Tens	Ones
Numbers	10,00,00,000	1,00,00,000	10,00,000	1,00,000	10,000	1000	100	10	1

Commas are used after each period while writing a number. This helps us to read the numbers easily and to understand the place value of each digit of the number. The table given below shows the short forms for different places (O for ones, T for tens, H for hundreds, Th for thousands, TTh for ten thousands, L for lakhs, TL for ten lakhs, C for crores and TC for ten crores).

Indian Place Value Chart									Number	Name
Crores		**Lakhs**		**Thousands**		**Ones**				
TC	**C**	**TL**	**L**	**TTh**	**Th**	**H**	**T**	**O**		
			1	3	7	5	0	6	1,37,506	One lakh thirty-seven thousand five hundred six
		5	2	0	5	3	9	8	52,05,398	Fifty-two lakh five thousand three hundred ninety-eight
6	6	1	8	7	3	0	0	2	66,18,73,002	Sixty-six crore eighteen lakh seventy-three thousand two

Expanded Form

The expanded form of a number is a way of representation where the number is expressed as the sum of the place values of its digits.

> **Note**
>
> A number never starts with zero. For example, we never write two hundred thirty-five as 0235 or 00235. We always write it as 235.

Example 2: Insert commas to rewrite 7523864 as per the Indian place value system. Also write the number in words and in its expanded form.

75,23,864

In words: Seventy-five lakh twenty-three thousand eight hundred sixty-four

Expanded form: 70,00,000 + 5,00,000 + 20,000 + 3000 + 800 + 60 + 4

Example 3: Write the number corresponding to ninety-four crore seventy-three lakh two thousand nine hundred one. Also, write the number in its expanded form.

Number: 94,73,02,901

Expanded form: 90,00,00,000 + 4,00,00,000 + 70,00,000 + 3,00,000 + 2000 + 900 + 1

International Place Value System

The international place value system of writing and reading numbers is widely used across the world. In this system, the places are ones, tens, hundreds, thousands, ten thousands, hundred thousands, millions, ten millions, hundred millions, etc. Also, every three places are grouped into one period. The following table gives the details of the periods and their place values.

Billions	Millions			Thousands			Hundreds		
Billions	Hundred Millions	Ten Millions	Millions	Hundred Thousands	Ten Thousands	Thousands	Hundreds	Tens	Ones
1,000,000,000	100,000,000	10,000,000	1,000,000	100,000	10,000	1000	100	10	1

> **Remember**
>
> The largest 5-digit number is 99,999.
>
> On adding 1 to it, we get the smallest 6-digit number 1,00,000.
>
> The largest 6-digit number is 9,99,999.
>
> Similarly, we can find the largest and the smallest 7-digit numbers, 8-digit numbers, 9-digit numbers and so on.

Let us consider the examples given in the following table.

Number	Use of Commas	Number Name
65321	65,321	Sixty-five thousand three hundred twenty-one
803640	803,640	Eight hundred three thousand six hundred forty
9538542	9,538,542	Nine million five hundred thirty-eight thousand five hundred forty-two
81256307	81,256,307	Eighty-one million two hundred fifty-six thousand three hundred seven

Try These!

Write the number corresponding to fifty-six million forty-five.

Expanded Form

Example 4: Write the expanded form of the following numbers using the place value of the digits.

a. 6,422,891 = 6,000,000 + 400,000 + 20,000 + 2000 + 800 + 90 + 1

b. 60,240,012 = 60,000,000 + 200,000 + 40,000 + 10 + 2

Exercise 1.1

1 Write the predecessor and successor of each of the following numbers.

a. 2 b. 24,530 c. 78,90,214 d. 85,12,046

2 Write the number names of the following numbers in both Indian and international place value systems.

a. 135204 b. 9052020 c. 52147683 d. 50412565
e. 25386125 f. 50263050 g. 52010509 h. 24502012

3 Write the place value and face value of the underlined digits in each number. Also, write the numbers in the expanded form.

a. 57,495,702 b. 75,50,293 c. 140,849,021 d. 75,95,008
e. 17,003,004 f. 23,45,892 g. 6,80,36,203 h. 2,35,67,890

4 Write the numbers corresponding to the following number names in the Indian place value system.

a. Twenty-three crore seventy lakh forty thousand two hundred five
b. Nine crore one lakh thirty-three thousand eight hundred seven
c. Ninety-nine lakh forty-one thousand five hundred ninety
d. Sixty-seven lakh four

5 Write the numbers corresponding to the following in the international place value system.

a. Twenty-three crore seventy lakh fifty thousand two hundred five
b. Thirty-four million seven hundred thousand six
c. Five million four

Comparison of Numbers

Recall the symbols used for comparing numbers.

Symbol	Meaning
>	Greater than
<	Less than
=	Equal to

Rule 1: Compare the number of digits in both the numbers. If the number of digits is not equal, then the number with more digits is bigger than the other number.

For example, 30,245,879 > 9,856,784.

Rule 2: If the number of digits in both the numbers is equal, then start comparing the digits starting from the extreme left.

For example, consider the numbers 9,09,15,327 and 8,97,65,379. Both the numbers have 8 digits. So, we start comparing the digits at the extreme left that is, we compare the digits at the crores place.

9 > 8

C	TL	L	T Th	Th	H	T	O
9	0	9	1	5	3	2	7
8	9	7	6	5	3	7	9

We see that the digit at the crores place in 9,09,15,327 is greater than that in 8,97,65,379.

Therefore, 90,915,327 > 89,765,379.

But what if the digits at the leftmost place are same in both the numbers?

In such a case, we compare the digits on the immediate right of the leftmost digits. We continue this process till we find two unequal digits at the corresponding places.

Ordering of Numbers

Ascending order: The order in which numbers are arranged from the smallest to the largest is called ascending order or increasing order.

Descending order: The order in which numbers are arranged from the largest to the smallest is called descending or decreasing order.

Example 5: Arrange the following numbers in ascending order.

7862578 9009852 8521456 9109999 7872599

First, let us insert commas in the numbers according to the Indian system of numeration.

78,62,578 90,09,852 85,21,456 91,09,999 78,72,599

Now, on arranging the numbers in ascending order, we get

78,62,578 < 78,72,599 < 85,21,456 < 90,09,852 < 91,09,999

Example 6: Arrange the following numbers in descending order.

99999999 80009980 52056800 75600985 5007990

First, let us insert commas in the numbers according to the Indian system of numeration.

9,99,99,999 8,00,09,980 5,20,56,800 7,56,00,985 50,07,990

Now, on arranging the numbers in descending order, we get

9,99,99,999 > 8,00,09,980 > 7,56,00,985 > 5,20,56,800 > 50,07,990

Exercise 1.2

1 Compare the following numbers and fill in the blanks with > or <.

a. 12568958 ________ 12560998
b. 99999999 ________ 999999990
c. 895674269 ________ 900505801
d. 100000001 ________ 20000002
e. 456123001 ________ 456321001
f. 235782468 ________ 235784268
g. 724005789 ________ 7245030678
h. 98765421 ________ 123456789

2. **Arrange the following numbers in ascending order**
   a. 4345608, 3350720, 21007891, 3052608, 724562187
   b. 2000123, 20607812, 10200123, 204500123, 9999901, 1112222
   c. 120430156, 120102141, 230156701, 102067891, 1243015
   d. 700502369, 10024005, 790505100, 1000245, 705223690, 78045123
3. **Arrange the following numbers in descending order.**
   a. 1205679, 7856824, 5067891, 5026078, 1262187
   b. 81110203, 20104712, 28902823, 20450023, 20801503, 22102183
   c. 701301145, 701301102, 701306002, 701301145, 701301142
   d. 310102301, 312502024, 43551012, 25020245, 31251236, 31278451

Formation of Numbers

Let us learn how to form numbers using the given digits.

Example 7: What is the smallest 8-digit number that can be formed using the digits 2, 5, 1, 6, 0, 8, 4 and 7 only once?

The smallest 8-digit number formed using all the digits 2, 5, 1, 6, 0, 8, 4 and 7 only once can be obtained by writing the digits in ascending order.

0	1	2	4	5	6	7	8

With 0 at the beginning, the number obtained is not an 8-digit number. So, interchange the positions of 0 and 1.

The required number is 10245678.

1	0	2	4	5	6	7	8

Example 8: What is the greatest 9-digit number that can be formed using the digits 0, 1, 5, 4, 3, 2, 9, 8 and 7 only once?

To find the greatest number, we arrange the given digits in descending order.

Therefore, the required number is 987543210.

Exercise 1.3

1. **Find the greatest and the smallest 6-digit numbers that can be formed using each of the following digits only once.**
   a. 7, 3, 5, 1, 2, 6   b. 3, 4, 5, 0, 9, 8
2. Find the greatest and the smallest 7-digit number that can be formed using the digits 3, 2, 6, 0, 7, 1 and 9 only once.
3. Find the greatest and the smallest 8-digit number that can be formed using the digits 8, 0, 6, 3, 5, 2, 9 and 4 only once.
4. How many 3-digit numbers can be formed using the digits 8, 3 and 0 only once? List them.

Properties of Whole Numbers Under Addition

You are familiar with the four basic operations (addition, subtraction, multiplication and division) on whole numbers. Let us now learn the properties of these operations on whole numbers.

Look at the following table showing the properties of the whole numbers under addition.Fill in the blanks where required.

Closure Property	a	b	$a + b$	Is $a + b$ a whole number?	Observation
	5	4	$5 + 4 = 9$	Yes	If a and b are any two whole numbers, then $(a + b)$ is also a whole number.
	4052	0	$4052 + 0 = 4052$	______	
	98,523	752	______	______	

Commutative Property	a	b	$a + b$	$b + a$	Is $a + b = b + a$?	Observation
	8	5	$8 + 5 = 13$	$5 + 8 = 13$	Yes	If a and b are any two whole numbers, then $a + b = b + a$.
	0	78,025	______	______	______	
	98,75,012	1,00,250	______	______	______	

Additive Identity	a	$a + 0$	$0 + a$	Is $a + 0 = 0 + a = a$?	Observation
	5	5	5	Yes	If a is any whole number, then $a + 0 = 0 + a = a$. 0 is the additive identity of whole numbers.
	452	______	______	______	
	8,723	______	______	______	

Associative Property	a, b, c	$(a + b) + c$	$a + (b + c)$	Is $(a + b) + c = a + (b + c)$?	Observation
	1, 3, 5	$(1 + 3) + 5 = 4 + 5 = 9$	$1 + (3 + 5) = 1 + 8 = 9$	Yes	If a, b and c are any three whole numbers, then $(a + b) + c = a + (b + c)$.
	0, 5, 9	______	______	______	
	3, 0, 8	______	______	______	

Example 9: Add the following numbers by suitably arranging them.

101, 102, 103, 104, 105, 106, 107, 108 and 109

(101 + 109) + (102 + 108) + (103 + 107) + (104 + 106) + 105

= 210 + 210 + 210 + 210 + 105 = 840 + 105 = 945

Example 10: Verify the following and name the property satisfied.

a. 7077 + 1023 = 1023 + 7077

LHS	RHS
7077 + 1023 = 8100	1023 + 7077 = 8100

LHS = RHS and the property satisfied is the commutative property of addition.

b. (3657 + 3043) + 980 = 3657 + (3043 + 980)

LHS	RHS
(3657 + 3043) + 980	3657 + (3043 + 980)
= 6700 + 980	= 3657 + 4023
= 7680	= 7680

LHS = RHS and the property satisfied is associative property.

Properties of Whole Numbers Under Subtraction

Look at the following table showing the properties of the whole numbers under subtraction. Fill in the blanks where required.

Closure Property	a	b	$a - b$	Is $a - b$ a whole number?	Observation
	5	4	$5 - 4 = 9$	Yes	$(a - b)$ is a whole number if $a > b$ and $(a - b)$ is not a whole number if $b > a$. The difference $(a - b)$ may or may not be a whole number.
	4	5	$4 - 5 = -1$	No	
	98,523	99,752	______	______	Conclusion: Closure property does not hold true for subtraction.

Commutative Property	a	b	$a - b$	$b - a$	Is $a - b = b - a$?	Observation
	5	4	$5 - 4 = 1$	$4 - 5 = -1$	No	If a and b are any two unequal whole numbers, then $a - b \neq b - a$.
	0	708	______	______	______	Conclusion: Commutative property does not hold true for subtraction.

Subtraction Property of 0	a	$a - 0 = a$	$0 - a = -a$	Observation
	5	$5 - 0 = 5$	$0 - 5 = -5$	If a is any whole number, then $a - 0 = a$, but $0 - a$ is not a whole number.
	801	______	______	

Associative Property	a, b, c	$(a - b) - c$	$a - (b - c)$	Is $(a - b) - c = a - (b - c)$?	Observation
	7, 0, 5	$(7 - 0) - 5 = 7 - 5 = 2$	$7 - (0 - 5)$ $= 7 - (-5)$ $= 7 + 5 = 12$	No	If a, b and c are three unequal whole numbers, then $(a - b) - c \neq a - (b - c)$.
	8, 5, 2	______	______	______	Conclusion: Associative property does not hold true for subtraction.
	6, 1, 0	______	______	______	

Exercise 1.4

1 **Complete the following.**

a. 6107 + 3049 = ________ + 6107

b. 7021 + ________ = 90333 + 7021

c. 48026 + ________ = 48026

d. 6031 + 0 = ________

2 **Verify the following.**

a. 72091 + 30054 = 30054 + 72091

b. 43001 + 362 = 362 + 43001

c. 3003 + (80251 + 6007) = (3003 + 6007) + 80251

d. (50106 + 4084) + 33707 = 50106 + (4084 + 33707)

3 **Verify the associative property under subtraction for each of the following groups of whole numbers.**

a. 25, 8, 0 b. 45, 8, 21 c. 317, 312, 50 d. 87, 082, 2018

Properties of Whole Numbers Under Multiplication and Division

Now let us try to understand the properties of whole numbers under the operations of multiplication and division.

Look at the following table showing the properties of the whole numbers under multiplication and division. Fill in the blanks where required.

Closure Property	a	b	a × b	Is a × b a whole number?	Observation
	15	2	15 × 2 = 30	Yes	If *a* and *b* are any two whole numbers, then (*a* × *b*) is also a whole number.
	0	1,45,201	______	______	
	12,405	2	______	______	
	a	**b**	**a ÷ b**	**Is a ÷ b a whole number?**	If *a* and *b* are any two non-zero whole numbers, then *a* ÷ *b* is not always a whole number.
	50	2	50 ÷ 2 = 25	Yes	
	0	201	0 ÷ 201 = 0	Yes	
	3	2	$3 \div 2 = \frac{3}{2}$	no	Conclusion: Closure property is true for multiplication but it does not hold true for division.

Commutative Property	a	b	a × b	b × a	Is a × b = b × a?	Observation
Under multiplication	15	4	15 × 4 = 60	4 × 15 = 60	Yes	If *a* and *b* are any two whole numbers, then *a* × *b* = *b* × *a*.
	0	4821	______	______	______	If *a* and *b* are any two non-zero unequal whole numbers, then *a* ÷ *b* ≠ *b* ÷ *a*.
	785	5	______	______	______	
	a	**b**	**a ÷ b**	**b ÷ a**	**Is a ÷ b = b ÷ a ?**	
Under division	15	3	15 ÷ 3 =5	$3 \div 15 = \frac{1}{3}$	No	Conclusion: Commutative property is true for multiplication but it does not hold true for division.
	0	4821	0 ÷ 4821 = 0	4821 ÷ 0 is undefined	No	
	785	5	______	______	______	

Multiplicative Identity	a	a × 1	1 × a	Is a × 1 = 1 × a = a?	Observation
	5	5 × 1 = 5	1 × 5 = 5	Yes	If *a* is any whole number, then *a* × 1 = 1 × *a* = *a*. 1 is the multiplicative identity of whole numbers.
	452	______	______	______	
	8723	______	______	______	

Associative Property	a, b, c	(a × b) × c	a × (b × c)	Is (a × b) × c = a × (b × c)?	Observation
Under multiplication	2, 3, 5	(2 × 3) × 5 = 6 × 5 = 30	2 × (3 × 5) = 2 × 15 = 30	Yes	If *a*, *b* and *c* are any three whole numbers, then (a × b) × c = a × (b × c).
	0, 5, 9	______	______	______	If *a*, *b* and *c* are any three unequal whole numbers, then (a ÷ b) ÷ c ≠ a ÷ (b ÷ c).
	3, 0, 8	______	______	______	
	a, b, c	**(a ÷ b) ÷ c**	**a ÷ (b ÷ c)**	**Is (a ÷ b) ÷ c = a ÷ (b ÷ c)?**	
Under division	24, 6, 3	(24 ÷ 6) ÷ 3 = 4 ÷ 3 = $\frac{4}{3}$	24 ÷ (6 ÷ 3) = 24 ÷ 2 = 12	No	Conclusion: Associative property is true for multiplication but it does not hold true for division.
	16, 8, 2	______	______	______	
	6, 1, 2	______	______	______	

Distributive Law of Multiplication Over Addition

Complete the table given below.

a, b, c	a × (b + c)	(a × b) + (a × c)	Is a × (b + c) = (a × b) + (a × c)?
2, 4, 3	2 × (4 + 3) = 2 × 7 = 14	(2 × 4) + (2 × 3) = 8 + 6 = 14	Yes
5, 8, 7	______	______	______
12, 18, 20	______	______	______

If a, b and c are any three whole numbers, then a × (b + c) = (a × b) + (a × c).

Distributive Law of Multiplication Over Subtraction

Example 11: Complete the table given below.

a, b, c	a × (b − c)	(a × b) − (a × c)	Is a × (b − c) = (a × b) − (a × c)?
18, 12, 0	18 × (12 − 0) = 18 × 12 = 216	(18 × 12) − (18 × 0) = 216 − 0 = 216	Yes
13, 8, 5	______	______	______
120, 15, 14	______	______	______

If a, b and c are any three whole numbers, then a × (b + c) = (a × b) + (a × c).

Special Properties

1. If a is a whole number, then $a \times 0 = 0$.

Examples: $15 \times 0 = 0$; $234 \times 0 = 0$

2. If a is a non-zero whole number, then $0 \div a = 0$.

Examples: $0 \div 1505 = 0$; $0 \div 30501203 = 0$;

3. If a is a whole number, then $a \div 0$ is not defined.

Example: $4520150 \div 0$ = Not defined

4. If a is any whole number, then $a \div 1 = a$.

Examples: $110502 \div 1 = 110502$;
$50005 \div 1 = 50005$

Example 12: Find the product by suitably arranging the numbers.

a. $50 \times 204 \times 20$

$(50 \times 20) \times 204 = 1000 \times 204 = 204000$

b. $375 \times 24 - 375 \times 4$

$375\ (24 - 4) = 375 \times 20 = 7500$

Example 13: Find the product using distributive laws.

a. 90702×102

By the distributive law of addition,

$$90702\ (100 + 2) = 90702 \times 100 + 90702 \times 2$$
$$= 9070200 + 181404$$
$$= 9251604$$

b. 308002×97

By the distributive law of subtraction,

$$308002\ (100 - 3) = 308002 \times 100 - 308002 \times 3$$
$$= 30800200 - 924006$$
$$= 29876194$$

Division Algorithm

Dividend = (Divisor × Quotient) + Remainder

On dividing 601 by 18, we get 33 as the quotient and 7 as the remainder.

$\therefore$ $601 = (18 \times 33) + 7$

If a and b are two whole numbers such that $a > b$, and if a is divided by b, then $a = bq + r$, where q is the quotient and r is the remainder, where $0 \leq r < b$. This result is known as **division algorithm**.

Example 14: Find the number which when divided by 43 gives 103 as the quotient and 5 as the remainder.

Given: Divisor = 43, Quotient = 103, Remainder = 5

By division algorithm,

Dividend = (Divisor × Quotient) + Remainder
$= (43 \times 103) + 5 = 4429 + 5 = 4434$

Therefore, the number is 4434.

Think and Discuss

Do all these properties also hold true for natural numbers?

Exercise 1.5

1. **Complete the following statements.**

   a. $604 \times 3081 = 3081 \times$ ______
   b. $70704 \times$ ______ $= 0$
   c. $673 \times$ ______ $= 673$
   d. $4090 \times (806 \times 31) =$ ______ $\times (4090 \times 31)$
   e. $802 \times 205 + 802 \times 705 = 802 \times ($ ______ $+$ ______ $)$

2. **State the property in each of the following.**

   a. $20340 \times 10030 = 10030 \times 20340$
   b. $302 \times (604 \times 7090) = (302 \times 604) \times 7090$
   c. $701080 \times 0 = 0$
   d. $90200 \times 1 = 90200$

3. **Find the products by suitably arranging the numbers.**

   a. $400 \times 2037 \times 2005$
   b. $2000 \times 4305 \times 5005$
   c. $5000 \times 10042 \times 1004$
   d. $40004 \times 2009 \times 2025$
   e. $25 \times 6025 \times 120 \times 80$
   f. $400 \times 500 \times 1025 \times 800$

4. **Solve the following.**

   a. $1846125 \div 45$
   b. $23577392 \div 23$
   c. $161375832 \div 18$
   d. $19408519 \div 19$

5. **Find the quotient and the remainder by actual division and check the answer by division algorithm.**

   a. $60742 \div 23$
   b. $500505 \div 101$
   c. $701773 \div 300$
   d. $890422 \div 312$
   e. $5570624 \div 571$
   f. $8840422 \div 230$

6. The product of two numbers is 1,41,705. If one of the numbers is 705, find the other.

7. **Find the missing term in the following using the division algorithm.**

   a. $459 = ($ ______ $\times 38) + 3$
   b. ______ $= (22 \times 305) + 18$
   c. $33333 = (22 \times 1515) +$ ______
   d. $424284 = (42 \times$ ______ $) + 0$

Roman Numerals

Roman number system is one of the ancient systems of writing numerals. In this system, seven symbols I, V, X, L, C, D and M are used to represent any number. The basic seven symbols and their values in Hindu-Arabic system are given in the table below. Remember that there is no 0 in Roman numerals.

Symbol	Value in Hindu-Arabic Number System
I	1
V	5
X	10
L	50
C	100
D	500
M	1000

Let us recall some of the rules that we discussed in the previous classes.

Rule 1: If a symbol is repeated, then its value is added as many times as it occurs. However, a symbol can be repeated only three times, not more than that. The symbols V, L and D are never repeated.

For example II = 2 and XX = 20, but we cannot write LL.

Rule 2: If a smaller number is written to the left of a bigger number, then it has to be subtracted from the bigger number. The symbol 'I' can only be written to the left of V and X. Also, V, L and D are never written to the left of a bigger number. The symbol X can be subtracted from L and C only. Similarly, C can be subtracted from D and M only.

For example, IV = 5 – 1 = 4 and XL = 50 – 10 = 40. But, we cannot write VX, IL and DM.

Rule 3: If a smaller number is written to the right of a bigger number, then it has to be added to the bigger number.

For example, XI = 10 + 1 = 11 and LV = 50 + 5 = 55.

Rule 4: If a smaller number is written in between two greater values, then it is subtracted from the greater number that follows it immediately.

For example, XXIV = 10 + 10 + (5 – 1) = 20 + 4 = 24 and MCIX = 1000 + 100 + (10 – 1) = 1109.

Example 15: Write the Roman numerals corresponding to the following Hindu-Arabic numbers.

a. 654 = 600 + 50 + 4 = 500 + 100 + 50 + (5 – 1) = DCLIV

b. 994 = 900 + 90 + 5 = (1000 – 100) + (100 – 10) + 5
= CMXCV

Example 16: Write the Hindu-Arabic numbers corresponding to the following Roman numerals.

a. MCCCXCI = 1000 + 100 + 100 + 100 + (100 – 10) + 1 =
1000 + 300 + 90 + 1 = 1391

b. MCMLXI = 1000 + (1000 – 100) + 50 + 10 + 1 = 1961

Note

In order to represent a number which is a multiple of 1000, use a bar (–) over the number (IV = 4000)

Exercise 1.6

1 Write the given Hindu-Arabic numbers in Roman numerals.

a. 1532 b. 1025 c. 620 d. 850 e. 504

f. 2504 g. 999 h. 358 i. 782 j. 888

2 Write the given Roman numerals in Hindu-Arabic numbers.

a. MMMMCMXCI b. MMCMX c. MMDCCXXII

d. MMDXLVIII e. MCMIV f. MDCCXCIX

For the Curious Mind

How many 4-digit numbers can be formed using 2, 4, 3 and 0 only once? Explain your logic.

Summary

1. A unit or unity means a single quantity.
2. A number is a value in mathematics used for measuring or counting a certain quantity. A number written in figures is called numeral, while a number written in words is called numeration.
3. All counting numbers are called natural numbers. The set of natural numbers N = {1, 2, 3, 4, 5, 6, ...}.
4. Natural numbers along with zero are called whole numbers. The set of whole numbers W = {0, 1, 2, 3, 4, 5, 6, ...}. 0 is the smallest whole number.
5. We use the Hindu-Arabic Number System to write numerals. The numerals are formed using the digits 0, 1, 2, 3, 4, 5, 6, 7, 8 and 9.
6. Two important place value systems that are used to read and write numbers are the Indian and the international place value systems.
7. Face value of a digit is the digit itself.

   Place value of a digit = (Face value of the digit) × (Value of its place)
8. Roman number system is an ancient system used to represent numbers. It uses 7 basic symbols (I, V, X, L, C, D and M) as per some rules to represent any number. In order to represent a number which is a multiple of 1000, use a bar (–) over the number ($\overline{\text{IV}}$ = 4000).
9. Closure property holds true for addition and multiplication of whole numbers, but not for subtraction and division.
10. Commutative property holds true for addition and multiplication of whole numbers, but not for subtraction and division.
11. Additive property and multiplicative property of zero: $a + 0 = 0 + a = a$ and $a \times 0 = 0 \times a = 0$
12. Associative property holds true for addition and multiplication of whole numbers, but not for subtraction and division.
13. Distributive property of multiplication holds true over addition as well as subtraction.
14. Multiplicative property of 1: $a \times 1 = 1 \times a = a$

Revision Exercise

1 **Write the following numbers in both Indian and international place value systems. Also, write the number names and identify the largest number and the smallest number among the given numbers.**

a. 6045896 b. 20456087 c. 20850135

d. 5021369 e. 7894562154 f. 208500140

g. 90001009 h. 410302410 i. 102380014

2 **Write the numbers corresponding to the following number names. Also, arrange the numbers in ascending order.**

a. Forty-nine crore ninety-two lakh four thousand two hundred six
b. Five billion nineteen million seventy-one thousand nine hundred thirty-eight
c. Seven crore thirteen lakh twenty-four thousand nine hundred nine
d. Two billion ninety-two million four thousand two hundred eleven
e. Seventy-eight crore seventy-five lakh forty thousand one hundred fifty
f. Two billion nine-hundred seventy-four million fourteen thousand nine hundred five

3 **Arrange the following in descending order.**

a. 1825790, 1825970, 185297, 1089201, 1825901
b. 7852015, 78543012, 9985214, 78596541, 7852016
c. 98562104, 98562140, 98568025, 98562001, 98562875
d. 900856029, 900856092, 900860012, 98752149, 900856379

4 **Write the given Roman numerals in Hindu-Arabic numbers.**

a. DXVI b. DCLXXIV c. MCCXXVII

d. MCCCLXXXVIII e. MMMCXXVII f. MMMCMXC

5 **Compare the numbers and fill in the blanks with > or <.**

a. 200,400,825 ______ 50,501,099 b. 546,709,021 ______ 546,221,036

c. 18,11,14,520 ______ 20,15,57,025 d. 91,62,00,008 ______ 826,000,000

e. 2,183,687 ______ 22,87,256 f. 312,002,891 ______ 312,002,059

6 **Form the greatest and the smallest.**

a. 6-digit number using the digits 5, 2, 0, 4, 3 and 1 only once
b. 8-digit number using the digits 8, 5, 6, 0, 4, 9, 7 and 3 only once
c. 7-digit number using the digits 9, 2, 0, 4, 3, 5 and 7 only once

7 **Solve the following using suitable rearrangement.**

a. 7082 + 30033 + 2018 b. 9091 + 9092 + 9093 +9097 + 9098 + 9099

c. $500 \times 451 \times 18$ d. $104 \times 106 \times 205 \times 705$

8 **Solve the following using properties of whole numbers.**

a. 1004×555 b. 98×6023

c. $70641 \times 93 + 70641 \times 2 + 70641$ d. $88765 \times 1005 - 88765 \times 5$

UNIT 1

Integers

2

What I shall learn

- To understand the concept of integers
- To represent integers on a number line
- To perform the basic operations on integers

Let's Get Started

In some situations in our daily lives, we use this idea of opposites of natural numbers. For example, we use this concept to distinguish above sea level from below sea level, hot temperature from cold temperature, profit from loss, etc. Therefore, there are numbers below zero (that is, less than zero) and they are called **negative numbers**. For easy understanding, these numbers are written with a negative or minus sign before them, for example, –1, –2 and –3.

Therefore, negative numbers (–1, –2, –3, ...) are the opposites of positive numbers (1, 2, 3, ...).

Let us see some examples.

Note

Conventionally, we do not write the + sign before a positive number. However, it is necessary to write the – sign before a negative number.

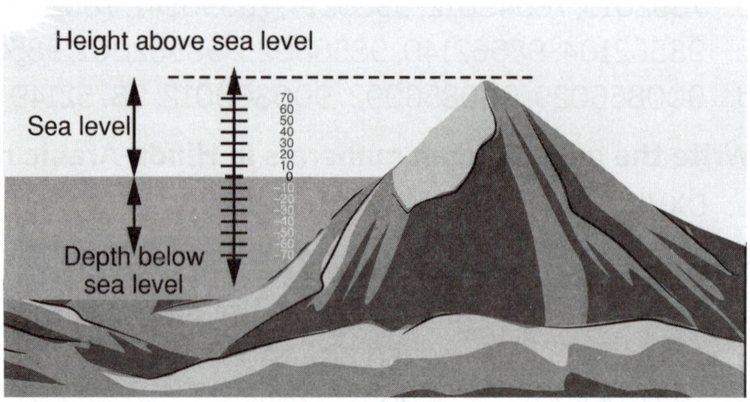

The Mount Everest peak is about 8848 m above sea level.	+8848 m
Sea level is considered as 0. Height measured above sea level is positive and depth measured below sea level is negative.	0 m
The submarine is 500 m below sea level.	–500 m

Integers

The collection of whole numbers along with the collection of negative numbers is known as **integers**. That is, the set of all positive numbers, negative numbers and zero put together is called integers and is denoted by the letter 'I' or 'Z'.

Integers, Z or I = {... –3, –2, –1, 0, 1, 2, 3, ...}

Positve integers, Z^+ or $I^+ = \{1, 2, 3, ...\}$

Negative integers, Z^- or $I^- = \{..., -3, -2, -1\}$

Observe that zero is neither a negative nor a positive integer.

Note

The letter Z stands for the German word 'Zahlen', which means 'numbers'.

Let us relate natural numbers, whole numbers and integers with the following diagrammatic representation.

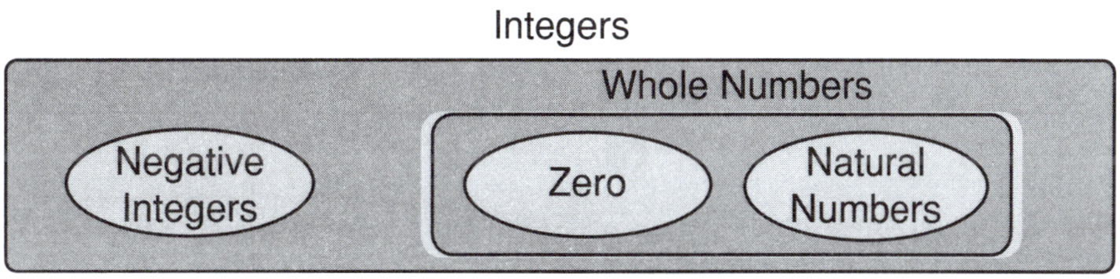

Use of Integers as Directed Numbers

Positive and negative integers together are known as **directed numbers**. There are many situations where directed numbers are used. Here are some examples.

1. When +15 m means 15 m above sea level, –15 m means 15 m below sea level.
2. When +₹60 means a profit of ₹60, – ₹60 means a loss of ₹60.

Representing Integers on a Number Line

Let us observe the following pattern of numbers.

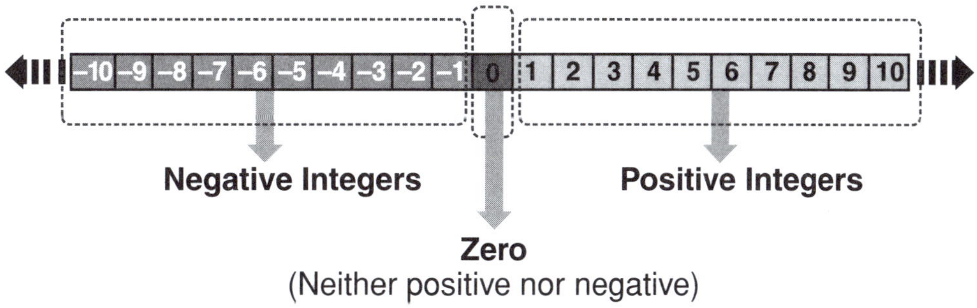

Interesting Facts

All positive integers are greater than negative integers because when we represent two integers on a number line, the integer on the right is greater than that on the left.

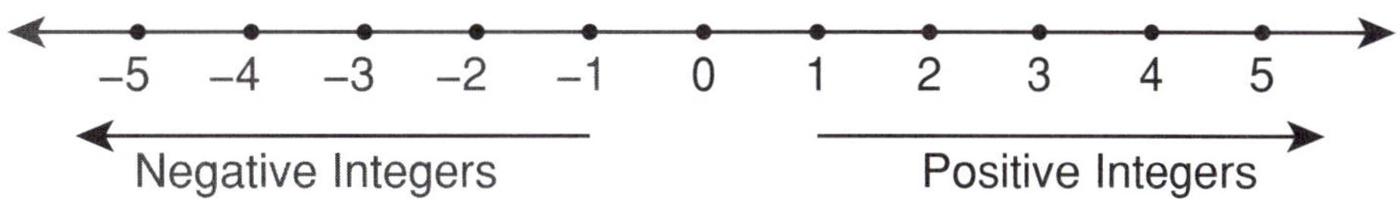

Zero is in the middle and all the positive integers are on its right and all negative integers are on its left side. So, zero is less than every positive integer and greater than every negative integer.

If a natural number is greater than another natural number, its negative is less than the negative of the other number and vice versa. For example, as $7 > 4$, we have $-7 < -4$; as $3 < 5$, we have $-3 > -5$.

The greatest negative integer is –1 since $-1 > -2 > -3 > -4 > ...$

Let us conduct an activity to represent the positive numbers and negative numbers on a number line.

Activity

Tie a thread with hooks at equal distances to represent a number line and hang the 0 number card at the centre as shown below.

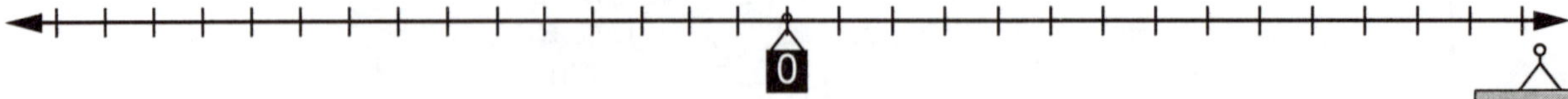

Divide the class into small groups. Distribute a set of cards numbered from –15 to +15 to each group. Ask students from each group to hang the number cards on the number line in their appropiate places.

For example, if the number is –6, the student moves six places to the left of 0 and hangs the integer –6 as shown below.

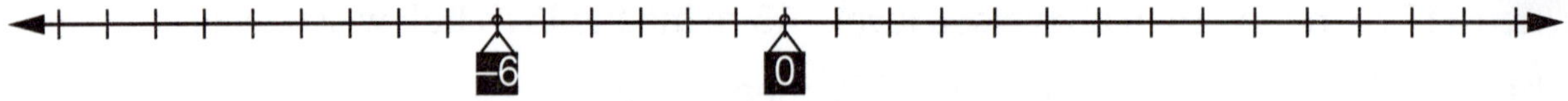

Conclusion: The numbers to the right of 0 are positive numbers (natural numbers), while the numbers to the left of 0 are negative numbers.

Example 1: Represent –4 on a number line.

–4 is marked on the number line four units to the left of 0.

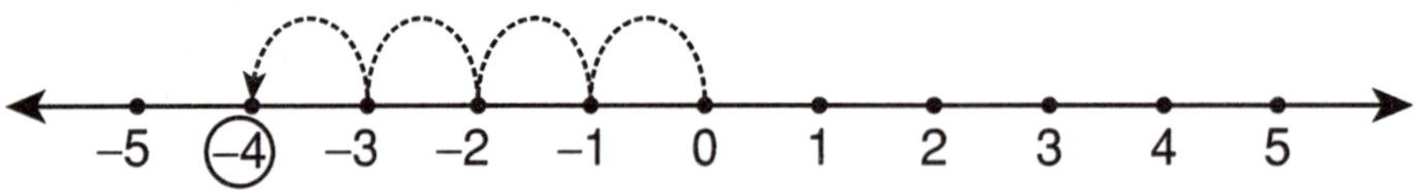

Example 2: Represent 3 on a number line.

3 is marked on the number line three units to the right of 0.

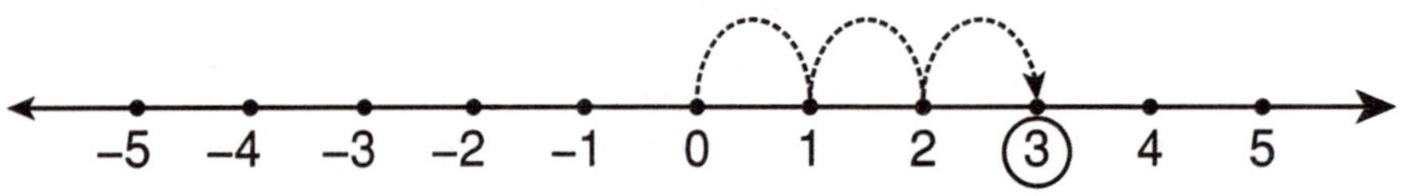

Example 3: Compare the following pairs of integers using the symbol '>' or '<'.

a. 3 ( ) –5

First, let us represent 3 and – 5 on the number line.

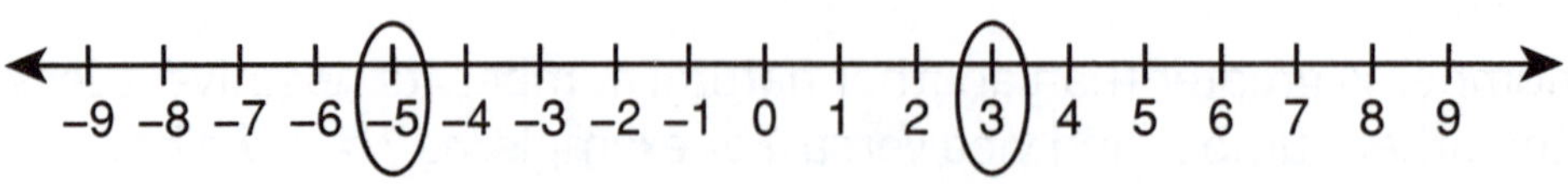

3 is on the right of zero and –5 is on the left of zero. So, 3 is greater than – 5. Therefore, 3 > –5

b. –10 ( ) –8

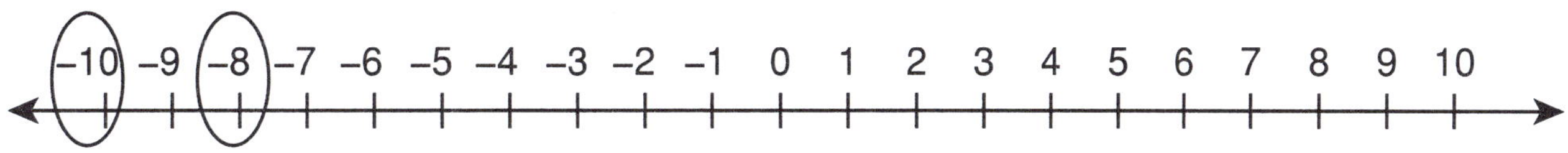

–10 is on the left of –8 in the number line. Therefore, –10 < –8.

Mental Maths

Circle the lowest temperature and underline the highest temperature.

14°C 4°C –19°C

–3°C –9°C

Example 4: Arrange the following set of integers in ascending order.

4, –7, 0, 2, –1, –13

Represent the numbers on a number line. Then, order the numbers from the smallest to the greatest.

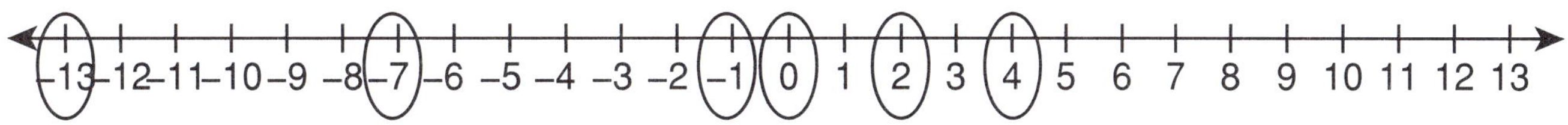

Numbers in ascending order: –13 < –7 < –1 < 0 < 2 < 4

Example 5: Arrange the following set of integers in descending order.

0, –4, 13, –11, –5, 6, 1

Numbers in descending order: 13 > 6 > 1 > 0 > –4 > –5 > –11

Example 6: Using a number line, find all integers from –5 to –1. State which of them is the greatest and which of them is the smallest integer.

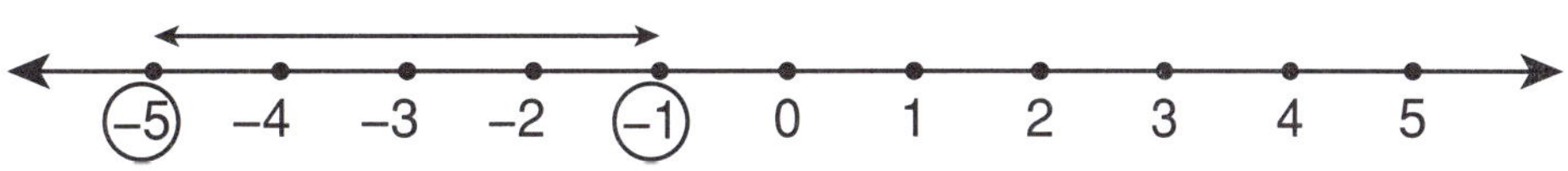

The integers are –5, –4, –3, –2 and –1.

The greatest integer is –1 and the smallest integer is –5.

Absolute Value of an Integer

Observe the given figure.

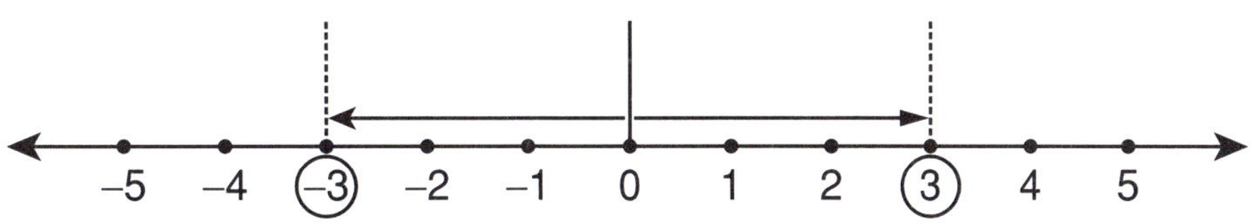

On the number line, –3 and 3 are on the opposite sides of 0 and at the same distance from 0. We say that they have the same absolute value and the value is 3 (not plus 3 or minus 3).

Thus, the absolute value of an integer is the numerical value of the integer regardless of its sign. It is the distance of the number from 0 on the number line. Since the distance cannot be negative, the absolute value of a number is always positive or zero. The symbol for absolute value is two vertical bars on either side of the number, for example, the absolute value of 10 is represented as $|10|$.

Note

The absolute value of 0 is 0 that is, $|0| = 0$

Look at the following example.

The absolute value of 4 is 4, that is, $|4| = 4$.

The absolute value of −4 is 4, that is, $|-4| = 4$.

Example 7: Compare $-|5|$ and $|-5|$.

The absolute value of 5 is 5. That is, $|5| = 5 \Rightarrow -|5| = -5$

The absolute value of −5 is 5. That is, $|-5| = 5$

$-5 < 5$ (since a negative integer is always less than a positive integer)

Therefore, $-|5| < |-5|$.

Try These!

Compare

a. 15 and $|-17|$

b. −9 and $|-9|$

Exercise 2.1

1 **Read the statements and write the numbers with appropriate signs (+ or −).**

a. A bird is flying at a height of 25 m above sea level.

b. The average temperature at the Mount Everest in January is 36°C below 0°C.

c. She lost about 2 kg of weight in a month.

d. Water freezes at 0°C.

e. The fish is swimming 10 m below the water surface.

f. He deposited ₹1000 in my bank account.

2 Write any six integers that are less than −2.

3 Mark the integers 6, −3, −7, −1, 4, −5 and 3 on the number line given below.

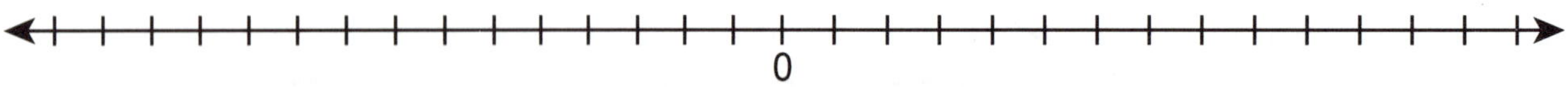

4 **Put the appropriate symbol '<' or '>' in the blanks below.**

a. −2 ____ 20 b. 3 ____ −50 c. $|-4|$ ____ −5

d. 0 ____ −10 e. 0 ____ 40 f. 100 ____ −100

5 **Write the following sets of integers in the ascending order.**

a. −4, 0, −10, 1, −2, 4, 5 b. −9, −11, 3, −2, −24, 8, −5

6. **Write the following sets of integers in the descending order.**

   a. −3, 4, −10, 10, −5, 7, −13
   b. −9, −11, 3, −2, −24, 8, 0

7. **Find all the integers that lie between the given two integers. Also, represent them on a number line.**

   a. −5 and 3
   b. −11 and −3
   c. −4 and 0

8. **Write the value of each of the following.**

   a. |−3|
   b. |232|
   c. |0|
   d. −|3|
   e. −|−3|
   f. −|0|

9. **Fill in the blanks.**

   a. Whole numbers and negative integers together form the set of ________.
   b. ________ is neither a negative nor a positive integer.
   c. ________ is the negative integer that is nearest to 0.
   d. The opposite of 'gain of ₹100' is '________ of ₹100'.

10. **State whether the following statements are true or false.**

    a. The greatest negative integer is −1.
    b. 0 is a positive integer.
    c. 0 is on the right side of −2 on a number line.
    d. The absolute value of 7 is −7.
    e. The opposite of 0 is 0.
    f. The opposite of −5 is 5.
    g. 7 is on the right of −9 on the number line.
    h. 1 is an integer that lies between −2 and 0 on a number line.
    i. −5 and +5 represent the same integer on the number line.
    j. Every negative integer is greater than 0.

Addition and Subtraction of Integers

Addition of Integers

In the previous section, we learned how to represent integers on a number line and how to compare them. Now, let us learn how to add integers.

Addition of Integers Using Number Line

We move towards the right to add a positive number and we move towards the left to add a negative number on the number line.

Example 8: Add (−4) and (+2) using a number line.

Starting from −4, move 2 units towards the right to get −2.

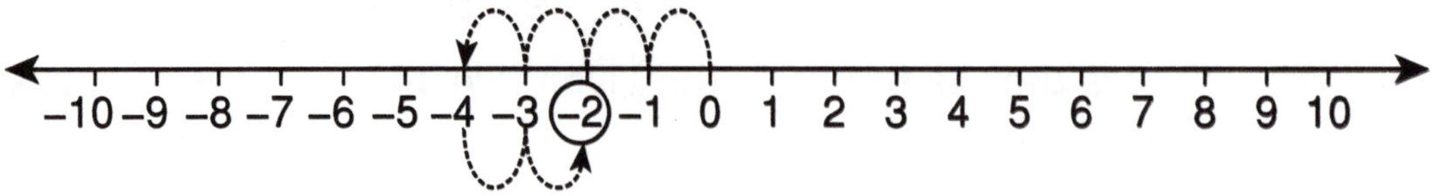

∴ (−4) + (+2) = (−2)

Example 9: Add (+4) and (−3) using a number line.

Starting from +4, move 3 units towards the left to get (+1).

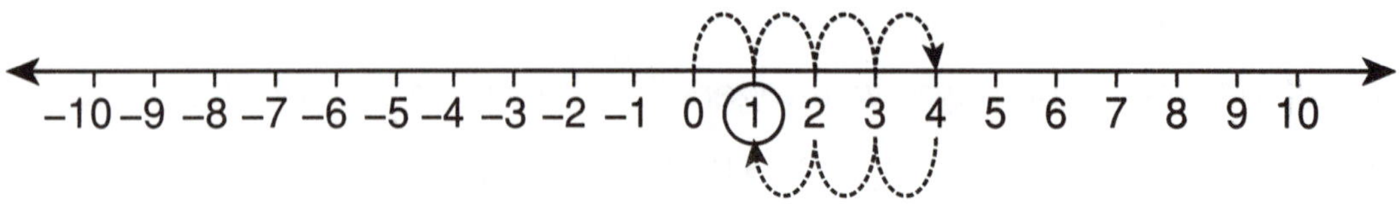

∴ (+4) + (−3) = (+1)

Example 10:

a. Add the positive numbers 4 and 3 on a number line.

b. Add the negative numbers (−4) and (−3) on a number line.

a. First move 4 steps to the right from 0 to reach 4. Then, move 3 steps to the right of 4 to reach 7.

∴ 4 + 3 = 7

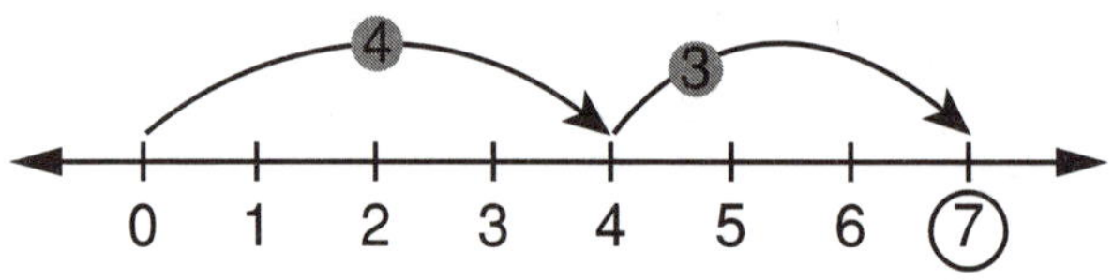

4 + 3 = 7

b. First move 4 steps to the left from 0 to reach −4. Then, move 3 steps to the left of −4 to reach −7.

∴ (−4) + (−3) = (−7)

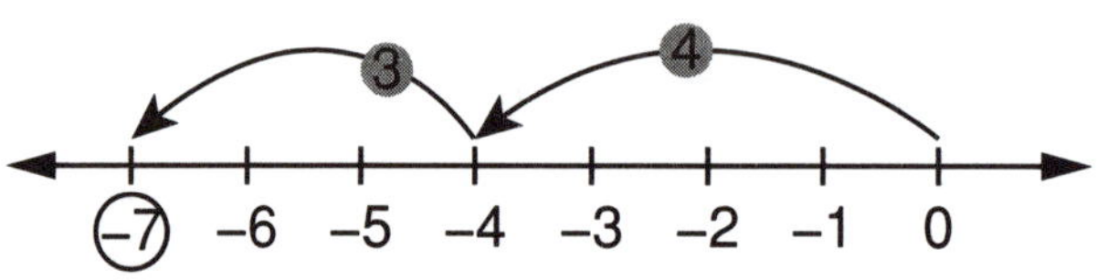

(−4) + (−3) = −7

Thus, from the above examples we can conclude that:

- The sum of two positive integers is always positive and the resulting integer is greater than the given integers.
- The sum of two negative integers is always negative and the resulting integer is lesser than the given integers.

Addition of Integers Without Using Number Line

1. If 2 numbers have the same sign, we
   - add them and
   - then put their sign
2. If 2 numbers have different signs, we
   - find the difference between the bigger number and the smaller number (without the signs) and
   - then put the sign of the bigger number

Example 11: Find the sum of (+10) and (+16).

(+10) + (+16) = +10 + 16 = +26

Example 12: Find the sum of (−11) and (−22).

(−11) + (−22) = −11 − 22 = −33

Example 13: Find the sum of (−72) and (+49).

(−72) + (+49) = −72 + 49 = −23

Note

If we have the '+' sign outside a bracket and we remove the bracket, the sign of the number inside the bracket is taken.

+(+3) = 3

+(−3) = −3

Note

If two signs are together one after the other, we put the bracket after the first sign to avoid confusion.

2++5 is written as 2 + (+5).

Properties of Integers under Addition

1. Closure Property

Study the given problems on addition and complete the table.

Statement	Conclusion
4 + 3 = 7	The sum is an integer.
(−3) + (−15) =	
8 + (−5) =	The sum is an integer.

Is the sum of two integers always an integer? Yes. Thus, we say that integers satisfy the closure property under addition.

For any two integers *a* and *b*, their sum, that is, $a + b$ is also an integer.

2. Commutative Property

Study the given problems on addition and complete the table.

Statement 1	Statement 2	Conclusion
4 + 3 = 7	3 + 4 = 7	4 + 3 = 3 + 4 = 7
−12 + 7 =	7 + (−12) =	

Did you find any pair of integers whose sum is different when the order is changed?

No. Thus, we say that integers satisfy the commutative property under addition.

For any two integers *a* and *b*, $a + b = b + a$.

3. Associative Property

Study the following problems on addition and complete the table.

Statement 1	Statement 2	Conclusion
$7 + (5 + 8) = 7 + 13 = 20$	$(7 + 5) + 8 = 12 + 8 = 20$	$7 + (5 + 8) = (7 + 5) + 8$
$(-3) + \{(-2) + 7\} =$	$\{(-3) + (-2)\} + 7 =$	

Did you find any pair of integers whose sum is different when grouping is changed? No. Thus, we say that integers satisfy the associative property under addition.

For any three integers a, b and c, $a + (b + c) = (a + b) + c$.

4. Additive Identity

Study the given problems on addition and complete the table.

Statement 1	Statement 2	Conclusion
$(-3) + 0 = -3$	$0 + (-3) = -3$	$(-3) + 0 = 0 + (-3) = -3$
$7 + 0 =$	$0 + 7 =$	

On adding 0 to an integer, did you get the same integer? Yes.
Thus, 0 is the additive identity for integers.

For any integer a, $a + 0 = 0 + a = a$.

5. Additive Inverse

Study the given problems on addition and complete the table.

Statement 1	Statement 2	Conclusion
$8 + (-8) = 0$	$(-8) + 8 = 0$	$8 + (-8) = (-8) + 8 = 0$
$13 + (-13) =$	$(-13) + 13 =$	

When the sum of two integers is 0, we say that one integer is the additive inverse of the other. We write the additive inverse of a as $-a$ and vice versa.

For any integer a, $a + (-a) = (-a) + a = 0$.

Subtraction of Integers

Subtraction of Integers Using Number Line

To subtract an integer from another integer, we add the additive inverse of the integer to be subtracted.

Example 14: Subtract (–3) from (–1) using a number line.

The additive inverse of –3 is +3.

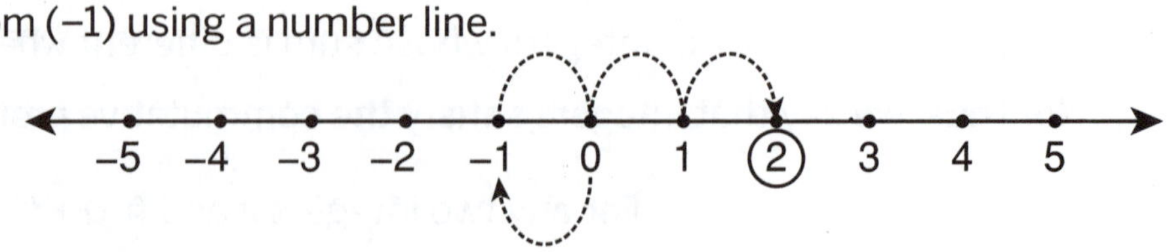

Instead of solving it as (–1) – (–3), we can solve it as (–1) + (+3).

Starting from –1, move 3 units towards right on the number line.

∴ (–1) – (–3) = 2

> **Note**
> In subtraction, the number immediately after 'from' is written first. After that the '–' sign is put, followed by the other number.

Example 15: Subtract (+4) from (–1) using a number line.

The additive inverse of +4 is –4.

Instead of solving it as (–1) – (+4), we can solve it as (–1) + (– 4).

Starting from –1, move 4 units towards left on the number line.

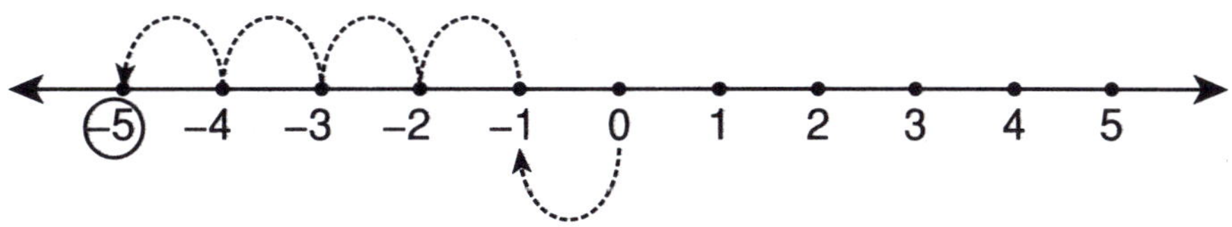

∴ (–1) – (+4) = –5

Subtraction of Integers without Using Number Line

We subtract integers in a way similar to the way we add them. The only difference is that if we have the '–' sign outside a bracket and we remove the bracket, the sign of the number inside the bracket changes.

Examples: –(+3) = –3; –(–3) = +3

Example 16: Subtract 5 from 2.

2 – 5 = –3

Example 17: Subtract (–2) from (–6).

(–6) – (–2) = –6 + 2 = –4

Example 18: Subtract –5 from (–58).

(–58) – (–5) = – 58 + 5

= – 53

Example 19: Subtract (–3215) from 6787.

6787 – (–3215) = 6787 + 3215

= 10002

Properties of Integers under Subtraction

1. Closure Property

Study the given problems on subtraction and complete the table.

Statement	Conclusion
10 – (–3) = 13	The difference is an integer.
(–32) – (–15) =	
(–54) – (+13) =	The difference is an integer.

Is the difference between any two integers always an integer? Yes. Thus, we say that the integers satisfy the closure property under subtraction.

> For any two integers *a* and *b*, their difference, that is, *a* – *b* is also an integer.

2. Commutative Property

Study the following problems on subtraction and complete the table.

Statement 1	Statement 2	Conclusion
7 – (–10) = 7 + 10 = 17	(–10) – 7 = –10 + –7 = –17	7 – (–10) ≠ (–10) – 7
9 – 4 =	4 – 9 =	
(–15) – (–8) =	(–8) – (–15) =	

Thus, we say that integers do not satisfy the commutative property under subtraction.

3. Associative Property

Study the following problems on subtraction and complete the table.

Statement 1	Statement 2	Conclusion
7 – (5 – 8) = 7 – (–3) = 10	(7 – 5) – 8 = 2 – 8 = –6	7 – (5 – 8) ≠ (7 – 5) – 8
(–3) – {(–2) – 7} =	{(–3) – (–2)} – 7 =	

From the table above, we find that for non-zero, unequal integers a, b and c, a – (b – c) ≠ (a – b) – c unless c = 0. Thus, we say that the integers do not satisfy the associative property under subtraction.

Exercise 2.2

1 **Solve the following using the number line.**

a. 7 + 4 b. 5 + (–8) c. (–3) + 6 d. (–4) + (–7)

2 **Solve the following without using the number line.**

a. 37 + 107 b. (–56) + (103) c. (–24) + (–76) d. 49 + (–54)

3 **Solve the following using the number line.**

a. (–7) – (–3) b. (–7) – (+3) c. 3 – (–2) d. 8 – 3

4 **Solve the following without using the number line.**

a. (–19) – (+21) b. 35 – (–18) c. (–17) – (+15) d. 0 – (+120)

5 **Fill in the blanks with >, = or <.**

a. (–3) + (–7) ______ (–7) – (–3) b. 55 – (–22) ______ 0 – (–77)

c. (–32) + (–23) ______ (–32) – (–23) d. 16 –(–16) ______ 42 – 10

6 **Fill in the blanks.**

a. (–36) + ______ = (–36) b. (–20) + ______ = 0

c. (–14) – ______ = –28 d. ______ – (–15) = +10

7 What number should be added to –14 to get –68?

8. The sum of two integers is 68. If one of them is −68, find the other.
9. The temperature on a particular morning is 14°C, but by midnight it falls to −2°C due to rain. By how many degrees does the temperature fall?
10. A bus travels 523 km north from Bangalore and then 201 km south on the same route. How far is the bus from Bangalore now?

Multiplication of Integers

We have learned that in case of whole numbers, multiplication is a process of repeated addition. Is it possible to give the same meaning to multiplication of integers? Yes.

Let us look at the following examples.

$3 \times 2 = 2 + 2 + 2 = 6$

And $3 \times (-2) = (-2) + (-2) + (-2) = (-6)$

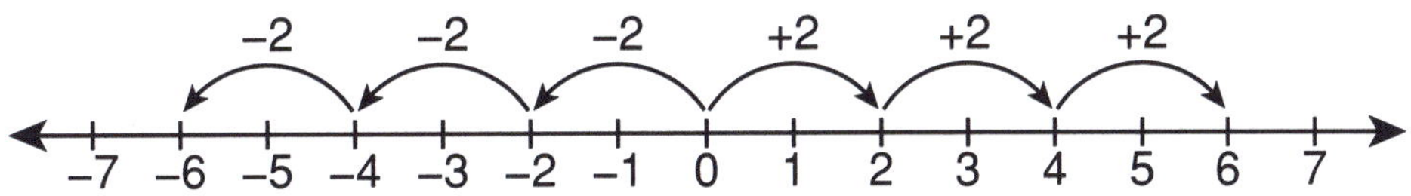

- The product of two positive integers is always a positive integer.
- The product of a positive integer and a negative integer is always a negative integer.

Remember

For any given integers a and b:

- $(+a) \times (+b) = (a \times b)$
- $(-a) \times b = -(a \times b)$ and $(a) \times (-b) = -(a \times b)$

For any two integers a and b, $-a \times -b = +(a \times b)$.

Now, observe the following pattern.

$3 \times -2 = -6$
$2 \times -2 = -4$
$1 \times -2 = -2$
$0 \times -2 = 0$
$-1 \times -2 = ?$
$-2 \times -2 = ?$
$-3 \times -2 = ?$

We observe that the first factor (the number in the first column) decreases by 1 each time and the product increases by 2 each time. Hence, $-1 \times -2 = 2$, $-2 \times -2 = 4$, $-3 \times -2 = 6$ and so on.

Thus, the product of two negative integers is always a positive integer.

To find the product of two integers, we multiply the signs separately and then the numbers (without the signs) separately.

Examples 20: Multiply (+7) and (+13).

+ × **+** = **+** and 7 × 13 = 91. So, (+7) × (+13) = 91

Examples 21: Multiply (−7) and (−13).

− × **−** = **+** and 7 × 13 = 91. So, (−7) × (−13) = 91

To find the product of two integers with unlike signs, we find the product of their absolute values and assign a minus sign to the product.

Example 22: Multiply (+7) and (–13).

+ × **–** = **–** and 7 × 13 = 91. So, (+7) × (–13) = –91

Example 23: Multiply (–7) and (+13).

– × **+** = **–** and 7 × 13 = 91. So, (–7) × (+13) = –91

Properties of Integers under Multiplication

1. Closure Property

Study the given problems on multiplication and complete the table.

Statement	Conclusion
15 × 8 = 120	The product is an integer.
(–7) × (–16) =	
8 × (–5) =	

Is the product of two integers always an integer? Yes. Thus, we say that integers satisfy the closure property under multiplication.

For any two integers *a* and *b*, their product, that is, $a \times b$ is also an integer.

2. Commutative Property

Study the given problems on multiplication and complete the table.

Statement 1	Statement 2	Conclusion
14 × (–3) = –42	(–3) × 14 = –42	14 × (–3) = (–3) × 14
10 × (–5) =	(–5) × 10 =	

Did you find any pair of integers whose product is different when the order is changed?

No. Thus, we say that integers satisfy the commutative property under multiplication.

For any two integers *a* and *b*, $a \times b = b \times a$.

3. Associative Property

Study the following problems on multiplication and complete the table.

Statement 1	Statement 2	Conclusion
7 × (5 × 8) = 7 × 40 = 280	(7 × 5) × 8 = 35 × 8 = 280	7 × (5 × 8) = (7 × 5) × 8
(–9) × {(–2) × 7} =	{(–9) × (–2)} × 7 =	

Did you find any pair of integers whose product is different when the grouping is changed? No. Thus, we say that integers satisfy the associative property under multiplication.

For any three integers *a*, *b* and *c*, $a \times (b \times c) = (a \times b) \times c$.

4. **Multiplicative Identity**

Study the given problems on multiplication and complete the table.

Statement 1	Statement 2	Conclusion
$(-14) \times 1 = -14$	$1 \times (-14) = -14$	$(-14) \times 1 = 1 \times (-14)$
$217 \times 1 =$	$1 \times 217 =$	

On multiplying any integer by 1, do you get the same integer as product? Yes. Thus, 1 is the multiplicative identity for integers.

> For any integer a, $a \times 1 = 1 \times a = a$.

5. **Multiplicative Inverse**

$6 \times ? = 1$

Can you find a number that gives the product as 1 when multiplied by 6? Yes.

$6 \times \frac{1}{6} = 1$. But $\frac{1}{6}$ is not an integer.

Can you find an integer that gives the product as 1 when multiplied by 6? No.

Therefore, we can say that just like in whole numbers, multiplicative inverse does not exist in integers also.

6. **Multiplication by 0**

$(-7) \times 0 = 0$ $8 \times 0 = 0$ $0 \times (-6) = 0$

> For any integer a, $a \times 0 = 0 \times a = 0$.

Thus, we can say that the product of an integer and 0 is always 0.

7. **Distributive Property**

Study the following problems on multiplication.

Statement 1	Statement 2
$-4 \times (-3 + 5)$	$(-4 \times -3) + (-4 \times 5)$
$= -4 \times 2$	$= 12 + (-20)$
$= -8$	$= -8$

$\therefore$ Statement 1 = Statement 2

Verify $15 \times \{(-4) + (-6)\} = \{15 \times (-4)\} + \{15 \times (-6)\}$.

You will find that in each case, the left-hand side is equal to the right-hand side.

Thus, multiplication distributes over addition of integers.

> For any three integers a, b and c, $a \times (b + c) = (a \times b) + (a \times c)$.

Now, study the following problems on multiplication.

Statement 1	Statement 2
$-6 \times \{7 - (-4)\}$	$\{(-6 \times 7)\} - \{(-6 \times -4)\}$
$= -6 \times 11$	$= -42 - 24$
$= -66$	$= -66$

$\therefore$ Statement 1 = Statement 2

Verify $(-3) \times \{(-5) - 2\} = \{(-3) \times (-5)\} - \{(-3) \times (2)\}$.

You will find that in each case, the left-hand side is equal to the right-hand side.

Thus, multiplication distributes over subtraction of integers.

For any three integers a, b and c, $a \times (b - c) = (a \times b) - (a \times c)$.

Division of Integers

We have learned that in case of whole numbers, division is the inverse operation of multiplication. Is it possible to give the same meaning to the division of integers? Yes.

Write the corresponding division statements for the multiplication statements in the following table. One example has been done for you.

Multiplication Statement (First Number × Second Number = Product)	Corresponding Division Statements	
	Statement 1 (Product ÷ First Number)	Statement 2 (Product ÷ Second Number)
$(3) \times (-4) = -12$	$-12 \div (3) = -4$	$-12 \div (-4) = 3$
$(-5) \times (-7) = 35$		
$(-2) \times (8) = -16$		
$(7) \times (4) = 28$		

Now, observe the following examples.

$a \div (-b)$	$(-a) \div (b)$	$-(a \div b)$	$(-a) \div (-b)$	$a \div b$
$12 \div (-4) = -3$	$(-12) \div (4) = -3$	$-(12 \div 4) = -3$	$(-12) \div (-4) = 3$	$12 \div 4 = 3$
$18 \div (-9) = -2$	$(-18) \div (9) = -2$	$-(18 \div 9) = -2$	$(-18) \div (-9) = 2$	$18 \div 9 = 2$
$25 \div (-5) = -5$	$(-25) \div (5) = -5$	$-(25 \div 5) = -5$	$(-25) \div (-5) = 5$	$25 \div 5 = 5$

Is $a \div (-b) = (-a) \div b = -(a \div b)$ for any integers a and b?

Yes. Thus, we can say that if the dividend and the divisor are of opposite signs, then the quotient is always negative.

Is $(-a) \div (-b) = a \div b$ for any integers a and b?

Yes. Thus, if both the dividend and the divisor have like signs, then the quotient is always positive.

Example 24: Solve the following.

a. $15 \div 5$

$15 \div 5 = \frac{15}{5}$

$= 3$

b. $(-28) \div 7$

$(-28) \div 7 = \frac{-28}{7}$

$= -4$

c. $(-42) \div (-6)$

$(-42) \div (-6) = \frac{-42}{-6}$

$= 7$

d. $240 \div (-48)$

$240 \div (-48) = \frac{240}{-48}$

$= -5$

Properties of Integers under Division

1. Closure Property

Study the following problems on division and complete the table.

Statement	Conclusion	Statement	Conclusion
$12 \div (-4) = -3$	The result is an integer.	$(-4) \div 12 = \frac{-1}{3}$	The result is not an integer.
$(-21) \div (-7) =$		$(-7) \div (-21) =$	

From the above table, can you say that the result obtained after dividing two integers is always an integer? No.

Thus, we say that integers do not satisfy the closure property under division.

2. Commutative Property

Is $a \div b = b \div a$, for any two integers a and b?

From the above table, we see that for non-zero, unequal integers a and b, $a \div b \neq b \div a$.

Thus, we can say integers do not satisfy the commutative property under division.

3. Associative Property

Study the following problems on division and complete the table.

Statement 1	Statement 2	Conclusion
$16 \div (8 \div 2) = 16 \div 4 = 4$	$(16 \div 8) \div 2 = 2 \div 2 = 1$	$16 \div (8 \div 2) \neq (16 \div 8) \div 2$
$\{(-54) \div 9\} \div (-3) =$	$(-54) \div \{9 \div (-3)\} =$	

From the above table, we see that for non-zero, unequal integers a, b and c, $a \div (b \div c) \neq (a \div b) \div c$ unless $c = 1$.

Thus, we can say that integers do not satisfy the associative property under division.

4. **Division by 1**

Study the following problems on division and complete the table.

Statement 1	Statement 2	Conclusion
$(-7) \div 1 = -7$	$1 \div (-7) = \frac{-1}{7}$	$(-7) \div 1 \neq 1 \div (-7)$
$7 \div 1 =$	$1 \div 7 =$	

For any integer a, $a \div 1 \neq 1 \div a$ and $a \div 1 = a$.

5. **Division of a Number by Itself**

$? \div 6 = 1$

Can you find a number that gives 1 as the quotient when divided by 6? Yes.

$6 \div 6 = 1$

For any integer a, $a \div a = 1$ $(a \neq 0)$.

6. **Division by 0**

$(-7) \div 0 = ?$

Suppose $(-7) \div 0 = a$

Then, we should have $a \times 0 = (-7)$.

But for any integer a, $a \times 0 = 0$ and hence $a \times 0 = (-7)$ is not possible.

Therefore, division by zero is not defined.

7. **Division of 0 by a Number**

$0 \div (-7) = ?$

Suppose $0 \div (-7) = a$

Then, $(-7) \times a = 0$

Since the product of the two whole numbers is 0, at least one of them has to be 0. Since $(-7) \neq 0$, a must be 0.

$\therefore 0 \div (-7) = 0$

For any integer a, $a \div 0$ is not defined, but $0 \div a = 0$ $(a \neq 0)$.

8. **Distributive Property**

$40 \div \{-2 + -8\}$
$= 40 \div (-10)$
$= -4$

$\{40 \div (-2)\} + \{40 \div (-8)\}$
$= (-20) + (-5)$
$= -25$

$40 \div (-2 + -8) \neq \{40 \div (-2)\} + \{40 \div (-8)\}$

Thus, division is not distributive over addition of integers.

For any three integers a, b and c, $a \div (b + c) \neq (a \div b) + (a \div c)$.

Order of Performing Operations

You may come across some problems where more than one operation is used. Consider the examples $5 \times \{(-4) + (-3)\}$, $3 + (-4) \times 5$ and $(-60) \div 5 \times 3$. How do you simplify them? Which operation would you perform first?

In order to solve such problems, we have to follow certain rules.

BODMAS Rule

The rule we generally follow during simplification is the BODMAS rule. This rule tells us the order of operations that is to be followed.

B	O	D	M	A	S
Brackets	Of	Divide	Multiply	Add	Subtract

First, you need to look for brackets in a given problem and simplify it.

Types of Brackets

( ) are known as round brackets or parentheses.

{ } are known as curly brackets or braces.

[ ] are known as square brackets or box brackets.

When an expression is enclosed inside a bracket, we simplify it separately. This is called the removal of the brackets. The preferences for brackets are given as follows.

1. First, we remove ( ).
2. Next, we remove { }.
3. Finally, we remove [ ].

Some examples are given below for simplification according to BODMAS rule.

Example 25: Simplify $(-9) + 45 + \{(-7) + (-4)\} \times 6 \div 3$

$(-9) + 45 + \{(-7) + (-4)\} \times 6 \div 3$

$= (-9) + 45 + (-11) \times 6 \div 3$ — **B**rackets

$= (-9) + 45 - 11 \times 2$ — **D**ivision $(6 \div 3 = 2)$

$= (-9) + 45 - 22$ — **M**ultiplication $(11 \times 2 = 22)$

$= 36 - 22$ — **A**ddition $(45 + 9 = 54)$

$= 14$ — **S**ubtraction $(54 - 22 = 32)$

Exercise 2.3

1 Find the products of the following.

a. $(-12) \times 12$ b. $20 \times (-70)$ c. $(-5) \times (-125)$ d. $(+13) \times (+8)$

e. $(-935) \times 0$ f. $1029 \times (-1)$ g. $(-643) \times 1$ h. $(-243) \times (-1)$

2 Find the quotients of the following.

a. $63 \div (-9)$ b. $(-144) \div 18$ c. $(-625) \div (-25)$ d. $(+1024) \div (+32)$

e. $756 \div 1$ f. $5785 \div 5785$ g. $0 \div 357$ h. $357 \div 0$

3 **Fill in the blanks.**

a. $(-6) \times$ ______ $= 36$ b. $7 \times$ ______ $= -49$ c. ______ $\times 25 = -200$

d. ______ $\times (-9) = 108$ e. $(-720) \times$ ______ $= 720$ f. $(-13) \div$ ______ $= 13$

g. ______ $\div 1 = -31$ h. $15 \div 0 =$ ______ i. $0 \div 3 =$ ______

4 **Verify the following.**

a. $17 \times \{5 + (-4)\} = (17 \times 5) + \{17 \times (-4)\}$

b. $(-25) \times \{10 - (-5)\} = \{(-25) \times 10\} - \{(-25) \times (-5)\}$

5 The product of two integers is –136. If one of them is 17, find the other integer.

6 **Use the BODMAS rule to simplify the following.**

a. $\{78 - (-3)\} \div (-9) \times 6$ b. $12 - 36 \div (-6)$ c. $17 - 3 \times (-5)$

d. $(-18) + \{6 - (-3)\} + 4$ e. $(-9) - 27 \div (-9)$ f. $(-8) + (-11) - 5 \times 6$

g. $9 + (-7) \times 2 - 5$ h. $\{9 - (-18) \div 9\} - (-2)$

Summary

1. The collection of whole numbers along with the collection of negative numbers is known as integers.
2. The absolute value of an integer is the numerical value of the integer regardless of its sign.
3. Operations on integers:

Addition of integers	Subtraction of integers	Multiplication of integers	Division of integers
(+) + (+) = (+) (–) + (–) = (–)	If we have the '–' sign outside a bracket and we remove the bracket, the sign of the number inside the bracket changes.	Sign of the First Number × Sign of the Second Number = Sign of the Product +1 × +1 = +1 +1 × –1 = –1 –1 × +1 = –1 –1 × –1 = +1	For any two integers a and b $a \div (-b) = (-a) \div b$, where $b \neq 0$ $(-a) \div (-b) = a \div b$, where $b \neq 0$ Sign of Number a ÷ Sign of Number b = Sign of $a \div b$ +1 ÷ +1 = +1 +1 ÷ –1 = –1 –1 ÷ +1 = –1 –1 ÷ –1 = +1

4. Zero is the additive identity for integers.
5. Two distinct numbers are said be additive inverse of each other if their sum is 0.
6. The integer 1 is the multiplicative identity for integers.
7. For any integer a, $a \times 0 = 0 \times a = 0$.
8. Distributivity under multiplication over addition $a \times (b + c) = (a \times b) + (a \times c)$.
   Distributivity under multiplication over subtraction $a \times (b - c) = (a \times b) - (a \times c)$.
9. For any integer a, $a \div 1 = a$; and for any integer a, $a \div a = 1$ for $a \neq 0$.
10. For any integer a, $a \div 0$ is not defined, but $0 \div a = 0$ for $a \neq 0$.
11. BODMAS stands for: B Brackets, O Of, D Divide, M Multiply, A Add, S Subtract

Revision Exercise

1 **Write the positive and the negative signs for the following statements.**

a. Depth of the ocean
b. Deposit in bank account
c. Height of a mountain
d. Spending money on shopping
e. Lift button indicating basement level

2 **Choose the correct number from the given options and fill in the blanks.**

+7, +3, +5, −5, −3

a. Number to the right of −6: ____________
b. Number that is six places to the left of 3:____________
c. Number that is 5 places to the right of −2: ____________
d. Number that is a predecessor of 6: ____________
e. Number that is 8 places to the right of −3: ____________

3 **State whether the following statements are true or false.**

a. Every positive integer is larger than every negative integer.
b. Farther a number from zero towards the right, smaller is its value.
c. Zero is larger than every negative integer.
d. Zero is larger than every positive integer.
e. The smallest negative integer is –1.

4 **Compare the integers and write '<' or '>'.**

a. (−22) ( ) (−13) b. 100 ( ) (−101) c. −142 ( ) −143
d. 23 ( ) 32 e. −130 ( ) 15 f. 100 ( ) 99

5 Write any four integers that are smaller than −2.

6 Write any four integers that are bigger than −23.

7 **Write all the integers (in the ascending order) between the given pairs.**

a. −6 and 1 b. 4 and −4 c. 7 and 2 d. −2 and −9

8 **Represent the following numbers on the given number line.**

a. 4 b. −7 c. −1
d. 6 e. −5 f. 7

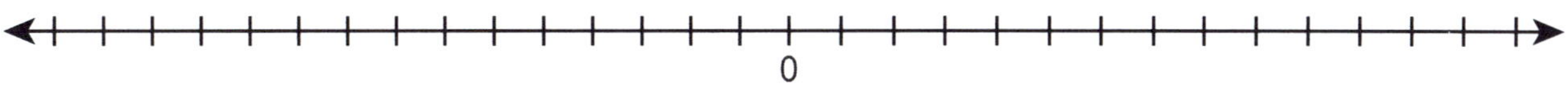

9 **Write the expression corresponding to the following addition problem.**

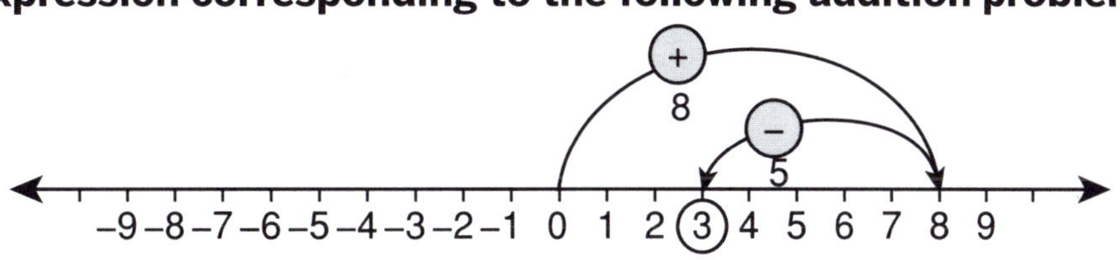

10. **Simplify the following expressions.**

a. (–15) + 8 b. (–110) + (–32) c. –215 + (+150) d. (–10) + (–19)

11. **Simplify the following expressions.**

a. 70 – (25) b. 67 – (–5) c. (–25) – (–75) d. –29 – (+14)

12. **Simply the following expressions.**

a. –9 + 7 + 6 – 4 b. 9 + 8 – 6 – 5 – 4 + 3

c. 4 + 0 + 9 – 7 + 1 d. 1 + 9 – 2 – 2 + 1

13. **Multiply the following.**

a. 12 by –10 b. 6 by –18 c. –1000 by 7 d. 0 by –94578

14. **Divide the following.**

a. –121 by 11 b. –288 by 18 c. 0 by –140 d. –224 by –224

15. **Use the BODMAS rule and simplify the following:**

For the Curious Mind

Using negative integers from –1 to –8, fill in the following circles such that the sum along any side is –15. What is such a square called? Try to form more such squares with positive and negative integers.

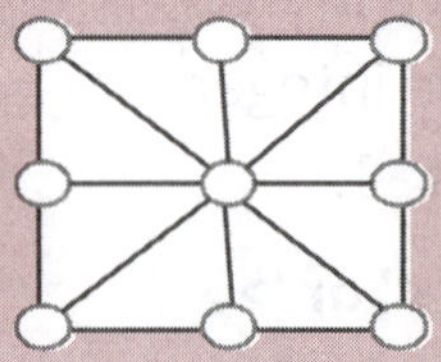

UNIT 1

Factors and Multiples

3

Let's Get Started

The numbers 1, 2, 3, 4, ... are called natural numbers. Natural numbers are denoted by the letter **N**.

All natural numbers that are divisible by 2 are even numbers. Even numbers end with the digits 0, 2, 4, 6 and 8.

All natural numbers that are not divisible by 2 are odd numbers. Odd numbers end with the digits 1, 3, 5, 7 and 9.

What I shall learn

- To understand the properties of factors and multiples
- To apply the divisibility rules and identify composite numbers
- To learn about HCF and LCM of numbers and their real-life application

Factors and Multiples

A factor of a number is a number that divides the number exactly without leaving any remainder.

Examples: The factors of 15 are 1, 3, 5 and 15.

The factors of 20 are 1, 2, 4, 5, 10 and 20.

Properties of Factors

- 1 is a factor of every number.
- Every number is a factor of itself.
- Number of factors of a number is finite.
- Every factor of a number is less than or equal to the given number.
- Every factor of a number is an exact divisor of that number.

Multiples of a number are obtained by multiplying that number by a natural number.

Examples: The multiples of 7 are 7, 14, 21, 28, 35,...

The multiples of 10 are 10, 20, 30, 40...

Properties of Multiples

- Every number is a multiple of itself.
- Every multiple of a number is greater than or equal to that number.
- Number of multiples of a number is infinite.

Exercise 3.1

1 State whether the following statements are correct or incorrect.

a. 6 is a factor of 42.

b. 24 is not a multiple of 5.

c. 20 is a multiple of 3.

d. 3 and 15 are factors of 54.

2 Write all the possible factors of the following numbers.

a. 40 b. 65 c. 90 d. 150

3 Write the first 5 multiples of the following.

a. 3 b. 11 c. 8 d. 4

4 Answer the following.

a. The smallest factor of 55 other than 1

b. The largest factor of 10

c. The 5th multiple of 9

Classification of Natural Numbers

Natural numbers are classified into prime and composite numbers based on the number of factors.

Natural Numbers

Prime Numbers
A prime number has only two factors, that is, 1 and the number itself. The smallest prime number is 2.
Examples: 2, 3, 5, 7 and 11

Composite Numbers
A composite number has more than two factors, that is, it has factors other than 1 and the number itself. The smallest composite number is 4.
Examples: 4, 6, 9, 10 and 12

Twin Prime Numbers
If the difference between two prime numbers is 2, then they are said to be twin primes.
Examples: 3 and 5, 11 and 13

Co-prime Numbers
Two numbers are said to be co-prime or relatively prime if their common factor is only 1.
Examples: 2 and 5, 3 and 8

Note

- The number 1 is neither prime nor composite.
- The number 2 is the only even prime number. All other even numbers are composite.
- Co-prime numbers need not be prime numbers.
  Examples: 13 and 15, 16 and 25

Exercise 3.2

1. **Define the terms and give examples.**
   a. Prime numbers
   b. Co-prime numbers
   c. Composite numbers
   d. Twin prime numbers
2. **Identify the composite numbers from the given numbers.**
   a. 17 b. 15 c. 23 d. 91
3. **Write the prime numbers between each of the following.**
   a. 3 and 21
   b. 15 and 50
   c. 64 and 87
   d. 21 and 79
4. **State whether the following statements are true or false and justify your answers.**
   a. All odd numbers are prime numbers.
   b. All even numbers are composite numbers.
   c. Two consecutive odd prime numbers are twin primes.
   d. 2 is the only even prime number.
   e. All co-primes are prime numbers but all prime numbers need not be co-primes.
5. How many composite numbers are there from 1 to 100? Out of these, list the composite numbers with digit 3 in the ones place?
6. Identify the seven consecutive composite numbers between 1 and 100 so that there is no prime number between them.

Test of Divisibility of Numbers

The test of divisibility helps to identify whether a number is a prime number or a composite number. Tests of divisibility by a few numbers are given below.

Test	Rule	Example
Divisibility by 2	All even numbers are divisible by 2.	52, 68 and 304 are even numbers; therefore, they are divisible by 2. 47, 67 and 307 are odd numbers; therefore, they are not divisible by 2.
Divisibility by 3	If the sum of the digits of a number is divisible by 3, then the number is divisible by 3.	396 $3 + 9 + 6 = 18$ 18 is divisible by 3; therefore, 396 is divisible by 3.

Divisibility by 4	If the last two digits of a number is divisible by 4, then the number is divisible by 4.	852 52 is divisible by 4; therefore, 852 is divisible by 4.
Divisibility by 5	If the digit in the ones place of a number is 0 or 5, then the number is divisible by 5.	230, 595, 120 and 765 have the digit 0 or 5 in their units place; therefore, they are divisible by 5. 459, 567, 602 and 703 do not have the digit 0 or 5 in their units place; therefore, they are not divisible by 5.
Divisibility by 6	If a number is divisible by both 2 and 3, then it is divisible by 6.	204 204 is an even number; therefore, it is divisible by 2. $2 + 0 + 4 = 6$ 6 is divisible by 3. 204 is divisible by both 2 and 3; therefore, it is divisible by 6.
Divisibility by 7	If the difference between twice the digit in the ones place and the remaining digits taken together is 0 or a multiple of 7, then the given number is divisible by 7. Continue the process until the difference is in 2 digits.	6804 $680 - (2 \times 4) = 672$ $67 - (2 \times 2) = 63$ (Checking divisibility of 672 by 7) 63 is divisible by 7; therefore, 6804 is divisible by 7. 1615 $161 - (2 \times 5) = 151$ $15 - (2 \times 1) = 13$ 13 is not divisible by 7; therefore, 1615 is not divisible by 7.
Divisibility by 8	If the last 3 digits of a number is divisible by 8, then the number is divisible by 8.	9864 864 is divisible by 8; therefore, 9864 is divisible by 8.
Divisibility by 9	If the sum of the digits of a number is a multiple of 9, then the number is divisible by 9.	684 $6 + 8 + 4 = 18$ 18 is divisible by 9; therefore, 684 is divisible by 9.
Divisibility by 10	If the ones digit of a number is 0, then the number is divisible by 10.	560, 2510, 3500 and 4050 have the digit 0 in the ones place; therefore, they are divisible by 10.
Divisibility by 11	If the difference between the sum of the digits in the even places and the sum of the digits in the odd places is 0 or a multiple of 11, then the number is divisible by 11.	928 $(9 + 2) - (3 + 8) = 11 - 11 = 0$ 0 is divisible by 11; therefore, 9328 is divisible by 11.

Properties of Divisibility of Numbers

- **If *a* is divisible by *b*, then *a* is divisible by all the factors of *b*.**

  For example, 48 is divisible by 12 and it is divisible by all the factors of 12. That is, 48 is divisible by 1, 2, 3, 4, 6 and 12.

- **If a number is divisible by each of the co-prime numbers, then it is divisible by the product of the co-prime numbers.**

  For example, 108 is divisible by the co-prime numbers 3 and 4. 108 is also divisible by the product of 3 and 4, that is, 12.

- **If a pair of numbers is divisible by a number, then the sum of or the difference between the given pair of numbers is also divisible by the same number.**

  For example, 65 and 35 are divisible by 5. The sum of 65 and 35, that is, 100 is also divisible by 5. Similarly, the difference between them, that is, 30 is also divisible by 5.

Exercise 3.3

1. **Complete the following table.**

Number	Divisible by									
	2	3	4	5	6	7	8	9	10	11
7020	Yes									
11,456					No					
7,31,541				No						
97,240		No							Yes	
7,89,430			No							

2. **State whether the following statements are true or false and justify your answers.**

   a. All numbers that are divisible by 9 are not necessarily divisible by 3.

   b. If two given numbers are divisible by a number, then their difference/sum is also divisible by that number.

   c. If a number is divisible by 2 and not by 3, then it is divisible by 6.

   d. If a number is divisible by 2 and 5, then it is also divisible by the sum of 2 and 5, that is, 7.

   e. 84 is divisible by 4 and also by the multiples of 4.

Prime Factorisation

A prime number that divides a number completely is a **prime factor** of that number.

For example, the factors of 48 are 1, 2, 3, 4, 6, 8, 12, 16, 24 and 48. Thus, the prime factors of 48 are 2 and 3. Similarly, the factors of 100 are 1, 2, 4, 5, 10, 20, 25, 50 and 100. So, the prime factors of 100 are 2 and 5.

Prime factorisation can be done either by the factor tree method or by the division method. Factor Tree method is very lengthy for big numbers. So, prime factor method is preferred. Henceforth, in this book we will call the division method of finding prime factors as the **prime factor method**.

Note

1 is not a prime factor of any number.

Example 1: Express 840 as the product of its prime factors.

Factor Tree Method

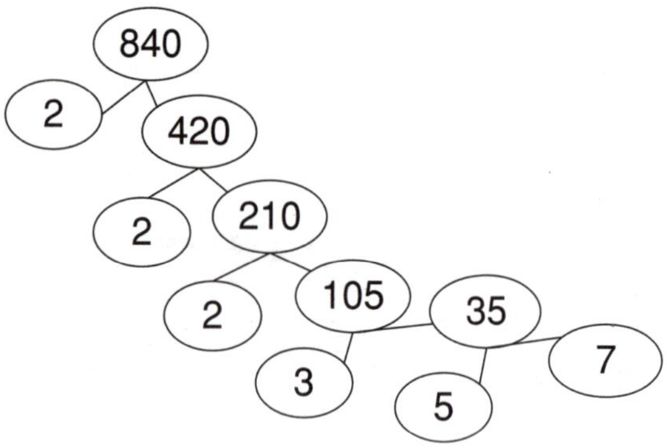

$840 = 2 \times 2 \times 2 \times 3 \times 5 \times 7$

Prime Factor Method

2	840
2	420
2	210
3	105
5	35
	7

Exercise 3.4

Express the following numbers as the product of their prime factors.

1. 136
2. 252
3. 9817
4. 1035
5. 13,915

Highest Common Factor (HCF)

The **highest common factor (HCF)** of any two numbers is the highest among the common factors. It is also known as the **greatest common divisor** (GCD). There are different ways to find the HCF for a given set of numbers. Let us discuss them one by one.

Method 1 Method of Common Factors

Step 1: List the factors of each number.

Step 2: Mark the common factors.

Step 3: Identify the highest common factor among all the common factors.

Example 2: Find the HCF of 64 and 120.

The factors of 64 are 1, **2, 4, 8,** 16, 32 and 64.

The factors of 120 are 1, **2**, 3, **4**, 5, 6, **8**, 10, 12, 20, 24, 30, 40, 60 and 120.

The common factors are 2, 4 and 8.

So, the HCF of 64 and 120 is 8.

Method 2 Prime Factorisation Method

Step 1: Factorise the given numbers into prime factors.

Step 2: Find the HCF by multiplying the common prime factors.

Example 3: Find the HCF of 45 and 108.

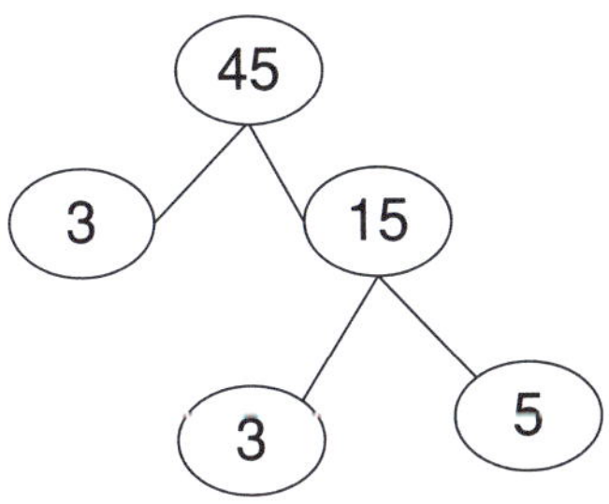

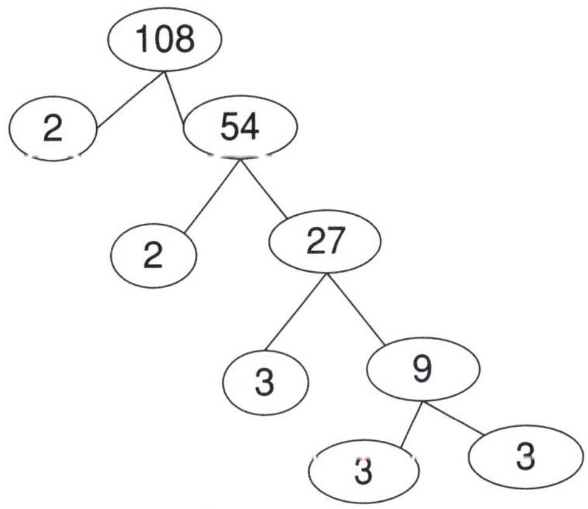

Prime factors of 45 = $\mathbf{3} \times \mathbf{3} \times 5$

Prime factors of 108 = $2 \times 2 \times 3 \times \mathbf{3} \times \mathbf{3}$

Therefore, the HCF of 45 and 108 is $3 \times 3 = 9$.

Method 3 Long Division Method

Step 1: Divide the greater number by the smaller number and then divide the previous divisor by the remainder.

Step 2: Repeat the process of division until the remainder is 0.

Step 3: The last divisor is the HCF of the number.

Example 4: Find the HCF of 144 and 84.

84) 144 (1
−84
60) 84 (1
−60
24) 60 (2
−48
12) 24 (2
−24
00

Therefore, the HCF of 144 and 84 is 12.

Example 5: Find the HCF of 936 and 864

864) 936 (1
−864
72) 864 (12
−72
144
−144
000

Therefore, the HCF of 936 and 864 is 72.

This answer can also be verified by the prime factorisation method as follows.

The factors of 144 are 1, 2, 3, 4, **6**, 12, 24, 36, 48, 72 and 144.

The factors of 84 are 1, 2, 3, 4, **6**, 7, 12, 14, 21, 28, 42 and 84.

So, the HCF is 12.

Real-life Applications of HCF

HCF is used to solve problems of arranging things into rows or columns, identifying the greatest number of things out of two or more quantities and so on.

Example 6: A rectangular hall of dimensions 60 feet by 24 feet is to be tiled with square tiles of certain dimension. All tiles have to be of same dimensions. Find the largest square tile that can be used to cover the hall completely.

```
       2
24 ) 60
    -48     2
    12 ) 24
        -24
         00
```

The HCF of 60 and 24 is 12.

Therefore, a square tile of dimension 12 feet would be the largest square tile that can be used to cover the hall completely.

Example 7: A library has 450 books on arts and 600 books on science. If the librarian wants to arrange them in the shelves in such a way that each shelf contains the same number of books of the same subject with no books left. Find the greatest number of books that can be arranged in each shelf. Also, find the total number of shelves needed.

```
          1
450 ) 600
     -450      3
     150 ) 450
          -450
           000
```

The HCF of 450 and 600 is 150.

The greatest number of books that can be arranged in each shelf is 150.

Total number of books = Number of books on arts + Number of books on science

= 450 + 600 = 1050

Number of shelves needed = 1050 ÷ 150 = 7

Therefore, 7 shelves are needed to arrange all the books.

Exercise 3.5

1. **Find the HCF of each pair of numbers by listing the factors.**

   a. 12 and 28 b. 30 and 12 c. 24 and 48 d. 45 and 72

2. **Find the HCF of each pair of numbers using the prime factorisation method.**

   a. 12 and 28 b. 64 and 120 c. 36 and 12 d. 40 and 88

3. **Find the HCF of each pair of numbers using the long division method.**

   a. 13 and 65 b. 120 and 280 c. 582 and 372 d. 658 and 770

4. A rectangular lawn of dimensions 168 m by 144 m is to be paved exactly with square grass patches of the same size. All grass patches have to be of the same size. What is the largest size of grass patch that can be used to cover the lawn?

5. 672 Boys and 480 girls are on a national learning trip. The boys and the girls are to be divided into separate smaller groups such that each group has the same number of girls or boys. What is the maximum number of students in each group such that no student is left out?

Least Common Multiple (LCM)

The **least common multiple (LCM)** or Greatest Common Denominator (GCD) of two numbers is the smallest among the common multiples of these numbers. There are different ways of finding the LCM of a given set of numbers. Let us learn them one by one.

Method 1 Common Multiple Method

Step 1: List the multiples of the given number.

Step 2: Identify the common multiples among them.

Step 3: Identify the least common multiple or LCM.

Example 8: Find the LCM of 5 and 6.

The multiples of 5 are 5, 10, 15, 20, 25, **30**, 35, 40, 45, 50, 55, **60**...

The multiples of 6 are 6, 12, 18, 24, **30**, 36, 42, 48, 54, **60**...

So, the common multiples of 5 and 6 are 30, 60....

Therefore, the LCM of 5 and 6 is 30.

Example 9: Find the LCM of 4 and 9.

The multiples of 4 are 4, 8, 12, 16, 20, 24, 28, 32, **36**, 40, 44, 48, 52, 56, 60, 64, 68, **72**...

The multiples of 9 are 9, 18, 27, **36**, 45, 54, 63, **72**...

The common multiples of 4 and 9 are 36, 72...

Therefore, the LCM of 4 and 9 is 36.

Mental Maths

Which of following are the common multiples of 6 and 8?

12, 16, 24, 32, 48

Method 2 Prime Factorisation Method

In this method, prime factorise the numbers and then indentify factors occurring maximum number of times in any of the numbers. Find their product to get the LCM.

Example 10: LCM of 20 and 30

$20 = \mathbf{2 \times 2 \times 5}$ $30 = \mathbf{2 \times 3 \times 5}$

2 occurs two times

Note that 2 occurs two times in 20, 5 occurs once in 30. So, the product 2 × 2 × 5 × 3 is the LCM.

∴ LCM of 20 and 30 = 2 × 2 × 5 × 3 = 60

Example 11: LCM of 18, 36 and 81

18 = 2 × 3 × 3

36 = 2 × 2 × 3 × 3

81 = 3 × 3 × 3 × 3

2 occurs twice in 36, 3 occurred four times in 81.

LCM of 18, 36 and 81 = 2 × 2 × 3 × 3 × 3 ×3

= 324

Example 12: LCM of 40, 50 and 75

40 = 2 × 2 × 2 × 5

50 = 2 × 5 × 5

75 = 3 × 5 × 5

LCM = 2 × 2 × 2 × 5 × 5 × 3 = 600

Method 3 Common Division Method

Step 1: Arrange the given numbers in a row in any order.

Step 2: Identify a prime number which divides at least two of the given numbers. Write the quotients and the undivided numbers below it.

Step 3: Identify another prime number which divides at least two numbers in the second row. Write the quotients and the undivided numbers (if any) below it.

Step 4: Continue this until all the numbers in a row are 1.

Step 5: LCM is the product of all these divisors.

Example 13: Find the LCM of 42 and 86.

2	42,	86
3	21,	43
7	7,	43
43	1,	43
	1,	1

Therefore, the LCM of 42 and 86 is $2 \times 3 \times 7 \times 43 = 1806$.

Example 14: Find the LCM of 210 and 250.

2	210,	250
3	105,	125
5	35,	125
5	7,	25
5	7,	5
7	7,	1
	1,	1

Therefore, the LCM of 210 and 250 is $2 \times 3 \times 5 \times 5 \times 5 \times 7 = 5250$.

Real-life Application of LCM

LCM is used in finding a common time frame when the individual time frame is given for different activities.

Mental Maths

What is the lowest common multiple of 6 and 10?

Example 15: If a patient is advised to take cough syrup every 4 hours and pills for fever at every 5 hours, then after how many hours will the patient take both the cough syrup and the pills?

Cough syrup is to be taken at hours which are multiples of 4 and pills are to be taken at hours which are multiples of 5.

The multiples of 4 are 4, 8, 12, 16, 20, 24, 28, 32, 36, 40...

The multiples of 5 are 5, 10, 15, 20, 25, 30, 35, 40, 45, 50...

The common multiples of 4 and 5 are 20 and 40.

The LCM of 4 and 5 is 20.

So, after 20 hours, the patient will take both the cough syrup and the pills.

Example 16: Two measuring rods are of lengths 66 cm and 84 cm. Find the shortest length that can be measured exactly by each one of these rods.

2	66 ,	84
2	33 ,	42
3	33 ,	21
7	11 ,	7
11	11 ,	1
	1 ,	1

The LCM of 66 and 84 is $2 \times 2 \times 3 \times 7 \times 11 = 924$.

Therefore, 924 m is the shortest length that can be measured exactly by each of the two rods.

Find the HCF and LCM of 36 and 60.

Exercise 3.6

1. **Find the LCM of each pair of numbers by the common multiple method.**

   a. 2 and 3 b. 4 and 7 c. 5 and 15 d. 10 and 25

2. **Find the LCM of each pair of numbers using the prime factorisation method.**

   a. 24 and 36 b. 24 and 80 c. 90 and 125 d. 160 and 112

3. **Find the LCM of each pair of numbers using the common division method.**

   a. 80 and 90 b. 108 and 180 c. 120 and 350 d. 700 and 490

4. Rahul goes to the market every 20 days and Marian goes to the same market every 45 days. They met each other today. After how many days will they meet again at the same market?

5. Find the least number which when divided separately by 28 and 36 leaves 9 as the remainder in each case.

Try This!

Find the HCF and LCM of

a. 40 and 100.

b. 54 and 72.

2	36
2	18
3	9
	3

2	60
2	30
3	15
	5

$36 = 2 \times 2 \times 3 \times 3 = 2^2 \times 3^2$

$60 = 2 \times 2 \times 3 \times 5 = 2^2 \times 3 \times 5$

HCF = $2^2 \times 3 = 12$ (For HCF, take the smaller powers of the common factors).

LCM = $2^2 \times 3^2 \times 5 = 180$ (For LCM, take the bigger powers of the common numbers. Then, take the left over numbers also).

Note

Use the prime factorisation method when both HCF and LCM are to be found in the same sum).

Summary

- A prime number has only two factors, that is, 1 and the number itself.
- A composite number has more than two factors.
- The number 1 is neither prime nor composite. The number 2 is the only even prime number.
- If the difference between two prime numbers is 2, then they are said to be twin primes.
- Two numbers are said to be co-primes if 1 is their only common factor.
- If a number is divisible by another number, then it is divisible by each of the factors of that number.
- If a number is divisible by two co-prime numbers, then it is divisible by their product also.
- If two given numbers are divisible by a number, then their sum is also divisible by that number.
- If two given numbers are divisible by a number, then their difference is also divisible by that number.
- A composite number can be expressed as the product of prime numbers. This way of writing a number is known as prime factorisation.
- Highest common factor (HCF) of numbers is the highest of their common factors. It is also known as the greatest common divisor (GCD).
- Lowest common multiple (LCM) of numbers is the lowest of their common multiples.

Revision Exercise

1 **Fill in the blanks.**

Number	Divisible by									
	2	3	4	5	6	7	8	9	10	11
12,453										
34,512										
78,145										
8,45,746										

2 **State whether the following statements are true or false and justify your answers.**

a. 3498 is divisible by 11 and 121.

b. If two numbers are divisible by a number, then their difference is also divisible by the same number.

c. The lowest number which is divisible by 7, 5 and 4 is 180.

d. The greatest number that will divide 197 and 269 leaving 5 as remainder in each case is 6.

3 **Find the HCF of each of the following pairs of numbers.**

a. 117 and 221 b. 145 and 232 c. 234 and 572 d. 693 and 1078

4 **Find the LCM of each of the following pairs of numbers.**

a. 42 and 63 b. 60 and 75 c. 36 and 78 d. 48 and 108

5 A carpenter has built a rectangular table and wants to tile the surface. If the table measures 360 cm by 1960 cm, what will be the largest square tile that can used without any cutting? How many square tiles will be used along the length of the table and how many will be used along the width of the table?

6 A school hallway has a long line of lockers. Every sixth locker has a pen and every eighth locker has an exercise book. What is the number of the first locker which has both a pen and an exercise book ?

For the Curious Mind

Find two composite numbers between 50 and 90 such that one of them is a square number and the difference between the numbers is the third multiple of 9. Find the sum and the difference between the HCF and the LCM of the composite numbers.

UNIT 1

Fractions 4

What I shall learn

- To find equivalent fractions
- To simplify fractions
- To compare fractions
- To perform basic operations on fractions
- To learn about real-life application of fractions

Quick Facts

Fraction as a Part of a Whole

$$\text{Fraction} = \frac{\text{Numerator}}{\text{Denominator}}$$

Some more examples:

Figure	Shaded Part	Fraction
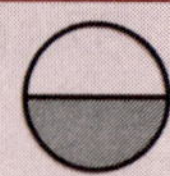	1 out of 2	$\frac{1}{2}$
	4 out of 5	$\frac{4}{5}$
	2 out of 6	$\frac{1}{3}$
	4 out of 7	$\frac{4}{7}$

Types of Fractions

Like Fractions: Like fractions have the same denominator.

Examples: $\frac{1}{6}, \frac{2}{6}, \frac{3}{6}, \frac{4}{6}$ and $\frac{5}{6}$

Unlike Fractions: Unlike fractions have different denominators.

Examples: $\frac{1}{2}, \frac{3}{4}, \frac{2}{5}, \frac{3}{7}$ and $\frac{6}{10}$

Unit Fractions: Unit fractions have 1 as its numerator.

Examples: $\frac{1}{2}, \frac{1}{3}, \frac{1}{4}, \frac{1}{6}$ and $\frac{1}{10}$

Proper Fractions: The numerator of a proper fraction is less than its denominator.

Examples: $\frac{5}{6}, \frac{2}{7}, \frac{1}{8}, \frac{2}{3}$ and $\frac{9}{10}$

Improper Fractions: The numerator of an improper fraction is more than its denominator.

Examples: $\frac{3}{2}, \frac{5}{4}, \frac{9}{7}, \frac{8}{3}$ and $\frac{10}{6}$

Mixed Fractions: Combination of a whole number and a proper fraction is a mixed fraction.

Examples: $1\frac{1}{3}, 2\frac{3}{7}, 4\frac{5}{8}, 4\frac{2}{3}$ and $1\frac{7}{10}$

Conversion of Fractions

Mixed Fraction to Improper Fraction

$$\text{Improper fraction} = \frac{(\text{Whole number} \times \text{Denominator}) + \text{Numerator}}{\text{Denominator}}$$

Example 1: Convert $3\frac{1}{2}$ into an improper fraction.

That is, $3\frac{1}{2} = \frac{(3\times2)+1}{2} = \frac{6+1}{2} = \frac{7}{2}$

Example 2: Convert $5\frac{1}{3}$ into an improper fraction.

That is, $5\frac{1}{3} = \frac{(5\times3)+1}{3} = \frac{15+1}{3} = \frac{16}{3}$

Common Errors

$1\frac{1}{2} = 1 + \frac{1}{2}$ ✓

$1\frac{1}{2} = 1 \times \frac{1}{2}$ ✗

Improper Fraction to Mixed Fraction

Divide the numerator by the denominator, then

$$\text{Mixed fraction} = \text{Quotient}\ \frac{\text{Remainder}}{\text{Divisor}}$$

Example 3: Convert $\frac{5}{2}$ into a mixed fraction.

$\therefore \frac{5}{2} = 2\frac{1}{2}$

```
    2 ──► Quotient
 2) 5
   -4
   ──
    1 ──► Remainder
```

Exercise 4.1

1 **Classify the following fractions into proper, improper and mixed fractions.**

$\frac{1}{4}, \frac{7}{3}, 1\frac{8}{9}, 2\frac{3}{5}, \frac{13}{7}, \frac{14}{5}, 2\frac{4}{7}, \frac{9}{11}, \frac{7}{10}, \frac{1}{8}, 5\frac{1}{7}, \frac{12}{11}$

2 **Classify the following pairs into like and unlike fractions.**

a. $\frac{1}{2}$ and $\frac{5}{2}$ b. $\frac{5}{6}$ and $\frac{1}{6}$ c. $\frac{7}{8}$ and $\frac{8}{7}$ d. $\frac{6}{10}$ and $\frac{7}{10}$ e. $\frac{4}{9}$ and $\frac{4}{7}$

3 **Convert the following into mixed fractions.**

a. $\frac{11}{6}$ b. $\frac{9}{2}$ c. $\frac{17}{10}$ d. $\frac{8}{3}$ e. $\frac{21}{11}$

4 **Convert the following into improper fractions.**

a. $2\frac{2}{5}$ b. $4\frac{2}{3}$ c. $1\frac{5}{7}$ d. $2\frac{3}{4}$ e. $3\frac{6}{10}$

Equivalent Fraction

Equivalent fractions have the same value.

Examples:

Remember

To get an equivalent fraction, multiply or divide the numerator and the denominator of the fraction by the same number.

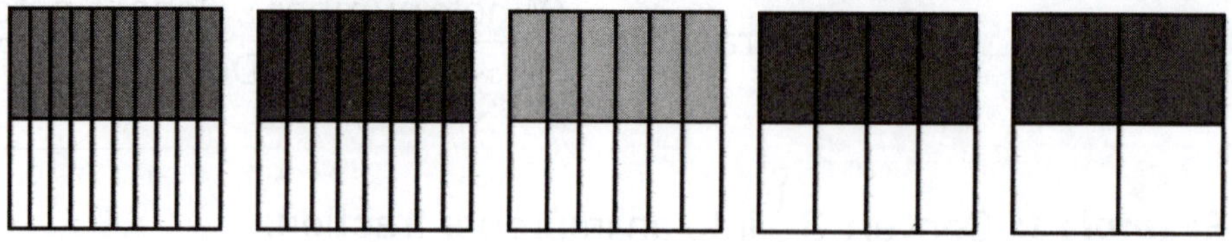

$\frac{10}{20}$ $\frac{8}{16}$ $\frac{6}{12}$ $\frac{4}{8}$ $\frac{2}{4}$

These fractions represent the same part of the whole.

That is, $\frac{10}{20} = \frac{8}{16} = \frac{6}{12} = \frac{4}{8} = \frac{2}{4} = \frac{1}{2}$

Example 4: Find the equivalent fractions of $\frac{3}{10}$.

Multiply both the numerator and the denominator of $\frac{3}{10}$ by the same number.

$\frac{3}{10} = \frac{3\times2}{10\times2} = \frac{6}{20}; = \frac{3\times3}{10\times3} = \frac{9}{30}; = \frac{3\times4}{10\times4} = \frac{12}{40}$

$\frac{3}{10} = \frac{6}{20} = \frac{9}{10} = \frac{12}{40} \ldots$

Therefore, three equivalent fractions of $\frac{3}{10}$ are $\frac{6}{20}$, $\frac{9}{30}$ and $\frac{12}{40}$.

How to Check Whether the given Fractions are Equivalent or not?

Let $\frac{a}{b}$ and $\frac{c}{d}$ be any two fractions. By cross multiplying the fractions, we get *ad* and *bc*. The given fractions are equal if the cross products are equal.

That is, $\frac{a}{b} = \frac{c}{d}$ if $ad = bc$.

Example 5: Find if the given fractions are equivalent of not.

a. $\frac{4}{25}$ and $\frac{8}{50}$

The cross products of $\frac{4}{25}$ and $\frac{8}{50}$ are $4 \times 50 = 200$ and $25 \times 8 = 200$.

Since the cross products are equal, the fractions are equivalent.

b. $\frac{3}{6}$ and $\frac{8}{12}$

The cross products of $\frac{3}{6}$ and $\frac{8}{12}$ are $3 \times 12 = 36$ and $6 \times 8 = 48$.

Since the cross products are not equal, the fractions are not equivalent.

Simplification of Fractions

A fraction is said to be in the simplest form if its numerator and denominator have no common factor except 1.

Example 6: Reduce $\frac{8}{24}$ to its simplest form.

Highest common factor of 8 and 24 is 8. So,

$$\frac{8}{24} = \frac{8 \div 8}{24 \div 8} = \frac{1}{3}$$

Now, 1 and 3 have no common factor except 1. Hence, $\frac{1}{3}$ is the simplest form of $\frac{8}{24}$.

Verification: Cross products of $\frac{8}{24}$ and $\frac{1}{3}$ are $8 \times 3 = 24$ and $24 \times 1 = 24$.

Since these are equal, the fractions are equivalent.

Example 7: Reduce $\frac{15}{25}$ to its simplest form.

Mental Maths

$$\frac{1}{10} = \frac{?}{100}$$

The HCF of 15 and 25 is 5. So,

$$\frac{15}{25} = \frac{15 \div 5}{25 \div 5} = \frac{3}{5}$$

Now, 1 and 5 have no common factor except 1. Hence, $\frac{3}{5}$ is in the simplest form.

Verification: Cross products of $\frac{15}{25}$ and $\frac{3}{5}$ are $15 \times 5 = 75$ and $25 \times 3 = 75$.

Since these are equal, the fractions are equivalent.

Exercise 4.2

1. **Write four equivalent fractions for the given fractions.**

   a. $\frac{4}{5}$ b. $\frac{6}{7}$ c. $\frac{3}{4}$ d. $\frac{5}{8}$

2. **Check whether the given fractions are equivalent or not.**

   a. $\frac{5}{8}$ and $\frac{8}{12}$ b. $\frac{1}{8}$ and $\frac{6}{10}$ c. $\frac{4}{9}$ and $\frac{12}{27}$ d. $\frac{5}{13}$ and $\frac{6}{14}$

3. **Reduce each of the given fractions into its simplest form.**

   a. $\frac{16}{24}$ b. $\frac{10}{50}$ c. $\frac{18}{72}$ d. $\frac{36}{54}$

Comparison of Fractions

Comparison of two fractions

- **When their denominators are same,** the fractions with the greater numerator is greater than the other fraction.
- **When their numerators are same,** the fraction with the greater denominator is smaller than the other fraction.
- **When their denominators are different,** we make the denominators equal by taking LCM and then compare the numerators.

Example 8: Compare $\frac{5}{8}$ and $\frac{3}{8}$.

$\frac{5}{8} > \frac{3}{8}$ (Since the denominators are same and $5 > 3$)

Example 9: $\frac{4}{9}$ and $\frac{4}{7}$

$\frac{4}{9} < \frac{4}{7}$ (Since the numerators are same and $7 < 9$)

Example 10: Compare $\frac{1}{5}$ and $\frac{2}{3}$.

Make the denominators equal and compare the numerators.

$\frac{1\times3}{5\times3} = \frac{3}{15}$ and $\frac{2\times5}{3\times5} = \frac{10}{15}$ — LCM of 5 and 3 is 15

$\therefore \frac{10}{15} > \frac{3}{15}$ (Since the denominators are same and $10 > 3$)

So, $\frac{2}{3} > \frac{1}{5}$.

Arranging the Fractions in Ascending Order and Descending Order

Example 11: Nisha, Deepa, Megha, Deeksha and Sanjana knitted the shawls measuring $\frac{1}{6}$m, $\frac{1}{2}$m, $\frac{1}{4}$m, $\frac{1}{3}$ m and $\frac{1}{10}$ m respectively. Arrange the given measurements in ascending order.

Since the numerators are same, arrange the denominators in order.

$$\frac{1}{10} < \frac{1}{6} < \frac{1}{4} < \frac{1}{3} < \frac{1}{2}$$

Example 12: Arrange these fractions in descending order.

$$\frac{4}{9}, \frac{2}{3}, \frac{5}{9}, \frac{1}{3}, \frac{8}{9}$$

Make the denominators equal $\frac{4}{9}, \frac{2\times3}{3\times3}, \frac{5}{9}, \frac{1\times3}{3\times3}, \frac{8}{9}$ — LCM of 5 and 3 is 15

$$\frac{4}{9}, \frac{6}{9}, \frac{5}{9}, \frac{3}{9}, \frac{8}{9}$$

Descending order: $\frac{8}{9} > \frac{6}{9} > \frac{5}{9} > \frac{4}{9} > \frac{3}{9}$

Exercise 4.3

1 Compare the fractions and insert the symbol '>' or '<'.

a. $\frac{3}{6}$ [ ] $\frac{3}{4}$ b. $\frac{2}{3}$ [ ] $\frac{4}{7}$ c. $\frac{1}{5}$ [ ] $\frac{4}{5}$

d. $\frac{7}{9}$ [ ] $\frac{1}{3}$ e. $\frac{2}{3}$ [ ] $\frac{1}{4}$ f. $\frac{3}{7}$ [ ] $\frac{5}{7}$

2 Arrange the following in ascending order.

a. $\frac{3}{10}, \frac{3}{7}, \frac{3}{11}, \frac{3}{4}, \frac{3}{5}$ b. $\frac{6}{7}, \frac{4}{7}, \frac{3}{14}, \frac{9}{14}, \frac{3}{7}$ c. $\frac{4}{5}, \frac{3}{5}, \frac{1}{5}, \frac{2}{5}, \frac{5}{5}$ d. $\frac{1}{2}, \frac{2}{3}, \frac{5}{6}, \frac{1}{3}, \frac{1}{6}$

3 Arrange the following in descending order.

a. $\frac{4}{9}, \frac{4}{5}, \frac{4}{8}, \frac{4}{7}, \frac{4}{10}$ b. $\frac{2}{3}, \frac{1}{5}, \frac{2}{5}, \frac{1}{3}, \frac{4}{5}$ c. $\frac{8}{10}, \frac{4}{10}, \frac{9}{10}, \frac{3}{10}, \frac{7}{10}$ d. $\frac{1}{8}, \frac{1}{2}, \frac{5}{8}, \frac{3}{4}, \frac{1}{4}$

Basic Operation on Fractions

Addition and Subtraction of like Fractions

The sum of like fractions is found by adding their numerators. Similarly, the difference between like fractions is found by subtracting their numerators.

Example 13: Find the sum of $\frac{5}{9}$ and $\frac{1}{9}$.

$$\frac{5}{9} + \frac{1}{9} = \frac{6}{9} = \frac{2}{3}$$

Therefore, the sum of $\frac{5}{9}$ and $\frac{1}{9}$ is $\frac{6}{9} = \frac{2}{3}$.

Example 14: Find the difference between $\frac{1}{5}$ and $\frac{4}{5}$.

$$\frac{4}{5} - \frac{1}{5} = \frac{3}{5}$$

Therefore, the difference between $\frac{4}{5}$ and $\frac{1}{5}$ is $\frac{3}{5}$.

Addition and Subtraction of Unlike Fractions

The sum of unlike fractions is found by making the denominators equal and then adding the numerators. Similarly, the difference between unlike fractions is found by making the denominators equal before subtracting the numerators.

Example 15: Find the sum of $\frac{2}{3}$ and $\frac{1}{4}$.

$$\frac{2}{3}+\frac{1}{4}=\frac{2\times4}{3\times4}+\frac{1\times3}{4\times3}$$

$$\frac{8}{12}+\frac{3}{12}=\frac{11}{12}$$

Therefore, sum of $\frac{2}{3}$ and $\frac{1}{4}$ is $\frac{11}{12}$.

Example 16: Find the difference between $\frac{1}{2}$ and $\frac{1}{7}$.

$$\frac{1}{2}-\frac{1}{7}=\frac{1\times7}{2\times7}-\frac{1\times2}{7\times2}$$

$$\frac{7}{14}-\frac{2}{14}=\frac{5}{14}$$

Therefore, difference between $\frac{1}{2}$ and $\frac{1}{7}$ is $\frac{5}{14}$.

Addition and Subtraction of Mixed Fractions

The sum or the difference of mixed fractions is found by converting them into improper fractions. Always retain the answer in its simplest form.

Example 17: Find the sum of $1\frac{1}{5}$ and $2\frac{1}{10}$.

$$1\frac{1}{5}+2\frac{1}{10}$$

$$=\frac{6}{5}+\frac{21}{10}$$

$$=\frac{6\times2}{5\times2}+\frac{21}{10}$$

$$=\frac{12}{10}+\frac{21}{10}=\frac{33}{10}=3\frac{3}{10}$$

Therefore, the sum of $1\frac{1}{5}$ and $2\frac{1}{10}$ is $3\frac{3}{10}$.

Example 18: Find the difference between $2\frac{2}{3}$ and $1\frac{1}{2}$.

$$2\frac{2}{3}-1\frac{1}{2}$$

$$=\frac{8}{3}-\frac{3}{2}$$

$$=\frac{8\times2}{3\times2}-\frac{3\times3}{2\times3}$$

$$=\frac{16}{6}-\frac{9}{6}=\frac{7}{6}=1\frac{1}{6}$$

Therefore, the difference between $2\frac{2}{3}$ and $1\frac{1}{2}$ is $1\frac{1}{6}$.

Hints and Tips

Shortcut for addition of mixed fractions:

1. Add the whole parts separately
2. Add the fractional parts separately.
3. Combine answers of steps (1) and (2) and write the answer.

Example: $3\frac{1}{2}+1\frac{1}{2}$
$=4+1=5$

Example 19: What should be added to $2\frac{1}{2}$ to get $4\frac{1}{4}$?

Let the number to be added be x.

$$2\frac{1}{2}+x=4\frac{1}{4}$$

$$x=4\frac{1}{4}-2\frac{1}{2}$$

$$=\frac{17}{4}-\frac{5}{2}$$

$$=\frac{17}{4}-\frac{5\times2}{2\times2}=\frac{17}{4}-\frac{10}{4}=\frac{7}{4}=1\frac{3}{4}$$

Therefore, $1\frac{3}{4}$ should be added to $2\frac{1}{2}$ to get $4\frac{1}{4}$.

Example 20: What should be subtracted from $6\frac{1}{4}$ to get $2\frac{1}{3}$?

Let the number to be subtracted be x.

$$6\frac{1}{4} - x = 2\frac{1}{3}$$

$$x = 6\frac{1}{4} - 2\frac{1}{3}$$

$$= \frac{25}{4} - \frac{7}{3}$$

$$= \frac{25\times3}{4\times3} - \frac{7\times4}{3\times4} = \frac{75}{12} - \frac{28}{12}$$

$$= \frac{47}{12} = 3\frac{11}{12}$$

Therefore, $3\frac{11}{12}$ should be subtracted from $6\frac{1}{4}$ to get $2\frac{1}{3}$.

Exercise 4.4

1. **Find the sum of the following.**

   a. $\frac{1}{9}$ and $\frac{4}{9}$ b. $\frac{2}{3}$ and $\frac{1}{6}$ c. $\frac{4}{5}$ and $\frac{1}{3}$ d. $1\frac{1}{2}$ and $5\frac{2}{7}$

2. **Find the difference between the following.**

   a. $\frac{4}{9}$ and $\frac{7}{9}$ b. $\frac{4}{5}$ and $\frac{3}{10}$ c. $\frac{3}{4}$ and $\frac{2}{3}$ d. $2\frac{1}{3}$ and $1\frac{3}{4}$

3. What should be added to $1\frac{1}{5}$ to get $4\frac{2}{3}$?

4. What should be deducted from $6\frac{4}{7}$ to get $2\frac{1}{4}$?

Multiplication of Fractions

$$\text{Product of fractions} = \frac{\text{Product of the numerators}}{\text{Product of the denominators}}$$

Note

Mixed fractions are converted into improper fractions before multiplying.

Example 21: Find the product of $\frac{2}{3}$ and 15.

$$\frac{2}{\cancel{3}_1} \times \frac{\cancel{15}^5}{1} = 10$$

Example 22: Find the product of $\frac{4}{5}$ and $\frac{2}{8}$.

$$\frac{{}^1\cancel{4}}{5} \times \frac{\cancel{2}^1}{\cancel{8}_{\cancel{4}_1}} = \frac{1}{5}.$$

Example 23: Find the product of $2\frac{6}{8}$ and 24.

$$2\frac{6}{8} = \frac{22}{8} \text{ and } 24 = \frac{24}{1}$$

$$\frac{22\times\cancel{24}^3}{\cancel{8}_1\times1} = \frac{22\times3}{1\times1} = \frac{66}{1} = 66$$

Example 24: Find the product of $1\frac{3}{4}$ and $2\frac{8}{9}$.

$$1\frac{3}{4} = \frac{7}{4} \text{ and } 2\frac{8}{9} = \frac{26}{9}$$

$$\frac{7\times\cancel{26}^{13}}{\cancel{4}_2\times9} = \frac{7\times13}{2\times9} = \frac{91}{18} = 5\frac{1}{18}$$

Exercise 4.5

1 Find the product of the following.

a. $\frac{1}{5} \times 45$ b. $\frac{5}{6} \times \frac{7}{11}$ c. $2\frac{1}{3} \times 3\frac{3}{5}$

d. $5\frac{3}{5} \times \frac{4}{7}$ e. $2\frac{1}{2} \times 15$ f. $\frac{1}{4} \times \frac{5}{8}$

Division of Fractions

To divide a whole number by any fraction, we multiply that number by the reciprocal of that fraction. Similarly to divide a fraction by a whole number, we multiply the fraction by the reciprocal of the whole number. To divide a fraction by another fraction, we multiply the first fraction by the reciprocal of the second fraction. Note that we always retain the answer in its simplest form.

Reciprocal of a fraction is written by interchanging the numerator and the denominator. For example, the reciprocal of $\frac{7}{4}$ **is** $\frac{4}{7}$ and the reciprocal of 9 **is** $\frac{1}{9}$.

The reciprocal of a proper fraction is an improper fraction and the reciprocal of an improper fraction is a proper fraction.

Example 25: $10 \div \frac{2}{3}$

$$\frac{10}{1} \div \frac{2}{3} = \frac{\overset{5}{\cancel{10}}}{1} \times \frac{3}{\cancel{2}_1} = 15$$

Example 26: $1\frac{6}{7} \div 26$

$$1\frac{6}{7} \div 26 = \frac{\overset{1}{\cancel{13}}}{7} \times \frac{1}{\underset{2}{\cancel{26}}} = \frac{1}{14}$$

Example 27: $\frac{4}{9} \div \frac{1}{6}$

$$\frac{4}{9} \div \frac{1}{6} = \frac{4}{9} \times \frac{6}{1} = \frac{4}{\cancel{9}_3} \times \frac{\cancel{6}^2}{1} = \frac{8}{3} = 2\frac{2}{3}$$

Example 28: $1\frac{5}{6} \div 2\frac{3}{4}$

$$1\frac{5}{6} \div 2\frac{3}{4} = \frac{11}{6} \times \frac{4}{11} = \frac{\cancel{11}}{\cancel{6}_3} \times \frac{\cancel{4}^2}{\cancel{11}} = \frac{2}{3}$$

Example 29: What should be multiplied by $3\frac{1}{9}$ to get $5\frac{4}{9}$ as a product?

$$5\frac{4}{9} = 3\frac{1}{9} \times x$$

$$x = 5\frac{4}{9} \div 3\frac{1}{9} = \frac{49}{9} \div \frac{28}{9}$$

$$x = \frac{\cancel{49}^7}{\cancel{9}} \times \frac{\cancel{9}}{\cancel{28}_4} = \frac{7}{4} = 1\frac{3}{4}$$

Exercise 4.6

1 Solve the following.

a. $9 \div \frac{2}{3}$ b. $\frac{4}{15} \div 6$ c. $\frac{3}{15} \div \frac{6}{20}$

d. $\frac{14}{15} \div 1\frac{1}{6}$ e. $2\frac{1}{4} \div 1\frac{1}{3}$ f. $2\frac{2}{3} \div \frac{8}{11}$

Simplification

Simplification is the process of simplifying a numerical expression containing a fraction. The mathematical operations are done according to the BODMAS principle.

B – Bracket Round brackets ( )
Flower or curly bracket or braces brackets { }
Square brackets [ ]

O – Of (works like multiplication but is performed before division)

D – Division (÷)

M – Multiplication (×)

A – Addition (+)

S – Subtraction (–)

Note

The usual calculators do not follow the BODMAS principle.

Example 30: Simplify $1\frac{1}{5}-\frac{1}{4}+\frac{1}{2}\div 3 \text{ of } 3\frac{1}{3}$

Solve the expression using the BODMAS principle.

$$1\frac{1}{5}-\frac{1}{4}+\frac{1}{2}\div 3 \text{ of } 3\frac{1}{3}$$

Operation of 'Of' $\quad \frac{6}{5}-\frac{1}{4}+\frac{1}{2}\div \cancel{3}^{1} \text{ of } \frac{10}{\cancel{3}_{1}} = \frac{6}{5}-\frac{1}{4}+\frac{1}{2}\div\frac{10}{1}$

Divide $\quad \frac{6}{5}-\frac{1}{4}+\frac{1}{2}\times\frac{1}{10} = \frac{6}{5}-\frac{1}{4}+\frac{1}{20} = \frac{6\times4-1\times5+1\times1}{20}$

Add $\quad \frac{6\times4}{5\times4}-\frac{1}{4}+\frac{1}{20} = \frac{24+1}{20}-\frac{1}{4} = \frac{25}{20}-\frac{1}{4}$

Subtract $\quad \frac{25}{20}-\frac{1\times5}{4\times5} = \frac{25-5}{20} = \frac{20}{20} = 1$

Example 31: Simplify $\frac{1}{3}+\frac{1}{2}-\left[\frac{2}{3}\div\frac{5}{6}+\left\{\frac{1}{4}\times\left(\frac{1}{3}+\frac{1}{3}-\frac{1}{2}\right)+\frac{5}{6}\right\}\div\frac{7}{8}\right]\div 5\frac{2}{5}$

Solve the expression using the BODMAS principle.

$$\frac{1}{3}+\frac{1}{2}-\left[\frac{2}{3}\div\frac{5}{6}+\left\{\frac{1}{4}\times\left(\frac{1}{3}+\frac{1}{3}-\frac{1}{2}\right)+\frac{5}{6}\right\}\div\frac{7}{8}\right]\div 5\frac{2}{5}$$

(Remove round brackets) $\quad = \frac{1}{3}+\frac{1}{2}-\left[\frac{2}{3}\div\frac{5}{6}+\left\{\frac{1}{4}\times\left(\frac{2+2-3}{6}\right)+\frac{5}{6}\right\}\div\frac{7}{8}\right]\div\frac{27}{5}$

(Remove curly brackets) $\quad = \frac{1}{3}+\frac{1}{2}-\left[\frac{2}{3}\div\frac{5}{6}+\left\{\frac{1}{4}\times\frac{1}{6}+\frac{5}{6}\right\}\div\frac{7}{8}\right]\div\frac{27}{5}$

$$= \frac{1}{3}+\frac{1}{2}-\left[\frac{2}{3}\div\frac{5}{6}+\left\{\frac{1}{24}+\frac{5}{6}\right\}\div\frac{7}{8}\right]\div\frac{27}{5}$$

(Remove square brackets) $= \frac{1}{3}+\frac{1}{2}-\left[\frac{2}{3}\div\frac{5}{6}+\frac{21}{24}\div\frac{7}{8}\right]\div\frac{27}{5} = \frac{1}{3}+\frac{1}{2}-\left[\frac{2}{\cancel{3}}\times\frac{\cancel{6}^{2}}{5}+\frac{\cancel{21}^{\cancel{3}^{1}}}{\cancel{24}_{3}}\div\frac{\cancel{8}_{1}}{\cancel{7}_{\cancel{1}_{1}}}\right]\div\frac{27}{5}$

$= \frac{1}{3}+\frac{1}{2}-\left[\frac{4}{5}+1\right]\div\frac{27}{5} = \frac{1}{3}+\frac{1}{2}-\left[\frac{4+5}{5}\right]\div\frac{27}{5} = \frac{1}{3}+\frac{1}{2}-\frac{9}{5}\div\frac{27}{5}$

(Divide) $= \frac{1}{3}+\frac{1}{2}-\frac{\cancel{9}}{\cancel{5}}\times\frac{\cancel{5}}{\cancel{27}_{3}}$

(Add and subtract) $= \frac{1}{3}+\frac{1}{2}-\frac{1}{3}=\frac{1}{2}$

Exercise 4.7

Solve the following.

a. $1\frac{1}{6}\div 1\frac{5}{9}\times 3\frac{1}{2}$

b. $\left(1\frac{1}{3}\div 3\frac{1}{10}\right)$ of $\left(2\frac{1}{2}\div\frac{1}{2}\right)$

c. $\left(1\frac{1}{3}\div\frac{3}{7}\right)$ of $\left(2\frac{5}{8}+1\frac{1}{9}\right)$

d. $\frac{3}{5}\div\left(\frac{5}{7}-\frac{3}{5}\right)-\frac{1}{2}$ of $\left(9\frac{7}{10}-2\frac{1}{5}\right)$

e. $\left(\frac{3}{4}-\frac{1}{5}\right)\div\left(\frac{3}{5}\times\frac{1}{2}\right)-\frac{1}{3}\div 2$

f. $\left(2\frac{4}{5}\times 1\frac{3}{7}\right)\div\left(1\frac{3}{4}\times 1\frac{1}{7}\right)$

Real-life Application of Fractions.

Example 32: If $\frac{1}{4}$ of an audience are women while $\frac{1}{3}$ are children, what part of the audience are men?

Number of men = Total audience – (Number of women + Number of children)

$$= 1-\left(\frac{1}{4}+\frac{1}{3}\right) = 1-\left(\frac{3+4}{12}\right) = 1-\left(\frac{7}{12}\right) = \frac{12-7}{12} = \frac{5}{12}$$

Thus, $\frac{5}{12}$ of the audience are men.

Example 33: A mug can hold $\frac{7}{14}\ell$ of water. How many mugs of water will be needed to fill up an empty bucket of capacity $4\frac{1}{2}\ell$?

Capacity of bucket = $4\frac{1}{2}\ell$ Capacity of mug = $\frac{7}{14}\ell$

Number of mugs of water needed to fill the bucket = $4\frac{1}{2}\div\frac{7}{14} = \frac{9}{\cancel{2}}\times\frac{\cancel{14}^{7}}{\cancel{7}} = 9$

Thus, 9 mugs of water will be needed to fill up the bucket.

Example 34: A man gave $\frac{5}{8}$ of his money to his daughter, $\frac{2}{3}$ of the remainder to his son and remaining to his wife. If wife gets ₹8500, what is the total amount?

Part of the money given to the daughter = $\frac{5}{8}$

Part of the money given to the son = $\frac{2}{3}$ of $\left(1-\frac{5}{8}\right) = \frac{2}{3}$ of $\frac{3}{8} = \frac{\cancel{2}}{\cancel{3}} \times \frac{\cancel{3}}{\cancel{8}_4} = \frac{1}{4}$

Part of the money given to the wife = $1-\left(\frac{5}{8}+\frac{1}{4}\right) = 1-\left(\frac{5+2}{8}\right) = 1-\frac{7}{8} = \frac{8-7}{8} = \frac{1}{8}$

If $\frac{1}{8}$ of the amount is ₹8500, then the total amount is 8500×8 = ₹68,000.

Example 35: There are 150 members in a committee. In a meeting, $\frac{7}{10}$ of them are present. How many members are absent?

Number of members present = $\frac{7}{10}$ of $150 = \frac{7}{1\cancel{0}} \times 15\cancel{0} = 7 \times 15 = 105$

Number of members absent = 150 − 105 = 45 Thus, 45 members are absent.

Exercise 4.8

1. In a school, $\frac{3}{8}$ students are boys and 850 are girls. Find the number of boys in the school.
2. A sum of money was divided between Anil and Karan. If Karan got $\frac{4}{9}$ of the whole amount and his share was ₹3500, find the total amount and Anil's share.
3. A drum of water was $\frac{2}{3}$ full. When 20 litres were drawn from it, it became half full. What was the capacity of the drum and how much water did the drum contain when it was $\frac{2}{3}$ full?
4. Three ballpoint pens cost ₹$22\frac{1}{2}$ and five sketch pens cost ₹$58\frac{3}{4}$. How much more does each sketch pen cost than each ballpoint pen?
5. An iceberg of total height 66 m is in the sea. $\frac{5}{6}$ part of the iceberg is under water. How many metres of the iceberg can be seen above the level of water?

Summary

- Make the denominators equal before adding or subtracting the numerators if the given denominators are different.
- To divide a fraction by a whole number, multiply the fraction by the reciprocal of the whole number.
- To divide a fraction by another fraction, multiply the fraction by the reciprocal of the other fraction.
- The order to be followed while simplifying an expression is given by the BODMAS principle.

  B – Bracket **O** – Of **D** – Division **M** – Multiplication **A** – Addition **S** – Subtraction

Revision Exercise

1 Choose the correct options.

a. The fraction equivalent to $\frac{3}{5}$ is ________.

i. $\frac{12}{15}$ ii. $\frac{9}{10}$ iii. $\frac{15}{25}$ iv. $\frac{36}{40}$

b. The simplest form of is $\frac{84}{108}$ is ________

i. $\frac{48}{54}$ ii. $\frac{24}{27}$ iii. $\frac{7}{9}$ iv. None of these

c. Which of the following is correct?

i. $\frac{2}{7} < \frac{2}{9}$ ii. $\frac{2}{7} > \frac{2}{9}$ iii. $\frac{2}{7} = \frac{2}{9}$ iv. $\frac{2}{7}$ and $\frac{2}{9}$ cannot be compared

d. The smallest of the fractions $\frac{4}{15}, \frac{2}{5}, \frac{1}{3}, \frac{3}{5}$ is ________.

i. $\frac{4}{15}$ ii. $\frac{2}{5}$ iii. $\frac{1}{3}$ iv. $\frac{3}{5}$

e. The largest of the fractions $\frac{1}{3}, \frac{2}{5}, \frac{8}{15}, \frac{13}{30}$ is ________.

i. $\frac{1}{3}$ ii. $\frac{2}{5}$ iii. $\frac{8}{15}$ iv. $\frac{13}{30}$

2 Solve the following.

a. $\frac{4}{5} + \frac{2}{5}$ b. $\frac{5}{9} + \frac{7}{10}$ c. $6\frac{2}{5} + 4\frac{3}{4}$ d. $8\frac{2}{3} + 9\frac{3}{8}$ e. $\frac{3}{6} + \frac{7}{9}$

3 Solve the following.

a. $\frac{7}{9} - \frac{5}{9}$ b. $\frac{13}{24} - \frac{11}{24}$ c. $\frac{2}{5} - \frac{1}{10}$ d. $\frac{5}{7} - \frac{6}{11}$ e. $4\frac{2}{3} - 3\frac{3}{4}$

4 Solve the following.

a. $\frac{2}{6} \times 36$ b. $\frac{2}{8} \times \frac{5}{6}$ c. $\frac{4}{7} \times \frac{14}{15}$ d. $\frac{5}{9} \times 2\frac{6}{15}$ e. $1\frac{7}{8} \times 3\frac{3}{5}$

5 Solve the following.

a. $\frac{2}{5} \div 16$ b. $\frac{3}{4} \div \frac{9}{10}$ c. $\frac{5}{8} \div \frac{15}{16}$ d. $1\frac{8}{10} \div 1\frac{6}{9}$ e. $\frac{2}{7} \div \frac{6}{14}$

6 **Solve the following.**

a. $1\frac{1}{2} \div 1\frac{1}{5} \times 2\frac{6}{7}$

b. $1\frac{1}{5} \div \left(1\frac{9}{15} \text{ of } 2\frac{1}{3}\right) \div \frac{1}{2}$

c. $1\frac{6}{8} \div \left(\frac{5}{8} \text{ of } 1\frac{2}{14}\right) + \frac{7}{10}$

d. $\frac{17}{20} \div \left(\frac{5}{8} - \frac{1}{5}\right) - \frac{1}{4}$

e. $\left(\frac{5}{7} - \frac{1}{2}\right) \div \left(\frac{1}{2} \times \frac{6}{7}\right) - \frac{1}{2}$

f. $\frac{1}{4} - \frac{2}{3} \text{ of } \frac{6}{7} + \frac{5}{12}$

7 **Solve the following word problems.**

a. Megha bought $1\frac{1}{5}$ kg of grapes and $2\frac{3}{4}$ kg of mangoes. What was the total weight of the fruits that Megha bought?

b. A petrol tank is filled with $4\frac{1}{4}$ litres of petrol. If $\frac{1}{8}$ of the petrol leaks out, then how many litres of petrol would be left?

c. If Rakesh has 16 CDs, out of which $\frac{1}{4}$ of them are classical music, then how many CDs are of classical music?

d. If it rains $\frac{3}{5}$ days in a year, how many days does it rain during the year?

e. Radhika spent $\frac{4}{7}$ part of her holidays completing her homework, $\frac{2}{7}$ part for a holiday trip and the rest she spent with her grandparents. If she spent 4 days with her grandparents then what is the total duration of the holidays.

For the Curious Mind

There are 672 students in the school. $\frac{1}{12}$ of them are studying in Class 6, $\frac{3}{7}$ of them are girls, and $\frac{1}{3}$ of the girls and $\frac{1}{2}$ of the boys participated in various sports. Find the number of students who did not participate in sports.

UNIT 1

Decimal Numbers 5

What I shall learn

- To compare decimal numbers
- To represent decimal numbers on the number line
- To perform basic operations on decimal numbers

Let's Get Started

The fractions in which the denominators are 10, 100, 1000 and so on are known as **decimal fractions**.

We have already learned how to represent tenths and hundredths in the pictorial form.

Look at the following.

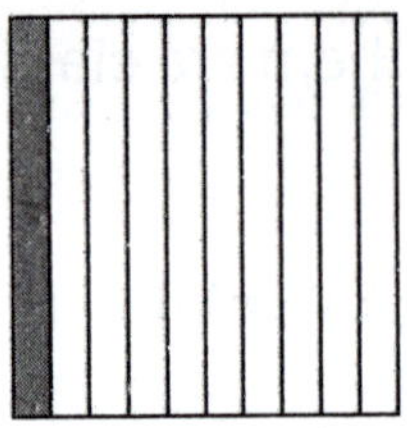

$\frac{1}{10}$ represents one-tenth of the figure and is written as 0.1. It is read as 'zero point one'.

$$\frac{1}{10} = 0.1$$

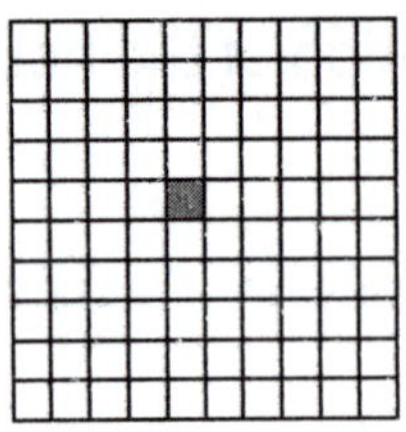

Similarly, $\frac{1}{100}$ represents one-hundredth and is written as 0.01. It is read as 'zero point zero one'.

$$\frac{1}{100} = 0.01$$

Now, let us learn about thousandths.

Thousandths

When one whole is divided into 1000 equal parts, each part represents $\frac{1}{1000}$. It is written as 0.001 and read as 'one thousandths' or 'zero point zero zero one'.

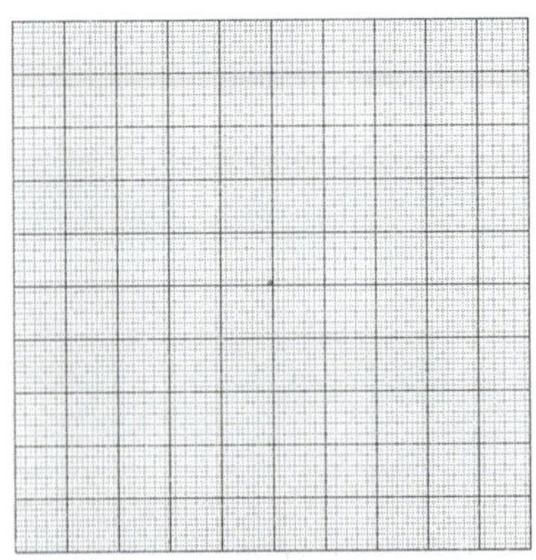

Try These!

Write the decimal form of each of the following fractions.

a. $\frac{7}{10}$ b. $\frac{7}{100}$

c. $\frac{27}{100}$ d. $\frac{1}{1000}$

Now, let us see how to write the place value of each digit in a place value chart for a decimal number, for example, 3618.925.

Thousands	Hundreds	Tens	Ones	Decimal Point	Tenths	Hundredths	Thousandths
3×1000	6×100	1×10	8×1	.	$9 \times \frac{1}{10} = \frac{9}{10}$	$2 \times \frac{1}{100} = \frac{2}{100}$	$5 \times \frac{1}{1000} = \frac{5}{1000}$

You might have noticed that a dot or a decimal point separates the whole number part of the number from the fractional part. The part on the left side of the decimal point is called the **integral or whole part** of the number. We read the integral part like a group as 'three thousand six hundred eighteen'. The part on the right side of the decimal point is called the **fractional or decimal part** of the number as it represents a part of 1. While reading this part, we do not group it. Thus, the number 3618.925 is read as 'three thousand six hundred eighteen point nine two five'.

Place Value Chart for Decimals

Whole Number Part				Decimal Number Part		
Thousands	Hundreds	Tens	Ones	Tenths	Hundredths	Thousandths
1000	100	10	1	$\frac{1}{10}$	$\frac{1}{100}$	$\frac{1}{1000}$

Example 1: Write the place value and value of each digit.

a. 23.62

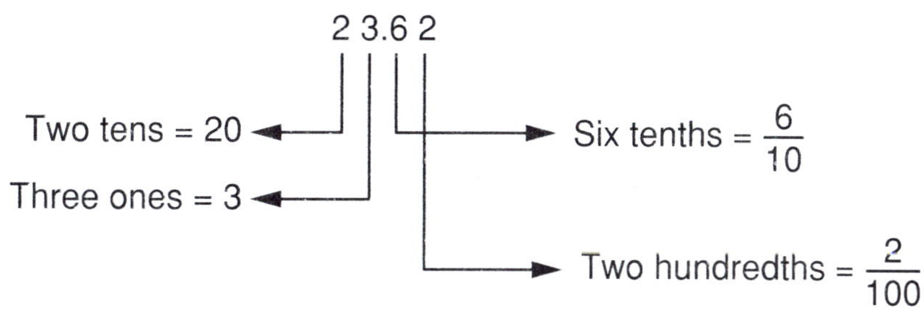

b. 5240.101

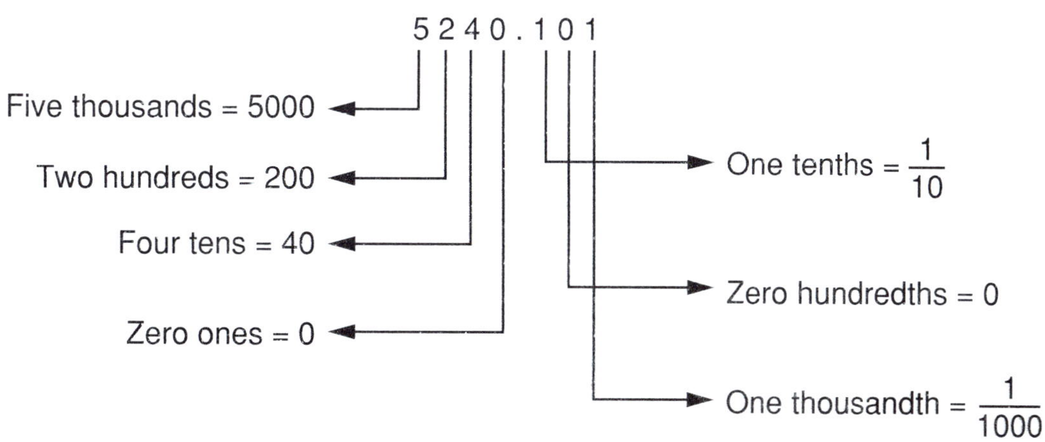

Example 2: Write the place value of the underlined number.

a. 34.5<u>6</u>

The place value of 6 in the number 34.56 is six hundredths or $\frac{6}{100}$.

b. 432.76<u>5</u>

The place value of 5 in the number 432.765 is five thousandths or $\frac{5}{1000}$.

More on Decimal Numbers

Decimal Places: The number of digits in the decimal part of a decimal number gives the number of decimal places.

For example, 6.06 is a decimal number with two decimal places and 7168.543 is a decimal number with three decimal places.

Like Decimal Numbers: Decimal numbers that have the same number of decimal places are called like decimals.

For example, 0.2, 31.1 and 721.3 are like decimals with one decimal place. Similarly, 3.78, 32.54 and 144.06 are like decimals with two decimal places.

Unlike Decimal Numbers: Decimal numbers that have different number of decimal places are called unlike decimals.

For example, 3.5, 6.94 and 51.905 are unlike decimals. Similarly, 43.12, 6.323 and 1.9 are also unlike decimals.

Comparison of Decimal Numbers

When we compare two decimal numbers that have different whole number parts, the decimal number with the greater whole number part is greater.

For example, 63.734 > 59.805.

When we compare two decimal numbers that have the same whole number part, we begin by converting the given numbers into like decimals by putting the required number of zeros to the right of the decimal point. Then we start comparing from the tenths place. The decimal number with the greater digit in the same place is greater.

For example, to compare 9.1 and 9.008, we first convert them into like decimals.

That is, 9.1 = 9.100. Now, 9.100 and 9.008 are like decimals.

On comparing, we get 9.100 > 9.008.

Converting Fractions into Decimals

Let us now try to find the decimal representations of some more fractions.

Case 1: When denominators are 10, 100, 1000 and so on

Example 3: Convert $\frac{501}{10}$, $\frac{501}{100}$ and $\frac{501}{1000}$ into decimal numbers.

The decimal form of $\frac{501}{10}$ is 50.1.

The decimal form of $\frac{501}{100}$ is 5.01.

And the decimal form of $\frac{501}{1000}$ is 0.501.

Case 2: When denominators are not powers of 10

If the denominator of a fraction is not a power of ten then we multiply both the numerator and the denominator by a whole number that makes the denominator a multiple of 10.

Example 4: Convert $\frac{25}{500}$ into a decimal number.

Multiply the numerator and the denominator by the same number to make it a power of 10.

That is, $\frac{25}{500} = \frac{25 \times 2}{500 \times 2} = \frac{50}{1000} = 0.050 = 0.05$

Example 5: Convert $1\frac{3}{4}$ into a decimal number.

To convert $1\frac{3}{4}$ into a decimal number, we need to find an equivalent fraction whose denominator is a power of 10.

That is, $1 + \frac{3}{4} = 1 + \frac{3 \times 25}{4 \times 25} = 1 + \frac{75}{100} = 1 + 0.75 = 1.75$

Fractions can also be converted into decimal numbers by the long division process.

Example 6: Convert $\frac{3}{25}$ into a decimal number using the long division process.

$$
\begin{array}{r}
0.12 \\
25\overline{)\,3.00} \\
-2\,5 \\
\hline
50 \\
-50 \\
\hline
0 \\
\hline
\end{array}
$$

$\therefore \frac{3}{25} = 0.12$

Convert $\frac{3}{25}$ into decimal form by making the denominator a multiple of 10 and verify the answer.

Think and Discuss

Look at the pattern between the denominator of the fraction and its decimal form in each case.

$\frac{1}{10} = 0.1$

$\frac{1}{100} = 0.01$

$\frac{1}{1000} = 0.001$

What do you observe?

Note

For any decimal number that has no integral number part, we generally place a zero on the left side of the decimal point to give prominence to the decimal point.

Interesting Fact

0.050 is same as 0.05

because there is no value for zero which is on the right of the decimal number after significant digit.

Note

When the digit on the right of the decimal point is brought down, a decimal point is added in the quotient.

Note

Once we have put the decimal, each time we divide, we can add one zero on our own.

Converting Decimals into Fractions

Now, let us learn how to convert decimal numbers like 0.7, 0.5 and 0.4 into fractions.

For example, $0.7 = 0 + \frac{7}{10} = \frac{7}{10}$

Remember

Steps to add unlike fractions

1. Find the LCM of the denominators.
2. Convert the unlike fractions into like fractions.
3. Add the like fractions.
4. Keep the sum in the simplest form.

Example 7: Convert 4.3 into a fraction and write the answer in the simplest form.

$$4.3 = \frac{4}{1} + \frac{3}{10} = \frac{40+3}{10} = \frac{43}{10} = 4\frac{3}{10}$$

Example 8: Convert 1.25 into a fraction and write the answer in the simplest form.

$$1.25 = 1 + \frac{25}{100} = 1 + \frac{1}{4} = \frac{4+1}{4} = \frac{5}{4} = 1\frac{1}{4}$$

To convert money, length, mass, etc. from one unit into another, we often use decimals. Given below are a few examples.

$5\text{ p} = ₹\frac{5}{100} = ₹0.05$ (₹1 = 100 p) $\qquad$ $220\text{ g} = \frac{220}{1000}\text{ kg} = 0.220\text{ kg}$ (1 kg = 1000 gm)

$25\text{ cm} = \frac{25}{100}\text{ m} = 0.25\text{ m}$ (1 m = 100 cm)

Example 9: Write the following numbers in the place value table. Also, write their expanded forms.

a. 12.43 $\qquad$ b. 947.526

a. 12.43

$= 1 \times 10 + 2 \times 1 + 4 \times \frac{1}{10} + 3 \times \frac{1}{100}$

$= 10 + 2 + \frac{4}{10} + \frac{3}{100}$

$= 10 + 2 + 0.4 + 0.03$

b. 947.526

$= 9 \times 100 + 4 \times 10 + 7 \times 1 + 5 \times \frac{1}{10} + 2 \times \frac{1}{100} + 6 \times \frac{1}{1000}$

$= 900 + 40 + 7 + \frac{5}{10} + \frac{2}{100} + \frac{6}{1000}$

$= 900 + 40 + 7 + 0.5 + 0.02 + 0.006$

Representation of Decimals on the Number Line

We know that fractions can be represented on the number line. Similarly, all decimal numbers also can be represented on the number line.

Example 10: Represent 0.3 on a number line.

$$0.3 = \frac{3}{10}$$

So, divide one unit of the segment into ten equal parts and take 3 parts to the right of 0 to represent 0.3 on the number line as shown below.

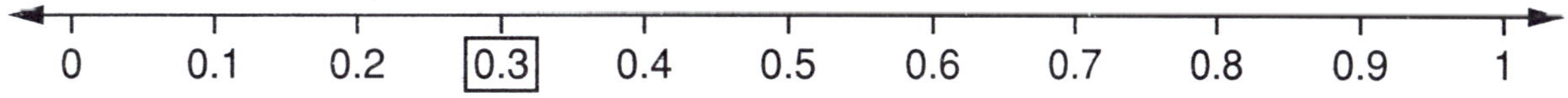

Example 11: Represent 1.4 on a number line.

$1.4 = \frac{14}{10}$

So, divide one unit of the segment into ten equal parts and take 4 parts to represent 1.4 on the number line as shown below.

Try These!

Represent the following decimals on a number line.

a. 0.3 b. 0.6 c. 0.9

d. 1.6 e. 1.8

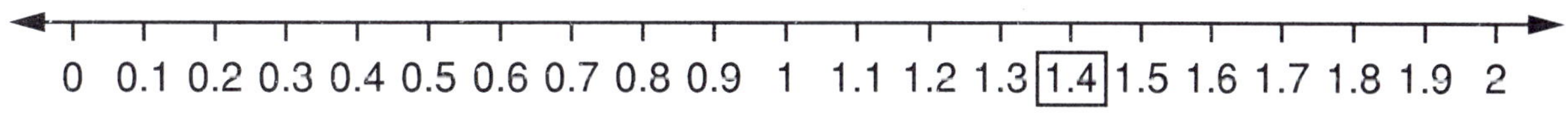

Exercise 5.1

1 Express the following decimals as numerals.

a. Five point five
b. Eighty-three point one seven
c. Two hundred sixty-seven point zero zero three
d. Fourteen point two zero three
e. Ten point zero eight seven

2 Write the place value of 7 in the following decimal numbers.

a. 9.746 b. 97.46 c. 671.009
d. 394.007 e. 3.071 f. 745.069

3 Write the expanded form of the following decimal numbers.

a. 495.6 b. 23.18 c. 14.087
d. 3527.17 e. 505.505 f. 7654.321

4 Write whether the following sets of decimal numbers are like or unlike decimals.

a. 3.56, 16.95, 780.54
b. 12.76, 16.7, 9.865
c. 1.1, 42.43, 435.768
d. 43.60, 47.8, 56.9
e. 0.81, 1.18, 23.45
f. 12.33, 0.97, 345.245

5 Compare the decimals and fill in the blanks with '<', '>' or '='.

a. 29.1 ☐ 291.1
b. 0.98 ☐ 9.08
c. 3.06 ☐ 3.006
d. 8.76 ☐ 8.706
e. 32.5 ☐ 32.500
f. 0.195 ☐ 0.19

6 **Arrange the following groups of decimal numbers in ascending order.**

a. 0.3, 0.003, 0.03, 3.3, 3.03, 0.33 b. 1.463, 4.643, 4.436, 4.346, 4.364

c. 2.45, 0, −4.25, −3.05, −1, 2.05, 3.92, 0.13 d. 1.7564, 1.5467, 1.4576, 1.8927

7 **Arrange the following groups of decimal numbers in descending order.**

a. 5.5, 5.05, 0.55, 55.5, 0.505, 50.5 b. 3.617, 3.712, 3.434, 3.279, 3.999

c. −1.75, −2, 0.404, −3.45, 1.78, 6.75 d. 0.6312, 0.63121, −0.936, 0.9366, −0.93661

8 **Convert the following fractions into decimals.**

a. $\frac{7}{100}$ b. $\frac{2}{5}$ c. $6\frac{18}{100}$

d. $\frac{52}{40}$ e. $65\frac{76}{1000}$ f. $\frac{16}{125}$

9 **Convert the following decimals into fractions.**

a. 0.58 b. 0.7 c. 1.308

d. 0.02 e. 12.042 f. 0.625

10 **Represent the following decimals on the number line.**

a. 0.2 b. 0.5 c. 1.9 d. 2.5

Remember

Short forms

Hundreds – H
Tens – T
Ones – O
Tenths – Tths
Hundredths – Hths
Thousandths – Thths

Addition and Subtraction of Decimals

Addition of Decimals

To add/subtract decimal numbers, arrange the decimal numbers in a column according to the place value of the digits such that the decimal point comes one below the other. Then add or subtract them and place the decimal point in the answer exactly below the decimal points of the given numbers.

Example 12: Add 9.38, 3.895, 109.5, 72.87 and 0.005.

	H	T	O		Tths	Hths	Thths
		2	2		2	1	
			9	.	3	8	0
			3	.	8	9	5
	1	0	9	.	5	0	0
		7	2	.	8	7	0
+			0	.	0	0	5
	1	9	5	.	6	5	0

∴ 9.38 + 3.895 + 109.5 + 72. 87 + 0.005 = 195.65

Note

In the above example, the numbers 9.38, 3.895, 109.5, 72.87 and 0.005 are called addends and 195.65 is the sum of addends.

Example 13: Ramesh went to the market to buy vegetables. He bought 3 kg 250 gm tomatoes, 7 kg 500 gm brinjals, 750 gm beans and 100 gm green chillies. What was the total mass of the vegetables Ramesh bought? Express the answer in kg.

Mass of tomatoes = 3 kg 250 gm = 3.250 kg

Mass of brinjals = 7 kg 500 gm = 7.500 kg

Mass of beans = 750 gm = 0.750 kg

Mass of green chillies = 100 gm = 0.100 kg

Therefore, total mass of the vegetables Ramesh bought was 11.6 kg.

	T	O		Tths	Hths	Thths
	1	1		1		
		3	.	2	5	0
		7	.	5	0	0
		0	.	7	5	0
+		0	.	1	0	0
	1	1	.	6	0	0

Subtraction of Decimals

Example 14: Find the difference between 218.302 and 34.111.

	H	T	O		Tths	Hths	Thths
	1	11			2	10	
	~~2~~	~~1~~	8	.	~~3~~	~~0~~	2
–		3	4	.	1	1	1
	1	8	4	.	1	9	1

∴ 218.302 – 34.111 = 184.191

Mental Maths

Observe the pattern and find the next number in the series.

0.25, 0.5, 0.75, 1.0, ________

Example 15: Marina bought 2.025 m of dress material for her elder daughter and 1.75 m for the younger one. What is the difference in the lengths of the two dress materials?

Length of the cloth bought for the elder daughter = 2.025 m

Length of the cloth bought for the younger daughter = 1.75 m

	T	O		Tths	Hths	Thths
		1		~~10~~ 9	12	
		~~2~~	.	~~0~~	~~2~~	5
–		1	.	7	5	0
		0	.	2	7	5

Therefore, the difference in the lengths of the two dress materials bought by Marina for her daughters is 0.275 m.

Note

In this example, the first number 218.302 is called the minuend, the second number 34.111 is called the subtrahend and the answer 184.191 is called the difference.

Mental Maths

What will you get if you take five hundredths from 1.72?

Exercise 5.2

1 **Solve the following.**

a. 97.71 + 1.3 b. 28.93 + 43.12 c. 77.5 + 71.615

d. 40.917 + 75.85 e. 71.92 + 3.963 + 55.5 f. 325.7 + 98.079 + 0.87 + 263.86

2 **Solve the following.**

a. 61.92 – 25.19 b. 99.61 – 30.3 c. 26.809 – 5.232

d. 100 – 0.001 e. 436.2 – 128.107 f. 55.5 – 5.777 – 7.55

3 **Fill in the blanks.**

a. 48.4 – 19.32 – 5 = ______ b. 7.4 – 3.6 + 2.82 = ______

c. 0.7 + 0.007 + 3.447 – 2.181 = ______ d. 127.5 – 84.1 – 13 + 4.39 = ______

e. 45.8 – ______ + 23.772 = 56.802 f. 82.672 – 30.54 – 10.012 + ______ = 107.535

4 What should be added to 67 to get 70.751?

5 What should be added to the difference of 3.14 and 1.674 to get 10?

6 Anil has ₹230.65 and Bhaskar has ₹125.35. How much money do they have altogether?

7 Tom and Tony were running a relay race. The distance to be run was 33.03 km in total. If Tom ran 16.93 km, how far did Tony run?

Multiplication of Decimals

Multiplication of decimal numbers is done in the same way as multiplication of whole numbers. The process is completed only after placing the decimal point in the appropriate place in the product.

Interesting Fact

Look at the pattern below and fill in the blanks. What do you observe?

$1.52 \times 10 = \frac{152}{100} \times 10 = 15.2$ $2.45 \times 10 =$ ____ $12.753 \times 10 =$ ____

$1.52 \times 100 = \frac{152}{100} \times 100 = 152$ or 152.0 $2.45 \times 100 =$ ____ $12.753 \times 100 =$ ____

$1.52 \times 1000 = \frac{152}{100} \times 1000 = 1520$ or 1520.0 $2.45 \times 1000 =$ ____ $12.753 \times 1000 =$ ____

When a decimal number is multiplied by 10, 100 or 1000 and so on, the digits in the product are same as in the decimal number, but the decimal point in the product is shifted to the right by as many places as there are zeros with one.

Multiplying Decimals by Whole Numbers

Example 16: Multiply 26.45 by 54.

Step 1: Multiply the decimal numbers as whole numbers.

$$\begin{array}{cccccc} & & 2 & 6 & 4 & 5 \\ \times & & & & 5 & 4 \\ \hline & 1 & 0 & 5 & 8 & 0 \\ 1 & 3 & 2 & 2 & 5 & 0 \\ \hline 1 & 4 & 2 & 8 & 3 & 0 \\ \hline \end{array}$$

Step 2: Calculate the total of the number of decimal places in the given decimal number and place the decimal point in the product by counting the same number of digits from the right.

That is, $26.45 \times 54 = 1428.30$.

Multiplying Two Decimals

Example 17: Multiply 8.732 by 9.6.

Step 1: Multiply the decimal numbers as whole numbers.

$$\begin{array}{cccccc} & & 8 & 7 & 3 & 2 \\ \times & & & & 9 & 6 \\ \hline & 5 & 2 & 3 & 9 & 2 \\ 7 & 8 & 5 & 8 & 8 & 0 \\ \hline 8 & 3 & 8 & 2 & 7 & 2 \\ \hline \end{array}$$

Step 2: Count the total number of decimal places in the two decimal numbers and then place the decimal point in the product by counting the same number of digits from the right.

That is, $8.732 \times 9.6 = 83.8272$.

Division of Decimals

Division of decimal numbers is done in the same way as division of whole numbers. The process is completed only after placing the decimal point in the appropriate place in the quotient.

Interesting Fact

Look at the pattern below and fill in the blanks. What do you observe?

$12.5 \div 10 = \frac{125}{10} \div 10 = \frac{125}{10} \times \frac{1}{10} = \frac{125}{100} = 1.25$ $\quad$ $159.7 \div 10 =$ _____ $\quad$ $12.75 \div 10 =$ _____

$12.5 \div 100 = \frac{125}{10} \div 100 = \frac{125}{10} \times \frac{1}{100} = \frac{125}{1000} = 0.125$ $\quad$ $159.7 \times 100 =$ _____ $\quad$ $12.75 \div 100 =$ _____

When a decimal number is divided by 10, 100 or 1000 and so on, the digits in the quotient are same as in the decimal number, but the decimal point in the quotient is shifted to the left by as many places as there are zeros with one.

Note

$$\begin{array}{r} 0.505 \\ 3\overline{)1.515} \\ -15 \\ \hline 015 \\ -15 \\ \hline 0 \\ \hline \end{array}$$

Hints and Tips

We remove the decimal in the denominator by shifting the decimal both in the numerator and in the denominator by number of decimal places in the denominator.

If there is a decimal in the numerator, usually we continue our calculation without removing this decimal. For example, $\frac{12.5}{5}$ can be calculated without removing the decimal point.

Dividing Decimals by Whole Numbers

Example 18: Divide 1.419 by 3.

Divide the decimal numbers as whole numbers.

$$\begin{array}{r} 0.473 \\ 3\overline{)1.419} \\ -12 \\ \hline 21 \\ -21 \\ \hline 09 \\ -9 \\ \hline 0 \\ \hline \end{array}$$

When the digit to the right of the decimal point is brought down or being considered, a decimal point is placed in the quotient.

$\therefore 1.419 \div 3 = 0.473$

Dividing Decimals by Decimals

Example 19: Divide 66.25 by 5.3.

Step 1: Convert the divisor into a whole number by multiplying the dividend and the divisor with a suitable power of 10.

$$\frac{66.25}{5.3} = \frac{66.25 \times 10}{5.3 \times 10} = \frac{662.5}{53}$$

Step 2: Divide the decimal numbers as whole numbers.

$$\begin{array}{r} 12.5 \\ 53\overline{)662.5} \\ 53 \\ \hline 132 \\ 106 \\ \hline 0265 \\ 265 \\ \hline 0 \\ \hline \end{array}$$

$\therefore 66.25 \div 5.3 = 12.5$

Exercise 5.3

1. **Solve the following.**

   a. 86.5×10 b. 34.754×10 c. 76.34×100
   d. 39.641×100 e. 7.8×1000 f. 8.59×1000

2. **Solve the following.**

   a. 15.8×7 b. 63.47×18 c. 2.375×135
   e. 5.6×3.8 e. 37.64×16.9 f. 8.735×9.6

3. **Solve the following.**

   a. $0.8 \div 10$ b. $24.75 \div 10$ c. $20.6 \div 10$
   d. $215.4 \div 100$ e. $2036 \div 1000$ f. $318.5 \div 1000$

4. **Solve the following.**

   a. $10.08 \div 9$ b. $1.001 \div 7$ c. $1.56 \div 1.3$
   d. $5.134 \div 1.7$ e. $13.455 \div 4.14$ f. $6.752 \div 5.275$

5. **Simplify the following.**
   a. $1.5 \times (4.125 - 3.25)$
   b. $(8.251 - 4.321) \times 4.5$
   c. $[4.6 \times -3.45] + [4.6 \times -1.25]$
   d. $6.739 \div 10 + 32.62$
   e. $14.95 \div 6.5 - 0.023 \times 100$
   f. $0.2 \times (1.7 + 1.1) + 1.84 - 7.36 \div 3.2$
6. If 1 kg of green grams contains 0.021 kg of protein, calculate the amount of protein present in 13 kg of green grams?
7. A motor bike can cover a distance of 56.575 km with 1 litre of petrol. How much distance can it cover with 100 litres of petrol?
8. If the cost of 15 pens is ₹78.75, find the cost of each pen.
9. A bottle holds 2.25 ℓ of cold drink. How many such bottles will be required to hold 56.25 ℓ of that cold drink?

Summary

1. $\frac{1}{1000}$ is one out of thousand equal parts and its decimal form is 0.001. It is read as 'zero point zero zero one'.
2. In the place value table, as we move from left to right, the value of a digit decreases by $\frac{1}{10}$ times of the decimal number.

Whole Number Part				Decimal Number Part		
Thousands	Hundreds	Tens	Ones	Tenths	Hundredths	Thousandths
1000	100	10	1	$\frac{1}{10}$	$\frac{1}{100}$	$\frac{1}{1000}$

3. Decimals having the same number of decimal places are called like decimals and decimals having different number of decimal places are called unlike decimals.
4. All fractions can be written as decimals and all decimals can be written as fractions.
5. All decimals can be represented on the number line.
6. When we compare two decimal numbers that have different whole number parts, the decimal number with greater whole number part is greater.
7. When we compare two decimal numbers that have the same whole number part, we begin comparing from the tenths place. The number with the greater digit in the same place is greater.
8. To add/subtract decimal numbers, arrange the decimal numbers in a column according to the place value of the digits such that the decimal point comes one below the other. Then add or subtract them and place the decimal point in the answer exactly below the decimal points of the given numbers.
9. Decimals are used in our day-to-day lives in representing units like money, length, weight and capacity.

Revision Exercise

1 Fill in the blanks.

a. The decimal form of $\frac{513}{1000}$ is ________.

b. In the decimal number 342.165, the place value of 1 and 4 is ________ and ________ respectively.

c. The fractional form of 1.16 is ________.

d. The point between the whole number part and the decimal number part of a decimal number is called the ________.

e. While expanding a decimal number, the place value of each digit is ________ by ________ times when we move from left to right.

2 Match the following.

i. 0.45	a. 0.75
ii. $\frac{256}{1000}$	b. 0.24
iii. $\frac{6}{25}$	c. $\frac{4}{5}$
iv. 0.8	d. $\frac{9}{20}$
v. $\frac{3}{4}$	e. 0.256

3 Answer the following questions.

a. Write the expanded forms of 12.2, 32.44 and 644.368.

b. Write the decimal forms of the following.

i. $4 + \frac{3}{10}$ ii. $30 + 2 + \frac{7}{10} + \frac{8}{100}$ iii. $100 + 20 + 1 + \frac{1}{10} + \frac{4}{1000}$

c. Write the place value of the underlined digit in each decimal.

i. 23.6$\underline{4}$ ii. 12.$\underline{5}$46 iii. 214.98$\underline{7}$

4 Convert the following fractions into decimals.

a. $\frac{3}{5}$ b. $\frac{4}{8}$ c. $\frac{12}{4}$ d. $\frac{16}{25}$

5 Convert the following decimals into fractions.

a. 0.5 b. 1.5 c. 0.123 d. 12.23

6. **Compare the following decimals and write ‘<’ or ‘>’ within the given brackets.**

a. 93.390 ( ) 93.039
b. 44.89( )43.580
c. 23.7( ) 27.3
d. 5.371( )5.731

7. **Solve the following.**

a. 80.5 + 72.10
b. 1.85 + 74.19
c. 86.1 + 72.346
d. 201.3 + 13.64 + 6.751

8. **Solve the following.**

a. 89.7 – 34.44
b. 16.57 – 7.4
c. 35.16 – 31.158
d. 68.2 – 41.71 – 24.541

9. **Solve the following.**

a. 53.67×49
b. 26.9×1.83
c. $6.35 \times 0.08 \times 1.5$
d. 8.46×10
e. 16.34×100
f. 9.5×1000

10. **Solve the following.**

a. $7.716 \div 8$
b. $67.984 \div 14$
c. $21.46 \div 3.7$
d. $29.24 \div 0.043$
e. $1.7 \div 10$
f. $15.27 \div 20$

For the Curious Mind

What is my decimal number if I have 5 in the tenths place, 9 in the thousandths place and 4 in the hundreds place?

UNIT 1

Powers and Roots

6

What I shall learn

- To understand the concept of powers
- To verify the laws of indices using examples
- To find the square roots of positive numbers by factor method
- To find the cube roots of positive numbers by factor method

Let's Get Started

Observe the following repeated additions and their short representations.

$2 + 2 + 2 + 2 + 2$

Here, 2 is added 5 times, that is, 5×2.

$8 + 8 + 8 + 8 + 8 + 8 + 8 + 8 + 8$

Here, 8 is added 9 times, that is, 9×8.

Now consider $10 \times 10 \times 10 \times 10 \times 10$.

Can we write it as 5×10 since 10 is multiplied 5 times? No, because in 5×10, 10 is added and not multiplied by itself 5 times. Then, how can we express such numbers? We express those using powers. Let us learn more about powers in this chapter.

Powers

When a number is multiplied by itself several times, we write it in the **exponential form** to make it brief. That is, we use exponents to represent repeated multiplication.

Thus, $10 \times 10 \times 10 \times 10 \times 10$ can be represented as 10^5, which is read as '10 raised to the power 5'. This form of representation of a number is known as the exponential form. In 10^5, 10 is called the base and 5 is called the exponent (power) or index. (The plural of index is indices.)

Note

Exponent or power or index of a number is how many times the same number is multiplied with itself.

Exponent

10^5

Base

Example 1: Express the following in exponential form.

a. $2 \times 2 \times 2 \times 2 \times 2 \times 2 \times 2$

Here, 2 is multiplied 7 times; therefore, the exponential form is 2^7.

b. $5 \times 5 \times 5 \times 5 \times 5$

Here, 5 is multiplied 5 times; therefore, the exponential form is 5^5.

We use the idea of exponents in algebraic expressions also, such as a^m, p^n, etc., with the same meaning.

Let a be any natural number and m be any positive integer. Then, $a^m = a \times a \times a \times \ldots$ m times, where a is the base and m is the exponent.

Remember

If the power of a number is 2, then it is called square and if the power of the number is 3, then it is called cube. If the power of a number is greater than three, then we say 'to the power of'.

Expressing Numbers in Exponential Form

To express a given number in its exponential form, first we find its prime factors by dividing it starting from the smallest prime number. Then, we write the product of its prime factors in the exponential form.

Example 2: Express the following numbers in exponential form.

a. 540

2	540
2	270
3	135
3	45
3	15
5	5
	1

∴ Prime factorisation of

$540 = 2 \times 2 \times 3 \times 3 \times 3 \times 5$

$= 2^2 \times 3^3 \times 5$

b. 3240

2	3240
2	1620
2	810
3	405
3	135
3	45
3	15
5	5
	1

∴ Prime factorisation of

$3240 = 2 \times 2 \times 2 \times 3 \times 3 \times 3 \times 3 \times 5$

$= 2^3 \times 3^4 \times 5$

Example 3: Find the value of the following.

a. $(5)^4$

$= 5 \times 5 \times 5 \times 5 = 625$

b. $(-3)^6$

$= (-3) \times (-3) \times (-3) \times (-3) \times (-3) \times (-3) = 729$

c. $(1000)^2$

$= 1000 \times 1000 = 10{,}00{,}000$

d. $(99{,}999)^1$

$= 99{,}999$

Law of Indices

Law of indices are used to manipulate expressions. These laws are applied only to manipulate expressions with the same base.

For any non-zero integer a,

1. $a^1 = a$

   Example: $4^1 = 4$

2. $a^{-1} = \frac{1}{a}$

   Example: $4^{-1} = \frac{1}{4}$

3. $a^0 = 1$

   Example: $4^0 = 1$

Example 4: Find the value of the following exponents.

a. 12502^1

Using $a^1 = a$, we get

$12502^1 = 12502$

b. 986521^0

Using $a^0 = 1$, we get

$986521^0 = 1$

c. 725^{-1}

Using $a^{-1} = \frac{1}{a}$, we get

$725^{-1} = \frac{1}{725}$

Do you know what is the value of $2^4 \times 2^3$?

Let us find it by writing them in the expanded form.

$2^4 \times 2^3 = (2 \times 2 \times 2 \times 2) \times (2 \times 2 \times 2) = 2 \times 2 \times 2 \times 2 \times 2 \times 2 \times 2 = 2^7$

Can you think of any other ways to find the value of $2^4 \times 2^3$?

Note that the numbers have the same base and the sum of their powers is equal to 7, that is, $4 + 3 = 7$,

$\therefore 2^4 \times 2^3 = 2^{4+3} = 2^7$

From the above example, we can conclude that for any non-zero integer a, $a^m \times a^n = a^{m+n}$, where m and n are integers.

Example 5: Find the value of the following.

a. $7^2 \times 7^3$

Using $a^m \times a^n = a^{m+n}$, we get

$7^2 \times 7^3 = 7^{2+3} = 7^5$

b. $(-5)^3 \times (-5)^4$

$(-5)^3 \times (-5)^4 = (-5)^{3+4} = (-5)^7$

Now, do you know what the value of $\frac{2^4}{2^3}$ is?

Let us find out by writing it in the expanded form.

$$\frac{2^4}{2^3} = \frac{\cancel{2} \times \cancel{2} \times \cancel{2} \times 2}{\cancel{2} \times \cancel{2} \times \cancel{2}} = 2^1$$

$$= 2$$

(By cancelling the common terms in the numerator and the denominator)

Can you think of any other ways to find the value of $\frac{2^4}{2^3}$?

Note that the numbers have the same base and the difference between their powers is equal to 1, that is, $4 - 3 = 1$.

$\therefore \frac{2^4}{2^3} = 2^{4-3} = 2^1 = 2$

From the above example, we can conclude that for any non-zero integer a, $\frac{a^m}{a^n} = a^{m-n}$, where m and n are integers and $m > n$.

Remember

Laws of Indices

$a^1 = a$

$a^{-1} = \frac{1}{a}$

$a^0 = 1$

$a^m \times a^n = a^{m+n}$

$\frac{a^m}{a^n} = a^{m-n}$

$(a^m)^n = a^{mn}$

Now, what is the value of $(2^3)^2$?

To find that, let us write it in the expanded form.

$(2^3)^2 = (2 \times 2 \times 2) \times (2 \times 2 \times 2) = 2 \times 2 \times 2 \times 2 \times 2 \times 2 = 2^6$

Is there any other way to find the value of $(2^3)^2$?

Note that the product of their powers is also equal to 6, that is, $3 \times 2 = 6$.

From the above example, we can conclude that for any non-zero integer a, $(a^m)^n = a^{mn}$, where m and n are integers.

Exercise 6.1

1 **Identify the base and the exponent in each of the following.**

a. 8^7 b. 5^6 c. 2^7 d. 9^4 e. 6^3

2 **Write the following in the exponential form.**

a. $8\times8\times8\times8\times8\times8$ b. $6\times6\times6\times6\times6\times6\times6$

c. $(-7)\times(-7)\times(-7)\times(-7)$ d. $(-1)\times(-1)\times(-1)\times(-1)\times(-1)\times(-1)$

e. $p\times p\times p\times p\times p\times p\times p\times p$

3 **Write the following in the exponential form using the prime factorisation method.**

a. 6125 b. 512 c. 729 d. 2401 e. 2310

4 **Calculate the following.**

a. 6^4 b. $3^2\times4^3$ c. $(-7)^4$ d. $(-2)^3\times(5)^3$ e. $(-1)^9\times(-9)^4$

5 **Simplify the following using suitable results.**

a. $3^6\times3^2$ b. $6^5\div6^3$ c. $(-2)^{12}\times(-2)^8\times(-2)^9$

d. $\dfrac{5^7\times5^5}{5^{10}}$ e. $10^0\times5^1$ f. $(2^0+5^0)^0$

Roots

Finding the root is the inverse procedure of raising to the power.

Squares and Square Roots

Consider the following.

$2\times2=2^2=4$; $3\times3=3^2=9$; $4\times4=4^2=16$ ... and so on.

Observe the products 4, 9 and 16. They are obtained by multiplying the same number by itself. Such products are called squares and the number which is multiplied is called its second root or square root.

In general, square root of a number is the number which when squared gives the given number. The symbol $\sqrt{\ }$ represents square root.

For example, $2^2 = 4$ and $\sqrt{4} = 2$.

4 is the square of 2 and 2 is the square root of 4.

We know that the square of the length of a square field gives its area. But how do you find the length of a square field when you know its area? The square root of the area gives the length of the square field. For example, if the area of a square field is 16 sq. m, then its length is $\sqrt{16} = 4$ m.

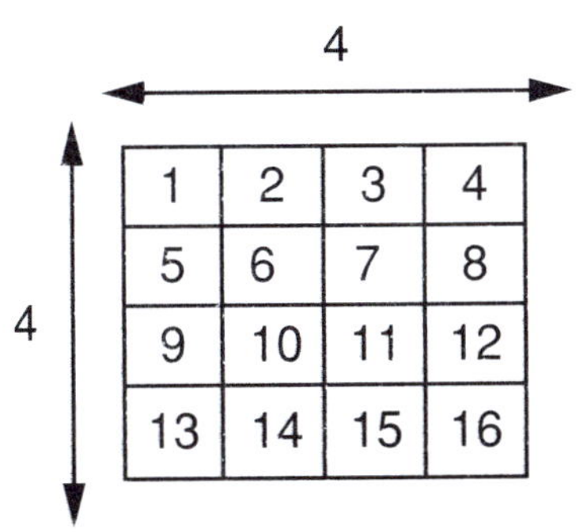

Example 6: Find the square of the following numbers.

a. 8

$8 \times 8 = 8^2 = 64$

b. 45

$45 \times 45 = 45^2 = 2025$

c. 100

$100 \times 100 = 100^2 = 10{,}000$

Finding Square Root of Numbers

Let us learn how to find the square root of a number with an example.

Consider a square number 144.

2	144
2	72
2	36
3	18
3	9
	3

Step 1: Find the prime factors of 144.

Step 2: Make pairs of the identical prime factors.

$\sqrt{\underline{(2 \times 2)} \times \underline{(2 \times 2)} \times \underline{(3 \times 3)}}$

Step 3: Take one factor from each pair and find their product. The product so obtained is the square root of the given number.

$\therefore\ 2 \times 2 \times 3 = 12$

That is, $\sqrt{144} = 12$.

Example 7: Find $\sqrt{324}$.

2	324
2	162
3	81
3	27
3	9
	3

$\sqrt{324} = \sqrt{\underline{(2 \times 2)} \times \underline{(3 \times 3)} \times \underline{(3 \times 3)}}$

$= 2 \times 3 \times 3 = 18.$

Cubes and Cube Roots

Consider the following.

$2 \times 2 \times 2 = 2^3 = 8$; $3 \times 3 \times 3 = 3^3 = 27$; $4 \times 4 \times 4 = 4^3 = 64$ ... and so on.

What do you observe? The products 8, 27 and 64 are obtained by multiplying the same number thrice. Such products are called cubes and the number which is multiplied is called its third root or cube root.

> In general, cube root of a number is the number which when cubed gives the given number. The symbol $\sqrt[3]{\ }$ represents cube root.

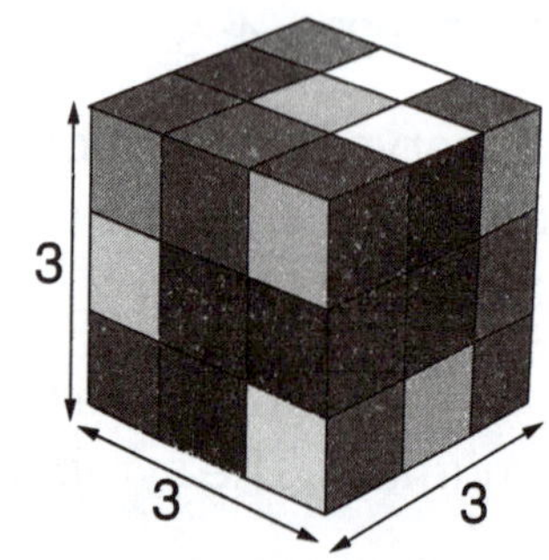

For example, $2^3 = 8$ and $\sqrt[3]{8} = 2$.

27 is the cube of 3 and 3 is the cube root of 27.

We know that the cube of the length of a side gives the volume of a cubical solid. But how do you find the side length of the cubical solid when its volume is given? The cube root of the volume gives the side of the cubical solid.

For example, in the above Rubik's cube, the volume is 27 cubic cm. Hence, length of its side is $\sqrt[3]{27} = 3$ cm.

Example 8: Find the cubes of the following numbers

a. 6

$6^3 = 6 \times 6 \times 6 = 216$

b. 11

$11^3 = 11 \times 11 \times 11 = 1331$

c. 112

$112^3 = 112 \times 112 \times 112 = 14{,}04{,}928$

Finding Cube Root of Numbers

Finding the cube root of a number is similar to finding a square root. The only difference is that instead of making pairs, we separate the identical factors into triplets and take one factor from each triplet and multiply them. The product obtained is the cube root of the given number.

Example 9: Find the cube root of 512.

2	512
2	256
2	128
2	64
2	32
2	16
2	8
2	4
	2

Step 1: Find the prime factors of 512.

Step 2: Make triplets or sets of three identical factors.

$\sqrt[3]{(\underline{2 \times 2 \times 2}) \times (\underline{2 \times 2 \times 2}) \times (\underline{2 \times 2 \times 2})}$

Step 3: Take one factor from each triplet and find their product.
The product obtained is the cube root of the given number, that is, $2 \times 2 \times 2 = 8$.

$\therefore \sqrt[3]{512} = 8$

Example 10: Simplify $\dfrac{\sqrt[3]{64}}{\sqrt[3]{216}}$

$\dfrac{\sqrt[3]{64}}{\sqrt[3]{216}} = \dfrac{4}{6} = \dfrac{2}{3}$

Exercise 6.2

1. **Evaluate the following.**

   a. $\sqrt{256}$ b. $\sqrt{324}$ c. $\sqrt[3]{729}$ d. $\sqrt[3]{1728}$ e. $\sqrt[3]{2197}$

2. **Find the values of the following.**

   a. $\sqrt{100 \times 64}$ b. $100 - \sqrt{100}$ c. $\dfrac{2}{3}$ of $\sqrt[3]{729}$ d. $\dfrac{\sqrt[3]{343}}{\sqrt{196}}$ e. $\dfrac{6 \times \sqrt{100}}{\sqrt[3]{27}}$

Summary

1. When a number is multiplied by itself several times, we write it in the exponential form to make it brief. For example: $a \times a \times a \times a \times a = a^5$
2. If a number is raised to the power 2, then it is called squared and if it is raised to the power 3, then it is called cubed.
3. $a^1 = a$; $a^0 = 1$, where a is any positive integer.
4. For any non-zero integer a, $a^m \times a^n = a^{m+n}$, $\dfrac{a^m}{a^n} = a^{m-n}$ where $m > n$, $(a^m)^n = a^{mn}$ where m and n are integers.
5. Finding the root is the inverse procedure of raising the power.
6. Squares are obtained by multiplying the same number by itself twice and the number which is multiplied is called its second root or square root.
7. Cubes are obtained by multiplying the same number thrice and the number which is multiplied is called its third root or cube root.

Revision Exercise

1 Choose the correct answer.

a. The square of 72 is

i. 5841 ii. 5184 iii. 5148 iv. 5814

b. The cube of 13 is

i. 2197 ii. 2971 iii. 2179 iv. 2917

c. The square root of 625 is

i. 5 ii. 15 iii. 25 iv. 35

d. The cube root of 2744 is

i. 14 ii. 24 iii. 34 iv. 16

e. The value of 125^0 is

i. 125 ii. 0 iii. 1 iv. 1250

2 Fill in the blanks.

a. The exponential form of $5 \times 5 \times 5 \times 5 \times 5 \times 5 \times 5 \times 5$ is ____________.

b. The value of 15^0 is ____________.

c. The product of 12^1 and 5 is ____________.

d. $\frac{6^5 \times 6^8}{6^{10}} =$ ____________

e. The cube root of 1000000 is ____________.

3 Match the following.

Squares/Cubes	Square roots/Cube roots
a. 625	i. 101
b. 2025	ii. 12
c. 512	iii. 45
d. 1728	iv. 25
e. 10201	v. 8

4 Evaluate the following.

a. $\sqrt{676}$ b. $\sqrt{2304}$ c. $\sqrt[3]{3375}$ d. $\frac{96 - \sqrt{3600}}{\sqrt[3]{216}}$ e. $\frac{50^0 \times 50^1}{\sqrt[3]{3375}}$

For the Curious Mind

Find the least number by which 675 is to be multiplied in order to make it a cube number and also find the cube root of the new number.

Unit Worksheet 1

Crossword

Complete the crossword using the given clues.

Across

1. $-2 \times 8 =$
2. $(-6) + (-9) =$
3. $\frac{1}{2}$ of $28 =$
5. $(-6) - (+7) =$
6. $15.28 + 3.72 =$
7. $-4 \times -4 =$
8. 6th multiple of 3 =
9. LCM of 2 and 5 –
11. HCF of 12 and 36 =
12. $\sqrt{196} =$

Down

1. $(-7) + (-4) =$
2. $-18 + 4 =$
3. $10.057 + 2.943 =$
4. $-15 - 4 =$
5. $-32 \div 2 =$
6. $-6 \times -3 =$
7. HCF of 17 and 34 =
8. $\sqrt[3]{1000} =$
9. $\sqrt{121} =$
10. LCM of 7 and 2

Mental Maths

1. What is the value of 1 crore in international number system? ___________
2. Write 1947 in Roman numerals. ___________
3. Which is the smallest composite number? ___________
4. What is the multiplicative inverse of 7? ___________
5. Which is the smallest number among 0.1, 0.01 and 0.001? ___________

UNIT 2

7 Average

Let's Get Started

What I shall learn

- **To understand the basic concept of average**

Study the information given below about the students of Class 6 in a school.

- The average age of the students is 11 years.
- The average height of the students is 121 cm.

On the basis of this data, can we say that the age of each student in Class 6 is 11 years? Can we say that the height of each student in Class 6 is 121 cm? Obviously, no. Some of the students may be 10 years old, while some others may be 12 years old. A similar situation holds true for the students with respect to their heights.

However, the average age of 11 years gives us an idea about the age of students in this particular class. It is the representative value of the age of each student. The same can be said about the heights.

Therefore, average is the value that is evenly distributed among a given number of quantities. Average is also called arithmetic mean or mean.

Average

Remember

Before calculating an average, make sure that all the measurements are in the same units.

The average of two numbers a and b is $\frac{a+b}{2}$.

And the average of three numbers a, b and c is $\frac{a+b+c}{3}$.

Thus, in general, average of n terms is given by

Hence, the formula for average is $\frac{1^{st}\text{term}+2^{nd}\text{term}+3^{rd}\text{term}+\ldots+n^{th}\text{term}}{n}$

$$\text{Average} = \frac{\text{Sum of the quantities}}{\text{Number of quantities}}$$

$\therefore$ Sum of the quantities = Average $\times$ Number of Quantities

And, number of quantities $= \frac{\text{Sum of the quantities}}{\text{Average}}$

Example 1: Find the average of 3 and 5.

$$\text{Average} = \frac{3+5}{2} = \frac{8}{2} = 4$$

Observe that 4 lies between 3 and 5.

Example 2: The average age of three girls is 16 years. One girl is 18 years old, while the second one is 13 years old. How old is the third girl?

Sum of the quantities = Average × Number of Quantities

18 + 13 + Age of the third girl = 16 × 3

31 + Age of the third girl = 48

Age of the third girl = 48 − 31 = 17

Example 3: The length of a rope is 225 m. The length of another rope is 120 m more than the first one, whereas the length of a third rope is 102 m more than the first one. Find the average length of the three ropes.

Length of the first rope = 225 m

Length of the second rope = 225 m + 120 m = 345 m

Length of the third rope = 225 m + 102 m = 327 m

$$\text{Average} = \frac{\text{Sum of the quantities}}{\text{Number of quantities}} = \frac{225+345+327}{3}$$

$$= \frac{897}{3} = 299$$

Therefore, the average length of the three ropes is 299 m.

Example 4: The average weight of a class of 40 students is 45 kg. Among 40 students, 25 students are boys and their average weight is 48 kg. What is the average weight of the girls in the class?

$$\text{Average} = \frac{\text{Sum of the quantities}}{\text{Number of quantities}}$$

∴ Sum of the quantities = Average × Number of quantities

Total weight of all the students in the class = 45 × 40
= 1800 kg

Total weight of the boys in the class = 48 × 25 = 1200 kg

To get the total weight of the girls, subtract the total weight of the boys from the total weight of all the students in the class.

Total weight of the girls in the class = 1800 − 1200 = 600 kg

Number of girls = 40 − 25 = 15

$$\text{Average weight of the girls} = \frac{600}{15} = 40 \text{ kg}$$

Note

The average lies between the greatest and the smallest observations.

Mental Maths

What is the average of 23, 24 and 25?

Remember

1. We cannot find the average of different quantities, for example, the age of 4 boys and their heights.
2. Before finding the average, we convert each quantity into the same unit.

Try These!

Ahmed kept a record of the amount of time he spent on his homework over 10 days.

$\frac{1}{2}$ h, 20 min, 35 min, $\frac{1}{4}$ h, 1 h, $\frac{1}{2}$ h, $1\frac{1}{2}$ h, $1\frac{1}{2}$ h, 40 min, $\frac{3}{4}$ h, 55 min

Find the average time he spent on his homework during those 10 days.

Exercise 7.1

1. **Find the averages.**

   a. 6.15 ℓ, 7 ℓ 500 mℓ and 6750 mℓ

   b. $\frac{1}{2}, \frac{2}{3}, \frac{1}{4}, \frac{5}{2}, \frac{2}{3}$

   c. The first ten natural numbers

   d. The first four prime numbers

2. **Given below are the timings of the practice sessions of the players of a cricket team for a week.**

Day	Mon	Tue	Wed	Thu	Fri	Sat	Sun
Minutes	150	120	115	133	150	125	180

   Find the average time spent by the players for their practice during that week.

3. The figures given below show the masses of four watermelons. Calculate the average mass of the watermelons in kg.

1.5 kg 1.405 kg 1.65 kg 1.077 kg

4. The earnings of a fruit vendor in a week are ₹650, ₹1500, ₹1250, ₹850, ₹1050, ₹1100 and ₹2000. Find the fruit vendor's average earning per day?

5. The maximum temperatures in a city from Monday to Sunday were 32.4°C, 33.1°C, 31.7°C, 35.3°C, 35.6°C, 28.7°C and 29.3°C respectively. What is the average temperature of the particular week?

6. On 3 consecutive days, Neha took 24 minutes, 42 minutes and $\frac{3}{4}$ hour respectively to finish her homework. Find the average time taken by Neha to finish her homework.

7. The lengths of three squares are 5 cm, 5 cm and 7 cm. Calculate the average area of the three squares.

Mental Maths

A newspaper agent sells 60 newspapers on a Sunday and an average of 25 newspapers on each of the other days of the week. What is the average for the whole week?

Summary

1. Average is the value that is evenly distributed among a given number of quantities.
2. The average lies between the greatest and the smallest observations.
3. Average = $\frac{\text{Sum of the quantities}}{\text{Number of quantities}}$
4. Sum of the quantities = Average × Number of quantities

Revision Exercise

1. **Find the average of the following.**
   a. ₹65,774 and ₹87,448
   b. 878.5 cm, 18.214 cm, 369.43 cm and 2984 cm
   c. 45.6 g, 67.8 g, 90.9 g and 12.2 g
   d. 3900, 8900, 4590, 9089
   e. Squares of the first five natural numbers
   f. The first six multiples of 6
   g. The first five prime numbers
   h. Composite numbers less than 9
2. In an annual exam, Afzal got 65, 72, 80, 90, 96, and 83 marks in six subjects. Find the average marks obtained by Afzal in his annual exam.
3. Shiva got 75 marks in a test. Satya got 5 marks more than Shiva and Sundar got 8 marks less than Shiva. What is their average score?
4. In a mathematics test, the average score of Class 6 students is 72 marks. If the total score of all the students is 2160, find the number of students in the class.
5. The average of 19 different quantities is 4. If one more quantity of 24 is added to it, then find the new average.
6. The average weight of 6 friends is 45 kg. What is their total weight?
7. The average marks of Rajeev in 4 subjects is 37. If he scored 33 in the fifth subject, what is his average score in all the five subjects?
8. The table given below shows the marks obtained by Harsh in two subjects—English and science. If the average score of Harsh is 75, find the marks he obtained in mathematics.

Subject	English	Science	Mathematics
Marks	58	72	

9. The average height of some basketball players is 175 cm. If the total height of the players is 10 m 50 cm, find the number of players.
10. The average weight of 12 students in a class is 42 kg. Three students of weights 41.5 kg, 40.5 kg and 44 kg, respectively leave the class. Find the average weight of the remaining students.

For the Curious Mind

A student has secured the following marks in 4 unit tests.

87, 95, 76 and 88

He has one more test to go and he wants to secure an average of 89 marks in all the five unit tests. What is the minimum mark that he needs to secure in the last unit test in order to achieve that average?

UNIT 2

Percentage

8

What I shall learn

- To understand the concept of percentage
- To relate fractions, decimals and ratios to percentage

Let's Get Started

Nelson told his friend Basha that he had scored 45 out of 50 in the mathematics test. Basha replied that he had scored more marks than Nelson, that is, 85 out of 100.

Whose score was better?

To find that let us calculate how much marks Nelson scored out of 100.

$$\frac{45}{50}=\frac{45\times 2}{50\times 2}=\frac{90}{100}$$

Thus, Nelson scored 90 out of 100 and Basha scored 85 out of 100. Hence, Nelson scored more marks than Basha.

In other words, Nelson got 90 per cent and Basha got 85 per cent in their respective mathematics tests.

Note

The term 'per cent' is made up of two words. It is derived from the Latin term 'per centum' which means 'per hundred'. One hundredth is $\frac{1}{100}$. Thus, 1% is same as one hundredth.

Percentage

Percentage is a fraction with denominator as 100.

The symbol for percentage is % and is read as 'per cent'. The term 'per cent' is another name of hundredths.

For example, 90% means 90 out of 100.

Example 1: The given figure consists of hundred squares of the same size. Calculate the percentage of the shaded region in the figure.

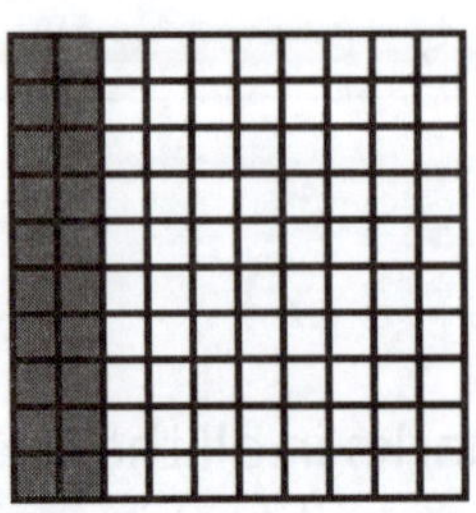

In the given figure, 20 out of 100 squares are shaded.

Thus, the percentage represented by the shaded region is

$\frac{20}{100}$ = 20% (read as 'twenty per cent')

Hence, 20% of the squares are shaded.

Converting Percentage to Fraction

To convert a percentage into a fraction, express the percentage numeral with 100 as the denominator; or multiply by $\frac{1}{100}$ and remove the % sign. Convert it into the simplest form, if required.

Example 2: Convert 35% into a fraction.

$$35\% = \frac{35}{100} = \frac{35 \div 5}{100 \div 5} = \frac{7}{20}$$

Example 3: Convert $2\frac{9}{8}\%$ into a fraction.

$$2\frac{9}{8}\% = \frac{25}{8}\% = \frac{\frac{25}{8}}{100} = \frac{25}{8} \times \frac{1}{100} = \frac{1}{32}$$

Example 4: Convert 125.8% into a fraction.

$$125.8\% = \frac{125.8}{100} = \frac{1258}{1000} = \frac{629}{500} = 1\frac{129}{500}$$

Mental Maths

Convert the following into fractions.

1. $3\frac{4}{5}\% =$ ________

Converting Fraction to Percentage

To convert a proper fraction into a percentage, multiply it by 100% or make the denominator as hundredths and put the % symbol.

Example 5: Convert $\frac{3}{10}$ into a percentage.

Change the denominator 10 of $\frac{3}{10}$ to 100 by multiplying the numerator and denominator by 10.

$$\frac{3}{10} = \frac{3}{10} \times \frac{10}{10} = \frac{30}{100} = 30\%$$

or

$$\frac{3}{1\cancel{0}} \times 10\cancel{0}\% = 3 \times 10\% = 30\% \quad \left(\text{because } 100\% = \frac{100}{100}\right)$$

Remember

Multiply both numerator and denominator by the same quantity.

Example 6: Express 18 out of 50 as percentage.

$$\frac{18}{50} = \frac{18}{50} \times \frac{2}{2} = \frac{36}{100} = 36\%.$$

or

$$\frac{18}{{}_{1}\cancel{50}} \times \overset{2}{\cancel{100}}\% = 18 \times 2\% = 36\%$$

Example 7: Convert $2\frac{3}{5}$ into percentage.

$$2\frac{3}{5} \times \frac{100}{100} = \frac{13}{5} \times 100\% = 13 \times 20\% = 260\%$$

Converting Percentage to Decimal

To convert a percentage into a decimal, express it as a fraction of hundredths and remove the % sign. Then, convert it into a decimal.

Example 8: Convert 52% into a decimal.

First, we divide the percentage by 100.

$$52\% = \frac{52}{100}$$

$$\frac{52}{100} = 0.52$$

$$\therefore 52\% = 0.52$$

Remember

While converting a fraction into a decimal number, the number of digits after the decimal point in the decimal number is the same as the number of zeros in the denominator of the fraction.

Example 9: Convert 0.5% into a decimal.

$$0.5\% = \frac{0.5}{100} = 0.005$$

Example 10: Convert 125% into a decimal.

$$125\% = \frac{125}{100} = 1.25$$

Converting Decimal into Percentage

To convert a decimal into a percentage, express it as a fraction of hundredths and then convert it to a percentage. Or multiply the decimal by 100 and put the % symbol in the answer.

Example 11: Convert 0.59 into a percentage.

$$0.59 = \frac{59}{100} = 59\%$$

or

$$0.59 = 0.59 \times 100\% = 59\%$$

Remember

The number of digits after the decimal point in the given decimal number is same as the number of zeros in the denominator of the fraction.

Example 12: Convert 0.05 into a percentage.

$$0.05 = 0.05 \times 100\% = 5\%$$

Example 13: Convert 1.35 into a percentage.

$$1.35 = 1.35 \times 100\% = 135\%$$

Converting Percentage into Ratio

To convert a percentage into a ratio, divide the percentage numeral by 100 or multiply by $\frac{1}{100}$ and write the fraction in terms of ratio.

Example 14: Convert 15% into a ratio.

$$15\% = \frac{15}{100} = \frac{15 \div 5}{100 \div 5} = \frac{3}{20} = 3:20$$

Example 15: Convert $33\frac{1}{3}\%$ into a ratio.

$$33\frac{1}{3}\% = \frac{100}{3}\% = \frac{\frac{100}{3}}{100} = \frac{100}{3} \times \frac{1}{100} = \frac{1}{3} = 1:3$$

Example 16: Convert 12.5% into a ratio.

$$12.5\% = \frac{12.5}{100} = \frac{\cancel{125}^{1}}{{}_{8}\cancel{1000}} = \frac{1}{8} = 1:8$$

Mental Maths

Convert the following percentage into ratios

1. 25 % ________
2. $4\frac{1}{5}$ % ________

Converting Ratio into Percentage

To convert a ratio into a percentage, first write the given ratio as a fraction and then multiply it by 100 and put the % symbol in the answer.

Example 17: Convert 5 : 8 into percentage.

$$\frac{5}{\cancel{8}_{2}} \times \cancel{100}^{25}\% = \frac{5}{2} \times 25\% = \frac{125}{2}\% = 62.5\%$$

Example 18: Convert 112 : 125 into percentage.

$$\frac{112}{\cancel{125}_{5}} \times \cancel{100}^{4}\% = \frac{112}{5} \times 4\% = \frac{448}{5}\% = 89.6\%$$

Exercise 8.1

1 **Write the percentage of the shaded portion in each square grid.**

a. 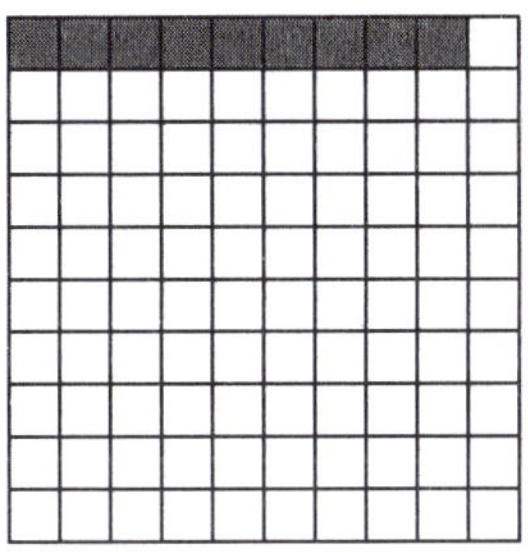

b. 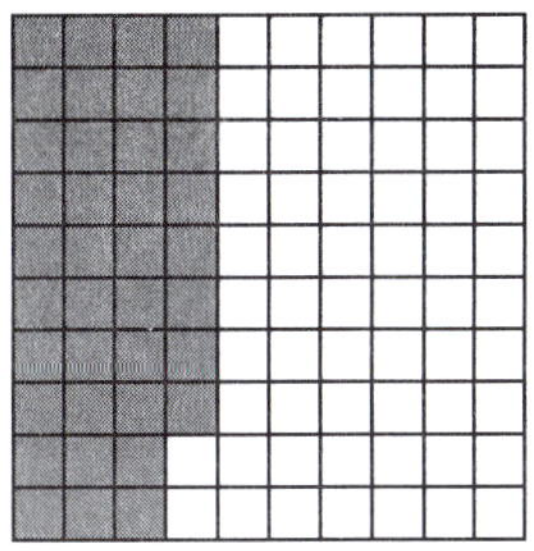

c. 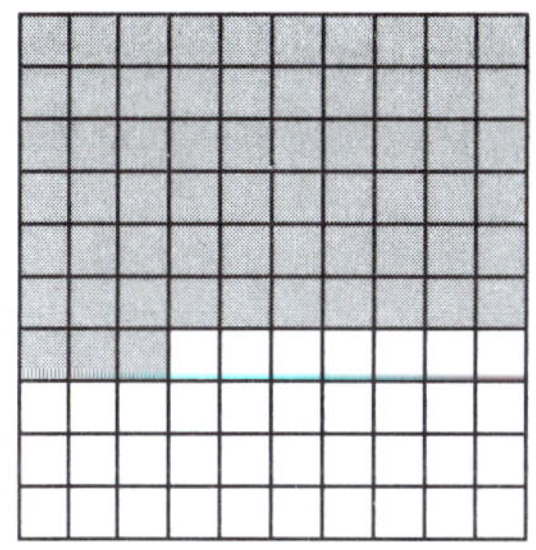

2 **Express the following percentages as fractions.**

a. 5% b. 75% c. $62\frac{1}{2}$% d. 2.75%

3 **Express the following fractions as percentages.**

a. $\frac{1}{8}$ b. $\frac{13}{20}$ c. $\frac{5}{12}$ d. $1\frac{5}{8}$

4 **Express the following percentages as decimals.**

a. 7% b. 44% c. $33\frac{1}{5}$% d. 16.4%

5 **Express the following decimals as percentages.**

a. 0.6 b. 0.07 c. 1.05 d. 1.625

6 **Express the following percentages as ratios.**

a. 2% b. 70% c. $6\frac{1}{2}$% d. 0.8%

7 **Express the following ratios as percentages.**

a. 1 : 10 b. 1 : 20 c. 1 : 4 d. 5 : 8

Expressing a Quantity as a Percentage of Another Quantity

To express one quantity as a percentage of another quantity, we first convert both the quantities into the same unit. Then, we divide the first quantity by the second quantity and multiply by 100, and put the % symbol.

Example 19: Suhail scored 24 out of 40 marks. Find the percentage of marks scored by him.

First quantity (marks scored) = 24

Second quantity (total marks) = 40

Percentage of marks = $\frac{\cancel{24}^{\,6}}{_{1}\cancel{40}} \times 10\cancel{0}\% = 60\%$

Example 20: What percent of 1 kg is 15 gm?

First quantity = 15 gm

Second quantity = 1 kg = 1000 gm

Percentage = $\frac{\cancel{15}^{\,3}}{_{2}\cancel{1000}} \times 1\cancel{00}\% = \frac{3}{2} = 1.5\%$

Example 21: What percent of 3.5 ℓ is 245 mℓ?

First quantity = 245 mℓ

Second quantity = 3.5 ℓ

= 3.5 × 1000 mℓ = 3500 mℓ

Percentage = $\frac{\cancel{245}^{\,7}}{_{1}\cancel{3500}} \times 1\cancel{00}\% = 7\%$

Percentage of a Given Quantity

To find the percentage of a given quantity, first, convert the percentage as a fraction and then multiply the fraction by the given quantity.

Example 22: Find 4.5% of 600.

4.5% of 600 = $\frac{4.5}{1\cancel{00}} \times 6\cancel{00} = 4.5 \times 6 = 27$

Example 23: Find 20% of 1820.

20% of 1820 = $\frac{2\cancel{0}}{10\cancel{0}} \times 182\cancel{0} = 2 \times 182 = 364$

Example 24: Find $1\frac{1}{5}$ % of 3500.

$1\frac{1}{5}$ % of 3500 = $\frac{6}{5} \times \frac{1}{100} \times 3500 = 6 \times 7 = 42$

Mental Maths

1. 10% of 100 = ______
2. 0.2% of 200 = ______

Increase or Decrease of Measures as Percentage

$$\text{Increase per cent} = \left(\frac{\text{New value} - \text{Old value}}{\text{Old value}} \times 100\right)\% = \left(\frac{\text{Increase in value}}{\text{Old value}} \times 100\right)\%$$

Note

When the value of an object is increased to another value, the second value is the new value of the object. The new value of the object is the sum of the original value and the increase in value.

Note

'Old value' can also be referred to as 'Original value' or 'Initial value'.

Example 25: The cost of a bicycle is increased from ₹5000 to ₹5500. Find the percentage of increase.

Old value of the bicycle = ₹5000

New value of the bicycle = ₹5500

$$\text{Increase per cent} = \left(\frac{\text{New value} - \text{Old value}}{\text{Old value}} \times 100\right)\%$$

$$= \left(\frac{5500-5000}{5000} \times 100\right)\%$$

$$= \left(\frac{500}{5000} \times 100\right)\% = 10\%$$

$$\text{Decrease per cent} = \left(\frac{\text{Old value} - \text{New value}}{\text{Old value}} \times 100\right)\% = \left(\frac{\text{Decrease in value}}{\text{Old value}} \times 100\right)\%$$

Example 26: A person's weight decreased from 75 kg to 69 kg. What was the percentage of decrease?

Decrease in value = 75 kg – 69 kg = 6 kg

Old value = 75 kg

$$\text{Decrease per cent} = \left(\frac{\text{Decrease in value}}{\text{Old value}} \times 100\right)\% = \left(\frac{6}{75} \times 100\right)\% = 8\%$$

Example 27: The ratio of students who have received excellent marks in mathematics, science and history is 20 : 18 : 12. Find the percentage of students who have received excellent marks in each of these subjects.

Given ratio = 20 : 18 : 12

Total parts of the ratio = 20 + 18+ 12 = 50

∴ Percentage of students who got excellent marks in mathematics $= \frac{20}{50} \times 100\% = 40\%$

Percentage of students who got excellent marks in science

$= \frac{18}{50} \times 100\% = 36\%$

Percentage of students who got excellent marks in history

$= \frac{12}{50} \times 100\% = 24\%$

Mental Maths

1. An advertisement shows 8 out of 10 babies prefer eat a particular brand of biscuits. What percentage is this?

   ____

2. Express $33\frac{1}{3}\%$ as a fraction.

Exercise 8.2

1 **What percent of the first quantity is the second quantity in each of the following?**

a. ₹6.25; ₹2.5 b. ₹320; ₹100 c. 7 km; 7000 m

d. 8 kg; 500 g e. $2\frac{1}{2}$ litres; $\frac{3}{4}$ litres f. 4 km; 400 cm

2 **Find the following.**

a. 20% of ₹75 b. 45% of 2 m 80 cm c. $6\frac{1}{4}$% of 5 km

d. 30% of 30 litres e. $33\frac{1}{3}$% of 1 kg 200 g f. 16% of 13 km 6cm

3 Virat got 27 marks out of 75 in mathematics. Find the percentage of marks obtained.

4 Units of scooters sold in India in 2008–2009 and 2009–2010 are 74.4 lakh and 93.7 lakh respectively. Find the percentage of increase in sales.

5 The ratio of copper, zinc and nickel in an alloy is 24 : 16 : 10. Find the percentage of each metal in the alloy.

6 Chetan earns ₹25,000 per month. He spends 80% of his earning and saves the remaining amount. How much does Chetan save every month?

Summary

1. The word 'per cent' is derived from the Latin word 'per centum' meaning 'per hundred' and it is denoted by the symbol %.

2. To convert a percentage to a fraction, divide the percentage numeral by 100 and remove the % sign. The fraction can also be changed into the form of a ratio.

3. To convert a ratio or fraction into percentage, change it into a fraction of hundredths and put the % sign.

5. To convert a decimal into a percentage, multiply the decimal by 100 and put the % symbol.

6. To express one quantity as a percentage of another quantity, divide the first quantity by the second quantity. Then, multiply by 100 and put the % symbol.

7. To find the percentage of a given quantity, convert the percentage into a fraction and multiply the fraction by the given quantity.

8. Increase per cent = $\left(\frac{\text{New value} - \text{Old value}}{\text{Old value}} \times 100\right)\% = \left(\frac{\text{Increase in value}}{\text{Old value}} \times 100\right)\%$

9. Decrease per cent = $\left(\frac{\text{Old value} - \text{New value}}{\text{Old value}} \times 100\right)\% = \left(\frac{\text{Decrease in value}}{\text{Old value}} \times 100\right)\%$

Revision Exercise

1. **Fill in the blanks.**
   a. A fraction having 8 in the numerator and 100 in the denominator is equal to ______%.
   b. Per cent means __________.
   c. Per cent is denoted by the symbol __________.
2. A family's savings and expenditure on various items given below as fractions. Express them in per cents.
   Food $\frac{3}{10}$, clothes $\frac{3}{25}$, housing $\frac{2}{10}$, savings $\frac{4}{25}$, miscellaneous expenses $\frac{11}{50}$
3. Shashidara's weight decreased from 60 kg to 55 kg. What was the percentage of decrease?
4. In a school, 15% of 920 students failed in the annual exam. Find the number of students who passed in the exam.
5. A bank announces two schemes for senior citizens, one with 9.25% interest on ₹10,500 and the other with 9.1% interest on ₹10,000. Which scheme would be preferable?
6. The present value of a bike is ₹44,000 after the depreciation of 12% after one year of purchase. Find the actual cost of the bike.
7. The price of a pair of jeans before discount is ₹984. What is the price of the pair of jeans after a discount of 5%?
8. 2,28,000 people constitute 96% of the population of a town. Find the total population of the town.
9. Asif's salary has been increased from ₹42,000 to ₹45,000. What is the percentage of increase in his salary?
10. In an exam, Deepak scored 45 out of 60 in physics and 50 out of 75 in mathematics. In which subject was his performance better?
11. Two candidates contested in an election. One got 65% of the votes and won by 30,000 votes. Find the number of votes polled.
12. If 72% of the students in a school are boys and the number of girls is 420, find the total number of boys.
13. A goldsmith mixes 0.05 grams of copper in every gram of gold. What are the percentages of gold and copper in a gram of gold?
14. The price of petrol decreased from ₹80. to ₹76. What was the percentage of decrease in the price of petrol?

For the Curious Mind

In School A, 68 students appeared for a public exam, out of which 51 students passed. In School B, 40 students appeared and 32 of them passed. Which school's performance can be called better and why?

UNIT 2

9 Ratio and Proportion

What I shall learn

- To compare two ratios
- To understand the concept of proportion
- To understand the concepts of direct variation and inverse variation

Let's Get Started

The comparison of two similar quantities by division is called **ratio**. We denote ratio using the symbol ':'.

In general, the ratio of two quantities *a* and *b* is written as $a : b$ and we read it as '*a* is to *b*'. The two quantities *a* and *b* are called the **terms** of the ratio. The first quantity *a* is called the first term or the **antecedent** and the second quantity *b* is called the second term or the **consequent**.

Now, let us look at the following situation.

The height of a young girl is 1 m 20 cm and her picture in a book is 4 cm. Do you think we can write the ratio of the actual height to the height of her picture, one being in metre and centimetre and the other being in centimetre?

No. This is because two quantities can be compared only if they are in the same unit.

Remember

- The order of terms in a ratio is important when we compare two quantities.
- The quantities to be compared must be in the same unit. A ratio is a pure number. So, it does not have a unit.

So, we need to convert the height of the girl into cm.

Height of the girl = 1 m 20 cm = 1×100 cm + 20 cm = 120 cm

Height of the picture = 4 cm

So, the ratio between the two heights is $\frac{120}{4} = 30 : 1$

So, we can say that the actual height is 30 times more than that of its picture in the book.

Also, the ratio of the height of the picture to the height of the girl = $\frac{4}{120} = \frac{1}{30}$.

So, we can easily say that 30:1 is different from 1:30

In general, $a : b \neq b : a$ (unless $a = b$).

Remember

Since ratio can be expressed as fraction, all the properties that hold good for fractions also hold good for ratios.

Therefore, the order of a ratio is important when we compare two quantities.

Example 1: Find the ratio of 30 min to 2 h.

Converting 2 hours into minutes, we get 2 h = 2×60 min = 120 min

$\therefore$ Required ratio = $30 : 120 = \frac{30}{120} = \frac{1}{4} = 1:4$

Equivalent Ratios

We have learned how to find equivalent fractions of a given fraction. If we multiply or divide the antecedent and the consequent of a ratio by the same non-zero number, the value of the ratio does not change. Such ratios are called equivalent ratios.

Example 2: Find two equivalent ratios of 2 : 4.

$$2 : 4 = \frac{2}{4} = \frac{2 \times 2}{4 \times 2} = \frac{4}{8}$$

Therefore, 4 : 8 is an equivalent ratio of 2 : 4.

Similarly, $2 : 4 = \frac{2}{4} = \frac{2 \div 2}{4 \div 2} = \frac{1}{2}$

So, 1 : 2 is another equivalent ratio of 2 : 4.

Example 3: Are 1 : 5 and 2 : 10 equivalent ratios?

$$2 : 10 = \frac{2}{10} = \frac{2 \div 2}{10 \div 2} = \frac{1}{5}$$

Therefore, 1 : 5 and 2 : 10 are equivalent ratios.

Example 4: Diya earns ₹1500 by working for 2 hours. If she works for 8 hours, how much money will she earn?

The ratio between the money Diya earns to the hours she works = 1500 : 2 = $\frac{1500}{2}$.

Here. we have to find the equivalent ratio with the second term as 8.

Money she earns in 8 hours = $\frac{1500}{2} \times \frac{?}{?} = \frac{1500 \times 4}{2 \times 4} = \frac{6000}{8}$

Therefore, she earns ₹6000 in 8 hours.

Ratio in Simplest Form

If the antecedent and the consequent of a ratio do not have any common factor except 1, then the ratio is said to be in its lowest terms or the simplest form.

For example: The ratios 3 : 5 and 5 : 8 are in their respective simplest forms.

To convert a given ratio into its simplest form, find the HCF of its antecedent and consequent and divide both the terms by the HCF.

Example 5: Convert the ratio 100 : 625 into its lowest term.

The HCF of 100 and 625 is 25.

$$\frac{\cancel{100}^{\,4}}{\cancel{625}_{\,25}} = 4 : 25$$

Example 6: Convert the ratio 60 : 132 into its lowest term.

The HCF of 60 and 132 is 12.

$$\frac{\cancel{60}^{\,5}}{\cancel{132}_{\,11}} = 5 : 11$$

If the antecedent or the consequent or both the terms of a ratio are fractions, then we find the LCM of the denominators of the fractions and multiply both the terms of the ratio by this LCM. This will convert the fractional terms into natural numbers.

Example 7: Simplify each of the following ratios.

a. $1:\frac{8}{3}$

$1:\frac{8}{3}=1\times3:\frac{8}{3}\times3=3:8$

b. $2:\frac{7}{5}$

$2:\frac{7}{5}=2\times5:\frac{7}{5}\times5=10:7$

c. $\frac{1}{15}:\frac{1}{10}$

The LCM of 15 and 10 is 30.

$\frac{1}{15}:\frac{1}{10}=\frac{1}{15}\times30:\frac{1}{10}\times30=2:3$

d. $\frac{1}{6}:\frac{2}{3}:\frac{1}{2}$

The LCM of 6, 3 and 2 is 6.

$\frac{1}{6}:\frac{2}{3}:\frac{1}{2}=\frac{1}{6}\times6:\frac{2}{3}\times6:\frac{1}{2}\times6=1:4:3$

Comparison of Ratios

We have already learned how to compare fractions. To compare ratios, we convert them into fractions and then compare. Look at the following examples.

Example 8: Compare 11 : 15 and 7 : 10.

11 : 15 can be written as $\frac{11}{15}$ and 7 : 10 can be written as $\frac{7}{10}$.

Now, let us compare $\frac{11}{15}$ and $\frac{7}{10}$.

The LCM of 15 and 10 is 30.

Now, making the denominators of each fraction equal to 30, we get

$\frac{11}{15}=\frac{11\times2}{15\times2}=\frac{22}{30}$ and $\frac{7}{10}=\frac{7\times3}{10\times3}=\frac{21}{30}$

$\therefore \frac{22}{30}>\frac{21}{30}\Rightarrow\frac{11}{15}>\frac{7}{10}$

Hence, 11 : 15 > 7 : 10.

Example 9: School A has 8 volleyball players and 10 football players. School B has 9 volleyball players and 4 football players. Which school has a higher ratio of volleyball players to football players?

Ratio of volleyball players to football players in School A = 8 : 10

Ratio of volleyball players to football players in School B = 9 : 4

Converting both the ratios into fractional form, we get $\frac{8}{10}$ and $\frac{9}{4}$.

$\frac{8\times2}{10\times2}=\frac{16}{20}, \frac{9\times5}{4\times5}=\frac{45}{20}$

On comparing these two ratios, we see that School B has a higher ratio of volleyball players to football players as compared to School A.

Remember

To compare two ratios, convert them into equivalent like fractions.

Proportion

Observe the following figures. Do you find any changes in the shape?

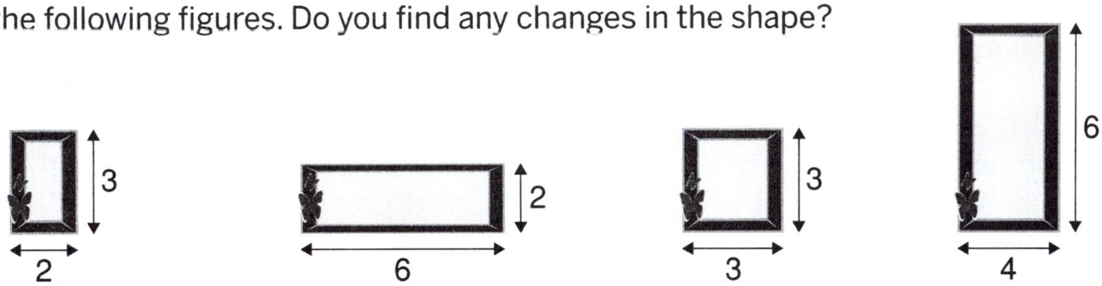

Original Image (i) (ii) (iii)

Now, let us find the ratio of length and breadth in all the figures.

Ratio of length and breadth in the original image = 3 : 2

Ratio of length and breadth in image (i) = 6 : 2 = 3 : 1 (in the simplest form)

Ratio of length and breadth in image (ii) = 3 : 3 = 1 : 1

Ratio of length and breadth in image (iii) = 6 : 4 = 3 : 2 (in the simplest form)

We notice that the ratio in image (iii) is equal to the ratio in the original image. This equality of ratios is called proportion. So, we can say that image (iii) is proportionate to the original image.

Observe the following table that provides the cost of different number of books.

Number of Books	1	5	10	15	18
Cost in Rupees	6	30	60	90	108

From the table, we see that the cost of 10 books is ₹60 and the cost of 18 books is ₹108.

Therefore, ratio of the number of books = 10 : 18 = 5 : 9

Ratio of their costs = 60 : 108 = 5 : 9

If two ratios are equal, then the four numbers forming the two ratios, written in order, are said to be in **proportion**.

In general, *a*, *b*, *c* and *d* are said to be in proportion if $a : b = c : d$. We write it as $a : b :: c : d$ and read it as '*a* is to *b* is as *c* is to *d*'.

Here, *a*, *b*, *c* and *d* are known as the first, second, third and fourth **terms** respectively of the given proportion.

The first and fourth terms are called the **extremes**. The second and third terms are called the middle terms or **means**.

Consider the proportion 10 : 18 = 60 : 108.

Here, 10 and 108 are the extremes, and 18 and 60 are the means.

Product of extremes = $10 \times 108 = 1080$

Product of means = $18 \times 60 = 1080$

$\therefore$ Product of extremes = Product of means

If four numbers are in proportion, then the product of the extremes is equal to the product of the means.

That is, if $a : b = c : d$, then $ad = bc$.

Consider the ratios 3 : 4 and 20 : 30.

Product of extremes = $3 \times 30 = 90$

Product of means = $4 \times 20 = 80$

$\therefore$ Product of extremes $\neq$ Product of means

Therefore, 3, 4, 20 and 30 are not in proportion.

Example 10: Test whether the following sets of numbers are in proportion.

a. 3, 9, 5, 15

In the given numbers,

Product of the extremes = $3 \times 15 = 45$

Product of the means = $9 \times 5 = 45$

$\therefore$ Product of extremes = Product of means

Therefore, 3, 9, 5 and 15 are in proportion.

b. 10, 15, 24, 30

Product of the extremes = $10 \times 30 = 300$

Product of the means = $15 \times 24 = 360$

$\therefore$ Product of extremes $\neq$ Product of means

Therefore, 10, 15, 24 and 30 are not in proportion.

Example 11: Find the fourth proportional of 12, 20 and 3.

Let d be the fourth proportional of 12, 20 and 3.

Thus, 12, 20, 3 and d are in proportion.

Product of extremes = Product of means

$\therefore 12 \times d = 20 \times 3 \Rightarrow 12d = 60 \Rightarrow d = 5$

Therefore, the fourth proportional of 12, 20 and 3 is 5.

Example 12: John bought 3 jars of tomato ketchup for ₹90. Jennifer bought 21 jars of tomato ketchup for ₹630. Check if the number of jars and the cost are in proportion.

If they are in proportion, then number of jars John bought : Cost paid by John : : Number of jars Jennifer bought : Cost paid by Jennifer. That is, 3 : 90 : : 21 : 630

Product of the extremes = $3 \times 630 = 1890$ Product of the means = $90 \times 21 = 1890$

Therefore, 3, 90, 21 and 630 are in proportion.

Exercise 9.1

1. **Express each of the following ratios in its simplest form.**

   a. 24 : 72 b. 80 : 112 c. 130 : 160 d. 629 : 407

2. **Find the ratio of the first quantity to the second quantity in its simplest form.**

   a. ₹7, ₹1.75 b. 5 m, 150 cm c. 6 h, 1 h 50 min d. 6 ℓ, 625 mℓ

3. **Rewrite the following ratios with their terms as natural numbers.**

   a. $1 : \frac{6}{7}$ b. $\frac{7}{12} : 2$ c. $\frac{3}{4} : \frac{5}{6}$ d. $5\frac{1}{2} : 3\frac{2}{3}$

4. **Which of the following sets are equivalent ratios?**

   a. 3 : 5, 27 : 45 b. 2 : 3, 30 : 20 c. 7 : 4, 126 : 64 d. 135 : 30, 9 : 2

5. **Compare the ratios in each of the following.**

   a. 5 : 6, 6 : 7 b. 19 : 25, 37 : 50 c. 24 : 13, 12 : 7 d. 21 : 50, 43 : 100

6. **Which of the following sets of numbers are in proportion?**

   a. 2, 3, 22, 33 b. 8, 6, 12, 9 c. 15, 30, 7, 14 d. 15, 21, 25, 40

7. **Find the missing numbers in the following proportions.**

   a. 24 : 18 = ________ : 9 b. 12 : 16 = 9 : ________

   c. ________ : 20 = $5 : 2\frac{1}{2}$ d. $10\frac{1}{2}$: ________ = $5\frac{1}{2} : 2\frac{3}{4}$

8. **Find the fourth proportional in each of the following.**

   a. 16, 12, 4 b. 9, 10, 18 c. 10, 20, 15 d. 24, 18, 12

9. 250 mℓ of mango squash requires 2 ℓ of water. Find the ratio of water to mango squash.

10. The length of a line segment is 114 cm. If it is divided in the ratio 9 : 10, find the length of the two parts.

11. A milkman mixes milk and water in the ratio 5 : 2. Find the amount of water mixed by him in 6.3 ℓ of milk.

12. If the ratio of three angles in a triangle is 1 : 2 : 3, then find the measure of each angle in the triangle. (Hint: The sum of the three interior angles in any triangle is 180°.)

13. In a class of 30 students, the number of boys is 16 and the remaining students are girls. Find the ratio between.

    i. the number of girls and boys. ii. the number of girls and the whole class.

14. A man earns ₹5000 and spends ₹3000. Find the ratio of his expenditure to

    i. his saving ii. his total income.

Variation

Look at the following pictures of some workers building a compound wall and the number of days required to build the same.

What did you observe? From the above picture, it is clear that if more number of workers share the same job, then the time taken to complete that particular job is less. Similarly, there are many situations in our daily life where a change in one quantity brings about a change in another. This is known as variation.

> **Note**
> "vary" means change.

If two quantities depend on each other in such a way that a change in one results in a corresponding change in the other, then the two quantities are said to be in **variation**.

Examples:

- As the number of members increase in a family, the consumption of water increases accordingly.
- When deforestation increases, the amount of rainfall decreases.
- As population increases, food consumption increases.

Now, let us learn about the different types of variation.

Direct Variation

If an increase in one quantity results in a corresponding increase in another quantity, or a decrease in one quantity results in a corresponding decrease in another quantity, then the two quantities are said to be in **direct variation**.

Suppose a bike is travelling with a constant speed of 50 km/h. The distance covered (d) by it in different time intervals (t) are given below.

Time Taken (t)	Distance Covered (d)
1 h	50 km
2 h	100 km
3 h	150 km
4 h	200 km
5 h	250 km
6 h	300 km

The table tells us that as t increases, d also increases and vice versa.

We can write it as, $\frac{d}{t} = \frac{50}{1}$ = constant

That is, $d = 50t$, where d is directly proportional to t.

Take any two values of t, say 2 and 6.

Ratio of values of $t = 2 : 6 = 1 : 3$

Ratio of the corresponding values of $d = 100 : 300 = 1 : 3$

Therefore, the two ratios of *t* and *d* are equal. That is, 100:300

So, 2, 6, 100 and 300 are in proportion.

Therefore, *t* and *d* are in direct proportion.

Note

If *x* and *y* are in direct variation, then we can also say that *x* is directly proportional to *y*.

Example 13: *x* and *y* are directly proportional and $x = 9$ when $y = 3$. Find *x* when $y = 5$. Also, find *y* when $x = 42$.

Since x and y are directly proportional,

$$\frac{\text{first value of } x}{\text{second value of } x} = \frac{\text{first value of } y}{\text{second value of } y}$$

So, $\frac{9}{x} = \frac{3}{5}$.

Product of means $= 3x$.

Product of extremes $= 9 \times 5 = 45$.

$3x = 45$

$x = \frac{45}{3}$

$= 15$.

$\frac{9}{42} = \frac{3}{y}$.

Product of means $= 42 \times 3 = 126$.

Product of extremes $= 9y$.

$9y = 126$

$y = \frac{126}{9}$

$= 14$.

Example 14: The expenditure per month for a family of 4 members is ₹2,252. Suppose in a month, 6 relatives come to the house. What will be the expenditure for that particular month?

Expenditure per month for 4 members = ₹2,250

If 6 relatives come to the house, then the total number of members would be 10.

Let the expenditure of the 10 members be *x*.

When the number of member increases, the expenditure also increases.

Alternative method:

Product of means $= 4x$

Product of extremes $= 2252 \times 10$

$4x = 2252 \times 10$

$x = 2252 \times \frac{10}{4}$

$= 5630$

So, the expenditure and the number of members are in direct proportion.

$$\therefore x : 10 = 2252 : 4 \Rightarrow \left(\frac{x}{10} = \frac{2252}{4} \Rightarrow x = \frac{2252}{4} \times 10 = 563 \times 10 = 5630\right)$$

The the expenditure in that particular month will be ₹5630.

Inverse Variation

If an increase in one quantity results in a corresponding decrease in another quantity, or if a decrease in one quantity results in a corresponding increase in another quantity, then the two quantities are said to be in **inverse variation**.

Example 15: x varies inversely as y and $x = 6$ when $y = -3$. Find y when $x = -9$.

Since x and y are inversely proportional, $\frac{\text{first value of } x}{\text{second value of } x} = \frac{\text{second value of } y}{\text{first value of } y}$

So, $\frac{6}{-9} = \frac{y}{-3}$

Product of means = $-9y$; product of extremes = $6 \times (-3) = -18$

$$-9y = -18$$

$$y = \frac{-18}{(-9)} = 2$$

Remember

Direct variation is also known as direct proportion. Indirect variation is also known as indirect proportion.

Example 16: 24 men can construct a wall in 15 days, but the owner wants to finish the work in 12 days. How many more men should he employ?

24 men are required to construct a wall in 15 days.

Let x be the number of men required to construct the wall in 12 days.

As the numbers of men increases, the number of days decreases.

The number of men and the number of days are always in inverse proportion.

Ratio of the number of days = Inverse ratio of the number of men

$x : 24$ = Inverse ratio of $12 : 15$

$x : 24 = 15 : 12 \Rightarrow \frac{x}{24} = \frac{15}{12} \Rightarrow x = \frac{15}{12} \times 24 = 15 \times 2 = 30$

Number of more men to be employed = $30 - 24 = 6$

Exercise 9.2

1. **Examine whether the following are in direct variation or inverse variation.**
   a. Speed of a vehicle and the distance covered in different time intervals
   b. Speed of a vehicle and the time taken to cover a fixed distance
   c. Number of days worked and the amount earned
   d. Number of students in a hostel and the number of days food lasts
   e. Number of people working and the amount of work done
2. a varies inversely as b and $a = 5$ and $b = \frac{1}{10}$. Find a when $b = 2$ and find b when $a = \frac{1}{10}$.
3. 15 bags of rice weigh 375 kg. How much do 8 bags weigh?
4. In a military camp, the ration available is enough for 8 weeks for 1200 people. 300 more people joined the camp. How long will the same amount of ration last now?
5. A bike can cover 405 km with 9 litres of petrol. How many litres of petrol will it require to cover 225 km?

Summary

1. The comparison of two similar quantities in terms of 'how many times' is called ratio.
2. In general, the ratio of two quantities *a* and *b* is written as $a : b$ and we read it as '*a* is to *b*'. The two quantities are called the terms of the ratio. The first quantity *a* is called the first term or the antecedent and the second quantity *b* is called the second term or the consequent.
3. An equivalent ratio can be obtained by multiplying or dividing each term of the ratio by the same number.
4. To convert a given ratio into its simplest form, we find the HCF of its antecedent and consequent and divide both the terms by the HCF.
5. Four quantities *a*, *b*, *c* and *d* are said to be in proportion if $a : b = c : d$. We write this as $a : b :: c : d$. We read it as '*a* is to *b* is as *c* is to *d*'. Here *a*, *b*, *c* and *d* are known as the first, second, third and fourth terms respectively of the given proportion. The first and the fourth terms are called the extremes, and the second and the third terms are called the means.
6. If an increase or decrease in one quantity results in a corresponding increase or decrease in another quantity, then the two quantities are said to be in **direct variation**.
7. If an increase or decrease in one quantity results in a corresponding decrease or increase in another quantity, then the two quantities are said to be in **inverse variation**.

Mental Maths

1. State if each pair forms a proportion.

   a. 12:24 and 3:4   b. 4:40 and 2:8   c. 6:10 and 15:25

2. Find the value of *x* in the following.

   a. $4:7 :: x :49$ b. $12:20 :: 3:x$ c. $2: 34:: 8: x$

Revision Exercise

1 **Express each ratio in its simplest form.**

a. 75 : 150 b. 37 : 47 c. 85 : 102 d. 425 : 750

2 **Which of the following sets of numbers are in proportion?**

a. 5, 7, 15, 21 b. 5, 10, 16, 8 c. 16, 18, 8, 9 d. 24, 30, 10, 15

3 **Find the ratio of each of the given set of quantities and express it in its lowest terms.**

First Quantity	50 p	750 g	1 h	5 m	5 min	30 mm
Second Quantity	₹1	1 kg	30 min	125 cm	5 s	1 cm

4 Two partners have invested in a business in the ratio 5 : 8. If they earn a profit of ₹1,04,000, then find the amount that each partner will receive according to their investment.

5 The ratio of the weights of two men is $\frac{1}{2}:\frac{1}{3}$. If the weight of the first person is $22\frac{1}{2}$ kg, then find the weight of the second person.

6 The length and the breadth of a rectangle are in the ratio 7 : 4. Find the perimeter of the rectangle if its length is 121 cm.

7 A farmer has enough grains to feed 120 cattle for 30 days. He sells 10 cattle. For how many days will the grain last now?

8 Two quantities a and b are directly proportional and $a = 6.5$ when $b = 13$. Find a when $b = 38$ and find b when $a = 7.5$.

9 The expenditure per month for 8 students in a hostel is ₹18,000. 7 more students join the hostel. What will be the monthly expenditure now?

10 Executives working at the rate of 8 hours a day can complete a work in $19\frac{1}{2}$ days. As per client's demand to finish the work early, they start working for 9 hours a day. In how many days will they finish the same work now?

11 A farmer has enough grain to feed 120 cattle for 30 days. He sells 10 cattle. For how many days will the grain last now?

For the Curious Mind

The sketch of a square field is drawn with a scale of 1 cm = 5 km. Find the actual area of the square field if its area is 16 sq. cm in the sketch.

UNIT 2

Unitary Method 10

Let's Get Started

In unitary method, first the price or value of one unit is calculated and then the price of many or a required number of units is calculated.

- Divide to find the value of one unit.
- Multiply to find the value of larger quantities.

What I shall learn

- To understand the concept of unitary method
- To apply unitary method and solve problems

Example 1: The cost of 1 pack of chocolates is ₹72. Find the price of 5 chocolates if there are 12 chocolates in each pack.

Cost of 12 chocolates = ₹72

We divide the price of 1 pack by the number of chocolates in the pack to get the cost of 1 chocolate.

Price of one unit = Price of many ÷ Number of units = $72 \div 12 = 6$

Thus, the price of one chocolate is ₹6.

Now, we multiply the price of one chocolate with the required quantity of chocolates, that is, 5.

Cost of 5 chocolates = $5 \times 6 = 30$

So, the cost of 5 chocolates is ₹30.

Example 2: If a transport company charges ₹1500 to carry 3 kg of weight, then find the charges to carry 8 kg.

Charges for 3 kg of weight = ₹1500

Charges for transporting 1 kg of weight = $1500 \div 3$ = ₹500

Charges for transporting 8 kg of weight = 500×8 = ₹4000

Therefore, the transport company charges ₹4000 to carry 8 kg of weight.

Example 3: If Afzal walks 18 km in 5 hours, how long would he take to walk 10.8 km?

Time taken to walk 18 km = 5 hours

Time taken to walk 1 km = $5 \div 18 = \frac{5}{18}$ hours

Time taken to walk 10.8 km = $10.8 \times \frac{5}{18} = 3$ hours

Therefore, Afzal would take 3 hours to walk a distance of 10.8 km.

Example 4: A car can travel 145 km with 10 ℓ of petrol. What is its mileage?

Distance travelled with 10 ℓ of petrol = 145 km

Distance travelled with 1 ℓ of petrol = 145 ÷ 10 = 14.5 km

Therefore, the mileage of the car is 14.5 km per litre.

Note

Mileage means the distance a vehicle covers using one litre of petrol.

Exercise 10.1

1 Find the missing quantities or values in the following cases.

Quantity	Value (in ₹)	Required Quantity	Value of Required Quantity (in ₹)
3 pen sets	180	5 pen sets	
5 kg flour	165		396
15 m ribbon	105	8 m ribbon	
2 dozen eggs	144		276

2 5 workers in a handicraft workshop produce 35 toys per day. How many toys does a worker produce in 15 days?

3 A car travels 120 km in 10 litres of petrol. What is its mileage?

4 56 books weigh 8 kg. How much will 10 books weigh?

5 987 bricks are required to build a 3-m-high wall. How many bricks will be required to build a 5-m-high wall?

Summary

1. The method in which we first find the value of one unit and then the value of the required number of units is known as unitary method.
2. We divide to find the value of one unit and we multiply to find the value of larger quantities.

Revision Exercise

1. The quantities of each ingredient needed to prepare a cake for 10 people are given below. Complete the table by calculating the quantities of these ingredients that would be needed to prepare a cake for 4 people and 25 people.

Ingredients	Quantity for 10 People	Quantity for 4 People	Quantity for 25 People
Flour	400 g		
Oil	350 g		
Essence	10 drops		
Eggs	5		
Baking powder	15 g		
Almonds	100		

2. A daily wage worker earns ₹630 for six days' of work. How much will he earn if he works for 22 days?
3. 985 bricks are needed to build a wall of height 5 m. How many bricks will be needed to build a wall of height 12 m?
4. A certain type of basmati rice is available in 25 kg and 15 kg packs. If the 25 kg pack costs ₹1250, then what will be the cost of the 15 kg pack?
5. 12 farmers harvest the crops in one acre of land in 24 hours. How many farmers will be required to do the same in 16 hours?
6. The weight of 60 books is 4 kg. What will be the weight of 135 such books? How many of such books will weigh 5 kg?
7. 44 people can complete a job in 28 days. In how many days will 56 people be able to do the same job?
8. At a particular time, the length of the shadow of the Qutub Minar, whose height is 72 m, is 80 m. What will be the height of an electric pole, the length of whose shadow at the same time is 600 cm?

For the Curious Mind

Mr Sharma sells a bag containing 12 kg onions for ₹90, whereas Mr Verma sells a bag containing 15 kg onions for ₹120. In whose shop are the onions cheaper and by how much?

UNIT 2

Profit or Loss

11

Let's Get Started

What I shall learn

- To find profit or profit percentage and loss or loss percentage
- To solve problems on profit and loss
- To solve situational problems on discount

Cost price is the price at which the goods are purchased from the wholesaler or producer. It is written as **CP**.

Overhead expenses are the expenses incurred during buying and selling. These include transportation, packing, rent, labour, fuel and are added to the cost price.

Thus, actual or total cost is the sum of the cost price and the overhead expenses put together.

Marked price is the price at which goods are available in the shop or market. It is written as **MP**.

Selling price is the price at which the shopkeeper sells the goods to the consumer or customer. Selling price may be different from the marked price. Selling price is written as **SP**.

Profit is earned when the selling price is more than the cost price.

Profit = SP – CP

Loss is incurred when the selling price is less than the cost price.

Loss = CP – SP

Example 1: Rohan bought 10 kg mushrooms from the market at ₹45 per kg. He spent ₹100 on fuel for transportation and ₹50 on packing. Then, he sold 6 kg mushrooms at ₹64 per kg, 3 kg mushrooms at ₹62 and the rest at the cost price. Find the profit or loss incurred during the sale.

CP of the mushrooms = 10 × ₹45 = ₹450

Overhead expenses = Cost of fuel + Cost of packaging

= ₹100 + ₹50 = ₹150

∴ Actual cost of 10 kg mushrooms = ₹450 + ₹150 = ₹600

Total SP of 10 kg mushrooms

= SP of 6 kg mushrooms at ₹64 per kg + SP of 3 kg mushrooms at ₹62 per kg + SP of 1 kg mushrooms at ₹45 per kg

= 64 × 6 + 62 × 3 + 45 × 1 = ₹615

Here, the total selling price is more than the actual cost. Therefore, Rohan made a profit of ₹615 – ₹600 = ₹15.

Hints and Tips

Distinguish between the terms Cost Price and Actual Cost. Always remember that if overhead expenses are mentioned in the question, then Actual cost = CP + Overhead expenses.

Example 2: A fruit seller bought 100 apples at ₹6 each and 50 oranges at ₹5 each. He spent ₹250 on transportation and storage. He sold all the apples and oranges for ₹1000. Find the profit or loss incurred by the fruit seller.

Cost of 100 apples = ₹100 × 6 = ₹600

Cost of 50 oranges = ₹50 × 5 = ₹250

Overhead expenses = ₹250

∴ Actual cost of the apples and oranges = ₹600 + ₹250 + ₹250 = ₹1100

Total SP of the apples and oranges put together = ₹1000

Here, the total SP is less than the actual CP. Therefore, the fruit seller incurred a loss of ₹1100 – ₹1000 = ₹100.

Exercise 11.1

1. A shopkeeper buys 25 pencils at ₹65. He sells them at ₹3.50 each. Find the profit or loss incurred by the shopkeeper.
2. A pen drive bought for ₹210 is sold for ₹250. Find the profit/loss.
3. Find the C.P. of a cell phone, if on selling it for ₹8,200 a gain of ₹540 is made.
4. Find the S.P. of a cricket bat which is bought for ₹990 and sold at a loss of ₹77.
5. Chocolates are bought at 3 for ₹30 and sold at 2 for ₹24. Find
   i. Profit/Loss made on selling 1 chocolate.
   ii. Profit/Loss made on selling 6 similar chocolates.

Profit % or Loss %

Profit % or loss % is calculated on the actual cost price for every ₹100.

$$\text{Profit }\% = \frac{\text{Profit}}{\text{CP}} \times 100$$

$$\text{Loss}\% = \frac{\text{Loss}}{\text{CP}} \times 100$$

Example 3: Mahesh bought a radio for ₹500. Find the SP and profit percent if he gains ₹45.

CP of the radio = ₹500

Profit = ₹45

SP = CP + Profit = ₹500 + ₹45 = ₹545

$$\text{Profit}\% = \frac{\text{Profit}}{\text{CP}} \times 100 = \frac{45}{500} \times 100 = \frac{\cancel{45}^{9}}{\cancel{500}} \times \cancel{100} = 9\%$$

Therefore, Mahesh earned 9% profit.

Example 4: Krishna bought a chair for ₹480 and sold it for ₹540. Find his gain or loss per cent.

CP of the chair = ₹480

SP of the chair = ₹540

∴ Profit = ₹540 – ₹480 = ₹60 as SP > CP

$$\text{Profit\%} = \frac{\text{Profit}}{\text{CP}} \times 100 = \frac{60}{480} \times 100 = \frac{\cancel{60}}{\underset{8}{\cancel{480}}} \times 100 = \frac{100}{8} = 12.5\%$$

Therefore, the profit percentage earned by Krishna was 12.5%.

Exercise 11.2

1. What is the profit percentage if a calculator worth ₹150 is being sold at ₹186?
2. What is the profit or loss per cent earned when a dozen bananas worth ₹48 are sold at ₹3.80 each?
3. Sushmita bought a dress for ₹600 and sold it for ₹690. Find the profit percentage.
4. Find the loss percentage if Pratyush incurred a loss of ₹310 when he sold cosmetics worth ₹1550.

Calculating Profit/Loss When Profit/Loss Percentage is Given

The amount of profit or loss is calculated on the total cost price. If the percentage of profit or loss is known to us, we can calculate the selling price by adding the profit or by deducting the loss from the cost price.

Profit or loss = Total cost price × % of profit or loss

Example 5: A calculator was bought for ₹300. It was sold at a profit of 8% after inserting a new battery worth ₹50. Find the price at which the calculator was sold.

CP of the calculator = ₹300

Overhead charges = ₹50

∴ Total CP = ₹300 + ₹50 = ₹350

Profit or loss = Total cost price × % of profit or loss

$$= \frac{8}{100} \times 350 = ₹28$$

∴ SP of the calculator = CP + Profit = ₹350 + ₹28 = ₹378

Example 6: Darshana bought an oil painting from an art gallery for ₹45,000 and spent ₹2100 on framing and packing it. She sold it at a profit of 12%. Find the selling price of the oil painting.

CP of the oil painting = ₹45,000

Overhead charges = ₹2100

Actual CP = ₹45000 + ₹2100 = ₹47100

Profit = $\frac{12}{100} \times 47100$ = ₹5652

SP of the oil painting = ₹47100 + ₹5652 = ₹52752

Therefore, the SP of the oil painting is ₹52,752.

Example 7: A shopkeeper buys sugar worth ₹1200 and flour worth ₹1800. Find the selling price and the total profit earned by the shopkeeper if he sells the sugar at 5% profit and the flour at 2% loss.

CP of the sugar = ₹1200

Profit percentage on sugar = 5%

Profit = $1200 \times \frac{5}{100}$ = ₹60

$\therefore$ SP of the sugar = ₹1200 + ₹60 = ₹1260

CP of the flour = ₹1800

Loss percentage on flour = 2%

Loss = $1800 \times \frac{2}{100}$ = ₹36

$\therefore$ SP of the flour = ₹1800 − ₹36 = ₹1764

The CP of both the sugar and the flour = ₹1200 + ₹1800 = ₹3000

The SP of both the sugar and the flour = ₹1260 + ₹1764 = ₹3024

SP > CP

$\therefore$ Profit = ₹3024 − ₹3000 = ₹24

Therefore, the shopkeeper made a profit of ₹24.

Exercise 11.3

1. **Find the selling price in each of the following.**
   a. Cost price = ₹750, profit = 10%
   b. Cost price = ₹600, loss = 9%
   c. Cost price = ₹1000, loss = 2%
   d. Cost price = ₹350, overhead expenses = ₹50, profit = 15%
2. Find the selling price of a television set that was bought for ₹15,000 and sold at a profit of 12%.
3. Find the selling price of a car worth ₹5,00,000 if it was sold at a loss of 6% or at a profit of 6%.

Discount

Discount is the amount that is reduced from the marked price during a sale or after bargaining. Discount is also called rebate, which is usually offered by the seller during clearance sale and festive seasons or to simply boost sales.

The percentage of discount is the discount rate and is multiplied by marked price to find the discount amount. Selling price is found by deducting the discount amount from the marked price.

Discount Amount = Percentage of Discount   MP

SP = MP – Discount

Example 8: A watch with marked price of ₹1850 was sold at a discount of 10%. Find the selling price of the watch and the profit or loss incurred by the shopkeeper if its cost price was ₹1500.

MP of the watch = ₹1850

Discount % = 10%

Discount $= 1850 \times 10\% = 1850 \times \frac{10}{100}$ = ₹185

SP of the watch = ₹1850 – ₹185 = ₹1665

CP of the watch = ₹1500

SP > CP

Profit = 1665 – 1500 = ₹165

Therefore, the shopkeeper made a profit of ₹165.

Example 9: A vendor sold a pair of shoes for ₹595. Find the discounted amount and the rate of discount if the marked price of the pair of shoes was ₹700.

MP of the pair of shoes = ₹700

SP of the pair of shoes = ₹595

Discount = MP – SP = ₹700 – ₹595 = ₹105

$$\text{Discount percentage} = \frac{\text{Discount}}{\text{MP}} \times 100\%$$

$$= \frac{105}{7\cancel{00}} \times 1\cancel{00}\% = \frac{105\%}{7} = 15\%$$

Therefore, the vendor sold the shoes at 15% discount.

Exercise 11.4

1. A shopkeeper sold a book worth ₹80 at a discount of 20%. Find the selling price of the book.
2. A washing machine worth ₹18,500 was sold at ₹14,800. Find the discount and the discount %.

3. A chocolate with the marked price of ₹25 was sold at ₹19. Find the discount and the discount %.
4. An exporter sold goods worth ₹4,50,000 for ₹3,60,000. Find the discount and the discount %.
5. Jayan got a mobile phone for ₹13,500 after a discount of 10%. Find the marked price of the mobile. If the cost price was ₹8,500, what is the profit or loss incurred by the shopkeeper?
6. Alan went to buy a two-wheeler with a marked price of ₹58,000. If he managed to get a discount of 10%, how much did he buy it for? What is the profit earned by the shopkeeper if the cost price was ₹18,000 less than the marked price?
7. Find the discount and the discount percentage if a laptop marked ₹60,000 is sold at ₹57,600?
8. Santosh bought a shirt for his friend Krishna for ₹2800, which was marked at ₹3500. Find the discount and the discount percentage.
9. Anuradha bought an air conditioner for ₹36,800, which was marked at a price of ₹40,000. Find the discount and the discount percentage.

Summary

- Cost price is the price at which a shopkeeper purchases goods from the wholesaler or producer. Overhead expenses are the expenses incurred during buying and selling. They include transportation, packing, rent, labour, fuel, etc. Actual cost is cost price and overhead expenses put together.
- Marked price is the price at which goods are available in the shop or market.
- Selling price is the price at which a shopkeeper sells goods to the consumer or customer. It may be different from the marked price due to discounts and bargaining during sale.
- Profit is earned when the selling price is more than the cost price.
- Loss is incurred when the selling price is less than the cost price.
- Discount is calculated on the marked price.
- Percentage of profit or loss is calculated on the cost price for every ₹100.
- Percentage of discount is calculated on the market price for every ₹100.

For the Curious Mind

A mechanic bought an old cycle for ₹500 and spent ₹750 on extra fittings and other spares. He expected ₹1500 but sold it for ₹1400. Find the expected profit percentage and actual profit percentage.

Revision Exercise

1. **Find the selling price in each case and complete the table.**

Cost Price (₹)	Overhead Expenses (₹)	Profit (₹)	Loss (₹)	Selling Price (₹)
85	25	–	10	
150	35	15	–	
300	25	–	15	
800	125	20	–	

2. **Find the profit or loss percentage and complete the table.**

Cost Price (₹)	Overhead Expenses (₹)	Selling Price (₹)	Profit %	Loss %
45	15	72		
165	0	176		
585	40	575		
5320	80	5238		

3. **State whether the following statements are true or false.**

a. Marked price usually includes cost price, overhead expenses and profit of the seller.

b. Selling price is different from marked price due to the discounts, offers and bargaining done during the sale.

c. Profit is earned when the selling price is less than the cost price.

d. Discount is calculated on the selling price.

4. **Solve the following.**

a. Find the profit or loss percentage when Parankush sells goods worth ₹1800 at ₹1440.

b. Find the selling price of a computer that was bought for ₹35,000 and sold at a profit of 9%.

c. Find the selling price if stationery worth ₹50,000 is sold at a discount of 15%.

d. A vegetable vendor bought vegetables worth ₹2000 and spent ₹400 on transportation and storage. Find the percentage of profit or loss if the vegetables are sold at ₹2520.

e. If the cost price of 25 articles is equal to the selling price of 10 articles, then what is the percentage of profit or loss incurred by the merchant?

f. A merchant who marked his goods up by 30% subsequently offered a discount of 20%. What is the profit percentage made by the merchant after offering the discount?

g. A shirt with marked price ₹800 was sold at ₹600. Find the rate of discount allowed on the shirt.

h. If the marked price of an article is ₹4000 and the selling price is kept ₹480 less than the marked price, what is the selling price? Find the discount and the discount percentage.

UNIT 2

Simple Interest

12

Let's Get Started

Remember

- The amount of money one borrows for his needs or one lends to others is called the **principal**. It is denoted by 'P'.
- The period for which the money is borrowed or given is known as the **time period**. It is denoted by 'T'.
- The rate at which the lender charges the borrower is known as the **rate of interest**. It is denoted by 'R'.
- Rate is calculated per unit of money and per unit of time. The rate of interest per ₹100 per annum is called **rate per cent**.
- The extra money that is repaid to the lender in addition to the money borrowed is called the **interest**. It is denoted by 'I'.
- The **amount** that is to be repaid is equal to the sum of the principal and the interest. It is denoted by 'A'.

  Amount = Principal + Interest

What I shall learn

- **To understand the concept of simple interest and its relation with principal, rate of interest and time period**

Note

Usually, time is taken in years and the yearly rate of interest is taken.

If the time is given in months, express it as a fraction with 12 as the denominator since 1 year = 12 months.

If it is given in terms of days, express it as a fraction with 365 as the denominator since 1 year = 365 days.

While calculating the number of days, do not include the starting date.

Simple Interest

If the interest is calculated only on the principal, then it is called **simple interest**. In this chapter, we have used the term 'interest' to mean only simple interest.

Formula for Calculating Simple Interest and Amount

Let us derive the general formula for finding interest and amount.

Let the principal be ₹P, the rate of interest per annum be R% and the time be T years.

Interest on ₹100 per year = ₹R

Interest on ₹1 per year = ₹$\frac{R}{100}$

Interest on ₹P per year = ₹$P \times \frac{R}{100}$

Interest on ₹P per T years $= ₹P \times T \times \frac{R}{100} = ₹\frac{P \times R \times T}{100}$

$$\text{Simple Interest (SI)} = \frac{P \times R \times T}{100}$$

Amount = Principal + Interest

$$\text{Amount (A)} = P + \frac{P \times R \times T}{100} = P\left(1 + \frac{R \times T}{100}\right)$$

We can find the principal, time and rate of interest if we know the other quantities using the following formulae.

$$P = \frac{SI \times 100}{T \times R}; T = \frac{SI \times 100}{P \times R}; R = \frac{SI \times 100}{R \times T}$$

Note

If two quantities are directly proportional, then any increase/decrease in one quantity implies a proportional increase/decrease in the other quantity.

Interest is directly proportional to the principal, rate of interest and time period.

Example 1: If the rate of interest is 5 paise per month per rupee, then calculate the following.

a. Interest per year per rupee

Rate of interest per month per rupee = 5 paise

Interest per year per rupee = 12×5 paise = 60 paise

b. Interest per month per ₹100

Interest per month per ₹100 = 5 paise $\times$ 100 = 500 paise = ₹5

c. Interest per year per ₹100

Interest per year per ₹100 = 60 paise $\times$ 100 = 6000 paise = ₹60 (Or ₹5 $\times$ 12 = ₹60)

d. Rate per cent

The rate per cent is 60%.

Example 2: Find the interest when principal is ₹30,000, rate of interest is 11% per annum and time is $2\frac{1}{3}$ years.

P = ₹30,000; R = 11%; T = $2\frac{1}{3}$ years = $\frac{7}{3}$ years

$$SI = \frac{P \times R \times T}{100} = \frac{30000 \times \frac{7}{3} \times 11}{100} = \frac{10000 \times 7 \times 11}{100} = 100 \times 7 \times 11 = 7700$$

$\therefore$ Interest = ₹7700

Example 3: Find the interest and amount when principal is ₹1,80,000, rate of interest is 30% and the time duration is from 10 January 2015 to 17 August 2015.

P = ₹1,80,000; R = 30%; T = 10 January 2015 to 17 August 2015 = 219 days = 219/365 year.

$$SI = \frac{P \times R \times T}{100} = \frac{180{,}000 \times 30 \times 219}{100 \times 365} = 1800 \times 6 \times 3 = 32400$$

Amount = Principal + Simple Interest = 1,80,000 + 32,400 = ₹2,12,400

Example 4: Sameera got an interest of ₹3080 for 2 years at 8% per annum. Find the principal.

I = ₹3080; T = 2 years; R = 8%

$$P = \frac{SI \times 100}{T \times R} = \frac{3080 \times 100}{2 \times 8} = 19250$$

∴ Amount lent by Sameera = ₹19,250

Example 5: Find the time when ₹36,000 amounts to ₹37,800 at $6\frac{2}{3}$% per annum?

P = ₹36,000; A = ₹37,800; Rate of Interest = $6\frac{2}{3}\% = \frac{20}{3}\%$

Interest = Amount – Principal = 37800 – 36000 = ₹1800

$$T = \frac{SI \times 100}{P \times R} = \frac{1800 \times 100}{36000 \times \frac{20}{3}} = \frac{1800 \times 100 \times 3}{36000 \times 20} = \frac{3}{4} \text{ year} = 9 \text{ months}$$

∴ Time taken = 9 months

Example 6: At what rate per cent will the principal double itself in 8 years 4 months?

T = 8 years 4 months = $8\frac{4}{12}$ years = $8\frac{1}{3}$ years = $\frac{25}{3}$ years

Let the principal be ₹x.

Then, the amount will be ₹$2x$.

Interest = $2x - x = x$

$$R = \frac{SI \times 100}{P \times T} = \frac{x \times 100}{x \times \frac{25}{3}} = \frac{100}{\frac{25}{3}} = \frac{100 \times 3}{25} = 4 \times 3 = 12$$

∴ Rate per cent = 12%

Exercise 12.1

1. **If the rate of interest is 1 paise per month per rupee, then calculate the following.**
   a. Interest per annum per rupee
   b. Interest per annum per ₹100
   c. Rate per cent
2. **If the rate percent is 36%, then calculate the following.**
   a. Interest per ₹100 per annum
   b. Interest per ₹100 per month
   c. Interest per rupee per month
3. Find the interest on ₹75 for 9 months at the rate of 2 paise per month per rupee.

4 **Find the interest in the following cases.**

a. Principal = ₹10,000, rate of interest = 10%, time = $3\frac{1}{3}$ years

b. Principal = ₹1000, rate of interest = 15%, time = 1 years 4 months

5 **Find the amount when**

a. Principal = ₹25,000, rate of interest = 5%, time = 6 months

b. Principal = ₹75,000, rate of interest = 16%, time = 2 years 3 months

6 **Find the interest and amount when**

a. Principal = ₹20,000, rate of interest = 24 % time = 11 February 2001 to 11 June 2001

b. Principal = ₹15,000, rate of interest = 36%, time = 26 February 2011 to 8 July 2011

7 What is the sum borrowed for which the simple interest at 8% per annum for $3\frac{1}{2}$ years is ₹9800?

8 Find the time period for which ₹4,50,000 invested at a rate of 6% per annum simple interest amounts to ₹5,17,500.

9 How long will it take for a sum of ₹5,00,000 invested at $7\frac{1}{2}$% per annum to become ₹7,81,250?

10 Find the rate per cent per annum for the sum that triples itself in 25 years.

Summary

1. The amount of money one borrows for his needs or one lends to others is called the principal (P).
2. Time (T) refers to the period for which money is borrowed or given.
3. The agreement between the lender and the borrower about the interest to be calculated is called the rate of interest (R).
4. Rate is calculated per unit of money and per unit of time.
5. The rate of interest per ₹100 per year is called the rate per cent.
6. The extra money that is repaid to the lender in addition to the money borrowed for some time is called the interest.
7. Amount = Principal + Interest
8. If the interest is calculated only on the principal, then it is called simple interest.
9. Simple interest = $\frac{P \times R \times T}{100}$
10. Amount = $P\left(1+\frac{R \times T}{100}\right)$

Revision Exercise

1 **Fill in the blanks.**

a. Rate of interest per ₹100 per year is called __________.

b. Amount = Principal + __________

c. The amount of money one borrows for one's needs is called __________.

d. The extra money that is repaid to the lender in addition to the money borrowed is called __________.

e. The total money that is repaid to the lender at the end of the agreed time is called __________.

2 **If the rate of interest is 2 paise per month, then calculate the following.**

a. Interest per ₹100 per month

b. Interest per ₹100 per year

c. Rate per cent

3 Bhaskar borrowed ₹500 at the rate of 3 paise per month per rupee and repaid the amount after 6 months. How much did he repay?

4 Find the simple interest on a sum of ₹9,12,500 at 18% per annum from 12 February 2011 to 30 September 2011.

5 Find the amount paid on ₹32,000 for 2 years 4 months at $7\frac{1}{2}\%$ per annum.

6 Find the simple interest and the amount on the sum of ₹5440 for $2\frac{1}{4}$ years at 11% per annum.

7 What sum will amount to ₹5,08,200 at 3% per annum in 7 years?

8 Helen took a loan from a bank for buying a two-wheeler on simple interest. After 3 years, she paid ₹48,260 and settled the loan. If the rate of interest was 9% per annum, what was the sum she borrowed?

9 Find the rate per cent when simple interest of ₹36,250 becomes ₹14500 after 5 years.

10 In how many years would a sum of money triple itself at $12\frac{1}{2}\%$ per annum?

11 Find the difference of interests on a sum of ₹2100 at 8% per annum for one year and three years.

12 In how many years will the simple interest on a certain sum be 4.05 times the principal at 13.5 per cent per annum?

For the Curious Mind

What will be the amount in 2 years 8 months at 9% rate of interest if the sum of money invested at 8% per annum for simple interest amounts to ₹12,500 in 2 years?

Unit Worksheet 2

Study the given information and answer the questions that follow.

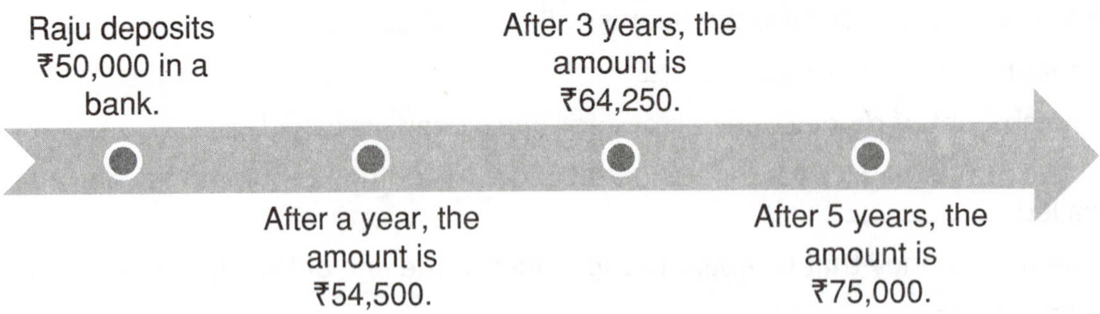

1 Calculate the interest earned after each of the following periods of time.

1 year	3 years	5 years

2 Calculate the rate of interest for each of the following periods of time.

1 year	3 years	5 years

3 Calculate the ratio between the following.

a. Interest earned after 1 year and interest earned after 3 years __________

b. Interest earned after 1 year and interest earned after 5 years __________

c. Interest earned after 3 years and interest earned after 5 years __________

4 Calculate the amount Raju gets after $2\frac{1}{2}$ years if the rate of interest is the same as in the first year.

____

____

Mental Maths

1. Find the average weight of 3 mangoes if they weigh 300 g, 250 g and 200 g respectively. ______
2. Find the value of x if $x : 3 :: 10 : 15$. ______
3. What is the value of $12\frac{1}{2}$ % in fraction? ______
4. How many seconds make an hour? ______
5. What is the percentage of discount if a product worth ₹200 is sold at ₹180? ______

UNIT 3

Introduction to Algebra

13

Let's Get Started

All of us are quite familiar with numbers. But do you know there is another branch of mathematics called **Algebra**, which uses letters to represent numbers? A letter can represent any number. The value represented by a letter can be determined depending upon the given conditions.

Let us learn more about algebra in this chapter.

What I shall learn

- To understand an algebraic statement
- To identify variables and constants

Know Your Mathematician – Diophantus (1890–1962)

Diophantus was an Alexandrian Greek mathematician born between 200 and 214 BC. He is called the **Father of Algebra** for his contributions to this branch of mathematics. He wrote a series of 13 books called *Arithmetica*, of which only the first six have survived.

Note

The word 'Algebra' is derived from the Arabic word *al-jabr*. It was coined from the title of the book *Kitab al-jabr wal-mugabala*, written by the Arab mathematician Al-Khwarizmi.

Indian mathematicians like Aryabhatta, Bhrahmagupta, Mahavir, Bhaskara II and Sridhara have also contributed significantly to algebra.

Numerical Statements and Algebraic Statements

Consider the following groups of mathematical statements.

First group	Second group
$100 \times 2 + 50$	$5y - 4c$
$30 - 7 + 2$	$10z \times 5$
$500 \div 5$	$18m \div 6$

Statements in the first group involve only numbers and mathematical operators, whereas those in the second group involve numbers, letters as well as mathematical operators.

Statements in the first group are known as **numerical statements** and those in the second group are known as **algebraic statements**.

Numerical Statements

A numerical statement is a mathematical statement involving only numbers and one or more mathematical operators (+, −, ×, ÷).

A numerical statement represents a number when it is evaluated.

Writing Numerical Statements

In the lower classes, we have solved many word problems involving basic arithmetic operations. It requires the skill of translating the word problem into a numerical statement and then evaluating it. Let us see an example.

Example 1: Electricity bill for two months is ₹1800, out of which only ₹975 is paid. How much more is to be paid? Write the numerical statement representing this situation.

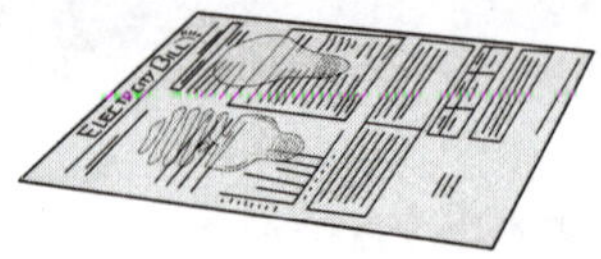

Electricity bill for two months = ₹1800

Amount paid = ₹975

Amount yet to be paid = Total bill amount – Amount paid

= ₹1800 – ₹975 = ₹825

Algebraic Statements

An algebraic statement is a mathematical statement involving letters, numbers and one or more mathematical operators (+, –, ×, ÷). Some examples of algebraic statements are

$16x + 7$ $\qquad$ $10z - 8$ $\qquad$ $17p + 32$

In the algebraic statement $16x + 7$, $16x$ means $16 \times x$. Similarly, $10z = 10 \times z$ and $17p$ means $17 \times p$.

Unlike numerical statements, algebraic statements do not represent a single number. Depending on the value assigned to the letter, the value of the algebraic statement changes.

For example, in the algebraic statement $16x + 7$, if the value of x is 1, then it evaluates to 23, if x is –1, then it evaluates to –9.

Let us learn in detail about algebraic statements in the following sections.

Note

Whenever a letter and a number are multiplied, the number is always written first in the product, followed by the letter. For example, $16 \times p = 16p$ and not $p16$.

Exercise 13.1

1 Identify the given statements. Write A for algebraic statements and N for numerical statements.

a. $25 + 6$ ☐ $\qquad$ b. $52 \times 7 + 3$ ☐ $\qquad$ c. $2d + 3$ ☐ $\qquad$ d. $36 \div 6 + 5$ ☐

2 Evaluate the following numerical statements.

a. $20 + 15 \div 3 - 10$ $\qquad$ b. $14 - 9 \times 2 + 10$ $\qquad$ c. $30 \div 5 + 3 - 7$ $\qquad$ d. $27 \times 4 \div 2 + 3$

3 Write the numerical statements for the following word problems and solve them.

a. In a stadium, there are 27,816 males and 14,908 females. Find the total number of people in the stadium.

b. In a theatre, there are 584 seats and each ticket costs ₹160. Find the total amount collected if all the seats are full.

4 What is the value of the algebraic statement $10m + 15$ for the following values of m?

a. 1 $\qquad$ b. –5 $\qquad$ c. 10

Variables and Constants

Look at the graph shown adjacent. It shows the amount of rainfall in different months of a year in Mysore. From the graph, we can see that the amount of rainfall changes every month, hence its value is not constant.

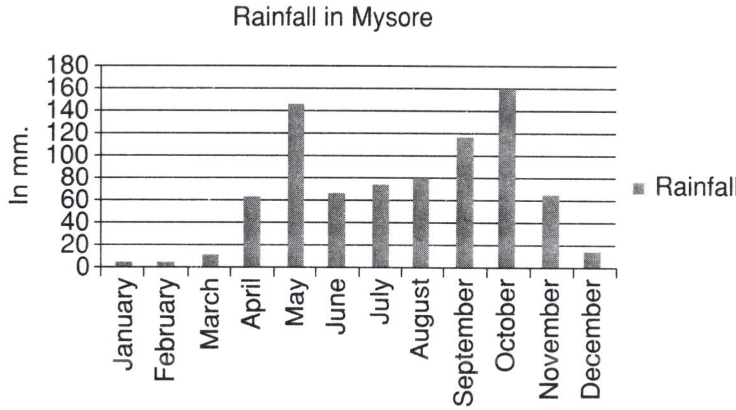

The quantities whose values are not fixed are known as **variables**. Variables can take different values. They are denoted by small letters like *l*, *m*, *o*, *x*, *y*, *p* and so on.

Some other examples of variables that we come across in our day-to-day life are population growth, cost of items, etc.

Observe the following statements. There are 7 days in a week; there are 12 months in a year; there are 24 hours a day. It is not possible to have any other numbers other than 7, 12 and 24 respectively.

The quantities whose values are fixed and do not vary are known as **constants**. Each constant stands for a fixed value.

Remember

All numbers are constants. as their values remain fixed.

A letter in an algebraic statement denotes a variable as its value may vary from one situation to another.

Power of a Variable

From the lower classes, you have been studying the multiplication tables. In each multiplication table, you can find one row where the number is multiplied by itself. For example, 1×1, 2×2, 3×3, ...

1×1 can be written as 1^2 and read as 'one-squared' or 'one raised to the power 2'; $2 \times 2 = 2^2$
and is read as 'two-squared' or 'two raised to the power of 2'; 3 $\times 3 = 3^2$ and is read as
'three-squared' or 'three raised to the power 2'; and so on.

In general, $a \times a$ is written as a^2. It is read as '*a* squared' or '*a* raised to the power 2', where *a* is any variable. Similarly, $a \times a \times a$ is written as a^3. It is read as 'a cubed' or 'a raised to the power 3'.

In general, $a \times a \times a \times a \times a \times a \times \ldots$ *n* times (multiplying the variable *a* by itself *n* times) is written as a^n in the exponential form and it is read as **'a raised to the power of *n*'**. In a^n, *a* is called the **base** and *n* is called the **exponent**.

Think and Discuss

Are your height and weight variables or constants?

Remember

a^1 is written as ***a*** as a convention. And the value of a^0 is **1**.

Operations with Variables and Numbers

Similar to numbers, different arithmetic operations can also be done with the combination of variables and numbers. The table below shows the four basic operations with numbers and the variable *p*.

Operation	Example	Algebraic Statement
Addition	25 is added to *p* to get 30.	$25 + p = 30$
Subtraction	10 is subtracted from *p* to get 3.	$p - 10 = 3$
Multiplication	15 is multiplied by *p* to get 60.	$15p = 60$
Division	*p* is divided by 2 to get 9.	$\frac{p}{2} = 9$

The variable *p* represents different values in each of these examples.

A variable combined with a number or another variable using the multiplication or division operator is a variable. For example, $8x$, xy, m^2n, $16pq$, $\frac{12}{x}$ and $\frac{-3}{pq}$ are all variables.

In $15p$, 15 is a constant and *p* is a variable. But the product $15p$ is a variable. Similarly, $\frac{p}{2}$ is also a variable.

Now, let us look at some properties that are true for operations with variables.

Let *a*, *b* and *c* be any three variables.

Properties of Addition

Commutative Property: $a + b = b + a$

Associative Property: $a + (b + c) = (a + b) + c$

Additive Identity: $a + 0 = 0 + a = a$

Properties of Multiplication

Commutative Property: $a \times b = b \times a$

Associative Property: $a \times (b \times c) = (a \times b) \times c$

Multiplicative Identity: $a \times 1 = 1 \times a = a$

Distributive Property of Multiplication over Addition: $a \times (b + c) = (a \times b) + (a \times c)$

Exercise 13.2

1. **Identify the variables and the constants in the following algebraic statements.**

   a. $5 - 6x$ b. $2 + m$ c. $3p + 10$ d. $56n$ e. 39

2. **Identify whether the following are variables (V) or constants (C).**

   a. Number of minutes in an hour
   b. Number of days in a month
   c. Number of colours in the rainbow
   d. Number of letters in the English alphabet

3. **a. Write the following powers in words.**

   i. y^6 ii. z^2 iii. p^4 iv. 6^9

   b. Express the following in powers.

   i. Seven raised-to the power of 2
   ii. Sixteen raised to the power of *p*
   iii. *m* raised to the power of 4
   iv. *x* raised to the power of *y*

4. Verify the commutative and the associative properties of addition and multiplication of variables by taking different values for the variables.

Algebraic Expressions

Consider the following situation.

You have to arrange a birthday party at your home. You have square tables that can accommodate one person on each side. You have to arrange the tables adjacent to each other in a row. If you are expecting 20 guests, how many tables need to be arranged?

From the above picture, we can see that in order to accommodate 20 guests, we require nine tables.

Can you say how many guests can be accommodated if 35, 50 or more tables are arranged? It is very difficult to draw the tables every time and count the number of guests that can be accommodated. Let us prepare a chart showing the number of tables and the number of guests that can be accommodated, and arrive at a general rule that gives us the number of guests that can be accommodated for a given number of tables.

Number of Tables	Number of Guests that can be Accommodated	Number of Guests Expressed in Terms of Number of Tables
1	4	$2 \times 1 + 2 = 4$
2	6	$2 \times 2 + 2 = 6$
3	8	$2 \times 3 + 2 = 8$
4	10	$2 \times 4 + 2 = 10$
5	12	$2 \times 5 + 2 = 12$

Rule: From the above table, we can say that ***n*** tables can accommodate $\mathbf{2n + 2}$ guests.

Now, we can easily find the number of guests for any given number of tables. For example, 20 tables can accommodate $(2 \times 20) + 2 = 42$ guests.

Observe the following T-patterns formed with matchsticks.

Rule: From the above table we can say that the number of matchsticks required is twice the number of shapes that are formed, that is, if ***n*** is the number of shapes formed, then the number of matchksticks required is $\mathbf{2 \times n}$.

Try these!

Using matchsticks, form more such patterns like C, E, F, triangle, square and so on and find the rule for each pattern.

Expressions like $2n$ and $2n + 2$ are algebraic expressions.

An **algebraic expression** is an expression that consists of variable(s) and constant(s) connected by arithmetic operators +, −, × and /. In the algebraic expression $2n + 2$, n is a variable and 2 is a constant and the arithmetic operation is addition.

Framing Algebraic Expressions

Till now, we have seen some examples of algebraic expressions. Now, let us understand how to frame an algebraic expression for a given situation.

Consider the algebraic expression $6x + 10$. It is formed by adding 10 to the product of 6 and x.

Consider the statement 'the sum of 4 and y is subtracted from the product of 2 and x.' The algebraic statement for this is $2x - (4 + y)$.

Try This!

Multiply a number n by 6 and then add 3 to the product. The sum is equal to 57. Write the algebraic expression representing this.

Algebraic Expressions in Real Life

Algebraic expressions are used widely in real life. Let us see an example

Example 2: A CD shop charges ₹20 for renting a video CD for the first day. It charges ₹2 extra for every additional day. What will be the algebraic expression for the amount that Akhila would pay if she rents a video cassette for p days?

Amount charged by the shop for the first day = ₹20

Extra amount charged per day = ₹2

Number of days Akhila rented the video cassette = p

∴ Total amount to be paid by Akhila is $20 + 2p$.

Exercise 13.3

1 Write the algebraic expressions for the following statements.

a. 7 added to the product of 5 and x

b. 13 added to the product of x and 4

c. 10 times a number taken away from 7

d. Half of the sum of $2x$ and $2y$

e. A number t decreased by 3

f. 4 divided by a

2 Write the statements for the following algebraic expressions.

a. $25p + 10 = 60$ b. $16m \div 2 = 24$ c. $10x + 7y - 15$ d. $100 - 15y$

3 Write the algebraic expressions representing the following situations.

a. Reshmi earns ₹500 a day working at a supermarket. How much money will she earn in p days?

b. A hotel manager has to distribute ₹10,000 equally among the workers of the hotel as bonus. How much money will each worker get if there are k workers?

c. The ages of two brothers can be represented as consecutive even integers. If the younger brother's age is $x + 3$, represent the age of the elder brother.

d. The ages of four sisters are in the ratio 3 : 5 : 7 : 10. The sum of their ages is 60 years.

Terms in an Algebraic Expression

Consider the algebraic expression $2a + 4b - 8$. This expression is made up of the terms $2a$, $4b$ and -8.

A **term** in an algebraic expression can be a number along with its sign, a variable or a constant multiplied by variable(s).

Each term is a product of its factors. For example, the term $2a$ is the product of the factors 2 and a.

When a term consists of a constant and a variable, the constant is called the **numerical coefficient** of the variable and the variable is called the **variable coefficient** or **the literal coefficient** of the constant. For example, in $4b$, 4 is the numerical coefficient of b and b is the variable coefficient or the literal coefficient of 4.

In the above algebraic expression, the power of the variables a and b is 1. In algebraic expressions, the power of the variable can be any number. For example, in $2x^2 + 3x^4 + 6$, the power of the variable x in the term $2x^2$ is 2 and in the term $3x^4$, it is 4. If the power of the variable is not written, it is considered to be 1.

Note

The value of any number or variable raised to the power 0 is always 1. For example, $2^0 = 1$, $y^0 = 1$, $x^0 y^0 = 1 \times 1 = 1$.

The term 6 can be written as $6 \times x^0$ since $x^0 = 1$.

Coefficient of any factor of a term is the product of the remaining factors eg.

Coefficient of 2 in $2xy$ is xy. Coefficient of x in $2xy$ is $2y$.

Look at the table below showing some algebraic expressions, the terms involved, the numerical coefficients of the variables and the powers of the variables.

Algebraic Expression	Term	Numerical Coefficient of the Variable	Power of the Variable
$15x + 27y + 10$	$15x$	15	1
	$27y$	27	1
	10	10	0
$4y^3 + 3y^2 + 2y + 1$	$4y^3$	4	3
	$3y^2$	3	2
	$2y$	2	1
	1	1	0
$7z^3 + 3z$	$7z^3$	7	3
	$3z$	3	1

Like and Unlike Terms

Terms in which same variables are used and each variable has the same exponent (that is, the variables are raised to the same power) are called **like terms**. The terms p, $4p$ and $-26p$ are like terms because they have the same variable (p) and the same exponent (1). Similarly, x^2, $-20x^2$ and $4x^2$ are like terms because they have the same variable (x) and the same exponent (2).

Remember

Like terms have the same variable with the same exponents. **Unlike terms** have different variables or the same variable with different exponents.

Terms in which the variables are different or the same variables have different exponents are called **unlike terms**. The terms $5x$, $6x^3$ and $-4x^2$ are unlike terms because even though all of them have the same variable (x), their exponents are different. Similarly, $46x^2$, $13y^2$ and $-20z^2$ are unlike terms because they have different variables even though their exponents are same.

Types of Algebraic Expressions

Consider the algebraic expressions $-6x$, $x + 2$ and $x + 7 + 4x^2$.

The first expression has one term, the second expression has two terms and the third expression has three terms. Based on the number of terms, algebraic expressions are classified as follows.

A **monomial** is a multinomial which has one term eg. $2x$, $2\frac{x}{y}$.

A **binomial** is a multinomial which has two terms $2x + 1$, $3x + \frac{y}{x}$.

A **trinomial** is a multinomial which has three terms $2x^2 + x + 1$, $2x^2 + \frac{x}{y} + 1$.

Polynomial is an algebraic expression with two or more terms. In a polynomial the power of the variable cannot be negative or fractional.

A monomial, binomial and a trinomial which are particular cases of a multinomial may or may not be polynomials. In general, monomials, binomials, trinomials etc fall under the category of polynomials.

Degree: Degree of a polynomial refers to the highest power of the variable in any of the terms of a polynomial.

Degree of $5x$ is 1. Degree of $5x + 4$ is 1. Degree of $5xy + x$ is 2.

A polynomial of degree 0 is called a constant. Example -5, $\frac{1}{2}$.

Exercise 13.4

1 **Identify the different terms (variable terms and constant terms) in the following algebraic expressions. Also identify the numerical coefficient and the power of the variable (exponent) in each term.**

a. $-25x^3 + 2x^2 + x$
b. $4a^3b^2 - 2b^2 + 3a - 4$
c. $52z^2 + 19zx$
d. $6x^4 + 4x^5 + 20x^3 - 6x^2 + 2$
e. $2l^3 + 24$
f. $(a + 4b + 5) \div 2$

2 **Identify the like terms in the following algebraic expressions.**

a. $10p^2q - 4pq^2 + 12q^2p - 6qp^2$
b. $5a - 8a + 12a^2 + 9a - 10a^2$
c. $2x^2y^3 + 5x^3y^2 - 10x^3y^2 + 11x^3y^3 - 3x^2y^3$
d. $24y^{10} + y^6 - 4y^{10} + 4y^2 + 7y^2 - 26y^6$

3 **Give reasons why the following groups of terms are unlike.**

a. $-5x^3, 5x^2, 2x$ b. $2a, 2b, 2c$ c. $14m^3, 5m^2n, 10$ d. $12p^2q, 11pq^2$

4. **Classify the following algebraic expressions based on the number of terms.**

a. $42b$ b. $0.5x^2$ c. $2p^2 + 2q^2$ d. $a^2 + 2ab + b^2$

e. $4y^{10} + 6y^3x + 72y^3 + 20$ f. $12abc$ g. $24x^2 + 12y^2$

5. **State the degree of the following polynomials:**

a. $2x + 1$ b. 5 c. 2 d. $24x^2 + 12y^2$ e. $2xy + 5x + 1$

Substitution

Monika wants to book a cab for sightseeing in Jaipur. She got the following information about the tariff.

Minimum Distance to be Travelled (km)	Minimum Charge (₹)	Charges per Additional km (₹)	Driver Charges (₹)
10	100	15	75

Let us write an expression to calculate the cab bill based on the number of kilometres travelled. Let the total distance travelled by Monika be x km. Then, the amount to be paid is given by

$100 + (x - 10)15 + 75 = 25 + 15x$

If she travels 15 km, then the bill would be $25 + 15(15) =$ ₹250.

If she travels 20 km, then the bill would be $25 + 15(20) =$ ₹325.

Here, we are substituting or replacing a particular value for a variable to find the value of the expression. Once the value of the variable is substituted in the expression, the algebraic expression changes into a simple arithmetic expression. Hence, its value can be calculated using arithmetic operations. This process of replacing variables with particular values to find the value of an algebraic expression is known as **substitution**.

Example 3: Find the values of the following algebraic expressions for the given values of the variables.

a. $25x + 15y$ when $x = 2$ and $y = 3$

Substituting the values of x and y in the algebraic expression $25x + 15y$, we get

$25(2) + 15(3) = 50 + 45 = 95$

b. $a^2 + 4ab$ when $a = 2$ and $b = 1$

Substituting the values of a and b in the algebraic expression $a^2 + 4ab$, we get

$2^2 + 4(2)(1) = 4 + 8 = 12$

c. $(2m^2n) \div 4mn$ when $m = 4$ and $n = 2$

Substituting the values of m and n in the algebraic expression $(2m^2n + n) \div 4mn$, we get

$[2 \times (4)^2 \times 2] \div [4 \times (4) \times (2)] = 64 \div 32 = 2$

Exercise 13.5

1 **Find the values of the following algebraic expressions for the given values of the variables.**

a. $2 + 3a + 6 - 7b$ when $a = -1$ and $b = 6$

b. $3(2x + 9)$ when $x = 10$

c. $2xy + 6x - 9y$ when $x = -1$ and $y = 2$

d. $\frac{1}{x^2} \times 125 \times \frac{y}{125} \times 0$ when $x = 5$ and $y = -4$

2 **Evaluate each of the following expressions using the given values of the variables.**

a. $-5p^3 + 2p^2 + p$ when $p = 6$

b. $52z^2 + 19zq$ when $z = 3$ and $q = 2$

c. $4a^3b^2 - 2b^2 + 3a - 4$ when $a = 4$ and $b = 3$

d. $\frac{25 + x^2 + 5x}{5}$ when $x = 5$

3 What is the value of the algebraic expression $10 + \frac{64}{x^2} + 6x$ when $x = 2, 4, 8$ and 10?

Summary

1. A numerical statement is a mathematical statement involving only numbers and one or more mathematical operators (+, −, ×, ÷).
2. An algebraic statement is a mathematical statement involving letters, numbers and one or more mathematical operators (+, −, ×, ÷).
3. The quantities whose values are not fixed are known as variables.
4. The quantities whose values are fixed and do not vary are known as constants.
5. An algebraic expression is an expression that consists of variable(s) and constant(s) connected by arithmetic operators.
6. Terms in which the same variables are used and each variable has the same exponent are called like terms.
7. Terms in which variables are different or the same variables have different exponents are called unlike terms.
8. A monomial is an algebraic expression that has only one term. Binomials have two terms and trinomials have three terms. Polynomials have more than three terms.
9. The process of substituting variables by particular values to find the value of an algebraic expression is known as substitution.
10. $x \times x$ can be written in exponential as x^2. Here, x called the base and 2 is called the exponent of x.

Revision Exercise

1 **Classify the following statements as numerical or algebraic statement.**

a. $5x + 10$ b. $12 + 10 \div 2$ c. $15 - 7 + 16y + z$ d. $26 - 10 + 16$

2 Write the differences between a variable and a constant.

3 **Classify the following as variables and constants.**

a. Planets in our solar system b. Number of states in a country

c. Number of oceans in the world d. Number of students in a class

4 **Write the following in words.**

a. x^{10} b. z^3 c. p^6

5 **Write the algebraic expressions for the following.**

a. The sum of three consecutive whole numbers

b. Four divided by a number reduced by 2

c. The difference between d and 3

d. Divide the product of 3 and x by 2

6 **Identify the various terms in the following algebraic expressions.**

a. $15x + 6y + z$ b. $16 + 6a$ c. $4x^2 + 16x - 16$ d. $a^3 + 4b - 3c$ e. $\frac{6+12x}{2}$

7 **Group the like terms together.**

$14x^3, -26y^2, 100x^2y, 36a^3, 42x^2, 49y^2, -19a^2b^2, 23a^3, -11x^3, -35a^2b, -12x^2, 30x^2y, 13a^2b^2$

8 **Find the value of $4a^3b^2c + 3a^2b - 12a$ when**

a. $a = b = 1$ and $c = 2$ b. $a = 1, b = 2$ and $c = 3$ c. $a = -1, b = 1$ and $c = 2$

9 The number of rose flowers is 8 more than the number of dahlias in the garden. Write an expression for this situation.

10 Hansita is x years old. Lisbeth is three times Hansita's age increased by 4 years. What is Lisbeth's age?

For the Curious Mind

A beautiful pearl necklace of a young lady was torn and the pearls were all scattered on the floor. One-third of the number of pearls was on the ground, one-fifth was on the bed, one-sixth was found by the lady herself, one-tenth was collected by her friend and six were seen hanging in the thread. Write an expression to find the total number of pearls.

UNIT 3

Operations on Algebraic Expressions

14

What I shall learn

- To be able to add, subtract, multiply or divide algebraic expressions

Let's Get Started

Let us learn now how to perform the four basic operations—addition, subtraction, multiplication and division—on algebraic expressions.

Addition of Algebraic Expressions

Look at the following example.

Sunil and Sudhir went to a bookshop. Sunil bought 8 books and Sudhir bought 5 books. If the cost of each book is ₹x, what is the amount spent by both of them?

Amount spent by Sunil = ₹$8x$ (Since the cost of each book is ₹x and Sunil bought 8 books)

Amount spent by Sudhir = ₹$5x$ (Since the cost of each book is ₹x and Sudhir bought 5 books)

$\therefore$ The total amount spent by them is ₹$8x + 5x$.

In order to solve the question, we need to know how to add algebraic expressions. Let us first understand some basic facts.

If there are 3 balloons in one bunch and 5 balloons in another bunch, then the total number of balloons is 3 balloons + 5 balloons = 8 balloons.

We can **add only like terms in algebraic expressions**. The like terms can be added by adding their numerical coefficients.

So, the total amount spent by Sunil and Sudhir = $8x + 5x = (8 + 5)x = 13x$

Example 1:

a. $9a + 15a = 24a$

b. $30xy + (-12xy) = 30xy - 12xy = 18xy$

Addition of Polynomials

Here are the two groups of ice creams and cupcakes.

What is the total number of eatables in both the groups?

Let us represent the ice creams by x and the cupcakes by y. Then the total number of eatables in A and B would be $(5x + 3y) + (4x + 6y)$

Now, let us see how to add these two algebraic expressions. It can be done in the following two ways.

Row Method or Horizontal Method

Example 2: Add $5x + 3y$ and $4x + 6y$ using the row or horizontal method.

Step 1	Write all the expressions to be added in a row with a '+' symbol in between them.	$(5x + 3y) + (4x + 6y)$
Step 2	Identify the like terms and rearrange them. Take the terms along with their signs while rearranging.	$= (5x + 4x) + (6y + 3y)$
Step 3	Add the coefficients of the like terms and write the resultant expression.	$= (5 + 4)x + (6 + 3)y$ $= 9x + 9y$

Try This!

Add $24x^2 + 16xy + 6$ and $-12xy + 22x^2 - 19$ using the row method.

Column Method or Vertical Method

Example 3: Add $5x^2 - 4y^2 + 2xy$ and $-3xy + 9x^2 - 7y^2$ using the column method.

Step 1	Write the expressions one below the other such that the like terms come in the same column.
Step 2	Add the coefficients of the like terms.
Step 3	Write the results in the respective columns.

$$\begin{array}{rcrcr} 5x^2 & - & 4y^2 & + & 2xy \\ 9x^2 & - & 7y^2 & - & 3xy \\ \hline 14x^2 & - & 11y^2 & - & 1xy \\ \hline \end{array}$$

Try This!

Add $24x^2 + 16xy + 6$ and $-12xy + 22x^2 - 19$ using the column method.

Subtraction of Algebraic Expressions

In the subtraction of algebraic expressions we use the concept of additive inverse. In Chapter 2, we have learned that to subtract x from y:

1. we first write y 2. Put '–' sign 3. write x 4. calculate

Subtraction of Monomials

Example 4: Subtract the following.

a. $32x$ from $75x$

$75x - 32x = (75 - 32)x = 43x$

b. $46y$ from $-12y$

$-12y - 46y = (-12 - 46)y = -58y$

c. $-15z$ from $25z$

$25z - (-15z) = 25z + 15z = (25 + 15)z$
$= 40z$

d. $-53p$ from $-23p$

$-23p - (-53p) = -23p + 53p = (-23 + 53)p$
$= 30p$

Subtraction of Polynomials

Let us understand the subtraction of polynomials in both horizontal and vertical methods using an example.

Example 5: Subtract $-3xy + 9x^2 - 7y^2$ from $5x^2 - 4y^2 + 2xy$ using the horizontal and vertical methods.

Horizontal Method

Step 1	Write the expressions in a row by writing a minus symbol in between them.	$(5x^2 - 4y^2 + 2xy) - (-3xy + 9x^2 - 7y^2)$
Step 2	Find the additive inverse of the expression to be subtracted and add it to the other expression.	$= 5x^2 - 4y^2 + 2xy + 3xy - 9x^2 + 7y^2$
Step 3	Identify and group the like terms.	$= (5x^2 - 9x^2) + (-4y^2 + 7y^2) + (2xy + 3xy)$
Step 4	Add/subtract the numerical coefficeints of the like terms and write the result.	$= -4x^2 + 3y^2 + 5xy$

Vertical Method

Step 1	Write the expressions one below the other such that the expression to be subtracted comes in the second row and the like terms come one below the other.
Step 2	Change the sign of every term in the second expression. Write the changed sign below the old sign of each term in the second line.
Step 3	Add the coefficients of the like terms and write the result in the respective columns.

$$\begin{array}{l} 5x^2 - 4y^2 + 2xy \\ 9x^2 - 7y^2 - 3xy \\ (+)\ (-)\ (-) \\ \hline 4x^2 + 3y^2 + 5xy \\ \hline \end{array}$$

Simplification of Algebraic Expressions

Example 6: Simplify the following algebraic expressions by performing the necessary addition and subtraction operations.

a. $-33t^2 + 30 - (25t - 45) - (11t^2 - 6 + 16t) = -33t^2 + 30 - 25t + 45 - 11t^2 + 6 - 16t$

$= -33t^2 - 11t^2 + - 25t - 16t + 30 + 45 + 6 = - 44t^2 - 41t + 81$

b. $-14p^3 - 15q^2 - (10p + 40p^3) + 20p + 50q^2 = -14p^3 - 15q^2 - 10p - 40p^3 + 20p + 50q^2$

$= -14p^3 - 40p^3 + - 15q^2 + 50q^2 + - 10p + 20p = -54p^3 + 35q^2 + 10p$

Exercise 14.1

1 **Add the following algebraic expressions.**

a. $-14ab^2$ and $3ab^2$

b. $10xyz$ and $100xyz$

c. $-3y^2$ and $26y^2$

d. $2x + y$ and $-16x + 3y$

e. $3x^2 - 4x + 10$ and $2x^2 + 6x - 12$

f. $4p^2 + 6p - 5$ and $3p^2 + 2p - 1$

2 **Subtract the second expression from the first expression in each of the following.**

a. $4b^3, 42b^3$

b. $-3abc, 16abc$

c. $19l^6, 27l^6$

d. $5p^2 - 6q + 3pq, 3p^2 - 5pq - 10p$

e. $2x^3 - 9y^3, 15y^3 - 4x^3$

f. $2ab + 7bc - 5ca, 15ab - 17bc + 20ca$

3 **Let X = $5x^2 - 4y^2 + 2xy$, Y = $-3xy + 9x^2 - 7y^2$ and Z = $16x^2 + 2y^2 - 15xy$. Find the following**

a. X + Y + Z

b. X + Y − Z

c. X − Y + Z

d. X − Y − Z

4 Add $17p^4 + 20p^3 - 15p + 6$ and $-45p^4 + 60p^3 - 12p^2 - 52$. Subtract the answer from the sum of $14p^3 + 32p^2 - 23$ and $48p^4 - 6p^2 + 12p$.

5 Find the algebraic expression to be added to $12x^5 + 10x^4 + 2x^2 - 5x + 6$ to get $45x^5 + 10x^3 - 20x^2 + 3x - 3$.

6 Simplify the following algebraic expressions.

a. $19ab + 15a + 16a^2b - (26b + 7a - 12a^2b + 7)$

b. $3x^2yz + 3xy^2z - xz^2 - 200 - (26 - 14xz^2 + 2x^2yz)$

c. $4pq^2 + 12p^2q^2 - 15pq - (26p^2q + p^2q^2 - (15pq^2 + 9p - 10))$

Multiplication of Algebraic Expressions

Samrud and Suhail have a rectangular field each. The dimensions of the fields are given below. Can you help them to find out the areas of the fields?

Samrud's Field

40 ft

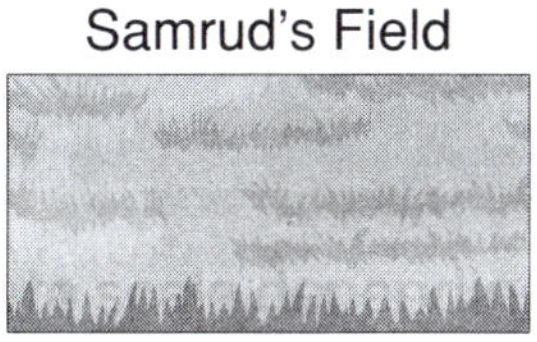

20 ft

Area = $40 \times 20 = 800$ sq. ft

Suhail's Field

(2x − 3) ft

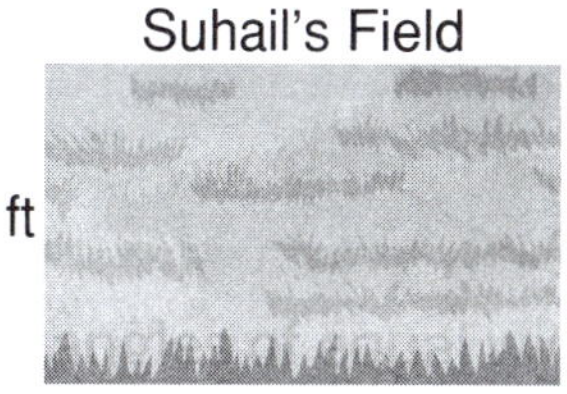

(5x + 5) ft

Area = $(2x - 3)(5x + 5)$ sq. ft

The dimensions of Suhail's field are in the form of algebraic expressions. In order to find the area of his field, we need to know how to multiply algebraic expressions.

Before learning the multiplication of algebraic expressions, let us recall some basic concepts that are essential here.

Remember

Product of signs

$(+) \times (+) = (+)$

$(+) \times (-) = (-)$

$(-) \times (+) = (-)$

$(-) \times (-) = (+)$

Law of Exponents (powers)

When two quantities with the same base are multiplied, their exponents are added.

That is, $\mathbf{a^m \times a^n = a^{m+n}}$

Multiplying a Monomial by a Monomial

Consider the expression $3m \times 9n$.

This can be written as

$(3 \times m) \times (9 \times n) = (3 \times 9) \times (m \times n) = 27mn$

Similarly, consider $4p^2q^3 \times 6pq^2$.

It can be written as

$4 \times p \times p \times q \times q \times q \times 6 \times p \times q \times q$

$= 4 \times 6 \times p \times p \times p \times q \times q \times q \times q \times q$

$= 24p^3q^5$

Which property of numbers has been used here?

Note

$4p^2q^3 \times 6pq^2$ can also be simplified using the law of exponent.

$\mathbf{a^m \times a^n = a^{m+n}}$

$4p^2q^3 \times 6pq^2$

$= 4 \times 6 \times p^2 \times p \times q^2 \times q^3$

$= 24p^{2+1}q^{2+3} = 24p^3q^5$

Example 7: Multiply the following.

a. $15a^3$ and $3a^5$

$15a^3 \times 3a^5$

$= 15 \times 3 \times a^3 \times a^5$

$= 45 \times a^{3+5}$

$= 45a^8$

b. $8a^6b^{10}$ and $-5a^9b^8$

$8a^6b^{10} \times -5a^9b^8$

$= 8 \times -5 \times a^6 \times a^9 \times b^{10} \times b^8$

$= -40a^{6+9}b^{10+8}$

$= -40a^{15}b^{18}$

Note

While multiplying algebraic terms, first multiply the numerical coefficients. Then, add the powers of the same variables separately.

Multiplying a Polynomial by a Constant

Consider the following product of a constant and a polynomial.

$5 \times (4x^3 + 3x^2 - 6x + 10)$

Using the distributive property of multiplication over addition, we can rewrite the product as

$5 \times 4x^3 + 5 \times 3x^2 - 5 \times 6x + 5 \times 10$

$= 20x^3 + 15x^2 - 30x + 50$

Note

Distributive Property

$a(b + c) = ab + ac$

Example 8: Multiply the following.

a. $4p^3 + 6p^2 + 3p - 5$ and -2

$-2 \times (4p^3 + 6p^2 + 3p - 5)$

$= -2 \times 4p^3 + -2 \times 6p^2 + -2 \times 3p - -2 \times 5$

$= -8p^3 - 12p^2 - 6p + 10$

b. $2a^5 + 6a^3 - 4a^2 + 5$ and 15

$15 \times (2a^5 + 6a^3 - 4a^2 + 5)$

$= 15 \times 2a^5 + 15 \times 6a^3 - 15 \times 4a^2 + 15 \times 5$

$= 30a^5 + 90a^3 - 60a^2 + 75$

Note

To multiply a polynomial by a constant, multiply each term in the polynomial by that constant.

$5 \times (4x^3 + 3x^2 - 6x + 10)$

Multiplying a Polynomial by a Monomial

Consider the expression $5p \times (8p^2 - 2p^2q + 16p + 5)$.

We have learned how to multiply a polynomial by a constant using distributive property. In the similar manner, we can multiply a polynomial by a monomial using the distributive property as shown below.

$= 5p \times 8p^2 - 5p \times 2p^2q + 5p \times 16p + 5p \times 5$

$= 5 \times 8 \times p \times p^2 - 5 \times 2 \times p \times p^2q + 5 \times 16 \times p \times p + 5 \times 5 \times p$

$= 40p^{2+1} - 10\, p^{2+1}q + 90\, p^{1+1} + 25p = 40p^3 - 10p^3q + 90p^2 + 25p$

Example 9: Find the product of $4a^3$ and $(2a^2 + 7a - 6)$.

$4a^3 \times (2a^2 + 7a - 6) = 4a^3 \times 2a^2 + 4a^3 \times 7a + 4a^3 \times -6 = 8a^5 + 28a^4 - 24a^3$

Multiplying Two Binomials

We can use the distributive property of multiplication over addition to multiply two binomials by applying it twice. Consider two binomials, $(a + b)$ and $(p + q)$. Using distributive property of multiplication over addition, we have

$(a + b) \times (p + q) = a \times (p + q) + b \times (p + q)$

$= [(a \times p) + (a \times q)] + [(b \times p) + (b \times q)]$

$= [ap + aq] + [bp + bq] = ap + aq + bp + bq$

$(a + b) \times (p + q)$

Let us solve some examples of multiplying a binomial by another binomial.

Example 10: Multiply $(4p^2 + 2q^2)$ and $(2p^2 - 5q^2)$.

$(4p^2 + 2q^2) \times (2p^2 - 5q^2) = 4p^2\,(2p^2 - 5q^2) + 2q^2(2p^2 - 5q^2)$

$= 4p^2 \times 2p^2 - 4p^2 \times 5q^2 + 2q^2 \times 2p^2 - 2q^2 \times 5q^2$

$= 8p^4 - 20p^2q^2 + 4q^2p^2 - 10q^4 = 8p^4 - 16p^2q^2 - 10q^4$

Now we know how to multiply two binomials. Let us find the area of Suhail's field in the example given above. It is given by,

$(2x - 3)(5x + 5) = 2x \times (5x + 5) - 3 \times (5x + 5)$

$= 2x \times 5x + 2x \times 5 - 3 \times 5 + 3 \times 5$

$= 10x^2 + 10x - 15x - 15 = 10x^2 - 5x - 15$

Exercise 14.2

1 Multiply the following monomials.

a. $6ap$ and $2p$ b. $5d^5$ and $3d^{10}$ c. $4y^4$ and $3y^6$

d. $9a^2b^8$ and $7ab^4$ e. $-5x^3y$ and $3y^4$ f. $-9ab$ and $-7b^2$

2 Multiply the following.

a. 15 and $2e^7 - 6e^5 + 4e^2 + 3e + 1$ b. -7 and $2k^9 - 5k^5 + 9$

c. $x^{10} + 4x^4 - 25x + 6$ and $-10x$ d. $15b^4 - 4b^{15} + 12b^8 + 7b^2$ and $7b$

e. $-3d$ and $4d^7 - 14d^5 + 4d^3 + 7d + 8$ f. $-9x + 5$ and $3x + 1$

g. $6m + 5n$ and $2m - 4n$ h. $a^3 + 5b^5$ and $3a^3 - 6b^2$

i. $5k^2 - 8k$ and $3k^2 + k$ j. $\left(\frac{3}{2}x - \frac{1}{2}y\right)$ and $\left(\frac{2}{3}x - 4y\right)$

Division of Algebraic Expressions

We have learned how to multiply different algebraic expressions. Let us now learn how to divide algebraic expressions. While multiplying algebraic expressions, we have used the addition law of exponents. While dividing algebraic expressions, we use the subtraction law of exponents.

For any non-zero integer a, $\boldsymbol{a^m \div a^n = \frac{a^m}{a^n} = a^{m-n}}$, where m and n are integers and $m > n$.

Dividing a Monomial by another Monomial

To divide a monomial by another monomial, divide the coefficient of the numerator by the coefficient of the denominator and then divide the variable part of the numerator by the variable part of the denominator. Let us understand it in detail using the following examples.

Example 11: Solve the following.

a. $12k^{10} \div 2k^7$

$$12k^{10} \div 2k^7 = \frac{\cancel{12}^{6}k^{10}}{\cancel{2}k^7} = 6k^{10-7} = 6k^3$$

b. $25p^2q^5 \div 5pq^2$

$$25p^2q^5 \div 5pq^2 = \frac{^{5}\cancel{25}p^2q^5}{\cancel{5}pq^2} = \left(\frac{25}{5}\right)\times\left(\frac{p^2}{p}\right)\times\left(\frac{q^5}{q^2}\right) = 5p^{2-1}q^{5-2} = 5pq^3$$

c. $343a^9k^7x^{21} \div 49a^{-5}k^3x^2$

$$343a^9k^7x^{21} \div 49a^{-5}k^3x^2 = \frac{^{7}\cancel{343}a^9k^7x^{21}}{\cancel{49}a^{-5}k^3x^2} = \left(\frac{343}{49}\right)\times\left(\frac{a^9}{a^{-5}}\right)\times\left(\frac{k^7}{k^3}\right)\times\left(\frac{x^{21}}{x^2}\right) = 7a^{9-(-5)}k^{7-3}x^{21-2}$$

$$= 7a^{14}k^4x^{19}$$

Dividing a Polynomial by a Monomial

To divide a polynomial by a monomial, we divide each term of the polynomial by the monomial. Let us solve a few examples.

Example 12: Solve the following.

a. $2k^7 - 4k^4 + 28k^2 \div 4k^3$

$$2k^7 - 4k^4 + 28k^2 \div 4k^3 = \frac{2k^7 - 4k^4 + 28k^2}{4k^3} = \left(\frac{\cancel{2}k^7}{\underset{2}{\cancel{4}}k^3}\right) - \left(\frac{\cancel{4}k^4}{\cancel{4}k^3}\right) + \left(\frac{\overset{7}{\cancel{28}}k^2}{\cancel{4}k^3}\right) = \frac{1}{2}k^4 - k + 7k^{-1}$$

b. $15p^5 + 125p^3 + 5p^2 - 10p \div 5p^2$

$$15p^5 + 125p^3 + 5p^2 - 10p \div 5p^2 = \frac{15p^5 + 125p^3 + 5p^2 - 10p}{5p^2}$$

$$= \left(\frac{\overset{3}{\cancel{15}}p^5}{\cancel{5}p^2}\right) + \left(\frac{\overset{25}{\cancel{125}}p^3}{\cancel{5}p^2}\right) + \left(\frac{\cancel{5}p^2}{\cancel{5}p^2}\right) - \left(\frac{\overset{2}{\cancel{10}}p}{\cancel{5}p^2}\right) = 3p^3 + 25p + 1 - 2p^{-1}$$

Exercise 14.3

1 Solve the following.

a. $51m^3 \div 17m$

b. $72p^8 \div 9p^2$

c. $1296a^7b^5c^2 \div 36a^2b^2c^2$

d. $1024x^9y^4z^3 \div 16x^3y^4z^5$

2 Divide the following polynomials by the given monomials.

a. $16b^5 + 8b^7 + 32b^3 \div 4b^2$

b. $12z^6 - 18z^4 + 27z^2 \div 3z^3$

c. $63t^{10} - 42t^8 + 84t^5 \div 21t^2$

d. $-256j^{16} + 60j^{12} - 36j^9 \div 6j^3$

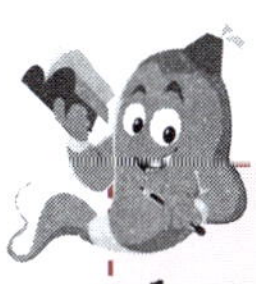

Summary

1. Addition and subtraction of algebraic expressions are done by combining the like terms and adding or subtracting their numerical coefficients.
2. While multiplying algebraic terms, first multiply the numerical coefficients and then add the powers of the same variables separately.
3. To multiply a polynomial by a constant, multiply each term in the polynomial by that constant.
4. We use the distributive property of multiplication over addition twice to multiply two binomials.
5. To divide a monomial by another monomial, divide the coefficient of the numerator by the coefficient of the denominator and then divide the variable part of the numerator by the variable part of the denominator.
6. To divide a polynomial by a monomial, divide each term of the polynomial by the monomial.
7. $a^m \times a^n = a^{m+n}$
8. $a^m \div a^n = \frac{a^m}{a^n} = a^{m-n}$

Revision Exercise

1 Add the given algebraic expressions.

a. $2x^2 - 5x - 6$ and $x^2 + 8x - 3$
b. $5x^3 + 2x^2 - 6x + 10$ and $-4x^3 + 6x^2 + 1$
c. $2y^2 + 2y - 7$ and $-6y^2 - 4y + 6$
d. $6a^5 + 10a^3 - 7a^2 + 6$ and $2a^5 + 4a^2 + 7a - 21$
e. $6p^2 - 15p + 10$ and $-14p^2 + 8p - 12$
f. $4m^7 + 5m^4 + 3m$ and $-7m^4$

2 Subtract the following algebraic expressions.

a. $-15ab$ from $21ab$
b. $12m^2n$ from $-25m^2n$
c. $2p^3 + 6p^2 - 15p$ from $-5p^3 + 9p^2 + 2p$
d. $12xz + z^2$ from $25xz + x - 5z^2$
e. $-7l^2 - 4x^2 + 2lx$ from $-5lx + 6x^2 - 25l^2$
f. $8m^4 + 5m^2 + 2m$ from $-9m^4 - 5m + 9$

3 Multiply the following monomials.

a. $9d^2$ and $4d^4$
b. $44p^3q^2r^5$ and $2p^2qr^2$
c. $7k^2 l^3m^5$ and $9k^3m$
d. $-2ab^2$ and $-4a^2b$

4 Multiply the following polynomials by the given monomials.

a. $-5k$ and $k^2 - 3k + 20$
b. $6r^3$ and $r^2 + 2rv - 6r^2$
c. $-4q^2$ and $8q^2 + 2q - 15$
d. $5s$ and $s^{15} - 3s^{12} + 4s^5$

5 Multiply the following binomials.

a. $4z + 10$ and $3z - 2$
b. $2p - 3q$ and $5p - 10q$
c. $4k^2 + 2l^2$ and $2k^2 - 9l^2$
d. $4m^2 + 3m$ and $-7m + 8$

6 Solve the following.

a. $12g^4 \div 2g^2$
b. $15i^8 \div -3i^2$
c. $-8u^2v^3w^4 \div 2uv^4w^2$
d. $45c^3d^2 \div -5c$

7 Divide the following polynomials by the given monomials.

a. $14s^5t^3 - 35st^3v$ by $7st^2v^3$
b. $18p^2q^3 + 21p^5q^3$ by $-3p^2q$
c. $64f^{12} - 72f^9 + 80f^5 + 8f^2$ by $8f^2$
d. $22m^7 + 11m^4$ by $-11m^4$

For the Curious Mind

A factory has 55 skilled employees, 42 employees with mediocre skills and 15 trainees. It pays ₹x to a skilled employee, ₹y to an employee having mediocre skills and ₹z to a trainee. If the number of holidays in a month is a, then write a simplified algebraic expression for the money spent on paying wages for the month. Assume that all the employees were present during the month and the number of days in that month was 30.

UNIT 3

Formulae

15

What I shall learn

- To be able to formulate relationship between the known and the unknown elements

Note

The plural of 'formula' is 'formulae'.

Let's Get Started

From the lower classes, we have been using various formulae to calculate and show the relationship between different quantities. A **formula** is an algebraic expression used to solve various problems of mathematics. We use alphabets to represent quantities in formulae. We refer to them as variables. In this chapter, let us discuss about the formulae.

Formulae in Geometry

In the previous classes, we have used formulae to find the perimeter and area of squares and rectangles. Let us recall them.

Perimeter and Area

Rectangle

Let the length of a rectangle be l and its breadth be b. Let its perimeter be P and its area be A.

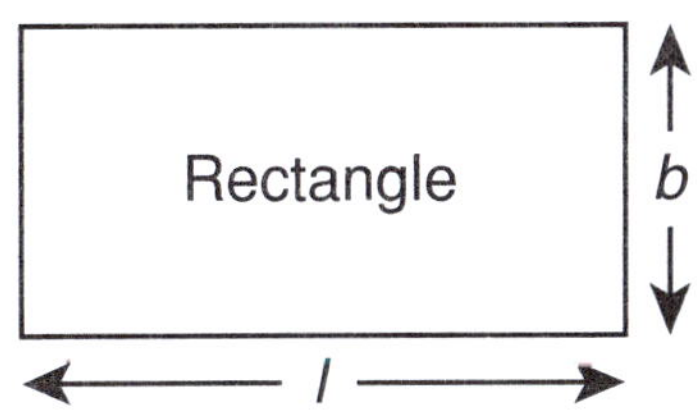

We know that the perimeter of a rectangle is given by two times the sum of its length and breadth.

Therefore, the perimeter of a rectangle is given by the formula $\mathbf{P = 2(l + b)}$.

Similarly, we know that the area of a rectangle is given by the product of its length and breadth.

Therefore, the area of a rectangle is given by the formula $\mathbf{A = l \times b}$.

Square

Let the side length of a square be a. Let its perimeter be P and its area be A.

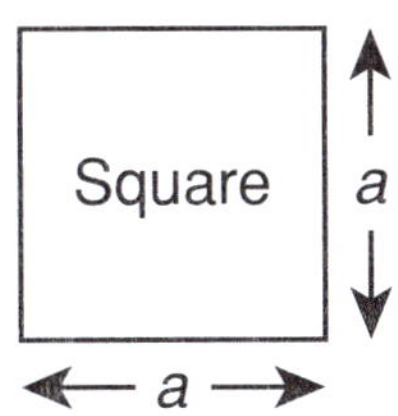

We know that the perimeter of a square is equal to four times the length of its side.

Therefore, the perimeter of a square is given by the formula $\mathbf{P = 4a}$.

Similarly, we know that the area of a square is given by the product of its length and breadth.

Therefore, the area of a square is given by the formula $\mathbf{A = a \times a = a^2}$.

Formulae in Patterns

	1st	2nd	3rd	4th	

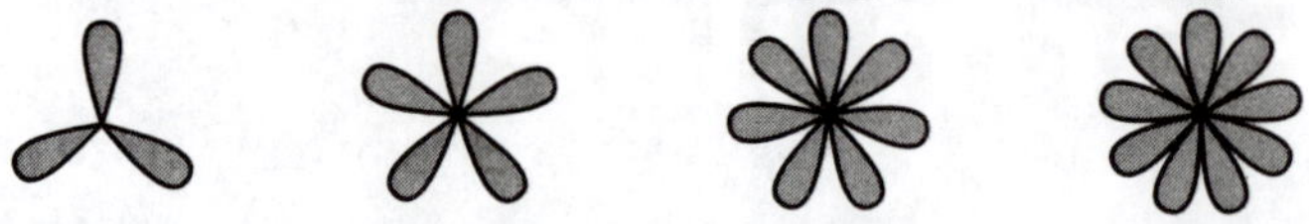

Number of Petals	3	5	7	9	. . .

The number of petals in the *n*th pattern is given by the formula **2*n* + 1**.

Even number pattern: 2, 4, 6, 8 ... *n*

The *n*th term of an even number pattern is given by the formula **2*n***.

Odd number pattern: 1, 3, 5, 7 ... *n*

The *n*th term of an odd number pattern is given by the formula **2*n* – 1**.

Formulae in Commercial Mathematics

Profit and Loss

Profit and Loss Let CP be *y*, SP be *x*, Profit be *P* and loss be *L*		Simple and Compound Interest Let sum be *P*, time period be *T* and rate of interest per annum be *R*%	
Profit	**Loss**	**Simple Interest (*I*)**	**Compound Interest (*CI*)**
$P = x - y$ Profit per cent = $\frac{p}{y} \times 100$	$L = y - x$ Loss per cent = $\frac{L}{y} \times 100$	$I = \frac{PTR}{100}$	$CI = P\left(1 + \frac{R}{100}\right)^T - P$

So far we have seen formulae that are formulated using the relationship between variables and constants. Let us now see some examples on how to frame a formula for a given situation.

Example 1: Five divided by a number reduced by 3 gives 10. Write the formula to find the number.

Let the number be *x*. Then, the number reduced by 3 is $x - 3$.

Thus, the formula to find the number is given by $\frac{5}{x-3} = 10$.

Example 2: Rahul's age is 5 years less than twice the age of Gokul. Write the formula to find Gokul's age if Rahul's age is 25.

Let Gokul's age be *x*. Then, Rahul's age is given by $2x - 5$.

Thus, Gokul's age can be found by using the formula $2x - 5 = 25$.

Example 3: Temperature is measured in two different units, Fahrenheit and Celsius. Fahrenheit temperature is 32 more than $\frac{9}{5}$ times that of Celsius. Write the formula for the conversion of temperature between these units.

Let Fahrenheit temperature be denoted by F and Celsius temperature be denoted by C.

Then, the conversion formula is given by $F = \frac{9}{5}C + 32$.

Revision Exercise

1. **Write the formulae for each of the following situations.**

   a. If 12 is subtracted from three times a number, then the result is 3.

   b. Three times a number divided by 2 gives 18.

   c. The square of a number added to five times the sum of the number and 6 gives 24.

2. The cost of one ball is ₹50. If Raghu spends ₹2500 to buy some balls, write the formulae to find the number of balls he buys.

3. The age of Ramesh is 20 years less than that of his mother. Write the formula to find his mother's age if Ramesh's age is 26?

4. The length of a rectangle is twice its breadth. If the perimeter of a rectangle is 192 m, then findind its length and breadth.

5. Students are standing in rows to attend the morning assembly. There are 8 students in a row. If there are 120 students in the assembly, write the formula to find the number of rows.

6. The circumference of a circle is given by twice the constant (π) times radius. Write the formula to find the circumference of a circle with radius k.

7. If 20% of a number is 450, then write the formula to find the number.

8. Write the formula to find the cost price of an article sold at 5% profit.

9. The volume of a sphere is given by $\frac{4}{3}$ of constant (π) times the cube of its radius. Write the formula to find the volume of a globe of radius y cm.

10. Write the values of B for the last column. Also choose the correct rule for the relationship between A and B.

A	0	1	2	3	4	5	n
B	−4	−3	−2	−1	0	1	?

$n - 2$ $5 - n$ $n - 4$ $2n - 5$

For the Curious Mind

Write the formula to find the area of the shaded region in the given figure.

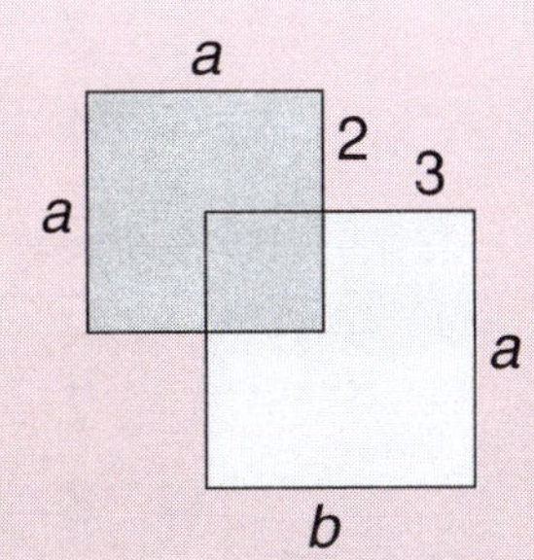

UNIT 3

Simple Equations 16

What I shall learn

- To find the solution of the given equation by different methods

Let's Get Started

In the previous chapters, we have learned that quantities whose values are not fixed are known as **variables** and quantities whose values are fixed and do not vary are known as **constants**. We have also learned how to write an algebraic expression for a given statement. Let us learn more about them in this chapter.

Algebraic Equations

Observe the following groups.

In Group A, the expressions do not have the equality sign, whereas each of the expressions in Group B, has been equated to another expression. Algebraic expressions that are equated to another expression are known as **algebraic equations**. Algebraic equations with only one variable (with power one) are known as **simple equations**.

Group A	Group B
$4g + 5$	$9t + 6 = 24$
$\frac{5r}{2} + 7$	$n + 5 = 92$
$2(k + 3) - 5$	$10s + 5 = 105$
$3y + 9$	$u - 2 = 5$
$15d - 2$	$7z - 3 = 18$
$5x + 6$	$\frac{5h}{2} = 7$

Consider an algebraic equation $u - 2 = 5$.

Does any value for the variable u satisfy this equation? Let us see by substituting certain values for u.

Value for the variable u	Value of the expression $u - 2$	Is it equal to 5? (Yes/No)
1	$1 - 2 = -1$	No
2	$2 - 2 = 0$	No
3	$3 - 2 = 1$	No
4	$4 - 2 = 2$	No
5	$5 - 2 = 3$	No
6	$6 - 2 = 4$	No
7	$\mathbf{7 - 2 = 5}$	**Yes**
8	$8 - 2 = 6$	No
9	$9 - 2 = 7$	No

The equation $u - 2 = 5$ is satisfied only for a particular value of u, that is, 7. No other value for u satisfies the equation. Hence, **an equation is a condition on a variable**. It is satisfied only for a definite value of the variable.

Observe that an equation has an equal sign (=) between its two sides.

The expression before the equal sign is called the left-hand side (LHS) of the equation.

The expression after the equal sign is called the right-hand side (RHS) of the equation.

RHS

↑

$$\underbrace{u - 2}_{\text{LHS}} = 5$$

Example 1: Write the equations for the following statements.

a. 7 less than a number is 40.

Let the number be x. Then, $x - 7 = 40$.

b. 3 more than 9 times a number is 21.

Let the number be y. Then, $9y + 3 = 21$.

c. The length of a rectangle is thrice its breadth and its perimeter is 96 metres.

Let the breadth be b.

Then its length would be $3b$ since it is given that the length of the rectangle is thrice its breadth.

Perimeter of the rectangle is given by

2(Length + Breadth) = 96

$\Rightarrow 2(3b + b) = 96$

$\rightarrow 2(4b) = 96$

$\Rightarrow 8b = 96$

Exercise 16.1

1. **Classify the following as algebraic expressions and algebraic equations.**

   a. $5k - 4$ b. $6p = 18$ c. $5m - 4 = 16$ d. $13g + 10$

2. **Find the LHS and RHS in the following algebraic equations.**

   a. $x - 8 = 11$ b. $10z + 2 = 18$ c. $5p - 7 = 23$ d. $\frac{5}{4}(m - 7) = 34$

3. **Write the equations for the following statements.**

   a. Three multiplied by a number gives 36.

   b. Five times a number subtracted from 9 gives –11.

4. There are 50 students in a class, out of which 22 are girls. Write the equation to calculate the number of boys.

5. Sukanya bought pencils worth ₹15. She spent ₹5 less than what Sudeshna spent. Write the equation to calculate the money spent by Sukanya.

Solution of an Equation

Earlier, we have seen that the equation $u - 2 = 5$ is satisfied only for a particular value of u, that is, 7. No other value for u satisfies this equation. Thus, the number 7 is the solution of the equation $u - 2 = 5$. The value of the variable that satisfies an equation is called the **solution of the equation** or the **root** of the equation.

Note

Satisfying an equation means LHS = RHS.

Solution of an equation can be found by the different methods which are discussed below.

Trial and Error Method

In this method, the solution of an equation is found by substituting different values for the variable randomly and picking up the value that satisfies the equation. Hence, this method is called trial and error method.

Example 2: Find the solution of the equation $2k + 6 = 16$ by trial and error method.

Value for k	Value of LHS ($2k + 6$)	Is LHS = RHS (16)?
1	$2(1) + 6 = 8$	No
2	$2(2) + 6 = 10$	No
3	$2(3) + 6 = 12$	No
4	$2(4) + 6 = 14$	No
5	$\mathbf{2(5) + 6 = 16}$	**Yes**
6	$2(6) + 6 = 18$	No

Since $k = 5$ satisfies the equation, $k = 5$ is the solution of the equation $2k + 6 = 16$.

Method of Balancing

Have you ever been to a market with your parents to buy vegetables? Have you observed the weighing balance used by the vegetable sellers? A weighing balance has pans on both sides. It is balanced only when both pans have the same weight; otherwise, the balance is disturbed.

An equation can be compared to a weighing balance. The LHS and the RHS of an equation should be equal just like the two pans of the balance. This balance should never be disturbed.

When the same quantity is added to or subtracted from both the sides of a balanced equation, the balance remains undisturbed. Similarly, when both the sides of the balanced equation are multiplied or divided by the same quantity, the balance stays undisturbed. Let us understand this using an example.

Consider the equation $x + 3 = 5$, where x represents the weight of a papaya. By trial and error method, we can find that the weight of the papaya is 2 kg (since $2 + 3 = 5$, $x = 2$ satisfies the given equation).

- Let us add 2 papayas of weight x kg to both the pans of the balance, that is, $(x + 3 + 2x = 5 + 2x)$, and check the weights of the pans.

  Weight on the left pan $= x + 3 + 2x = 3x + 3 = 3(2) + 3 = 6 + 3 = 9$ kg

  Weight on the right pan $= 5 + 2x = 5 + 2(2) = 5 + 4 = 9$ kg

Therefore, upon adding the same quantity to both the sides, the balance remains undisturbed.

- Let us remove 2 kg from each of the pans, that is, $(x + 3 - 2 = 5 - 2)$, and check the weights on both the sides.

  Weight on the left pan $= x + 3 - 2 = x + 1 = 2 + 1 = 3$ kg

  Weight on the right pan $= 5 - 2 = 3$ kg

Therefore, upon subtracting the same quantity from both the sides, the balance remains undisturbed.

- Let us double the weights on both the pans, that is, $[2(x + 3) = 2(5)]$, and check the weights.

  Weight on the left pan $= 2(x + 3) = 2(2 + 3) = 2(5) = 10$ kg

  Weight on the right pan $= 2(5) = 10$ kg

Therefore, upon multiplying both the sides by the same quantity, the balance remains undisturbed.

- Let us halve the weights on both the pans, that is, $\left(\frac{x+3}{2} = \frac{5}{2}\right)$, and check the weights.

  Weight on the left pan $= \frac{x+3}{2} = \frac{2+3}{2} = \frac{5}{2} = 2.5$ kg

  Weight on the right pan $= \frac{5}{2} = 2.5$ kg

Therefore, upon dividing both the sides by the same quantity, the balance remains undisturbed.

We can use this idea of balancing to solve equations. Let us see some examples.

Example 3: Solve $2k + 7 = 21$ by the method of balancing.

Given equation: $2k + 7 = 21$

Subtracting 7 from both sides of the equation, we get

$2k + 7 - 7 = 21 - 7 \Rightarrow 2k = 14$

Dividing both sides of the equation by 2, we get

$\frac{\cancel{2}k}{\cancel{2}} = \frac{\cancel{14}^{7}}{\cancel{2}} \Rightarrow k = 7$

Hence, the solution of the equation $2k + 7 = 21$ is 7.

Remember

Always verify the solution obtained by substituting it in the equation and checking whether it satisfies the equation.

Example 4: Solve $\frac{x}{2}+\frac{5}{2}=5$ by the method of balancing.

Given equation: $\frac{x}{2}+\frac{5}{2}=5$

Subtracting $\frac{5}{2}$ from both sides of the equation, we get

$\frac{x}{2}+\frac{5}{2}-\frac{5}{2}=5-\frac{5}{2} \Rightarrow \frac{x}{2}=\frac{10-5}{2} \Rightarrow \frac{x}{2}=\frac{5}{2}$

Multiplying both sides of the equation by 2, we get

$\frac{x}{\cancel{2}}\times\cancel{2}=\frac{5}{\cancel{2}}\times\cancel{2} \Rightarrow x=5$

Hence, the solution of the equation $\frac{x}{2}+\frac{5}{2}=5$ is 5.

Exercise 16.2

1 Solve the following equations by trial and error method.

a. $4r+7=3$ b. $5b-6=14$ c. $2p+7=19$ d. $7k=56$

e. $y+19=25$ f. $x-9=1$ g. $6m=30$ h. $\frac{2x}{3}=4$

2 Solve the following equations by the method of balancing.

a. $x+7=22$ b. $j+6=-4$ c. $5-t=20$ d. $x-8=10$

e. $g+7=49$ f. $r-10=2$ g. $5+3p=125$ h. $2y-10=8$

i. $k+30=94$ j. $8u-4=68$ k. $\frac{2e}{3}+6=2$ l. $\frac{a}{3}+\frac{1}{2}=1$

Method of Transposition

The word 'transpose' means to change the position. In context of algebra, 'transpose' means moving the terms (variables, constants or coefficients) from one side of an equation to the other. However, when we transpose the terms, they do not remain the same. Let us see what happens to the terms when we transpose them from one side to the other.

Consider the following equations that have been solved by the method of balancing.

Try These!

Write a few sentences using the word 'transpose' in general context.

Equation: $x-3=2$

$x-3+3=2+3$

$\Rightarrow x=2+3$

$\Rightarrow x=5$

When transposed from LHS to RHS, −3 becomes +3.

Equation: $y+6=9$

$y+6-6=9-6$

$\Rightarrow y=9-6$

$\Rightarrow y=3$

When transposed from LHS to RHS, +6 becomes −6.

Remember

Rule while transposing: Change side ↔ Change sign

From these examples, we can conclude that when we transpose terms from one side of an equation to the other, positive becomes negative and negative becomes positive.

Let us solve some equations by the method of transposing.

Example 5: Find the solution of the equation $k + 6 = 12$ by the method of transposing.

Given equation: $k + 6 = 12$

Transposing +6 to RHS, we get

$k = 12 - 6 \Rightarrow k = 6$

Therefore, the solution of the equation $k + 6 = 12$ is 6.

Example 6: Solve the equation $p - 8 = 20$ by the method of transposing.

Given equation: $p - 8 = 20$

Transposing −8 to RHS, we get

$p = 20 + 8 \Rightarrow p = 28$

Therefore, the solution of the equation $p - 8 = 20$ is 28.

Example 7: Solve the equation $3x - 5 = 22$ by the method of transposing.

Given equation: $3x - 5 = 22$

Transposing −5 to RHS, we get

$3x = 22 + 5 \Rightarrow 3x = 27$

Dividing both sides by 3, we get

$\frac{3x}{3} = \frac{27}{3} \Rightarrow x = 9$

Example 8: Solve the equation $\frac{x}{5} + 6 = 21$ by the method of transposing.

Given equation: $\frac{x}{5} + 6 = 21$

Transposing +6 to RHS, we get

$\frac{x}{5} = 21 - 6 \Rightarrow \frac{x}{5} = 15$

Multiplying both sides by 5, we get

$\frac{x}{5} \times 5 = 15 \times 5 \Rightarrow x = 75$

Exercise 16.3

Solve the following equations by the method of transposing.

1. $x + 5 = 9$
2. $t - 14 = 6$
3. $2y + 3 = 11$
4. $3k - 6 = 21$
5. $7r - 15 = 34$
6. $2p + 20 = 40$
7. $5d + 18 = 48$
8. $15 + 2r = 37$
9. $8l - 13 = 51$
10. $5g + 9 = 51$
11. $2(x - 5) = 8$
12. $\frac{3x}{5} = 9$
13. $\frac{6z}{5} = \frac{36}{15}$
14. $\frac{p}{2} + 4 = 17$
15. $\frac{w}{3} - 16 = 52$

Applications of Simple Equations

So far we have learned how to solve simple equations by various methods. Let us use them to solve some day-to-day problems.

Example 9: Amir is 5 years older than his sister Rizwana. If the sum of their ages is 31, find their ages.

Let Rizwana's age be x years.

Then Amir's age will be $(x + 5)$ years.

Sum of their ages $= x + x + 5 = 31 \Rightarrow 2x + 5 = 31$

$$\Rightarrow 2x = 31 - 5 \text{ [Transposing +5 to RHS]}$$

$$\Rightarrow 2x = 26 \Rightarrow x = \frac{26}{2} = 13$$

Therefore, Rizwana's age is 13 years and Amir's age is 13 + 5 = 18 years.

Verification: The sum of the ages of Amir and Rizwana is given as 31.

Let us add the ages we have calculated for Amir and Rizwana. We get 13 + 18 = 31.

Hence, the ages we calculated for Amir and Rizwana are correct.

Example 10: The length of a rectangle is three times more than twice its breadth. If the perimeter of the rectangle is 60 cm, find its length and breadth.

Let the breadth of the rectangle be x cm.

Then its length will be $(2x + 3)$ cm.

Perimeter of the rectangle = 2(length + breadth) $= 2(2x + 3 + x) = 60$ [Given]

$$\Rightarrow 2(3x + 3) = 60 \Rightarrow 3x + 3 = 30 \text{ [Dividing both sides by 2]}$$

$$\Rightarrow 3x = 30 - 3 \text{ [Transposing +3 to RHS]}$$

$$\Rightarrow 3x = 27 \Rightarrow x = \frac{27}{3} = 9$$

Therefore, the breadth of the rectangle is 9 cm and its length is $2x + 3 = 2(9) + 3 = 18 + 3 = 21$ cm.

Example 11: Sandhya has saved some money in her piggy bank. It contains two-rupee coins and five-rupee coins. The number of two-rupee coins is three more than half of five-rupee coins. Find the number of coins of each denomination if there are 60 coins in the piggy bank? Also find the amount in Sandhya's piggy bank.

Let the number of five-rupee coins be x.

Then, the number of two rupee coins will be $\frac{x}{2} + 3$.

Now, $\frac{x}{2} + 3 + x = 60$ [Given]

$$\Rightarrow \frac{3x}{2} + 3 = 60 \Rightarrow \frac{3x}{2} = 57$$

$$\Rightarrow 3x = 114 \Rightarrow x = \frac{114}{3} = 38$$

Mental Maths

1. If you multiply a number by 3 and subtract 5 from it, you will get 10. Find the number.
2. If you multiply a number by 6 and add 13 to it, you will get 85. Find the number.

Therefore, the number of five-rupee coins is 38 and the number of two-rupee coins is $\frac{38}{2} + 3 = 19 + 3 = 22$.

The amount in Sandhya's piggy bank = 22(2) + 38(5) = 44 + 190 = ₹234.

(Verify the solutions in all the above problems as done for Example 10).

Exercise 16.4

1. If 15 is subtracted from five times a number, the result is 30. Find the number.
2. Four subtracted from four times a number gives 40. Find the number.
3. If twice a number is six more than 12, then find the number.
4. If one-sixth of a number is added to twice the sum of the number and 5, the result is 62. Find the number.
5. The sum of three consecutive odd numbers is 106. Find the numbers.
6. The length of a rectangle is twice its breadth. The perimeter of the rectangle is 192 metres. Find its length and breadth.
7. Rakesh's age is 12 years less than his father's age. If the present age of Rakesh is 25 years, then what is his father's age?
8. There are 50 students in a class. The ratio of boys to girls is 3 : 2. Find the number of boys and girls in the class.
9. The number of elephants in a zoo is 20 less than thrice the number of giraffes. If their total number is 300, find the number of elephants and giraffes in the zoo.
10. Arya earns ₹250 per day working in a construction site. If he earns ₹3,750, find the number of days he works?

Summary

1. Expressions that have an equality sign are known as equations. An equation is a condition on a variable. It is satisfied only for a definite value of the variable.
2. The expression before the equal sign in an equation is called the left-hand side (LHS) of the equation. The expression after the equal sign is called the right-hand side (RHS) of the equation.
3. The value of the variable that satisfies an equation is called the solution of the equation.
4. Upon adding/subtracting/multiplying/dividing the same quantity on both sides of the equation, the balance remains undisturbed.
5. While transposing the terms from one side to the other, the sign changes.

Revision Exercise

1 **Solve the following equations.**

a. $y - 3 = 9$ b. $5t + 6 = 21$ c. $\frac{6r}{5} = 6$ d. $12x - 9 = -33$

2 **Solve the following equations.**

a. $3k - 10 = 2$ b. $7n - 2 = 19$ c. $8 + 15p = 113$ d. $28x = 112$

e. $2f + 4 = 16$ f. $4d - 6 = 26$ g. $15j = 165$ h. $\frac{t}{4} + 2t = 81$

i. $\frac{10x}{4} + 2 = 6$ j. $\frac{1}{2} + 3h = 5$ k. $\frac{8}{7}m + \frac{2}{7} = \frac{4}{7}$ l. $56n - \frac{3}{13} = \frac{10}{13}$

3 Twice a number added to 50 gives 72. Find the number.

4 Five times a number taken away from 12 gives −22. Find the number.

5 The quotient obtained when a number is divided by 8 is 40. Find the number.

6 Shashank's age is 4 times the age of his youngest brother. If they differ by 12 years, find their ages.

7 Dheeraj has a bag of chocolates. After he distributes 65 chocolates among his friends, 35 chocolates were left in the bag. How many chocolates were there in the bag initially?

For the Curious Mind

In the magic square, the magic sum is 34. Use the given clues to complete the magic square.

Note: Magic sum is the sum of the numbers along a row/column/diagonal.

A	B	C	13
E	11	G	H
I	7	J	K
D	M	L	1

Clues:

- A is 8 times B and C is 10 less than 13.
- A is 4 times D and E is 1 more than D.
- G is 2 times E and H is 2 times D.
- I is 3 more than J and J is half of K.
- L is 1 more than M.

Unit Worksheet 3

Find the value of the following expressions if $x = 1$, $y = -2$ and $z = 3$. Write them on the right side of the balances.

1. $x + y + z$

2. xyz

3. $3x - 2y + z$

4. $20xyz$

5. $5xyz - 2xyz$

Mental Maths

Find the value of the variables in the following.

1. $x + 5 = 15$ ________
2. $7x + 14 = 28$ ________
3. $-5x - 15 = 20$ ________
4. $\frac{2x}{3} = 2$ ________
5. $\frac{x}{4} + 8 = 13$ ________

UNIT 4

Fundamental Concepts of Geometry

17

Let's Get Started

Geometry is derived from an ancient Greek word where 'geo' means 'earth' and 'metron' means 'measurement'.

In ancient times, geometry was used to construct the pyramids in Egypt, the canals in Rome and *homa kundas* in India and to measure the distance of ships from the shore.

What I shall learn

- **To define point, line, line segment, ray, angle and collinear points**
- **To understand plane and classify a given surface as plane or curved surface**
- **To illustrate the concepts of parallel, perpendicular and concurrent lines through examples**

Pyramids of Egypt

Ship navigation

Point

Examples:

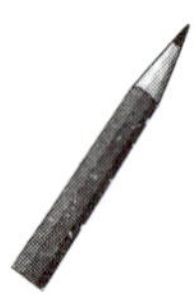

Tip of a pencil

A small dot drawn using the tip of a pencil on a plane paper illustrates a point. It has only position but no length, breadth and thickness (that is, it has no dimensions).

Points A, B and C are shown in the adjacent figure.

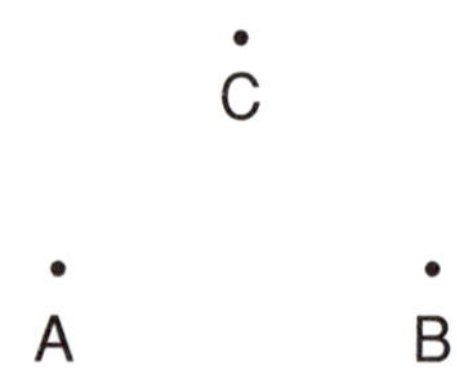

Line

A line is a straight path that has no breadth and no thickness; it only has length. Look at the image of a line given below, the arrows on both sides of the line signifies that it can be extended indefinitely from both the sides.

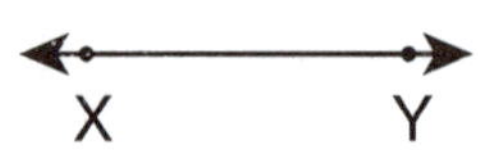

Line $\overleftrightarrow{XY}$

Line *m*

There are infinite number of points on a line and infinite number of lines can be drawn through a single point on a line.

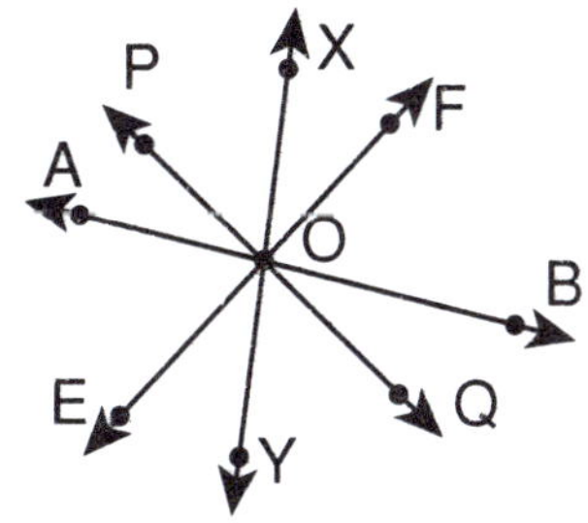

Examples:

Railway lines

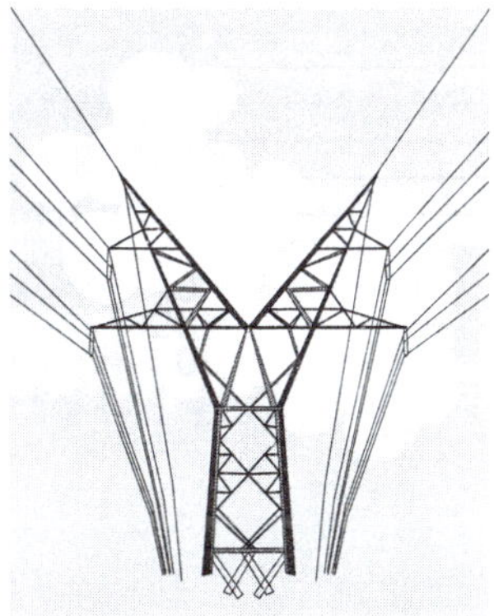

Electric wires

Remember

A line is a straight path that has no end points, no width and no breadth.

Line Segment

If we take two points on a line, then the two points and the part of the line between them is called a **line segment**. Any two points can be joined by only one line segment. A line segment has two end points. It has length but no width and thickness. There are infinite number of points on a line segment.

KL is a line segment which has K and L as its end points. The line segment KL is written as $\overline{KL}$. $\overline{KL}$ and $\overline{LK}$ denote the same line segment.

Examples:

Edges of a book

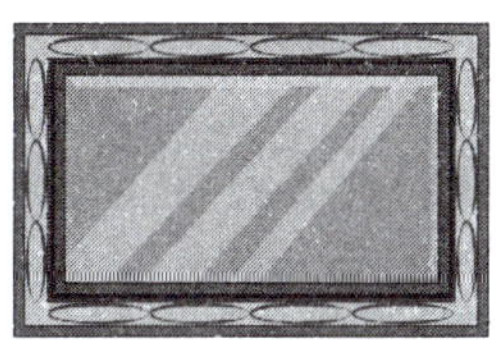

Edges of a photo frame

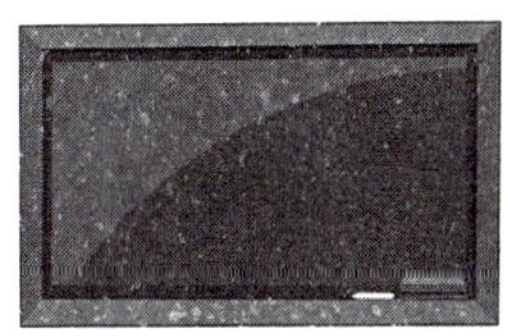

Edges of a board

Ray

Have you ever played with a laser beam light that forms an image at a distance? The images are formed due to the **rays** emerging out of the light.

Consider the line segment LK. If we extend the line indefinitely in one direction from point K, then we get the ray LK. Ray LK is written as $\overrightarrow{LK}$. L is called the **initial/end point** of the ray. Ray $\overrightarrow{LK}$ passes from point K, that is, point K provides the direction to the ray.

There are infinite number of points on a ray. And infinite number of rays can be drawn from a single point.

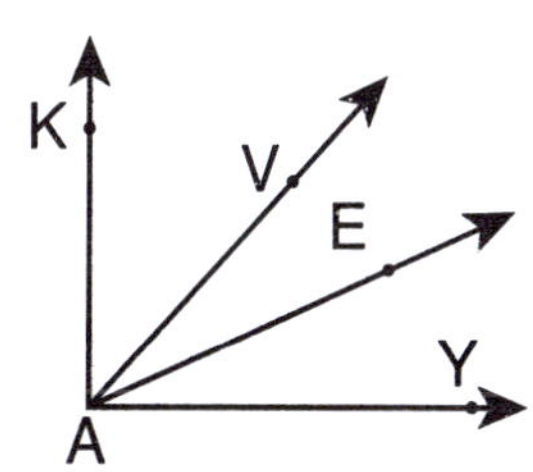

Examples:

Focus lights

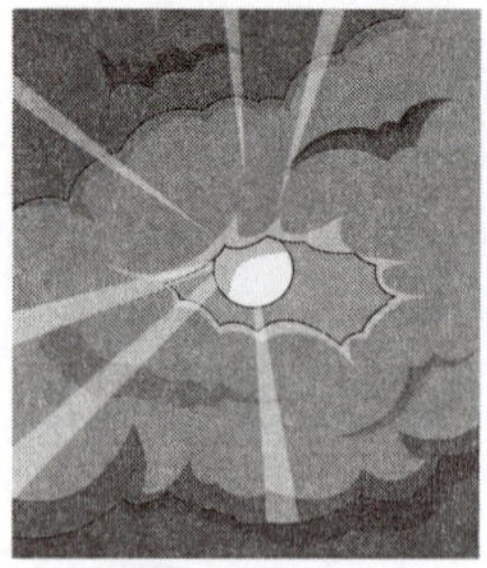

Sun rays

> **Note**
>
> $\overrightarrow{KL}$ is not same as $\overrightarrow{LK}$. Both the rays are different.

Parallel Lines

Have you ever noticed the railings of a bridge? Even if they are extended infinitely on both sides, they will never meet and the distance between them remains constant. Such lines are called parallel lines. Parallel lines are represented by the symbol II.

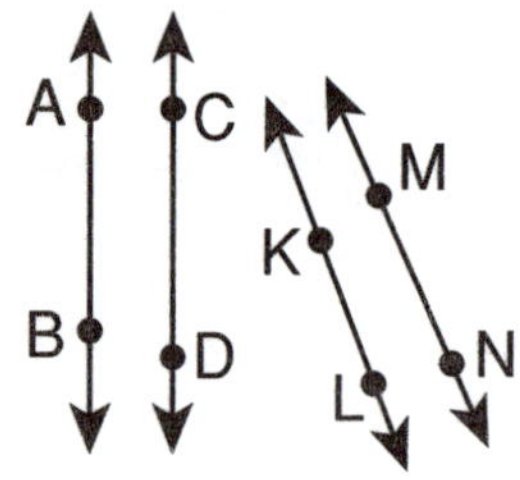

In the given figure, $\overleftrightarrow{AB}$ II $\overleftrightarrow{CD}$ and $\overleftrightarrow{KL}$ II $\overleftrightarrow{MN}$.

Examples:

Railings of a bridge

Wickets of a cricket game

Intersecting Lines

Two lines that are not parallel will meet each other at a particular point. Such lines are called **intersecting lines** and the point where they meet is called the **point of intersection**.

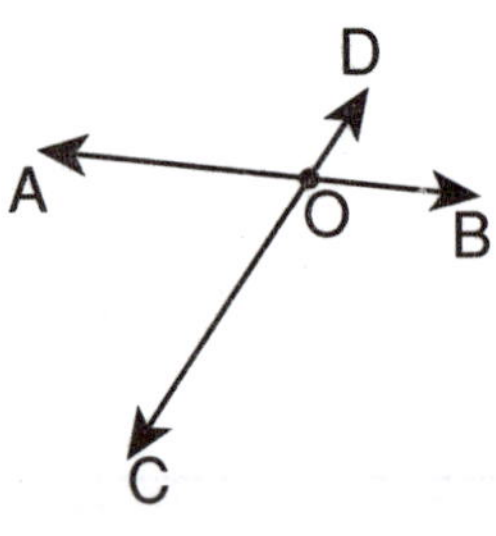

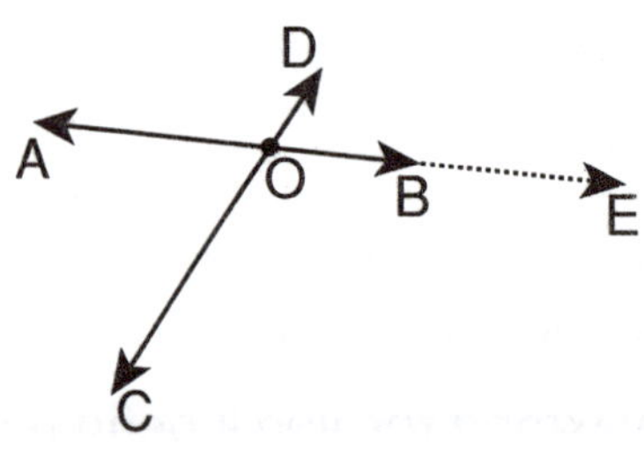

> **Remember**
>
> Lines that are not parallel are intersecting lines.

Perpendicular Lines

If two straight lines meet at a point to form a 90° angle, then the two lines are perpendicular to each other and are called **perpendicular lines**. Perpendicular lines are denoted by the symbol ⊥.

In the figure, AB ⊥ CP

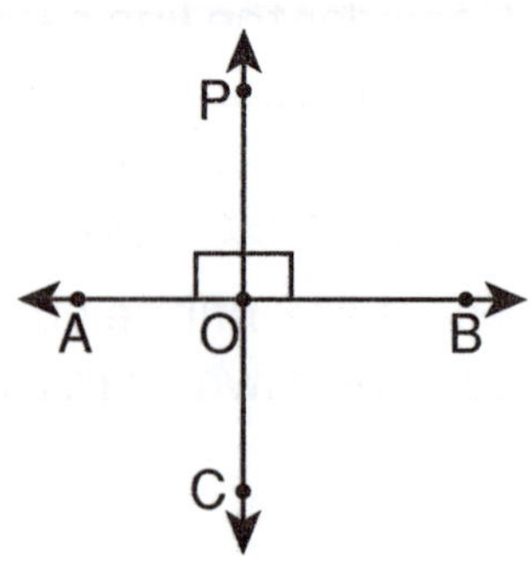

Examples:

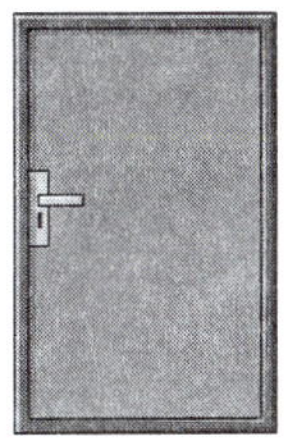

The height of the door is perpendicular to the floor.

One edge of the building is perpendicular to the other edge.

Concurrent Lines

If three or more lines intersect each other at a common point, they are said to be **concurrent lines**.

In the figure, point O is the point of concurrency.

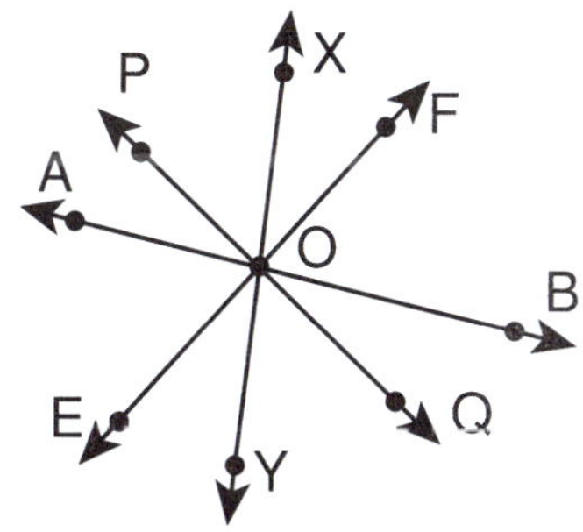

Collinear Points

The points which lie on the same straight line are called **collinear points**.

Collinear points always lie on the same plane.

In the figure, points E, G, B and A are collinear points as they lie on the same line *q*.

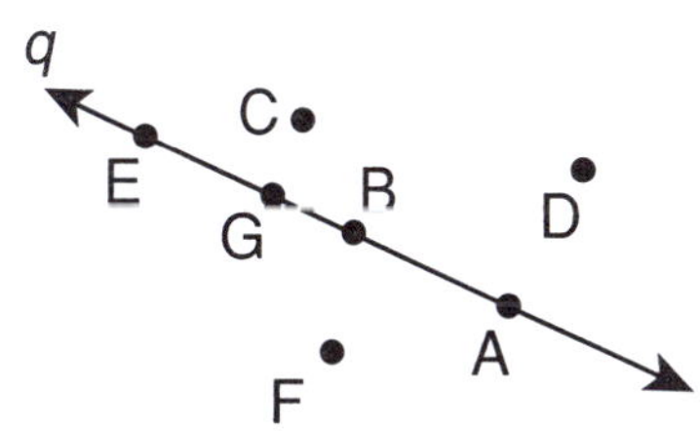

Angle

Draw a ray OA from a point O and then draw another ray OB from the same initial point. This forms an angle. An **angle** is the shape formed when two rays start from a common point. The two rays are known as the **arms** of the angle and the common point is known as the **vertex**.

Angle AOB is written as ∠AOB.

In ∠AOB, OA and OB are the arms of the angle and O is the vertex.

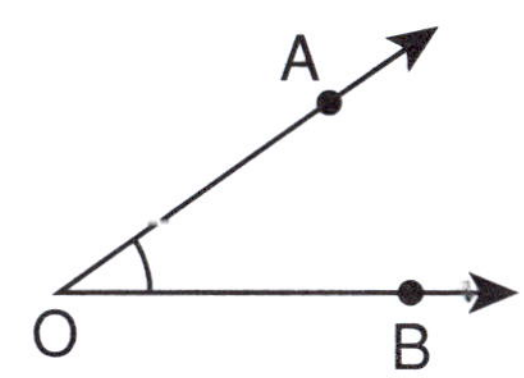

Examples:

The edges of this show piece form angles.

Plane

A plane is an infinite set of points that forms a flat surface extending infinitely in all directions.

A plane has

- infinite length,
- infinite width, and
- no thickness.

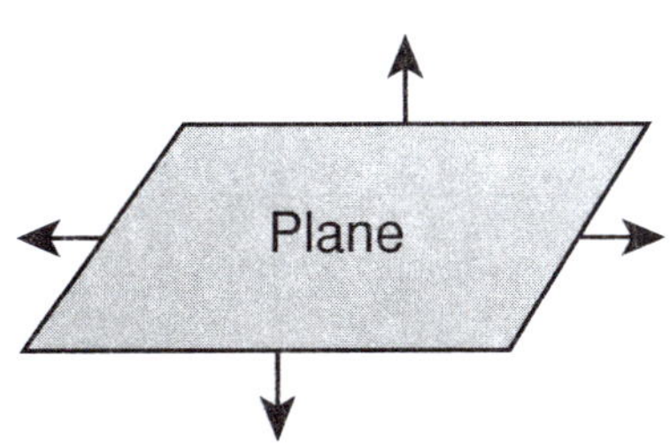

Plane and Curved Surfaces

Plane Surfaces

Observe the surface of a book. It has two dimensions, width and length, and perfectly flat surface that extends infinitely in all directions. It is an example of a plane surface.

More examples:

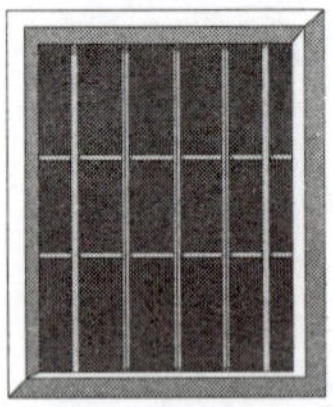

Window pane

Surface of a floor

Try these!

Consider the desk in your classroom and write the number of line segments, angles, parallel lines, perpendicular lines and plane surfaces present on it.

Curved Surfaces

Observe the following figures. They do not have flat surfaces. These objects have curved surfaces.

Cone

Globe

Cylinder

Ball

Apple

Constructing Perpendicular Lines

Tools Used for Construction

Ruler	Compass	Set Squares
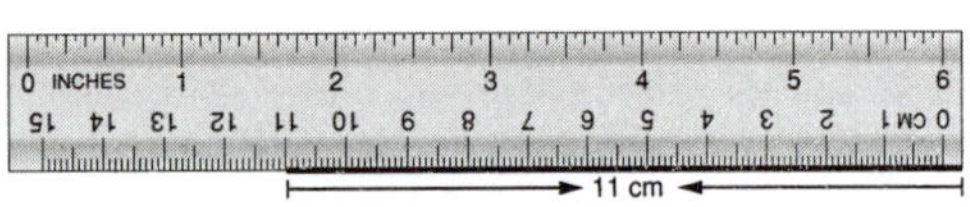		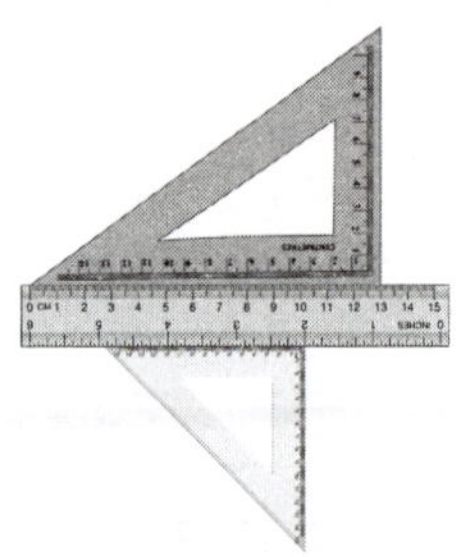
To draw and measure line segments	To draw arcs and circles	To draw lines and measure angles

Constructing Perpendicular Lines Using Set Squares

Example 1: Draw the perpendicular OC at a point O to a given line AB using the right-angled set square.

Step 1: Place the right angle of the set square such that the tip where the reading starts lies on the vertex O.

Step 2: Draw a line along the vertical edge of the set square perpendicular to line AB.

Step 3: Mark a point C on the perpendicular line drawn. OC is the required perpendicular line.

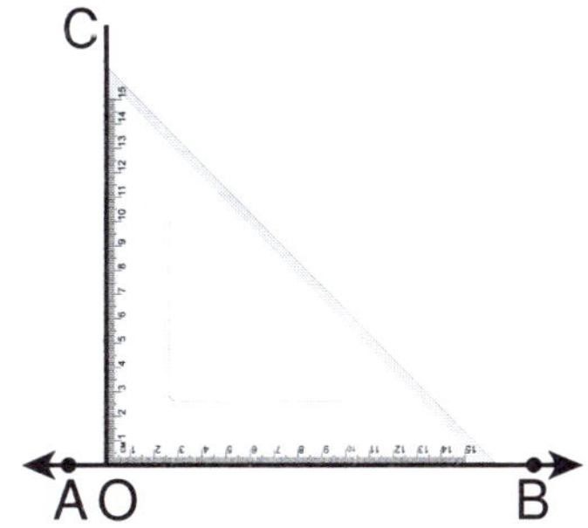

Constructing Perpendicular Lines Using Compass and Ruler

Example 2: Draw perpendicular OC at a point O on a given line segment AB using a compass and a ruler.

Step 1: Place the sharp edge of the compass at point O and with any radius, draw an arc that intersects AB at points P and Q.

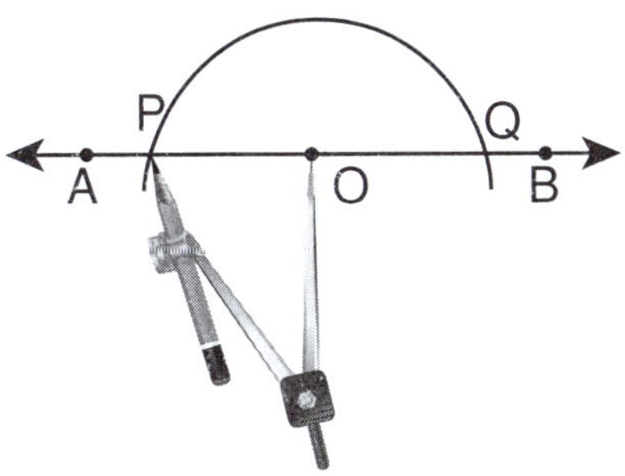

Step 2: Keeping P as the centre, with more than half of PQ as radius, draw an arc.

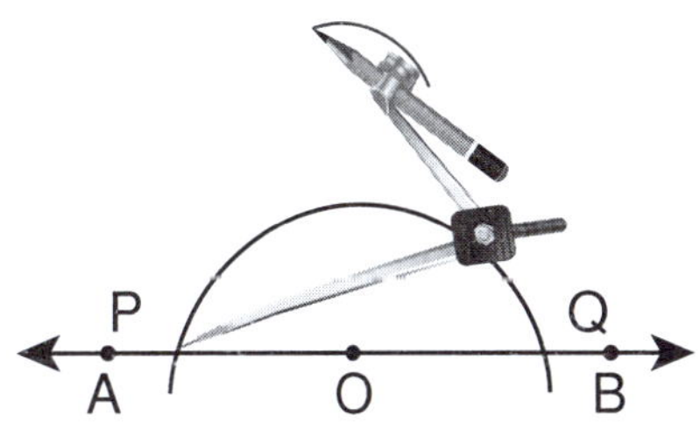

Step 3: Without changing the radius and keeping Q as the centre, draw another arc that intersects the previous arc.

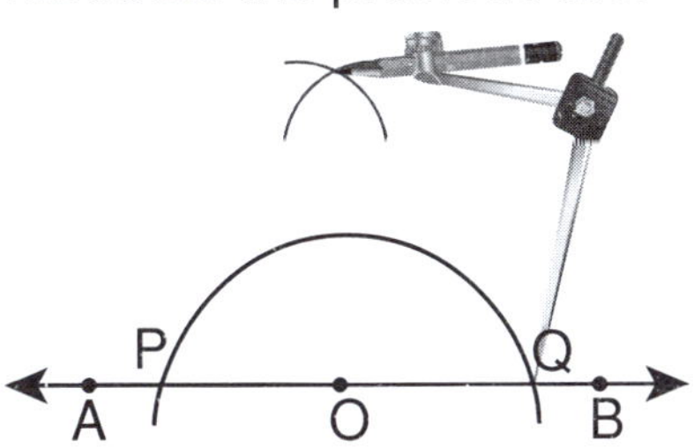

Step 4: Mark the point of intersection of the two arcs as C.

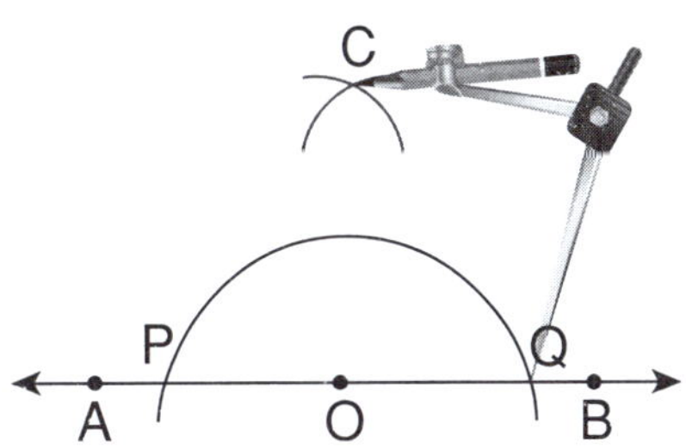

Step 5: Join O and C with a line using the ruler. OC is the required perpendicular line

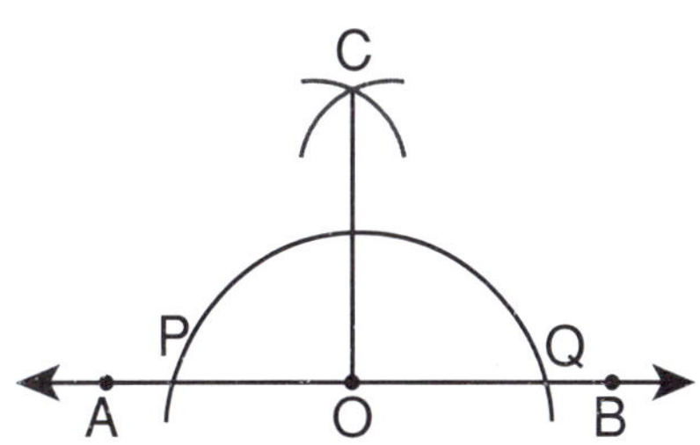

Constructing Perpendicular Bisectors of Line Segments

To bisect means to divide anything into halves. A perpendicular bisector divides a line segment exactly into two halves, making an angle of 90° at the point of intersection.

Example 3: With the help of compass, draw a perpendicular bisector to line segment AB of length 6 cm.

Step 1: Draw a line segment AB of length 6 cm.

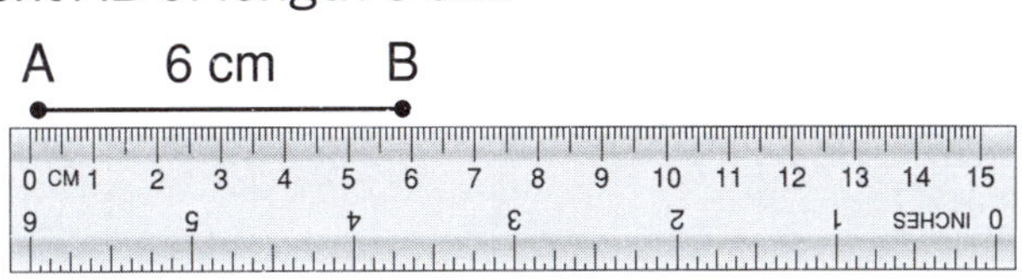

Step 2: With A as centre and more than half of AB as radius, draw a long arc.

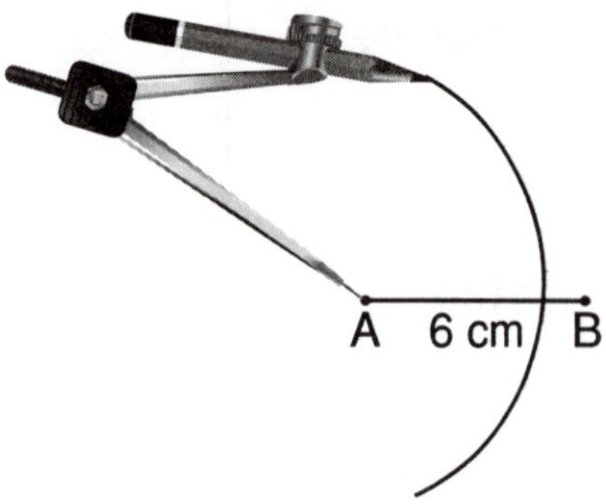

Step 3: With B as centre and without changing the radius, draw another arc that intersects the previously drawn arc at points E and F.

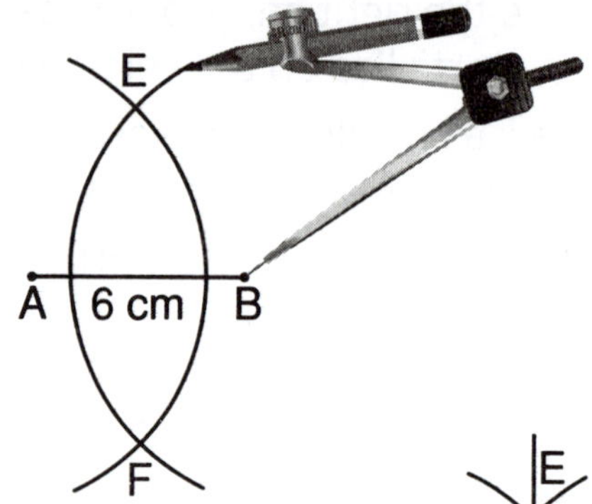

Step 4: Join E and F and name the point of intersection of EF and AB as O.

Step 5: We get the required bisector EF ⊥ AB and AO = OB = 3 cm.

We can verify this by measuring the lengths of AO and OB using the ruler.

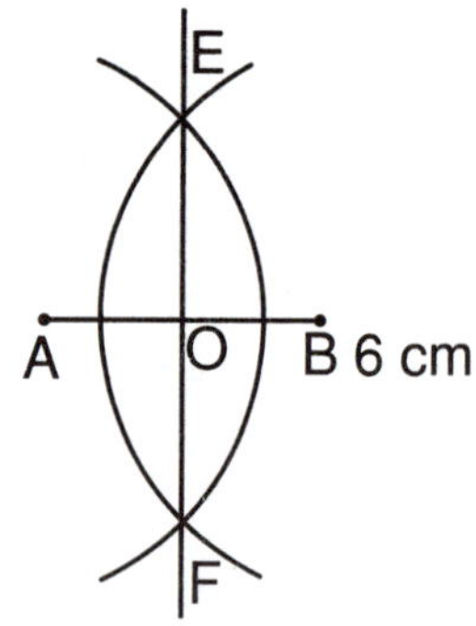

Summary

1. A point has a position but no dimension.
2. A line is a straight path that has no breadth and no thickness.
3. A line segment is a part of a line. It has two endpoints
4. A ray is an infinitely long part of a line which starts at a point called the vertex.
5. If three or more lines intersect each other at a common point, then they are said to be concurrent lines. The point at which they intersect is known as the point of concurrency.
6. Points that lie on a straight line are called collinear points.
7. An angle is a shape formed when two rays start from a common point.
8. A plane is an infinite set of points that forms a flat surface extending infinitely in all directions. A plane has infinite length, infinite width and no thickness.
9. Surfaces that have two dimensions (width and length), are perfectly flat and extend infinitely in all directions are called plane surfaces.
10. Surfaces that are not flat are called curved surfaces.

For the Curious Mind

1. While bisecting a line, can the angle be formed other than 90°? Justify your answer.
2. Draw a line segment AB. Mark a point X below it. Draw OX ⊥ AB using a set square.

Revision Exercise

1 **Identify and list the points, line segments, angles, parallel lines, perpendicular lines, collinear points and plane surfaces in the figure given below.**

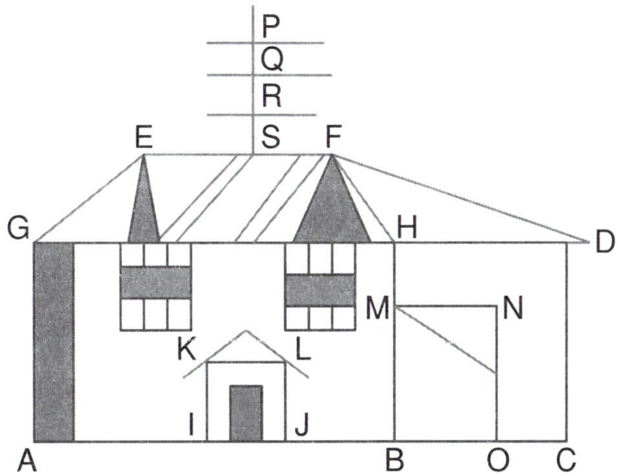

2 **State whether the lines are parallel or perpendicular.**

a. Opposite sides of a table top
b. Adjacent edges of a book
c. Adjacent edges of a blackboard
d. Two opposite edges of a fridge

3 **Draw the following in your notebook.**

a. Line segments AB, MN, FG and QR, which are parallel to each other
b. Line segment MN intersecting line segment PQ at point E
c. Line UV perpendicular to line WX at point O
d. Lines FG, HI, MN and JK, which intersect at point L

4 **Fill in the blanks.**

a. A ray has __________ endpoint.
b. A point has __________ dimension.
c. Two perpendicular lines intersect at __________ degrees.
d. A __________ extends endlessly on both sides.

5 Draw a line segment AB = 10 cm. Mark a point O on it such that AO = 4 cm and OB = 6 cm. Draw CO $\perp$ AB using set squares.

6 Draw a line segment AB = 12 cm. Mark a point O on it such that AO = 5 cm and OB = 7 cm. Draw OC $\perp$ AB using ruler and compass.

7 Draw a line segment AB = 10 cm. Draw OC $\perp$ AB such that AO = OB = 5 cm.

UNIT 4

Angles

18

What I shall learn

- To identify the types of angles made by the transversal cutting two lines
- To verify the properties of angles made by the transversal cutting parallel lines
- To check whether the two given lines are parallel or not

Let's Get Started

We have learned that an **angle** is a shape formed when two rays start from a common point. The two rays are known as the **arms** of the angle and the common point is known as the **vertex**.

Look at the followings pictures and identify the angles that are present in these pictures.

Angles

The word 'angle' is derived from the Latin word *angulus*, which means 'corner'. The Greeks and the Romans used angles widely in their architecture. Angles help in the construction of safer buildings and bridges. They can be used to support buildings and make them stronger in areas where earthquakes and other natural disasters are common.

Greek architecture: The Temple of Zeus is in the city of Olympia in Greece. It is an ancient temple dedicated to the Greek god Zeus.

Roman architecture: The Colosseum, is an elliptical amphitheatre in Rome, Italy.

Note

∠ABC = ∠CBA

The vertex is always written in the middle.

Naming an Angle

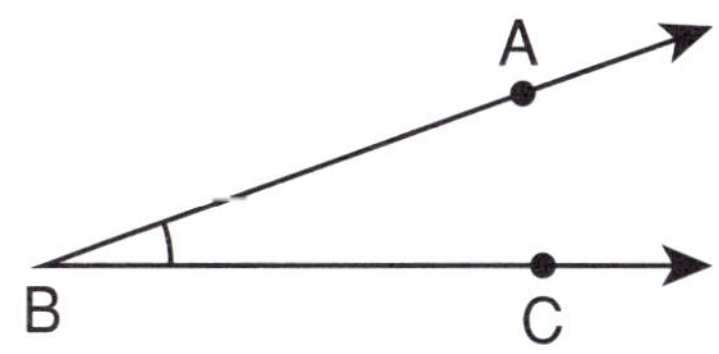

In this figure, $\overrightarrow{AB}$ and $\overrightarrow{BC}$ are the arms of the angle and B is the vertex. An angle is denoted by the symbol ∠ and is written as ∠ABC (read as 'angle ABC') or simply as ∠B (read as 'angle B').

Interior and Exterior of an Angle

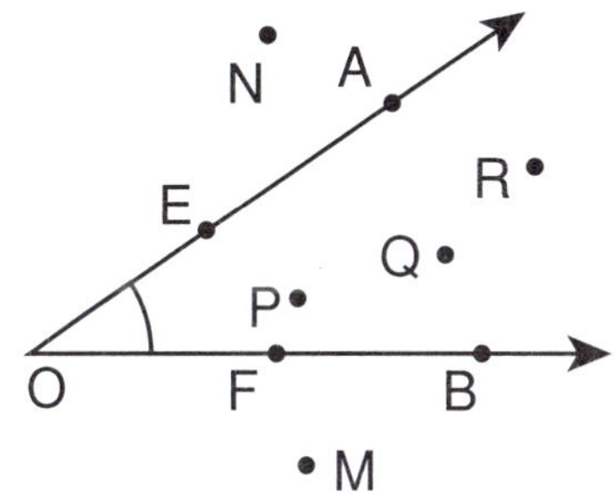

The region bounded by the arms of an angle is called the **interior** of the angle. In the figure, the points P, Q and R lie in the interior of ∠AOB.

The region outside the arms of an angle is called the **exterior** of the angle. In the figure, the points M and N lie in the exterior of ∠AOB.

All the points on the arms of an angle are said to lie on the angle. In the figure, the points E and F lie on ∠AOB.

Measurement of an Angle

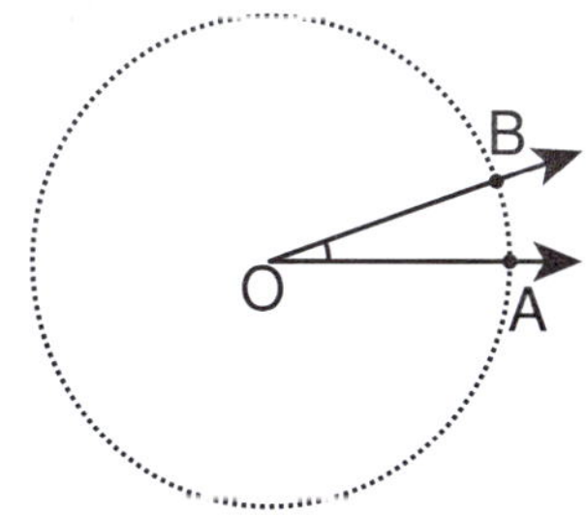

An angle is measured by a unit called degree, which is represented by the symbol °.

If one arm of an angle makes one complete rotation starting from the other fixed arm, then the angle made is of measure 360° (also called complete angle).

This 360° measure is divided into 360 equal parts and each part is measured as 1°.

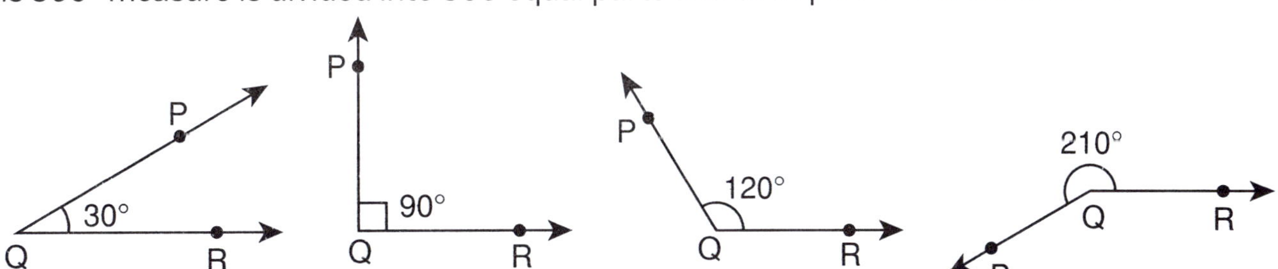

∠PQR = 30° ∠PQR = 90° ∠PQR = 120° ∠PQR = 210°

Measuring and Constructing Angles Using a Protractor

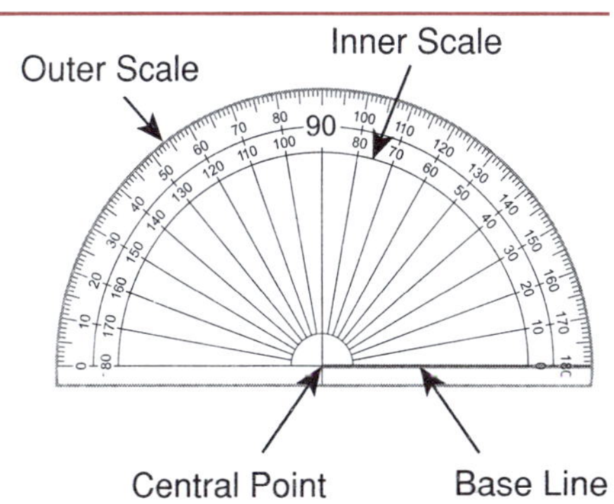

The D-shaped instrument in a geometry box is called the protractor.

Measuring Angles Using Protractor

In order to measure an angle PQR, place the protractor on the arm PQ so that the base line of the protractor coincides with the arm PQ and the midpoint/central point of the baseline coincides with the vertex Q. Starting from 0° in the inner scale, move in the anticlockwise direction. Read the measure of the angle by checking with which degree the other arm, that is, QR is coinciding. Here, the arm QR lies at 60°. Hence the measure of angle PQR is 60°.

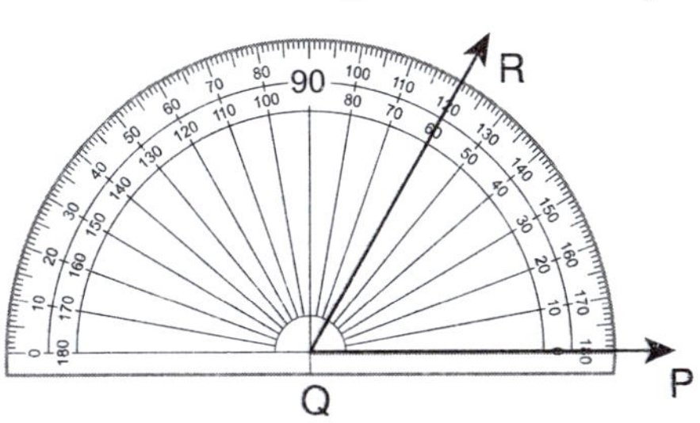

Constructing Angles Using Protractor

Example 1: Using a protractor, construct an angle of 50°.

Step 1: Draw a ray PQ.

Step 2: Place the protractor in such a way that the base line of the protractor coincides with the ray PQ and the midpoint of the base line coincides with the vertex P.

Step 3: Identify the 0° mark on the protractor and measure 50° in the anticlockwise direction and mark the point R.

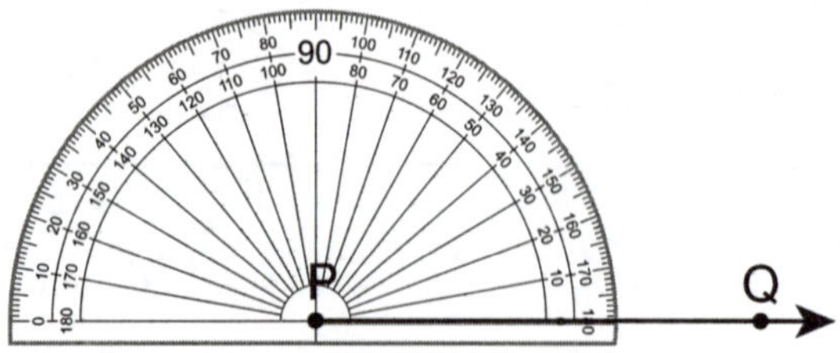

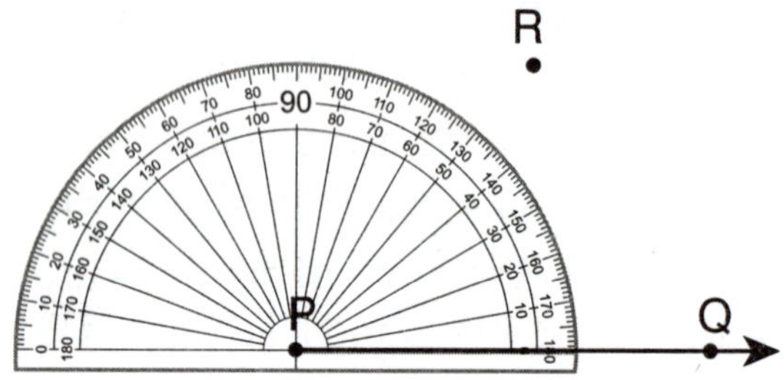

Step 4: Now remove the protractor and join P and R and extend it further to a suitable distance to form ray $\overrightarrow{PR}$.

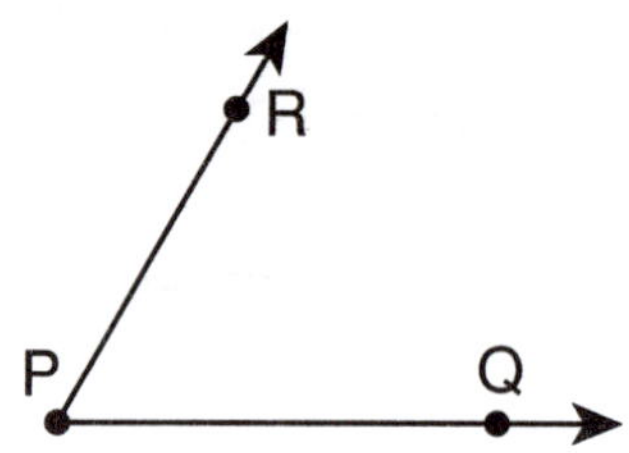

Thus, ∠QPR is the required angle.

Addition and Subtraction of Angles

While measuring an angle, the maximum angle one can measure is 360°, which can be divided into 360 equal parts of 1° each. Each 1° is further divided into 60 equal parts known as minutes, which in turn is divided into 60 equal parts known as seconds.

The symbol ′ is called prime.

1 minute is represented as 1′ (one prime) and read as 'one minute'. And 1 second is represented as 1″ (two primes) and read as 'one second'.

Remember

One complete angle = 360°

1° = 60′

1′ = 60″

Example 2: Add 63° 46′ 28″ and 12° 10′ 33″.

$$\begin{array}{r} 63° \; 46' \; 28'' \\ +\; 12° \; 10' \; 23'' \\ \hline 75° \; 56' \; 51'' \end{array}$$

Note

Do not confuse these minutes and seconds with the units of time with the same names as they are two entirely different concepts.

Example 3: Subtract 33° 44′ 22″ from 87° 56′ 05″.

$$\begin{array}{r} 87° \; 55' \; 65'' \\ -\; 33° \; 44' \; 22'' \\ \hline 54° \; 11' \; 43'' \end{array}$$

Classification of Angles

Angles are classified into the following types based on their measurements.

Zero angle
∠AOB = 0°

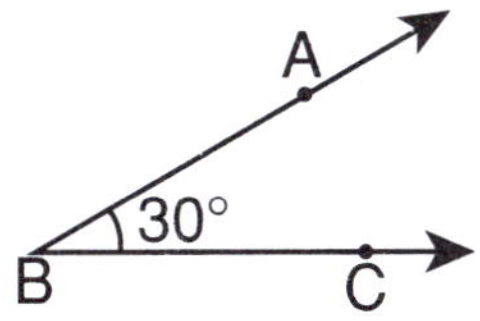

Acute angle
∠ABC = 0° < 30° < 90°

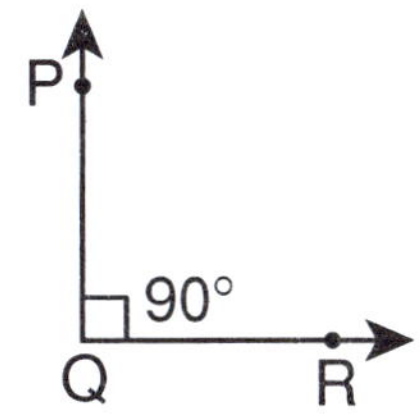

Right angle
∠PQR = 90°

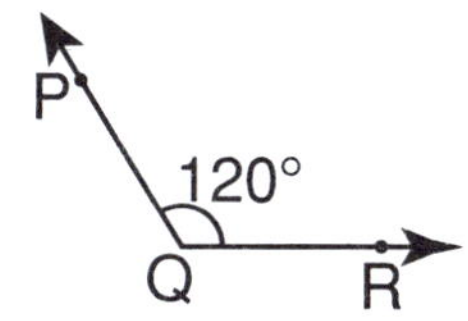

Obtuse angle
∠PQR = 90° < 120° < 180°

Straight angle
∠PQR = 180°

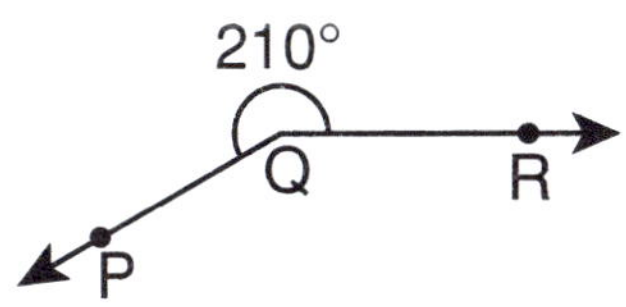

Reflex angle
∠PQR = 180° < 210° < 360°

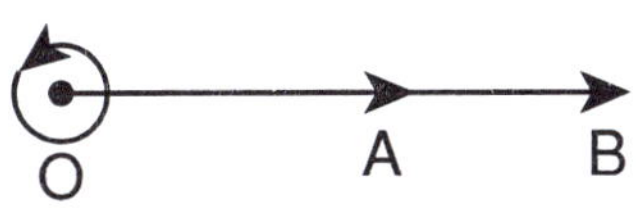

Complete angle
∠AOB = 360°

Remember

Right angle = 90°
Straight angle = 180°
Complete angle = 360°
0° < Acute angle < 90°
90° < Obtuse angle < 180°
180° < Reflex angle < 360°

Note

1 complete angle = 2 straight angles = 4 right angles

Exercise 18.1

1 **Name the points that lie on the angles, and in the interior and exterior of the angles.**

a.

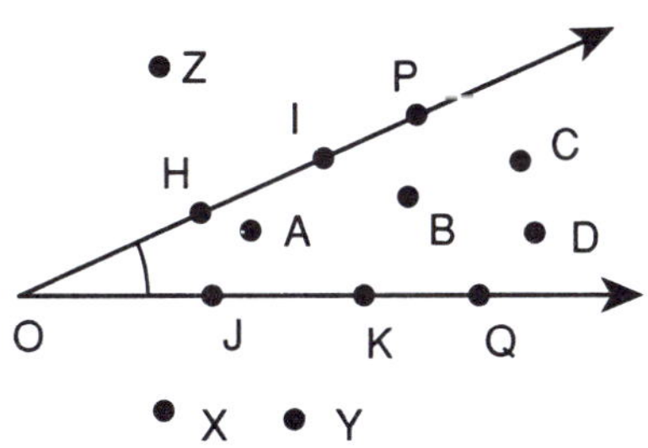

b.

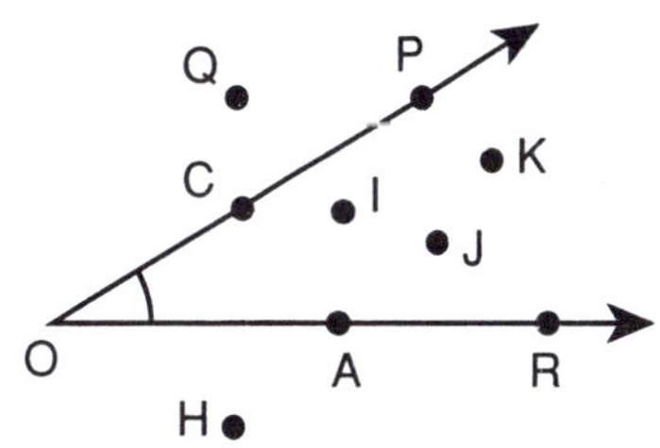

2 In the given figure, find ∠AQC if

∠PQR = 100° 44′ 33″

∠PQA = 54° 11′ 12″

∠RQC = 22° 21′ 31″

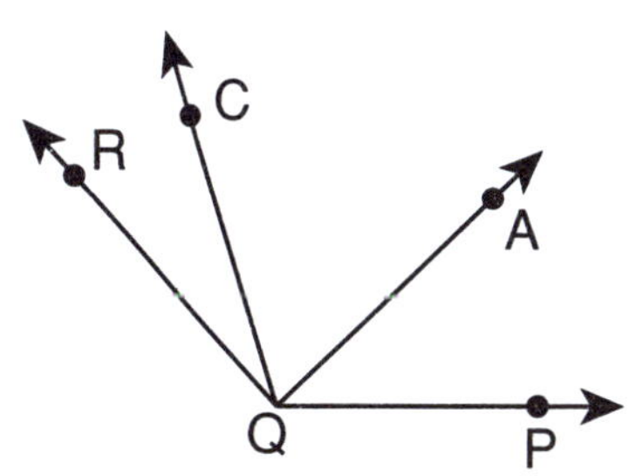

3 **Classify the following angles according to their magnitudes and construct them using a protractor.**

a. 23° b. 45° c. 87° d. 135° e. 270°

Special Pairs of Angles

Complementary Angles

If the sum of the measures of two angles is 90°, then the two angles are complementary angles.

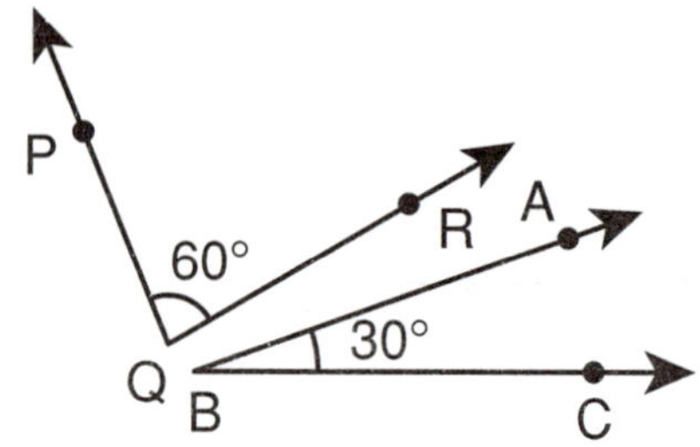

In the given figure, ∠PQR and ∠ABC are complementary angles since ∠PQR +∠ABC = 60° + 30° = 90°.

Can you think of other complementary angles?

Supplementary Angles

If the sum of the measures of two angles is 180°, then the two angles are supplementary angles.

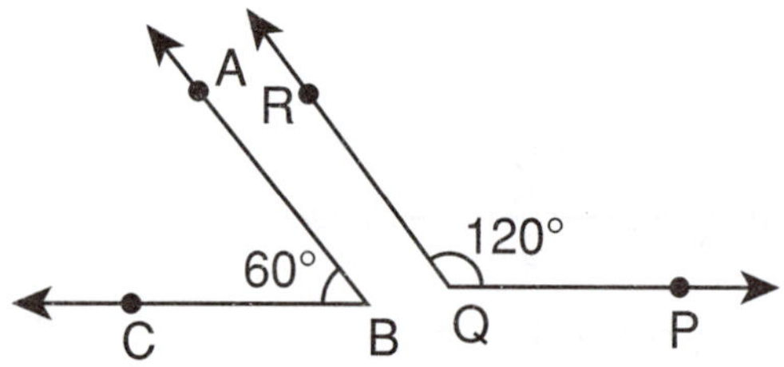

In the given figure, ∠PQR and ∠ABC are supplementary angles since ∠PQR + ∠ABC = 120° + 60° = 180°.

Are two right angles supplementary angles?

Congruent Angles

If two angles measure the same, then they are known as congruent angles.

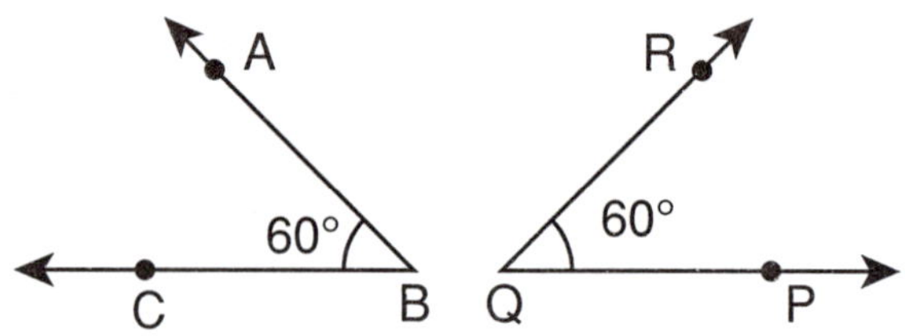

In the given figure, ∠PQR and ∠ABC are congruent angles.

Adjacent Angles

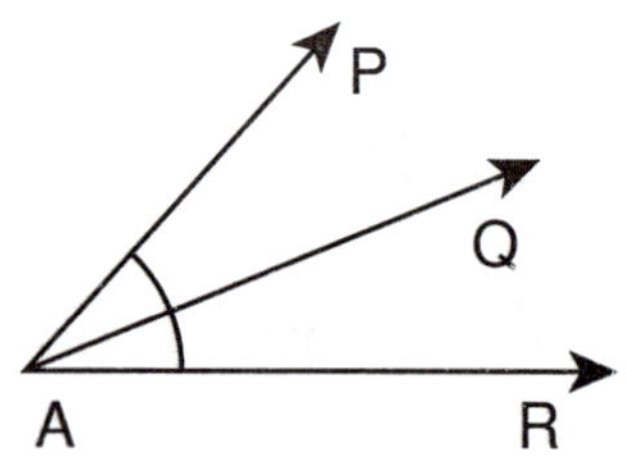

Angles like ∠PAQ and ∠QAR which have a common arm and common vertex are called adjacent angles. Sum of adjacent angles on a straight line is 180°.

Vertically Opposite Angles

In the given figure, ∠AOB and ∠COR are vertically opposite angles, and ∠AOC and ∠BOR are also vertically opposite angles.

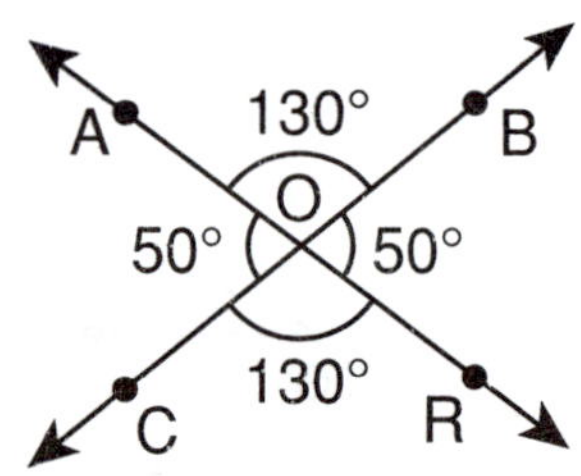

Linear Pair of Angles

If two angles are adjacent to each other and their sum is 180°, then they are known as a linear pair of angles.

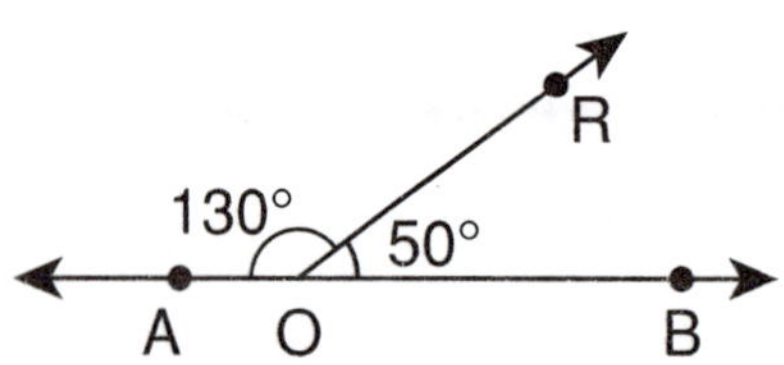

Note

Two arms of a linear pair make a straight line.

In the given figure, ∠AOR + ∠BOR = 180°, so they form a linear pair of angles.

Angles Formed by Transversal

Transversal

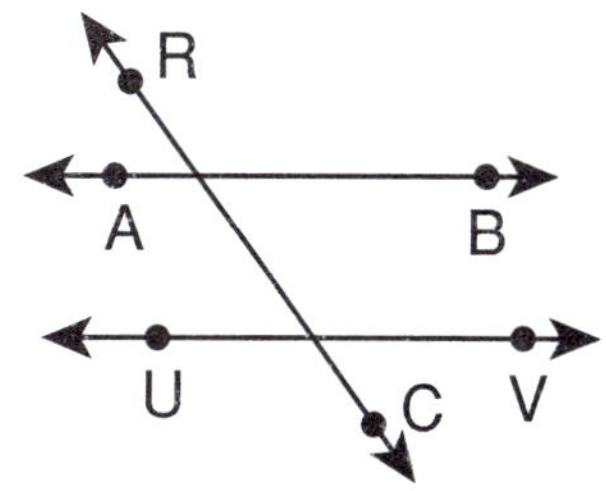

If a line intersects two or more lines, then it is known as a transversal. In the given figure, RC is the transversal intersecting the lines AB and UV.

Interior Angles

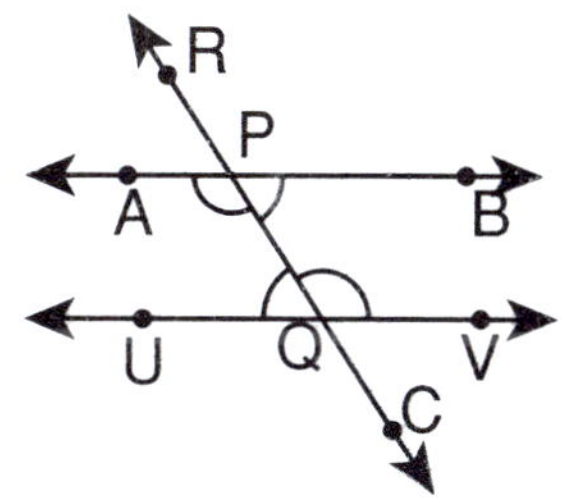

When a transversal intersects two lines, angles are formed on the interior of the two lines on either side of the transversal. Such angles are known as interior angles.

In the given figure, ∠APQ, ∠BPQ, ∠UQP and ∠VQP are interior angles.

Exterior Angles

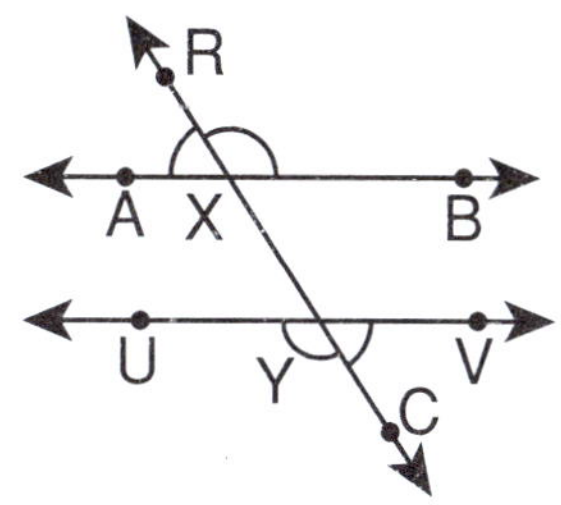

When a transversal intersects two lines, angles are formed on the exterior of the two lines on either side of the transversal. Such angles are known as exterior angles.

In the given figure, ∠AXR, ∠BXR, ∠UYC and ∠VYC are exterior angles.

Alternate Interior Angles

When a transversal intersects two lines, the pairs of interior angles formed on the opposite (alternate) side of the transversal are called alternate interior angles.

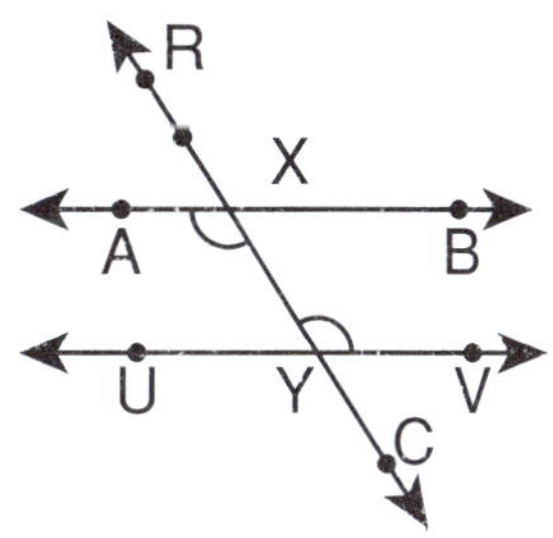

Note

When a transversal intersects two lines, two pairs of alternate interior angles are formed.

In the given figure, ∠AXY and ∠XYV are alternate interior angles. Similarly, ∠BXY and ∠XYU form another pair of alternate interior angles.

Alternate Exterior Angles

When a transversal intersects two lines, the pairs of exterior angles formed on the opposite (alternate) side of the transversal are called alternate exterior angles.

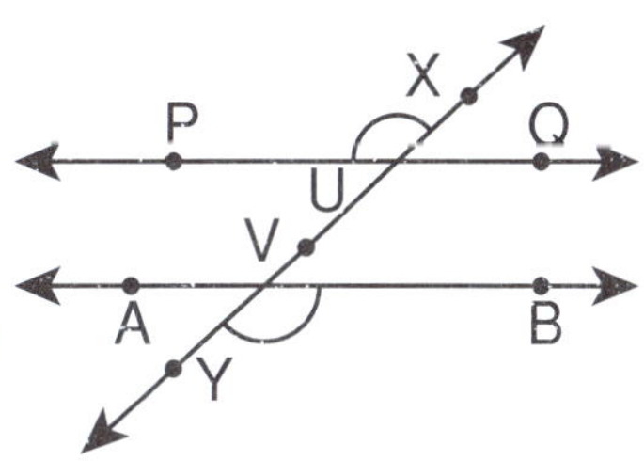

Note

When a transversal intersects two lines, two pairs of alternate exterior angles are formed.

In the given figure, ∠PUX and ∠YVB are alternate exterior angles. Similarly, ∠QUX and ∠YVA form another pair of alternate exterior angles.

Consecutive Interior Angles

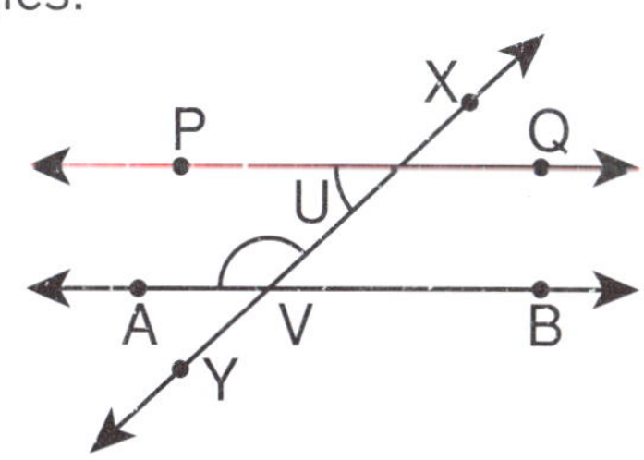

When a transversal intersects two lines, the pair of interior angles formed on the same side of the transversal are called consecutive interior angles.

In the given figure, ∠PUV and ∠AVU are consecutive interior angles. Similarly, ∠QUV and ∠BVU form another pair of consecutive interior angles.

Corresponding Angles

When a transversal intersects two lines, the pair of angles formed on one side of the transversal (in matching corners) are known as corresponding angles.

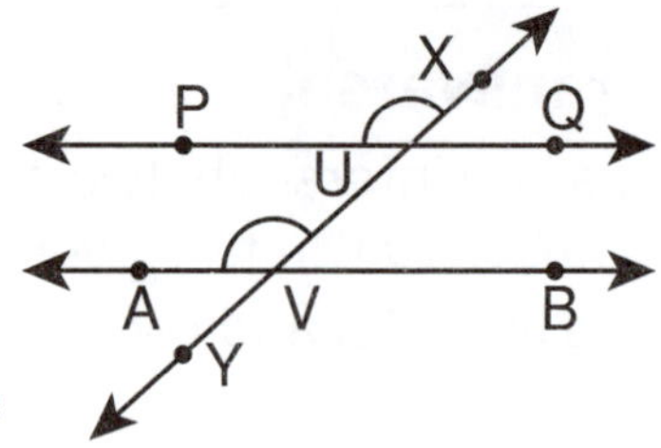

In the given figure, ∠PUX and ∠AVU are corresponding angles.

Can you find the other pairs of corresponding angles? There are 3 more pairs in the given figure.

Properties of the Angles Formed When a Transversal Intersects Two Parallel Lines

1. The pairs of **alternate interior** as well as the pairs of **alternate exterior** angles are equal.
2. The pairs of **corresponding angles** are equal.
3. The pairs of interior angles (**co-interior, conjoined or allied**) on the same side of the transversal are supplementary.

Applications of Angles in Real Life

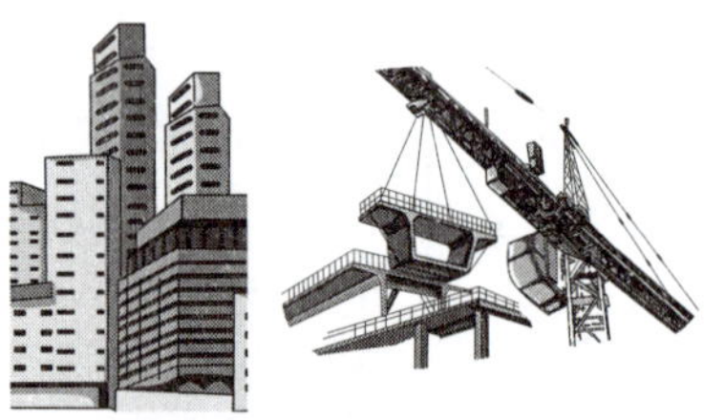

Angles in Construction

Angles in Sports

Banking Angle on road

Problems Based on Special Angles

Example 4: Find the complement of the following angle.

a. 32°

The complementary angle = 90° – 32° = 58°

Example 5: Find the supplement of the following angle:

a. 52°

The supplementary angle = 180° – 52° = 128°

Try These!

1. Find the complement of 45°. __________
2. Find the supplement of 90°. __________

Example 6: Two supplementary angles are in the ratio 5 : 13. Find the angles.

The ratio of the given angles = 5 : 13

Sum of the ratio = 5 + 13 = 18

Therefore, the angles are $\frac{5}{18} \times 180° = 50°$ and $\frac{13}{18} \times 180° = 130°$.

Exercise 18.2

1 **Find the measure of angle x and the measure of all the angles in the following figures. Also mention the properties used to find the answers.**

a.

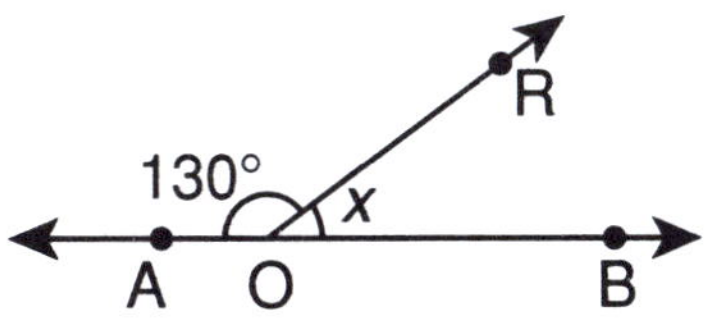

b.

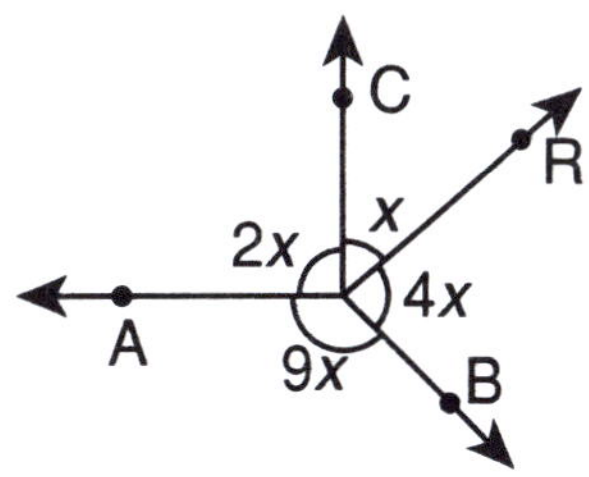

c.

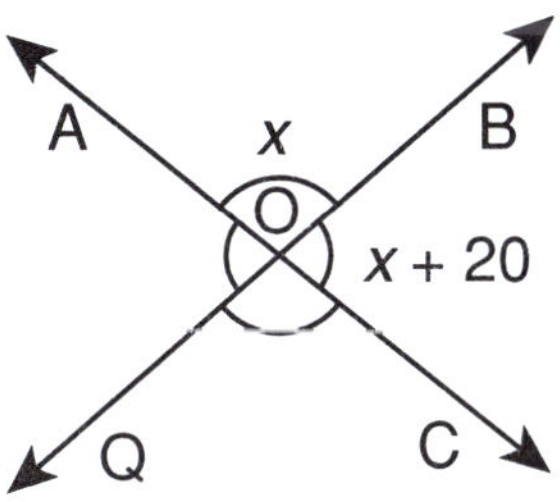

d.

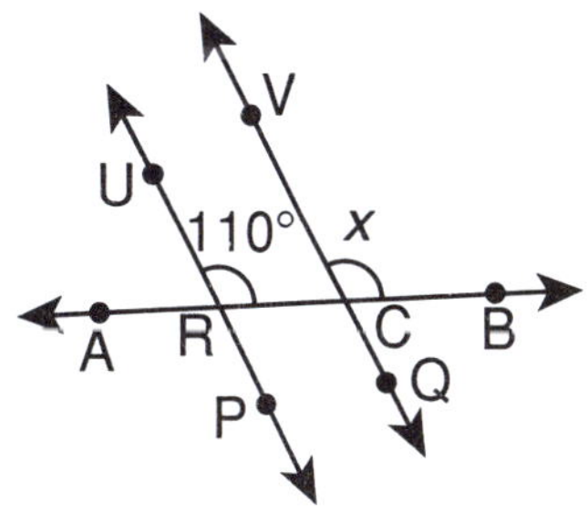

2 **Find the complement and supplement for each of the following angles.**

a. 48° b. 73° c. $x°$ d. $(20 + x)°$

e. 23° f. 90° g. 45° h. 87°

3 If two complementary angles are in the ratio 1 : 5, find the angles.

4 If two supplementary angles are in the ratio 3 : 7, find the angles.

Summary

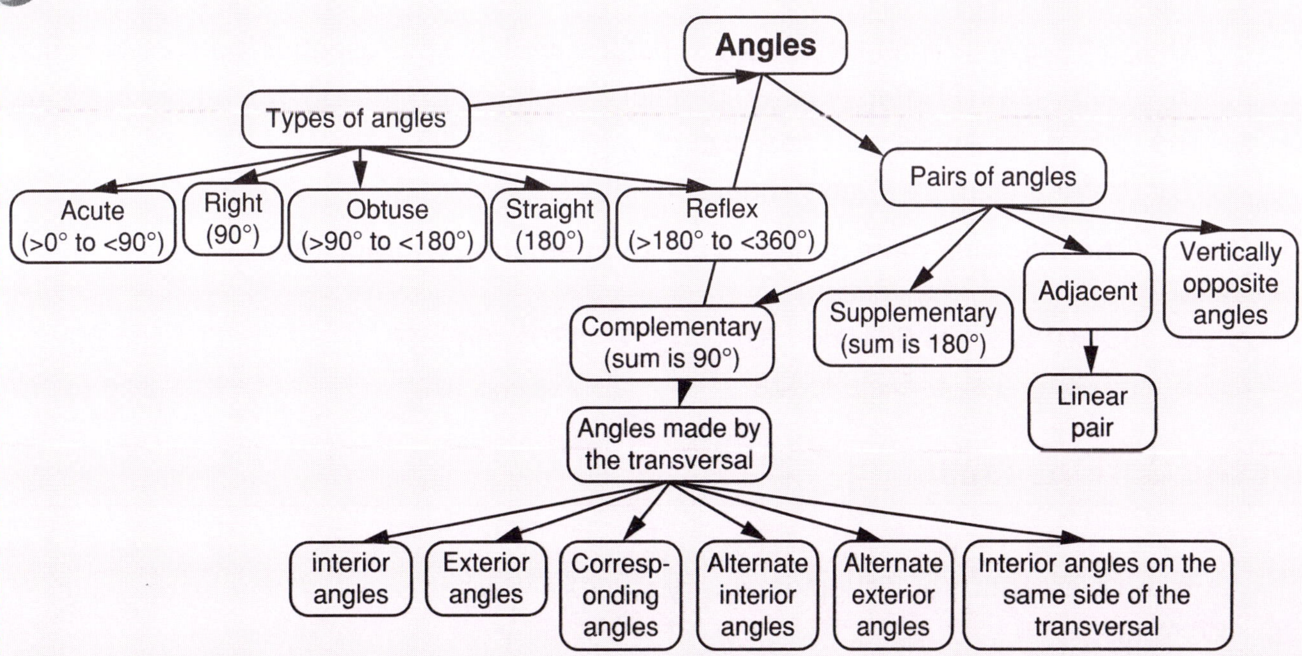

Revision Exercise

1 **Find the measure of x and the measure of all the angles in the following figures. Also mention the properties used to find the answers.**

a.

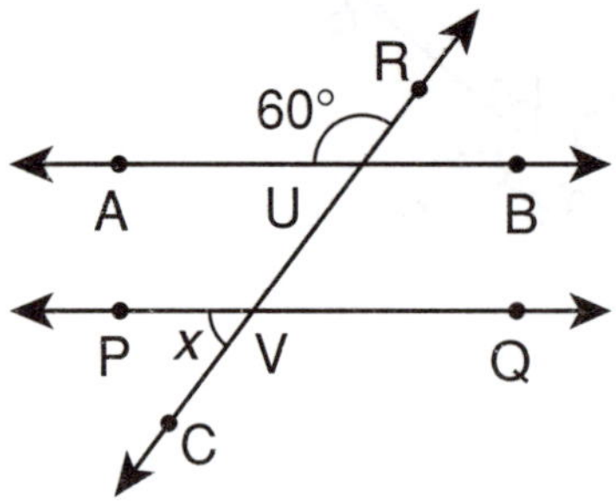

b.

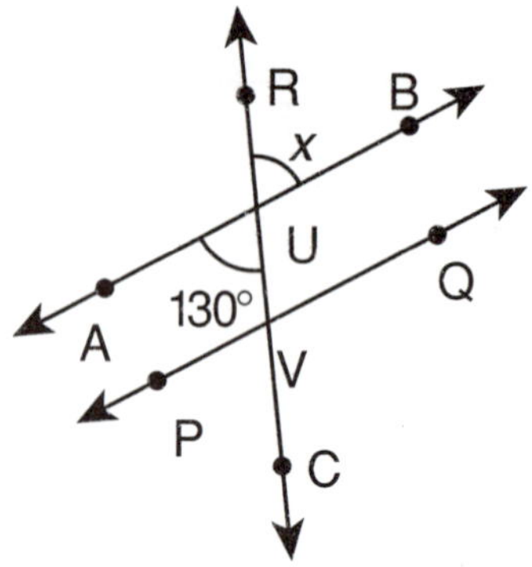

2 **Find the complement of the following angles.**

a. 12° b. 40° c. 56° d. 75° e. 79°
f. 33° g. 50° h. 67°55′22″ i. 14° j. 90°

3 **Find the supplement of the following angles.**

a. 35° b. 57° c. 92° d. 0° e. 180°
f. 150° g. 90° h. 123° i. 120° j. 157°66′33″

4 **State whether the following statements are true or false.**

a. A zero angle is drawn in a similar way as a complete angle.
b. An angle measuring 2° is an acute angle.
c. A transversal is a line that intersects only a set of two or more parallel lines.
d. The supplement of 90° is 90°.
e. When a transversal intersects two non-parallel lines, the corresponding angles are equal.
f. When a transversal intersects two parallel lines, the alternate exterior angles are equal.
g. The sum of the angles of a linear pair of angles is 90°.
h. Congruent angles are always equal and adjacent.

5 **Classify the following pairs of angles as complementary, supplementary or congruent.**

a. 70° and 20° b. 60° and 120° c. 130° and 130° d. 60° and 30°
e. 85° and 95° f. 55° and 125° g. 78° and 102° h. 180° and 180°

For the Curious Mind

1. Are complementary and supplementary angles always adjacent? If yes, justify your answer.
2. Construct an angle of 540° using a protractor.

UNIT 4

Construction of Angles

19

Let's Get Started

In the previous chapters, we have learned about the basic elements of geometry, like line segments, angles and perpendicular lines. Now, let us learn the purpose of each tool in your geometry box and how to construct angles using these tools.

What I shall learn

- To construct angles using protractor
- To construct special angles using compass or set squares
- To construct angle bisectors

Ruler

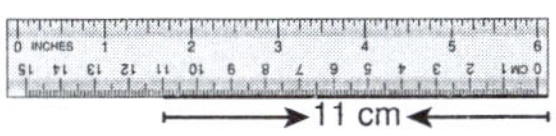

To draw and measure line segments

Protractor

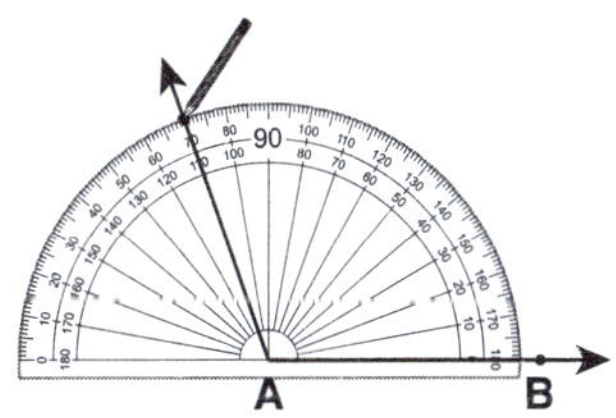

To draw and measure angles

Set Squares

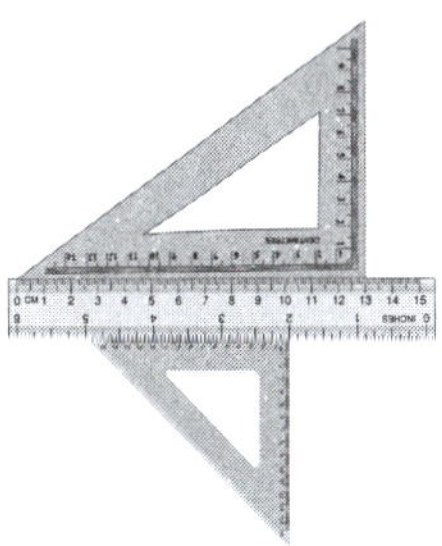

To draw parallel and perpendicular lines

Compass

To draw arcs and circles

Divider

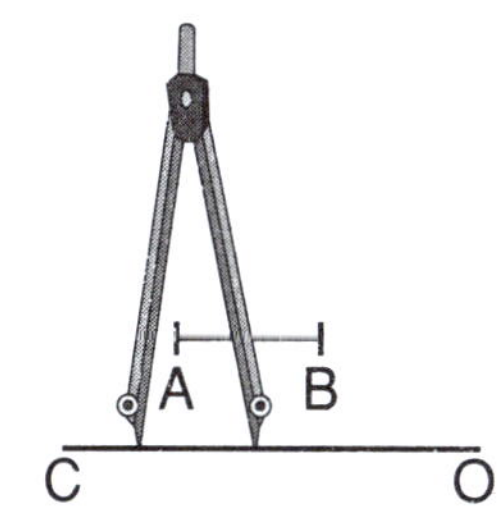

To compare lengths

Let us learn more about some of these tools.

1. **Ruler**: A scale or a ruler in a geometry box looks like this.

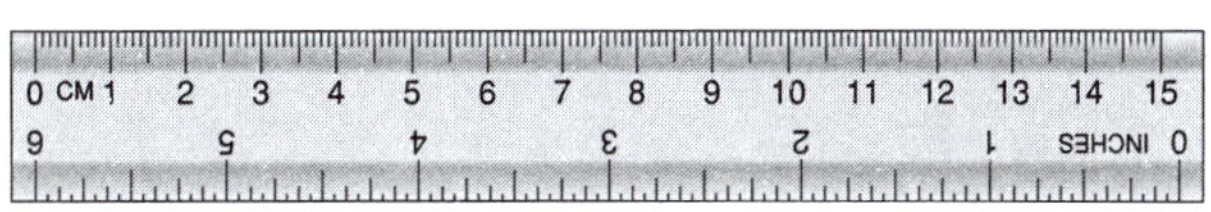

One of its edges is marked in **inches**. The other edge is divided into 15 divisions and each division represents a **centimetre**.

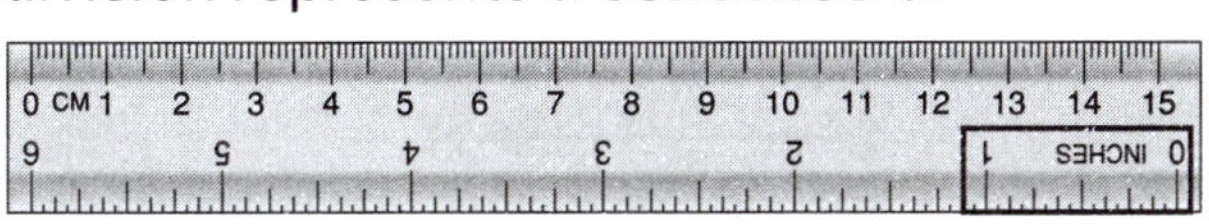

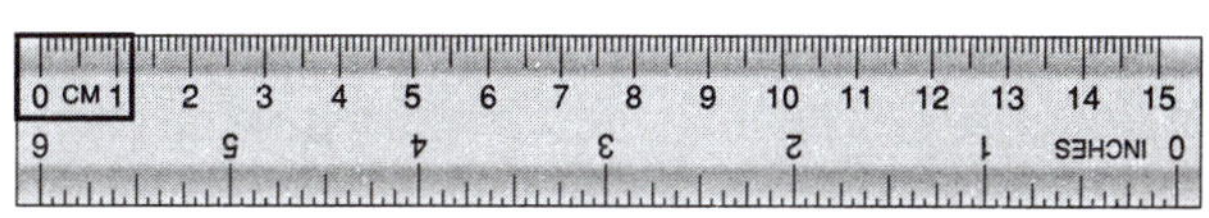

Each centimetre is further divided into 10 smaller divisions. Each smaller division represents $\frac{1}{10}$ of a centimetre and is known as a **millimetre**.

2. **Protractor**: The D-shaped instrument in a geometry box is called the protractor. It is used to measure and draw angles. There are two rows of measurements from 0° to 180° going in opposite directions. They are called **scales**. One is the inner scale and the other is the outer scale. There are 180 divisions between 0 and 180. Each division represents **one degree**. The bottom line is known as the **base line**. The point where the base line and the line corresponding to 90° meet is known as the **centre point**.

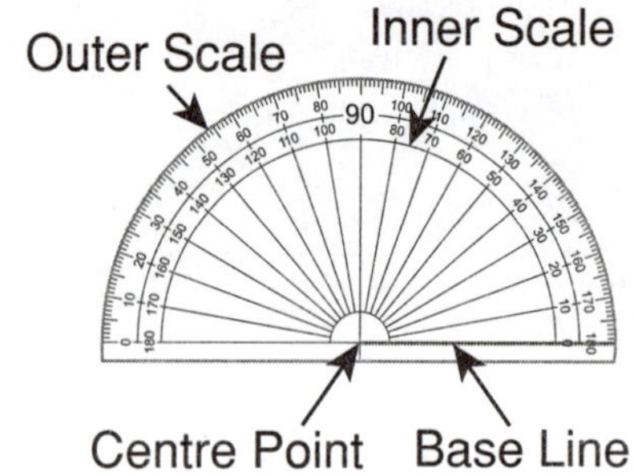

3. **Set Squares**: In a geometry box, there are two triangular instruments called set squares. Like a ruler, the set squares are graduated on the two outer edges. Set squares come in two forms, both right triangles, one with 90-45-45 degree angles and the other with 30-60-90 degree angles.

   Set squares are used to draw parallel lines, perpendicular lines and some specific angles.

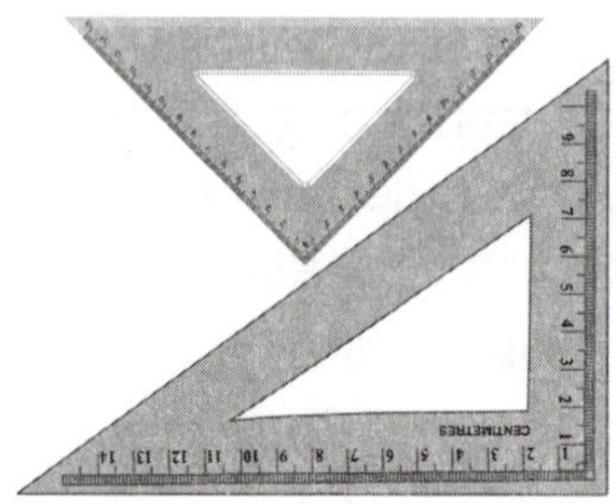

4. **Compass**: A compass has a metal pointed edge and a pencil holder.

   It is used to draw circles and arcs.

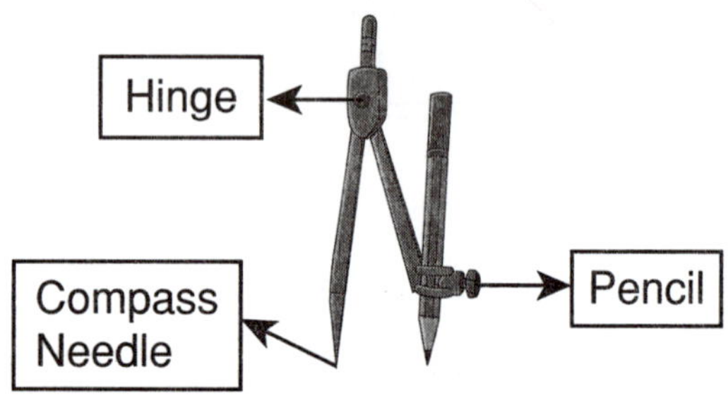

Constructing Angles of a Given Measurement Using a Protractor

Example 1: Construct a 75° angle using a protractor.

Step 1: Draw a ray AB. Place the centre of the protractor at point A and adjust it in such a way that its base line coincides with ray AB.

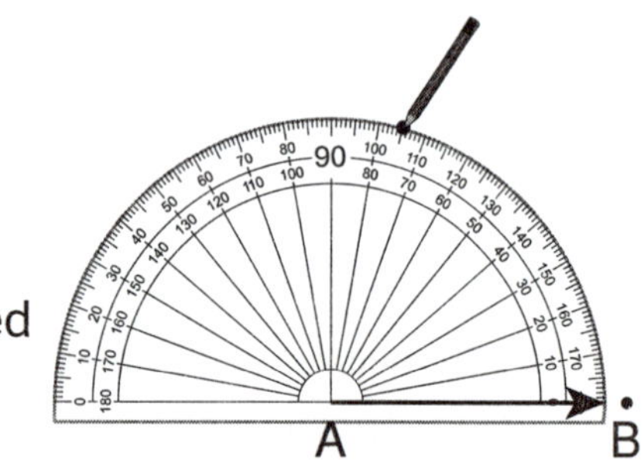

Step 2: Starting from the right, read the inner scale till the desired angle, that is, 75° is reached. Mark a point C at that reading.

Step 3: Draw ray BC. ∠CAB is the required angle.

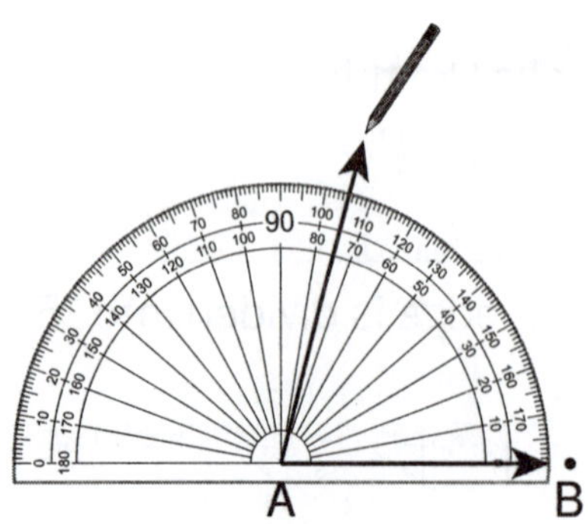

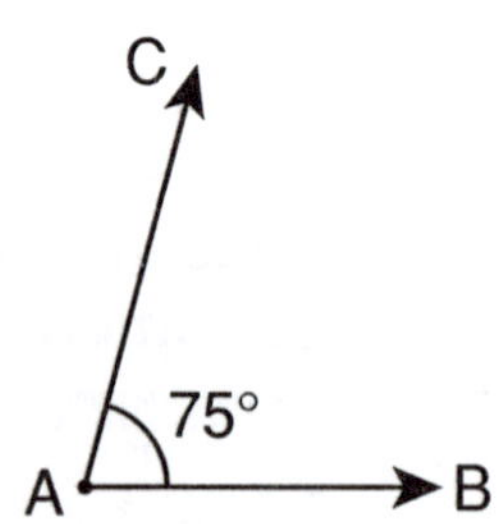

Constructing an Angle Equal to a Given Angle

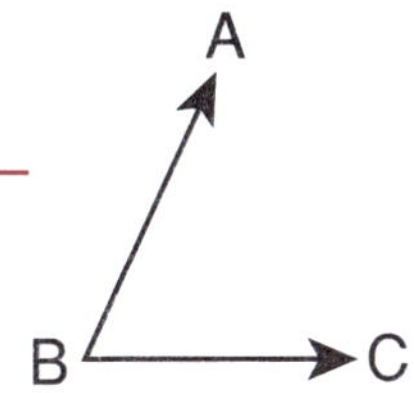

Example 2: Construct an angle whose measure is same as ∠ABC.

Step 1: Draw a line *l* and choose a point P on it.

Step 2: With B as the centre, draw any convenient arc, cutting the arms of the given ∠ABC at K and L.

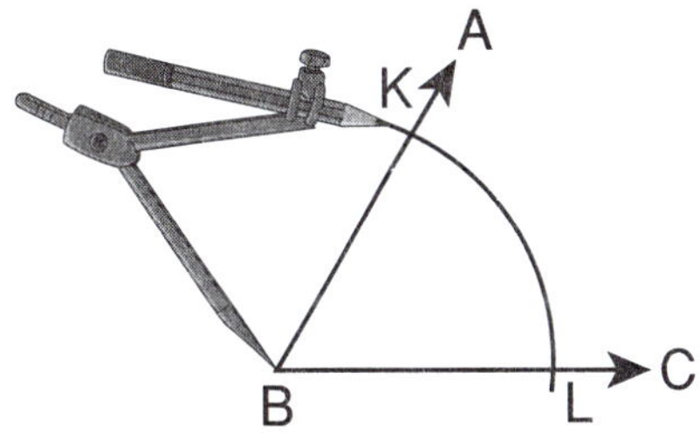

Step 3: Without changing the radius, keep the pointer at P and draw an arc cutting line *l* at Q.

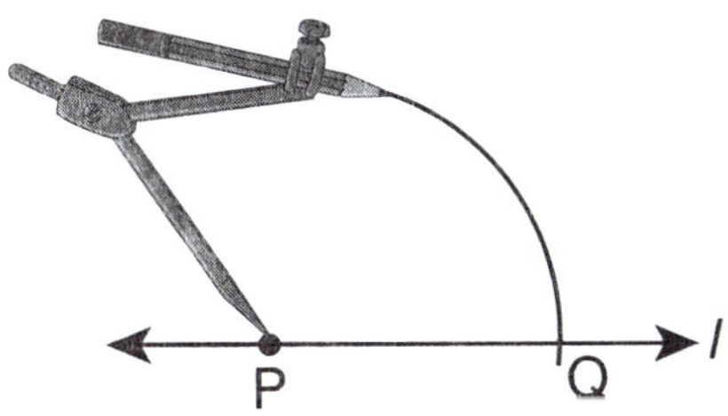

Step 4: Stretch the arms of the compass to the same length as KL.

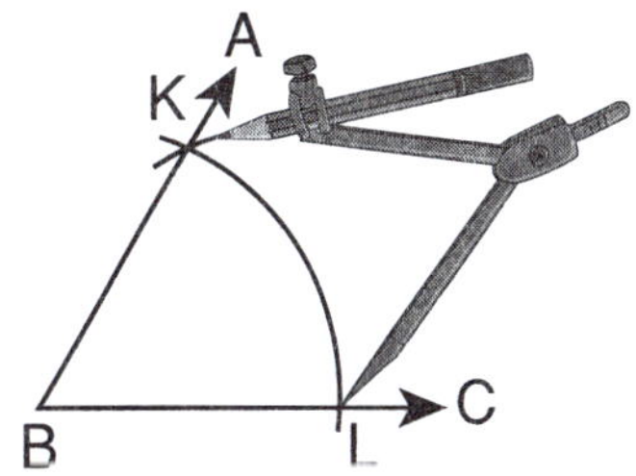

Step 5: With the same radius and point Q as the centre, draw an arc to cut the previous arc at R.

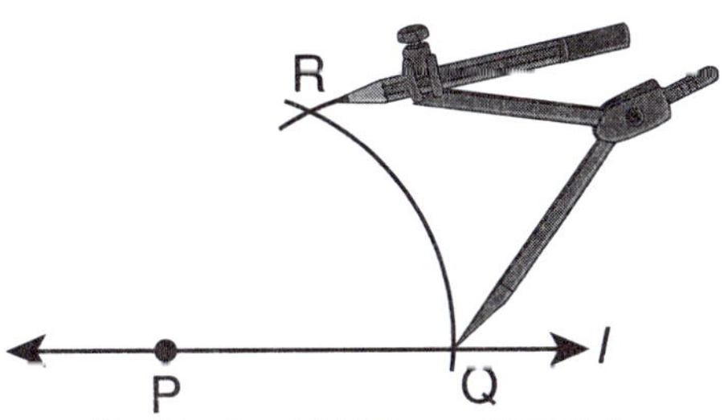

Step 6: Join the points P and R and extent it further to make $\overrightarrow{PR}$. ∠RPQ is the required angle whose measure is equal to ∠ABC.

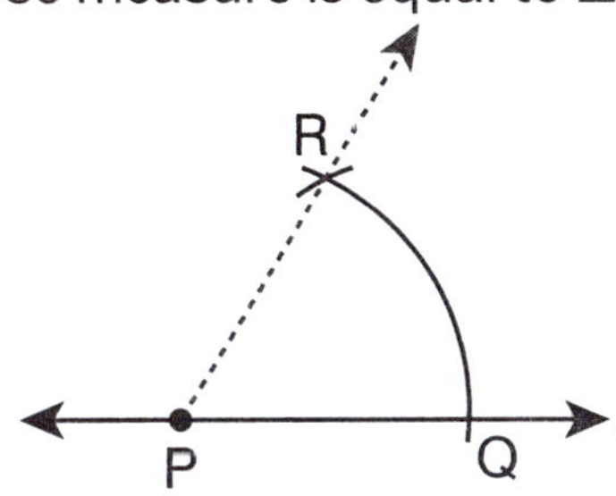

We can verify that ∠ABC = ∠RPQ by copying both the angles on a patty paper and then placing them one over the other or by measuring the angles using a protractor.

Constructing the Angle Bisector of a Given Angle

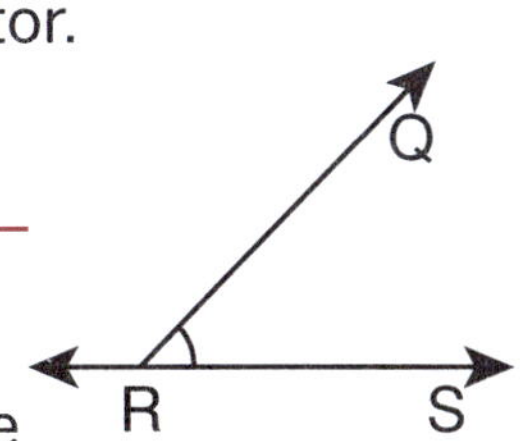

Example 3: Construct the angle bisector of ∠QRS.

Step 1: Draw an arc with R as the centre and any convenient radius to cut the two arms of the angle at points G and H.

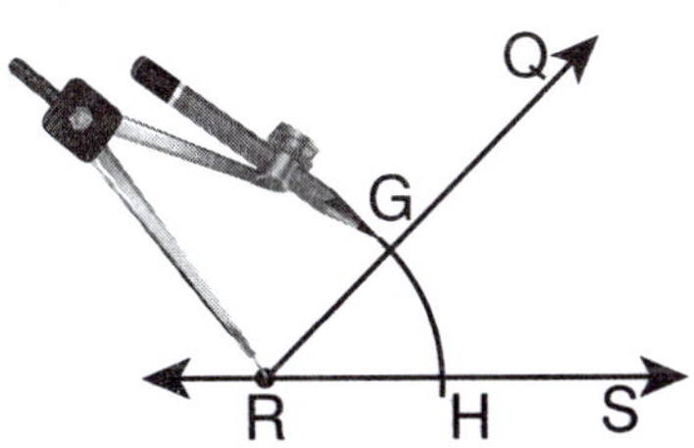

Step 2: With G as the centre and radius of more than half the length GH, draw an arc as shown.

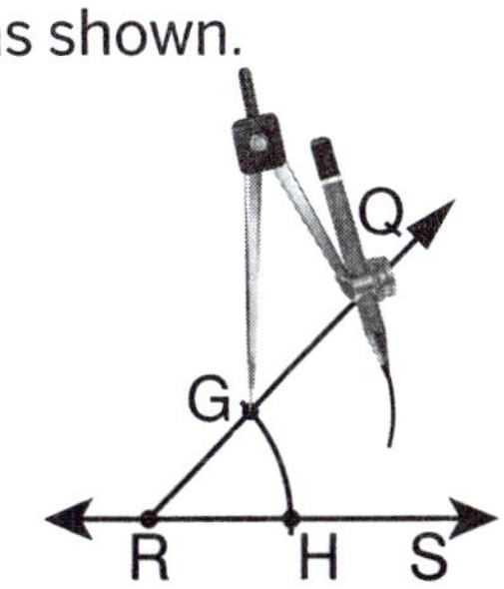

Step 3: With the same radius and H as the centre, draw another arc cutting the previous arc at B.

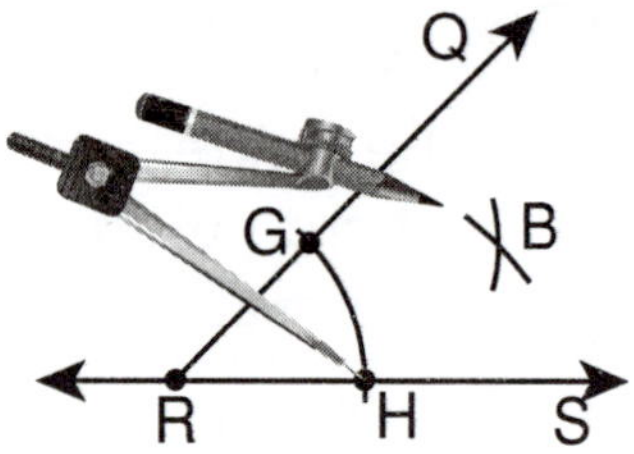

Step 4: Join points R and B to form Ray RB, which is the required angle bisector of ∠QRS.

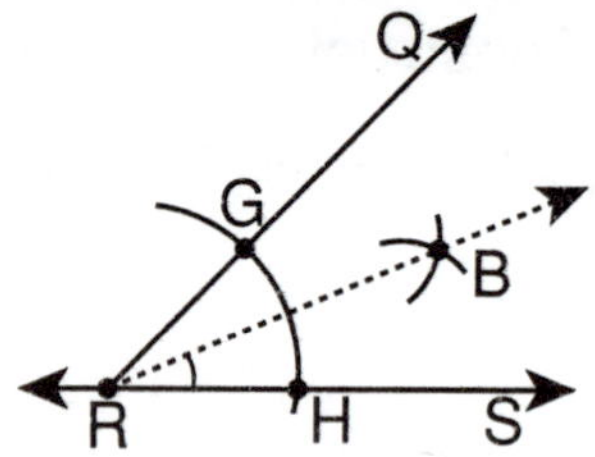

We can verify the above construction by measuring the bisected angles using a protractor or by copying ∠QRS on a patty paper and then folding the angle along RB.

Constructing Special Angles Using Ruler and Compass

1. Constructing an angle of measure 60°

Step 1: Draw a line *m* and mark a point O on it.

Step 2: With O as the centre and a convenient radius, draw an arc, cutting line *m* at R.

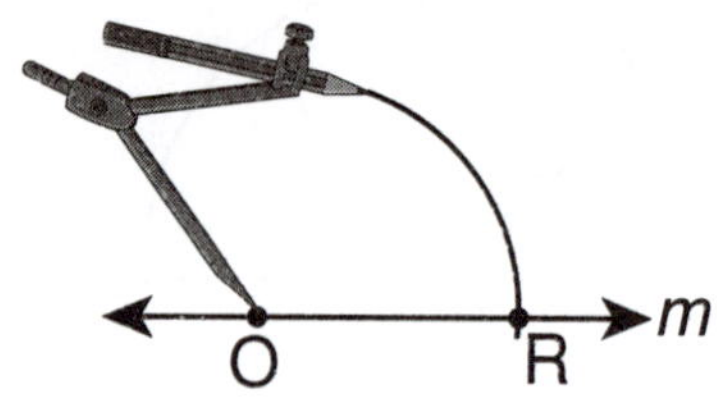

Step 3: With the same radius and R as the centre, draw another arc, cutting the previous arc at U.

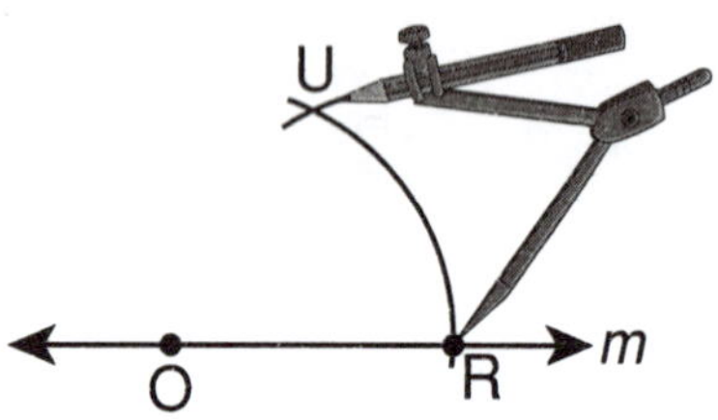

Step 4: Join points U and O and extend it to form ray OU. We get ∠UOR = 60°.

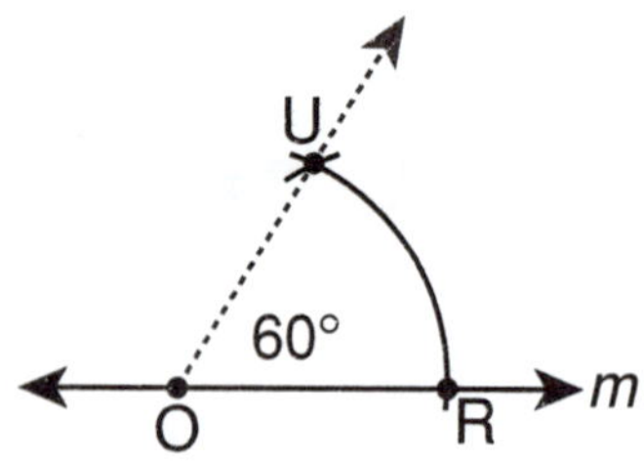

We can verify the above construction by measuring the angle using a protractor.

2. Constructing an angle of measure 30°

To construct a 30° angle, first construct an angle of 60° and then bisect the constructed angle to get two angles measuring 30° each.

Step 1: Construct an angle ∠PQR = 60° using the method described above.

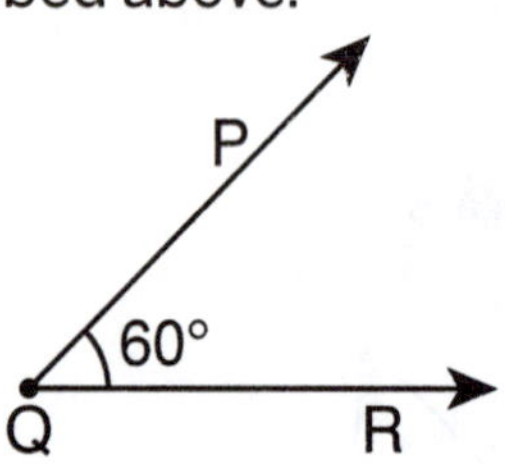

Step 2: Construct the angle bisector PS of ∠PQR.

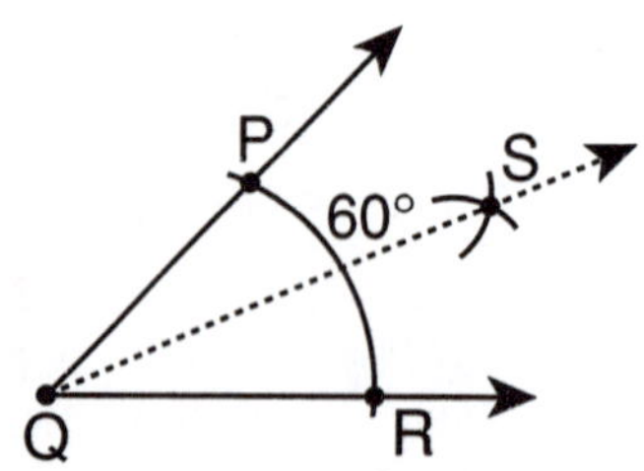

Step 3: ∠PQS = ∠SQR = 30°, which is the required angle.

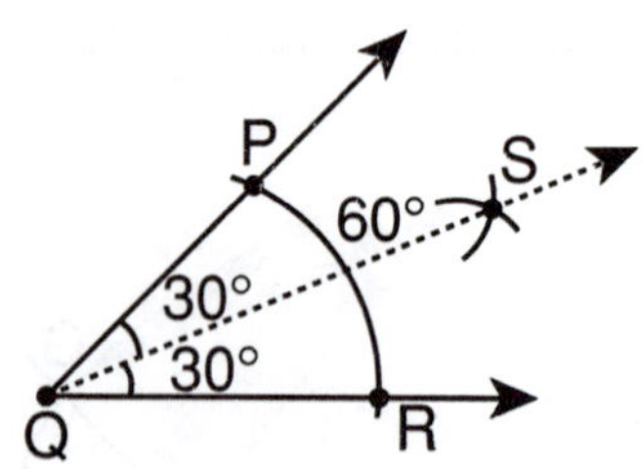

We can verify the above construction by measuring the angle using a protractor.

3. Constructing an angle of measure 120°

Step 1: Draw a line *m* and mark a point O on it.

Step 2: With O as the centre and any convenient radius, draw an arc (nearly a semicircle) that cuts the line *m* at x.

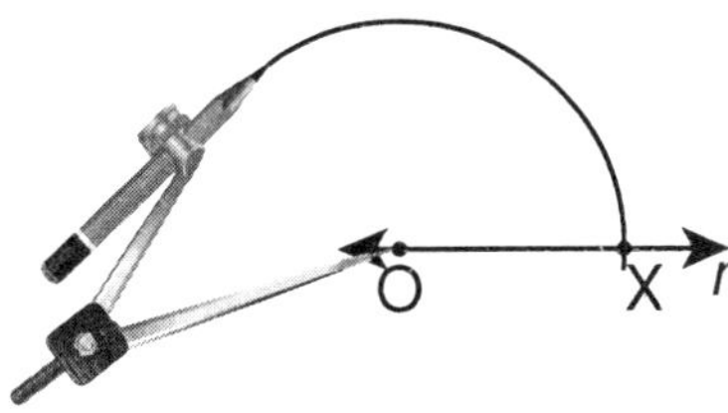

Step 3: With the same radius and x as the centre, draw an arc cutting the previous arc at Y.

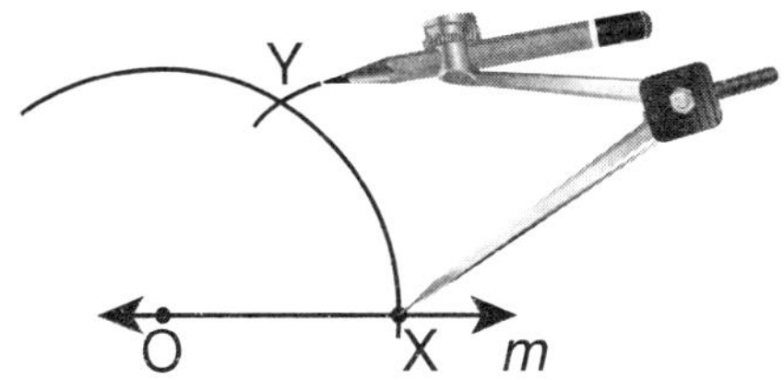

Step 4: With the same radius and Y as the centre, draw another arc cutting the first arc at Z.

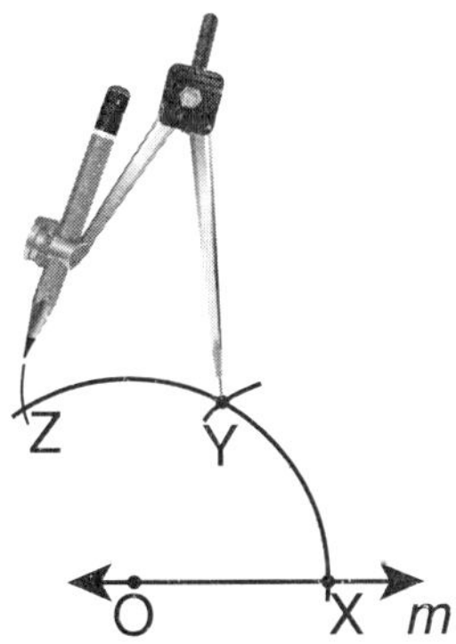

Step 5: Join O and Z and extend it to form ray OZ. ∠ZOX = 120° is the required angle.

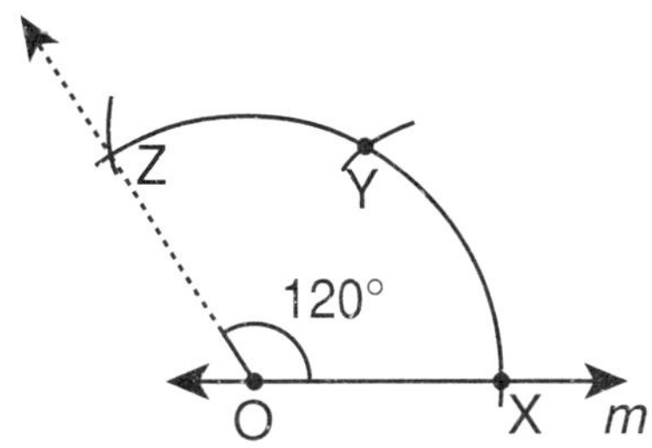

We can verify the above construction by measuring the angle using a protractor.

4. Constructing an angle of measure 90°

Step 1: Draw a line *m* and mark a point S on it.

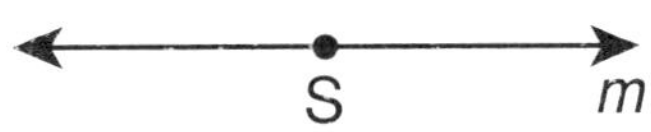

Step 2: With S as the centre and any convenient radius, draw an arc intersecting line *m* at U and T.

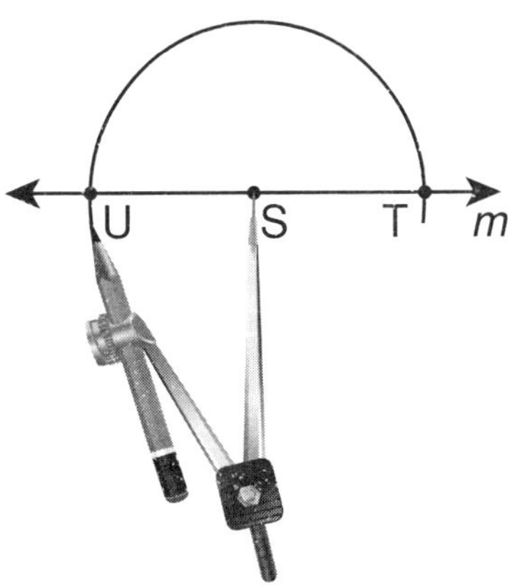

Step 3: With T as the centre and the same radius, draw an arc that cuts the previous arc at Y. With same radius and Y as the centre, draw another arc cutting the first arc at Z. Now with Y and Z as the centre and radius equal to more than half of YZ, cut the arcs and name the intersecting point as R. Join R and S. ∠RST is the required angle.

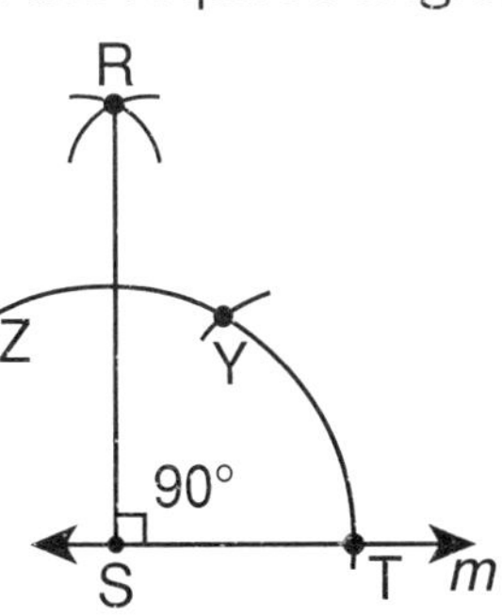

We can verify the above construction by measuring the angle using a protractor.

5. Constructing an angle of measure 45°

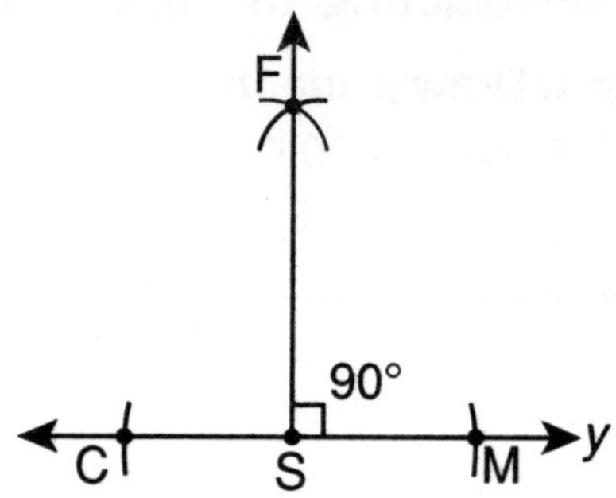

45° is exactly between 0° and 90°. So, we draw one arc from 0° position on the semicircle and the other arc from 90° position on the semi-circle.

We bisect 90° i.e. divide it into two equal halves.

Step 1: Construct an angle ∠FSM = 90° using the method described above.

Step 2: Construct the angle bisector ST of ∠FSM.

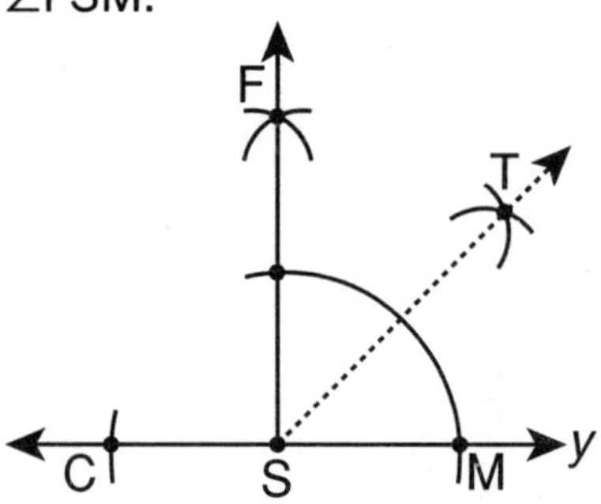

Step 3: We get ∠FST= ∠TSM = 45°

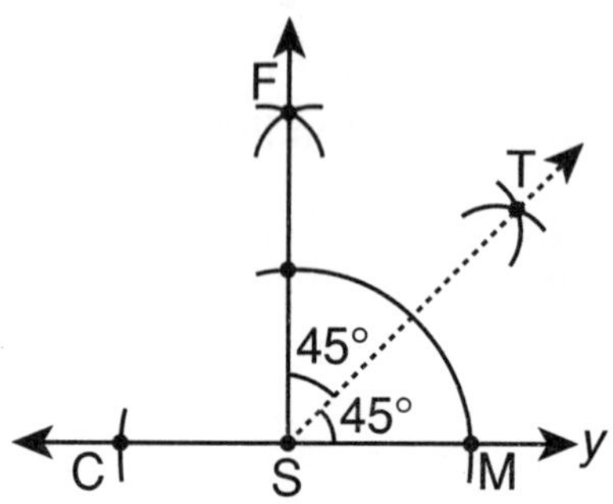

We can verify the above construction by measuring the angle using a protractor.

6. Constructing an angle of measure 105°

105° is exactly between 90° and 120°. So, we draw one arc from 90° position on the semicircle and the other arc from 120° position on the semi-circle.

Step 1: Draw a line *p* and mark a point O on it.

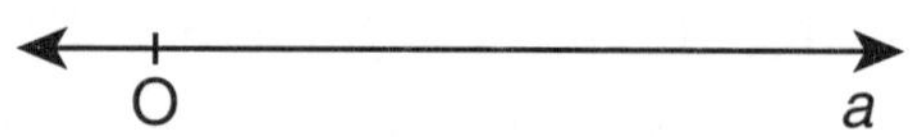

Step 2: Construct angles 90° and 120° using the steps discussed above.

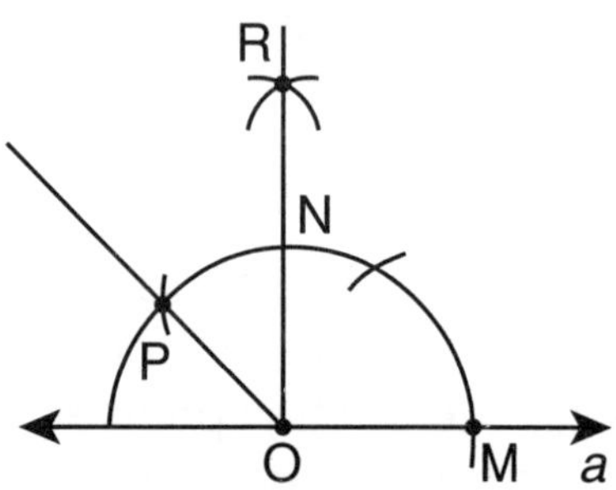

Step 3: Draw the angle bisector of ∠PON. We get ∠QOM = 105°, which is the required angle.

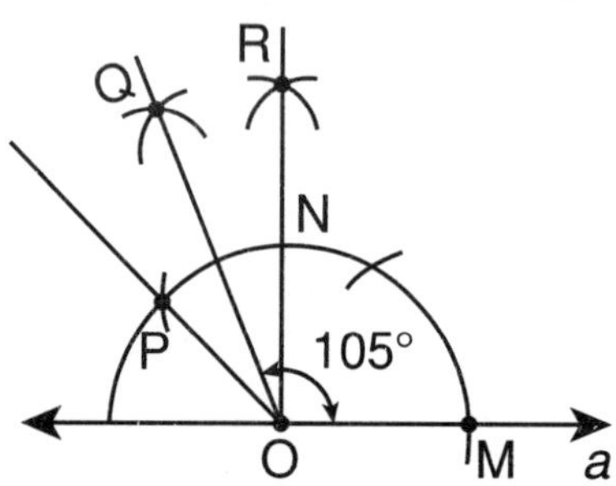

7. Constructing an angle of measure 135°

135° is exactly between 90° and 180°. So, we draw one arc from 90° position on the semicircle and the other arc from 180° position on the semi-circle.

135° is drawn on the left of 90° in the same way as we draw 45° to the right of 90°.

Step 1: Draw a line *m* and mark a point S on it.

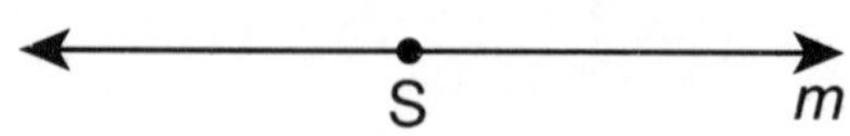

Step 2: Construct a 90° angle following the steps discussed above.

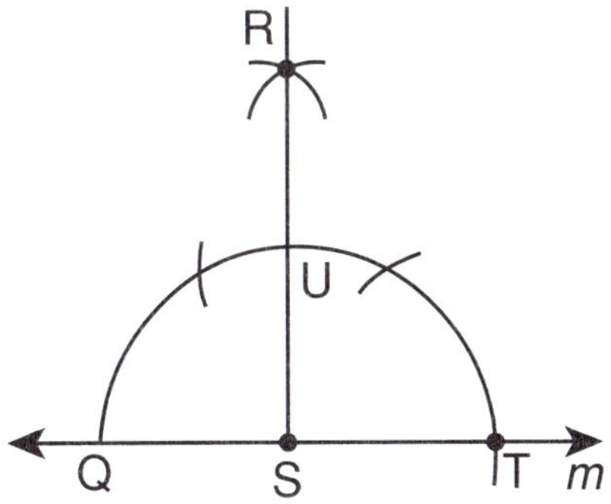

Step 3: Now bisect ∠QSU and mark the point of intersection of the arc as P. Therefore, ∠TSP 135° is the required angle.

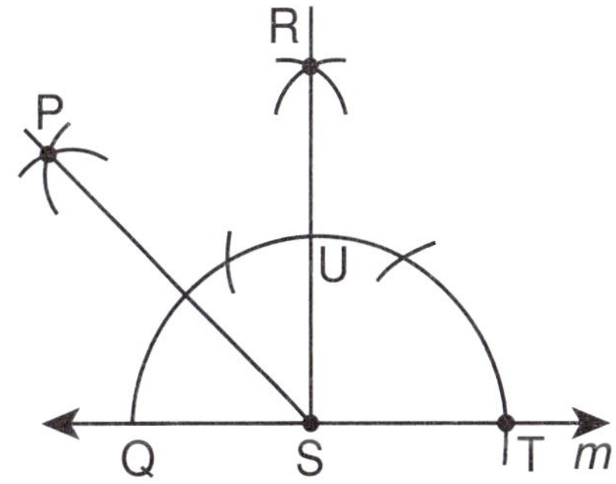

Construction of Special Angles Using Set Squares

To construct angles measuring 30°, 45°, 60°, 75°, 90° and 105° using set squares, draw a ray OA and place the set squares as shown below. Draw another ray OB to get the required angles.

1. 30°

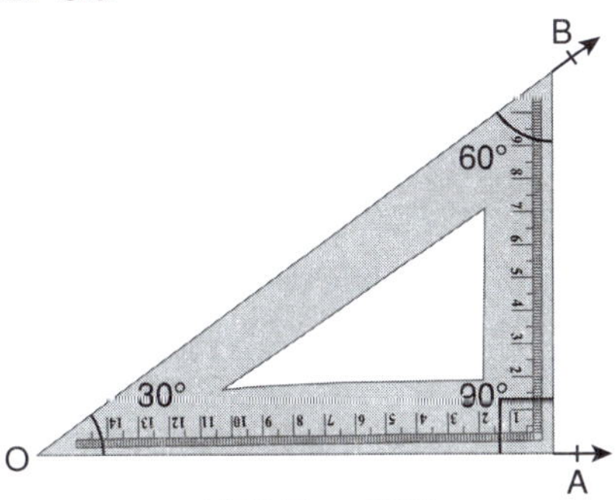

∠AOB = 30°

2. 45°

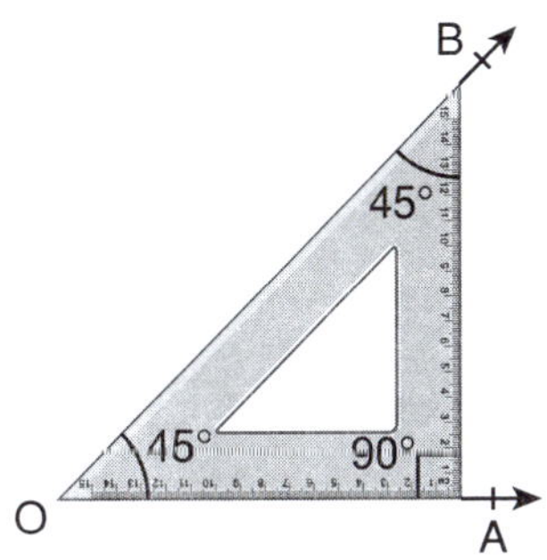

∠AOB = 45°

3. 60°

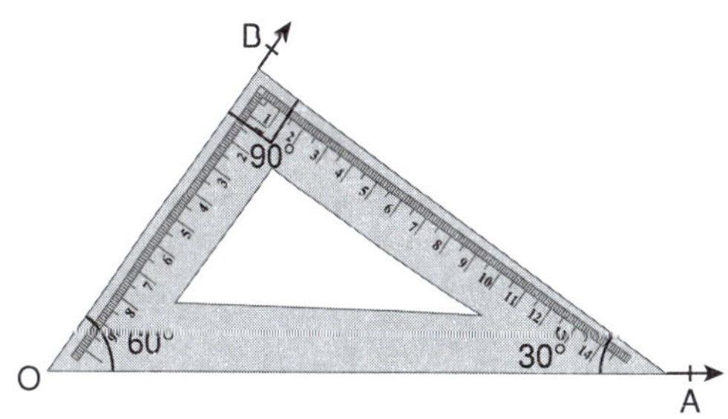

∠AOB = 60°

4. 75°

∠AOB = 75°

5. 90°

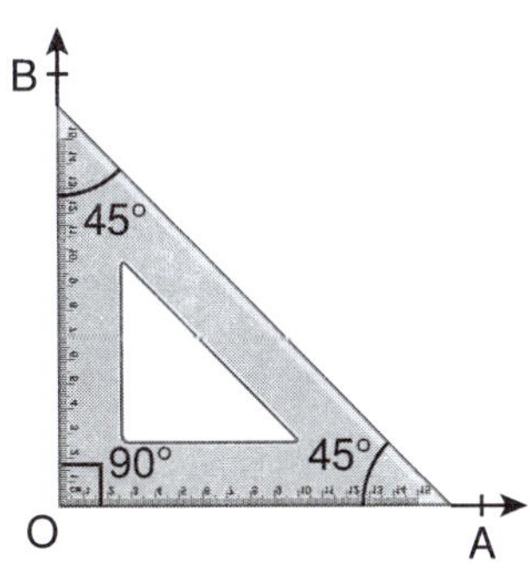

∠AOB = 90°

6. 105°

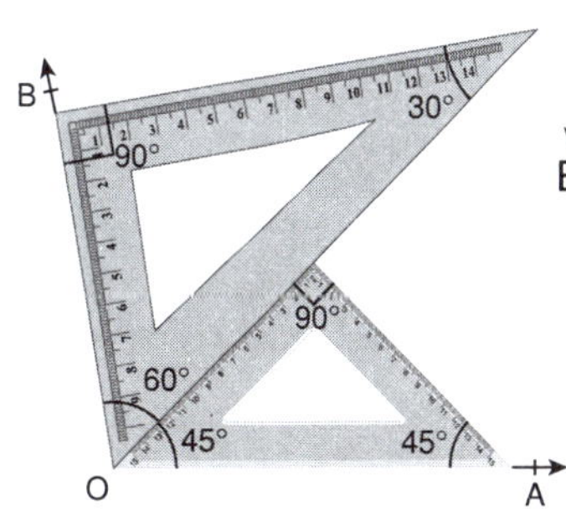

∠AOB = 105°

7. 135°

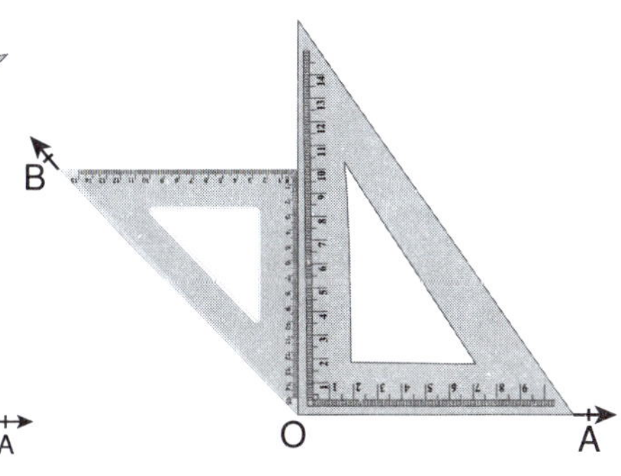

∠AOB = 135°

Summary

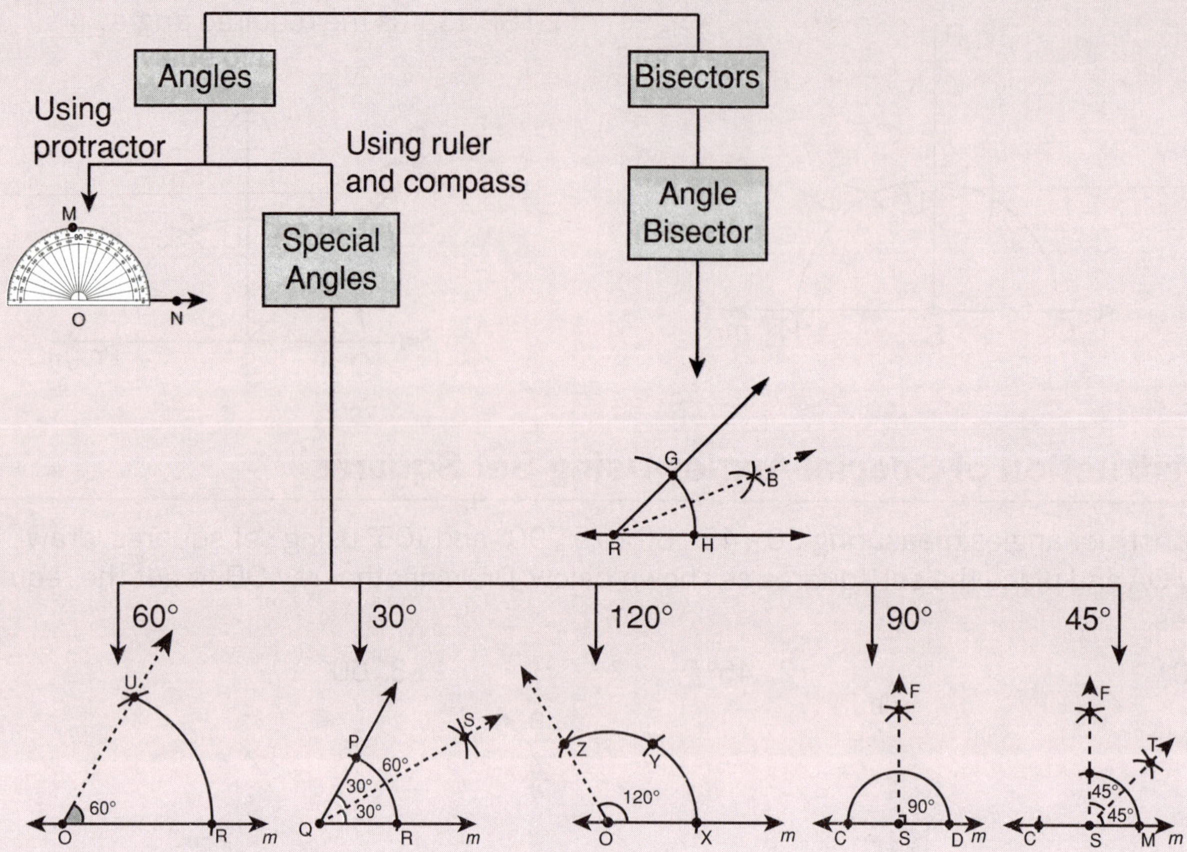
Angles
Bisectors
Using protractor
Using ruler and compass
Special Angles
Angle Bisector
60°
30°
120°
90°
45°

Revision Exercise

1. **Draw the following angles using a protractor and then bisect the angles.**

   a. 45° b. 80° c. 150° d. 125°

2. Construct angles measuring 90° and 30° using compass and ruler. Write the steps of construction.

3. Construct angles measuring 105° and 135° using compass and ruler. Write the steps of construction.

   (Hint: 105° = 90° + half of 30° and 135° = 90° + 45°)

4. Draw $\angle XYZ$ of your choice and then draw $\angle XYZ = \angle ABC$ using a ruler and a compass.

5. Construct angles measuring 60°, 90° and 120° using ruler and compass, and bisect the constructed angles.

6. **Choose the correct answers.**

   a. A rectangular geometrical instrument having graduated edges is called a

      i. divider ii. ruler iii. compass iv. set square

   b. How many scales does a protractor have?

      i. 1 ii. No Scale iii. 2 iv. 3

For the Curious Mind

Is it possible to construct an angle of 280° using a protractor? If yes, show your construction with steps.

UNIT 4

Triangles

20

What I shall learn

- To learn about triangles and their elements
- To classify triangles based on their sides and angles
- To list the properties of triangles
- To construct triangles using SSS, SAS and ASA criteria

Let's Get Started

Observe the following figures.

All the above figures are simple closed figures. The first two are closed curves, whereas the remaining figures are closed figures bounded by line segments.

A simple closed figure bounded by line segments is called a **polygon**. The line segments by which a polygon is bounded are called its sides.

We name a polygon according to its number of sides.

Triangle

A polygon with three sides is called a **triangle**. In other words, a triangle is a simple closed figure made up of three line segments.

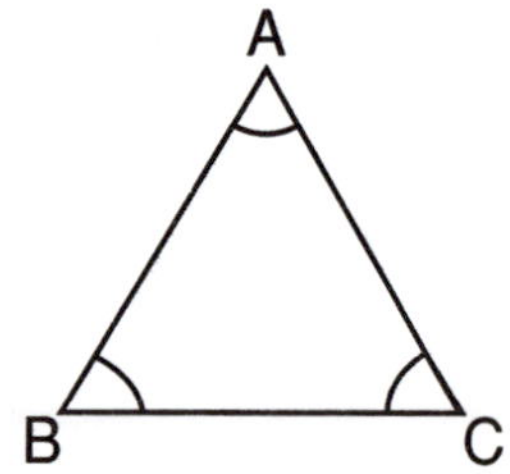

Elements of a Triangle

Sides: The line segments $\overline{AB}$, $\overline{BC}$ and $\overline{CA}$, which form the triangle are known as the three sides of the triangle ABC. Triangle ABC is denoted as ΔABC.

Angles: The sides $\overline{AB}$ and $\overline{BC}$ form $\angle$ABC. This angle can also be written as $\angle$CBA or $\angle$B.

The three sides and the three angles of a triangle are together known as the **six elements** of the triangle.

Vertex: The point where any two sides of a triangle meet is called the vertex. The plural of 'vertex' is 'vertices'. The points A, B and C are the three vertices of ΔABC.

Try These!

Identify the other angles of ΔABC.

In a triangle, no two sides are parallel (because they intersect each other). Also, the vertices of a triangle form a set of three non-collinear points.

Observe the given triangles and complete the table below. One has been done for you.

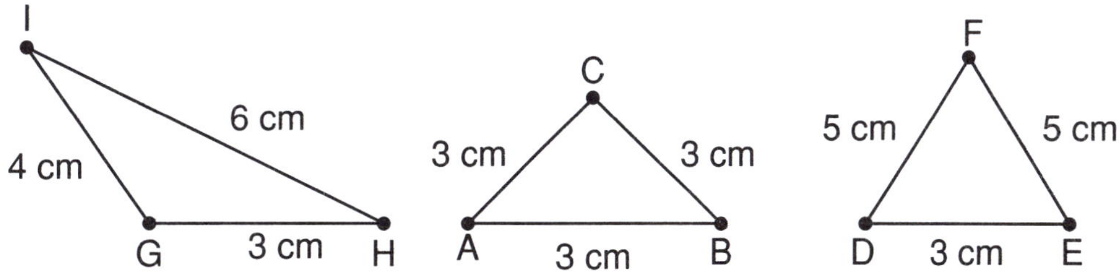

Name of the triangle	Length of a side	Sum of the lengths of the other two sides	Condition	Difference between the lengths of the other two sides	Condition
ΔGHI	$\overline{GH} = 3$ cm	$\overline{HI} + \overline{IG} = 6 + 4 = 10$	$\overline{HI} + \overline{IG} > \overline{GH}$	$\overline{HI} - \overline{IG} = 6 - 4 = 2$	$\overline{HI} - \overline{IG} < \overline{GH}$
	$\overline{HI} = 6$ cm	$\overline{IG} + \overline{GH} = 4 + 3 = 7$	$\overline{IG} + \overline{GH} > \overline{HI}$	$\overline{IG} - \overline{GH} = 4 - 3 = 1$	$\overline{IG} - \overline{GH} < \overline{HI}$
	$\overline{IG} = 4$ cm	$\overline{HI} + \overline{GH} = 6 + 3 = 9$	$\overline{HI} + \overline{GH} > \overline{IG}$	$\overline{HI} - \overline{GH} = 6 - 3 = 3$	$\overline{HI} - \overline{GH} < \overline{IG}$
ΔABC	$\overline{AB}$ = ____	$\overline{BC} + \overline{CA}$ = ____	$\overline{BC} + \overline{CA}$ __ $\overline{AB}$	$\overline{BC} - \overline{CA}$ = ____	$\overline{BC} - \overline{CA}$ __ $\overline{AB}$
	$\overline{BC}$ = ____	$\overline{AB} + \overline{CA}$ = ____	$\overline{AB} + \overline{CA}$ __ $\overline{BC}$	$\overline{AB} - \overline{CA}$ = ____	$\overline{AB} - \overline{CA}$ __ $\overline{BC}$
	$\overline{CA}$ = ____	$\overline{BC} + \overline{AB}$ = ____	$\overline{BC} + \overline{\Lambda B}$ __ $\overline{CA}$	$\overline{BC} - \overline{AB}$ = ____	$\overline{BC} - \overline{AB}$ __ $\overline{CA}$
ΔDEF	$\overline{DE}$ = ____	$\overline{EF} + \overline{FD}$ = ____	$\overline{EF} + \overline{FD}$ __ $\overline{DE}$	$\overline{EF} - \overline{FD}$ = ____	$\overline{EF} - \overline{FD}$ __ $\overline{DE}$
	$\overline{EF}$ = ____	$\overline{FD} + \overline{DE}$ = ____	$\overline{FD} + \overline{DE}$ __ $\overline{EF}$	$\overline{FD} - \overline{DE}$ = ____	$\overline{FD} - \overline{DE}$ __ $\overline{EF}$
	$\overline{FD}$ = ____	$\overline{EF} + \overline{DE}$ = ____	$\overline{EF} + \overline{DE}$ $\overline{FD}$	$\overline{EF} - \overline{DE}$ = ____	$\overline{EF} - \overline{DE}$ __ $\overline{FD}$

We can observe that **the sum of the lengths of any two sides of a triangle is greater than the length of the third side**. Also, **the difference between the lengths of any two sides of a triangle is less than the length of the third side**.

Interior and Exterior of a Triangle

The region within the boundary of a triangle is known as the **interior region**. The region outside the boundary of a triangle is known as the **exterior region**.

In the figure, A, B and C are in the interior region, K, L and M are in the exterior region, and P, Q and R are on the boundary of ΔXYZ. When we say ΔXYZ, it refers only to the boundary of the triangle and not its interior.

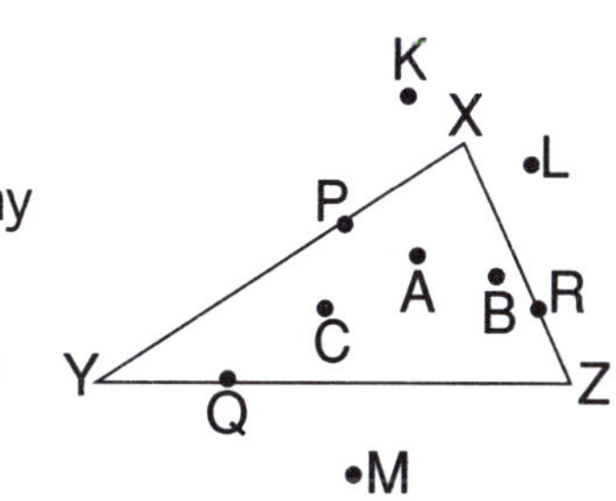

The interior region along with the boundary is known as the **triangular region**.

Classification of Triangles

Triangles can be classified into different types based on their sides and angles.

Classification Based on Sides

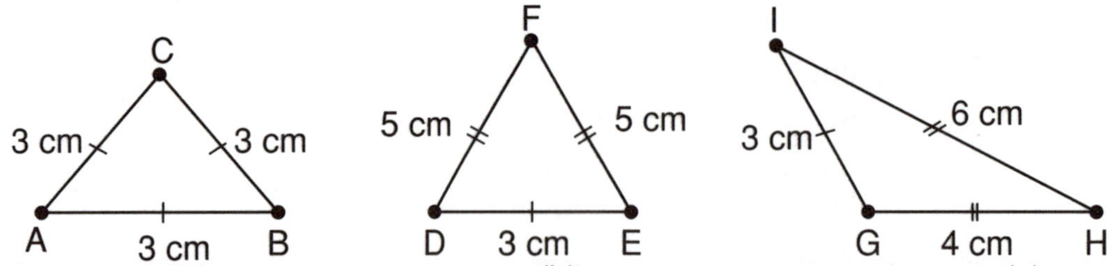

(a) (b) (c)

A triangle in which all sides are equal (Figure a) is known as an **equilateral triangle**.

A triangle in which two sides are equal (Figure b) is known as an **isosceles triangle**.

A triangle in which all sides are of different lengths (Figure c) is known as a **scalene triangle**.

Classification Based on Angles

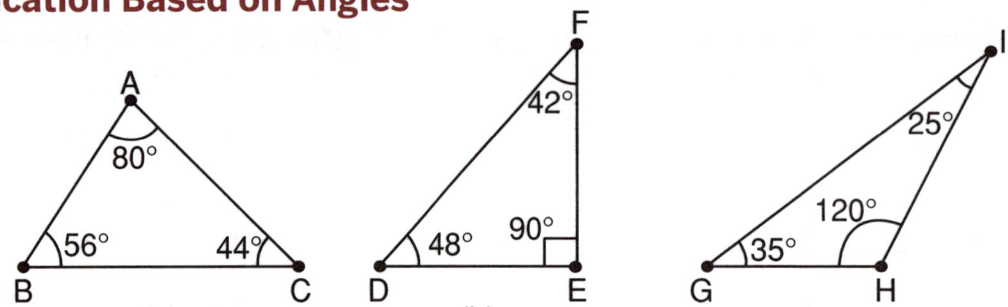

(a) (b) (c)

A triangle in which all the angles are acute (< 90°) is known as an **acute-angled triangle**.

A triangle in which one angle is a right angle (= 90°) is known as a **right-angled triangle**.

A triangle in which one angle is an obtuse angle (> 90°) is known as an **obtuse-angled triangle**.

Note

In a right-angled triangle, the side opposite to the right angle is called the **hypotenuse**. Hypotenuse is the largest side of such a triangle. The two acute angles in a right-angled triangle are complementary.

Properties of Triangles

Observe that, **in an equilateral triangle, all the angles are equal to 60°**.

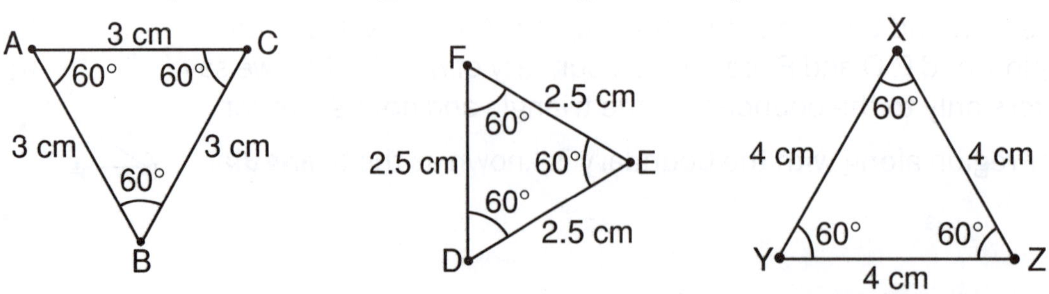

Now, observe the given isosceles triangle ABC.

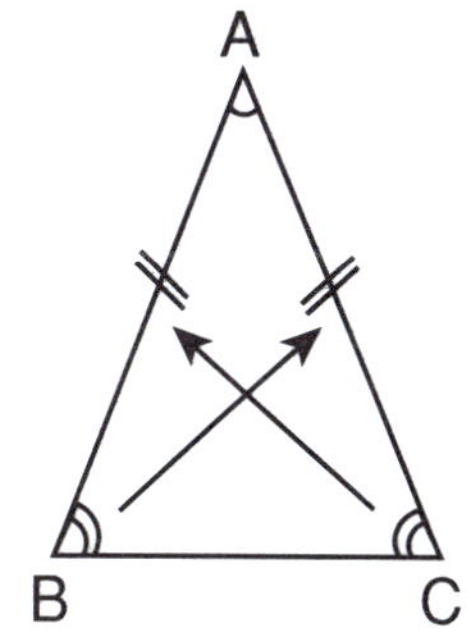

Here, the sides $\overline{AB}$ and $\overline{CA}$ are equal in length and side $\overline{BC}$ is the base. $\angle A$ is the vertex angle formed by the line segments $\overline{AB}$ and $\overline{CA}$. It is opposite to $\overline{BC}$. $\angle B$ and $\angle C$ are the base angles. $\angle B$ is opposite to $\overline{CA}$ and $\angle C$ is opposite to $\overline{AB}$.

Given below are a few isosceles triangles and scalene triangles. Measure the angles in each case and mark the angles that are equal. You will find that **in an isosceles triangle, the angles opposite to the equal sides are equal and in a scalene triangle, none of the angles are equal**.

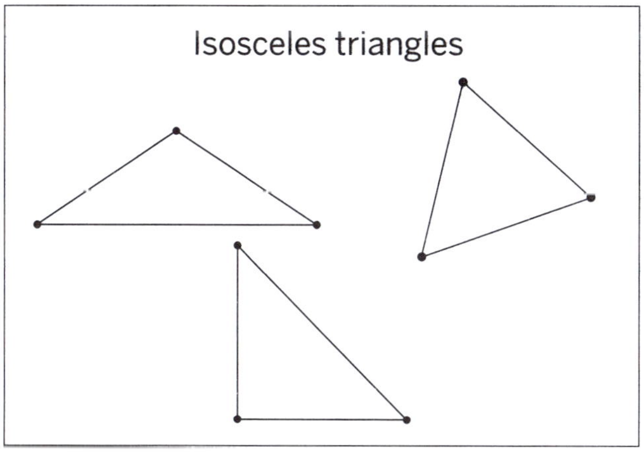

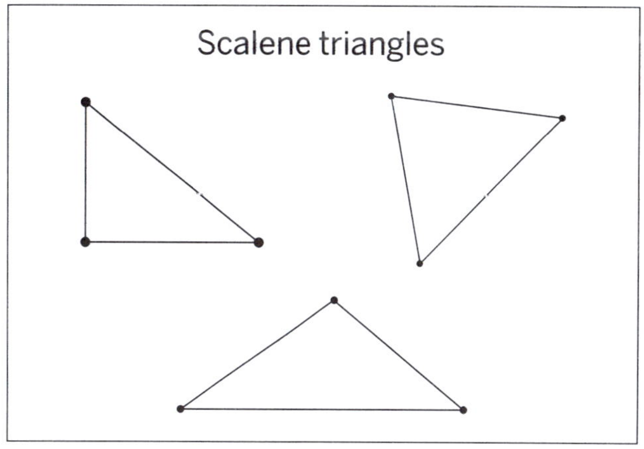

Exterior Angle of a Triangle

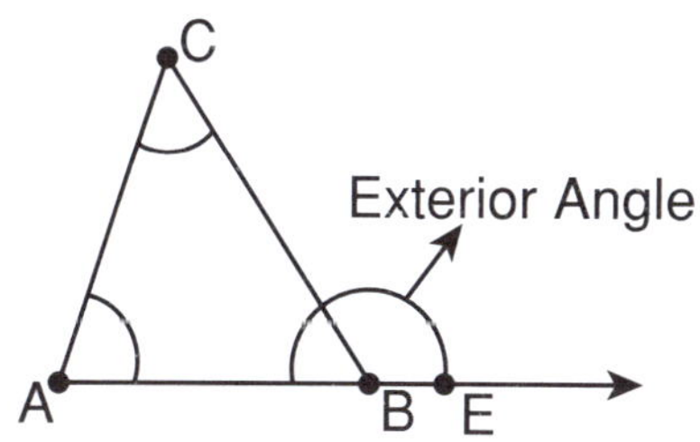

Consider a triangle ABC. We know that $\angle A$, $\angle CBA$ and $\angle C$ are the interior angles of the triangle. Let us extend the side AB towards E. The angle CBE formed between the lines BC and BE is known as the **exterior angle**. Observe that $\angle CBE$ forms a linear pair with the interior angle $\angle CBA$.

Thus, **an exterior angle of a triangle forms a linear pair with the corresponding adjacent interior angle of the triangle**, that is, $\angle CBE + \angle CBA = 180°$. $\angle A$ and $\angle C$ are the interior angles opposite to $\angle CBE$. Similarly, we can extend the other sides and find five more exterior angles. Find them and write them in your notebook.

Angle Sum Property of a Triangle

Take a sheet of paper and draw three different triangles—an acute, an obtuse and a right-angled triangle. Mark the interior angles for all the triangles. Cut all the interior angles of one triangle and arrange them to form a straight line as shown below. Repeat the same for the other triangles also.

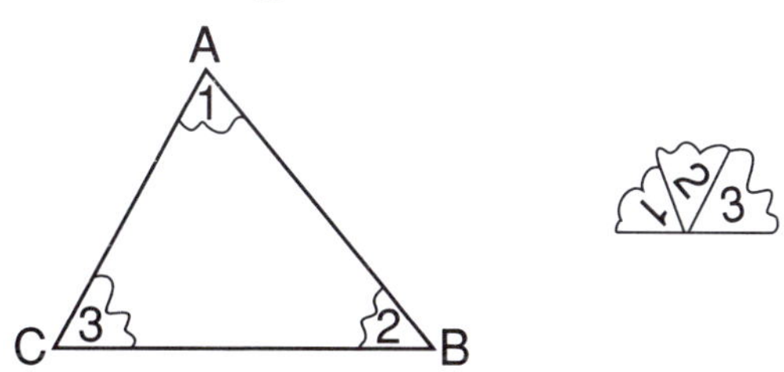

From the above activity, we can conclude that the sum of the interior angles of a triangle is 180°. This is known as the **angle sum property** of triangles.

Example 1: Find $\angle C$ in the given triangle ΔABC.

Mental Maths

In an isosceles ΔABC, if $\angle A = 100°$, then find the value of $\angle B$ ______.

We know that the sum of the interior angles of a triangle is 180°.

In ΔABC,

$\angle A + \angle B + \angle C = 180°$

$\angle C = 127°$

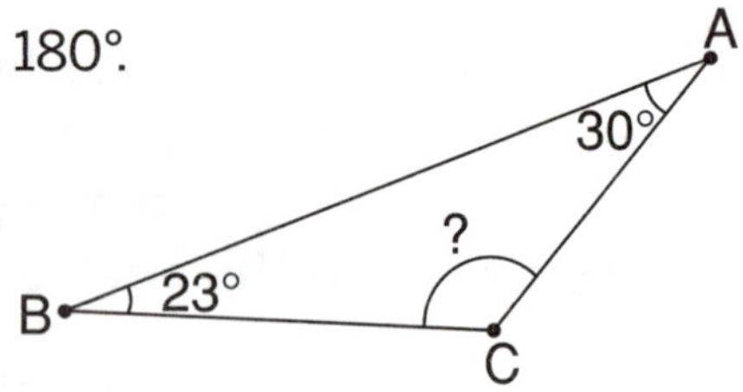

Example 2: If the angles in a triangle are in the ratio 1 : 2 : 3, then find the angles.

Let the angles of the triangle be x, $2x$ and $3x$.

$x + 2x + 3x = 180°$ (Angle sum property)

$6x = 180° \Rightarrow x = 30°$

Therefore, the angles of a triangle are $x = 30°$, $2x = 2(30°) = 60°$ and $3x = 3(30°) = 90°$.

Exterior Angle Property of a Triangle

Draw a triangle on a patty paper and mark its interior angles. Draw an exterior angle for a triangle by extending one of the sides. Cut the interior opposite angles and place them on the exterior angle. What do you observe?

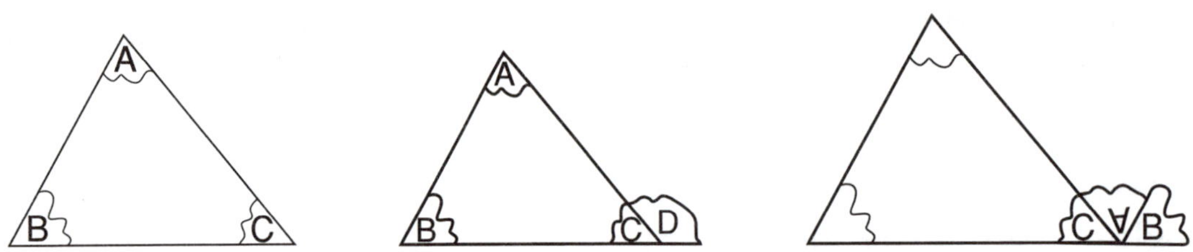

You can observe that the exterior angle of a triangle is equal to the sum of its interior opposite angles. This is known as the **exterior angle property** of a triangle. Let us prove this property.

Example 3: Find the measure of $\angle F$ in the given ΔDEF.

We know that the exterior angle of a triangle is equal to the sum of its interior opposite angles.

In ΔDEF, exterior angle $127° = \angle D + \angle F$

$\therefore \angle D + \angle F = 127°$

$59° + \angle F = 127°$

$\angle F = 127° - 59° = 68°$

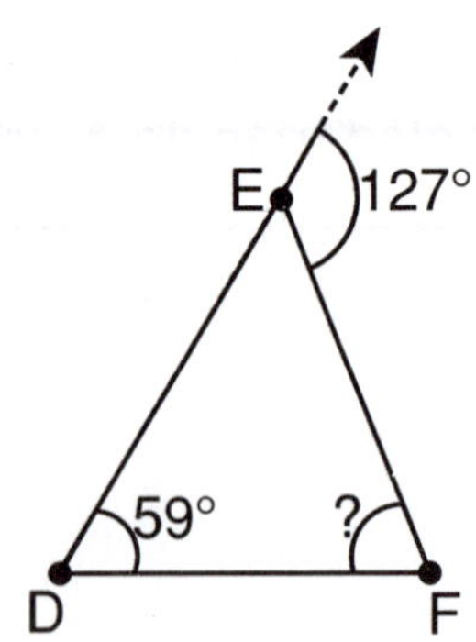

Example 4: An exterior angle of a triangle measures 117°. Its opposite interior angles measure $(2y^2 + 7)°$ and $(61 - y^2)°$. Find the measures of the three interior angles of the triangle.

$(2y^2 + 7°) + (61° - y^2) = 117°$ (Exterior angle property)

$\Rightarrow 2y^2 - y^2 + 7° + 61° = 117° \Rightarrow y^2 + 68° = 117° \Rightarrow y^2 = 117° - 68° = 49° \Rightarrow y = 7$

Two angles of a triangle are $(2y^2 + 7)° = 2 \times 7^2 + 7 = 2 \times 49 + 7 = 98 + 7 = 105°$ and $(61 - y^2)° = 61 - 7^2 = 61 - 49 = 12°$.

Third angle = $180° - (105° + 12°) = 180° - 117° = 63°$ (Angle sum property)

Thus, the three interior angles are 105°, 12° and 63°.

Exercise 20.1

1. **The measures of the sides of some triangles are given below. Based on the sides, state what kind of triangles they are.**

a. 12 cm, 8 cm, 8 cm b. 5 cm, 5 cm, 5 cm c. 3 cm, 4 cm, 5 cm

2. **The measures of the angles of some triangles are given below. Based on the angles, state what kind of triangles they are.**

a. 45°, 45°, 90° b. 50°, 60°, 70° c. 30°, 30°, 120°

3. **Which of the following are sets of interior angles of a triangle?**

a. 30°, 60°, 90° b. 40°, 60°, 70° c. 40°, 40°, 100° d. 40°, 60°, 100°

4. **Find the unknown angles specified below in each triangle.**

a.
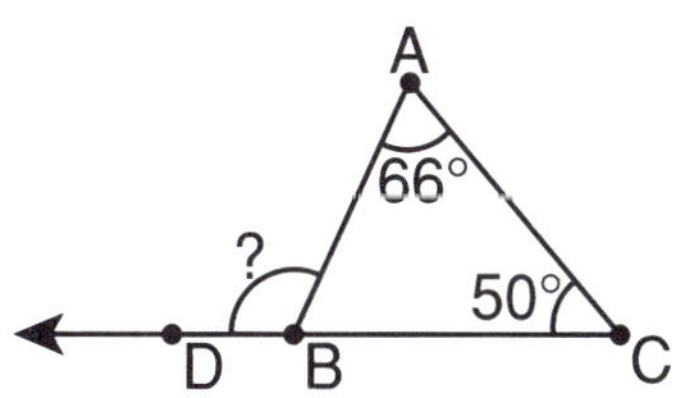

b.
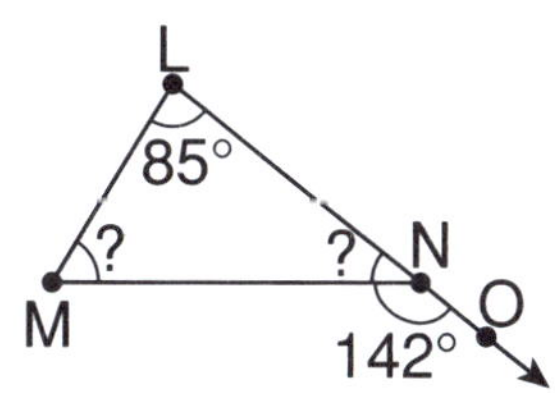

c.
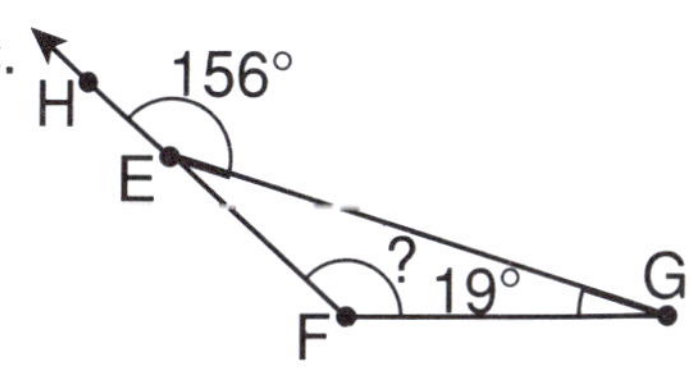

5. **Find the value of x and hence find all the angles of the following triangles.**

a.
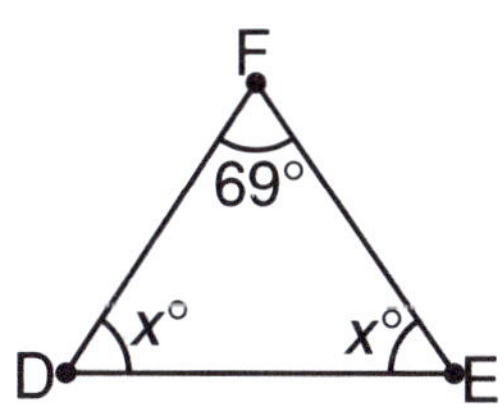

b.
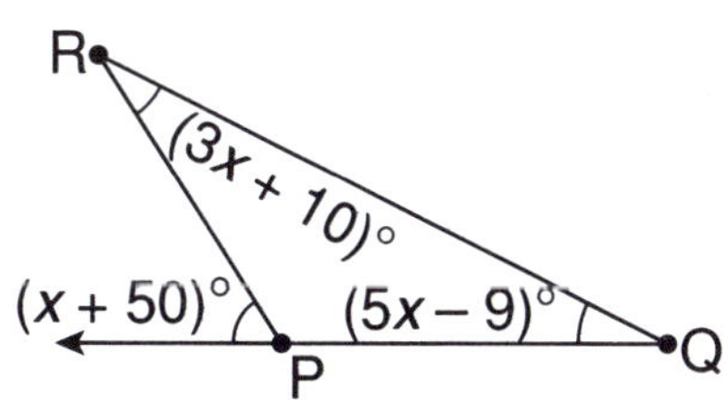

c.
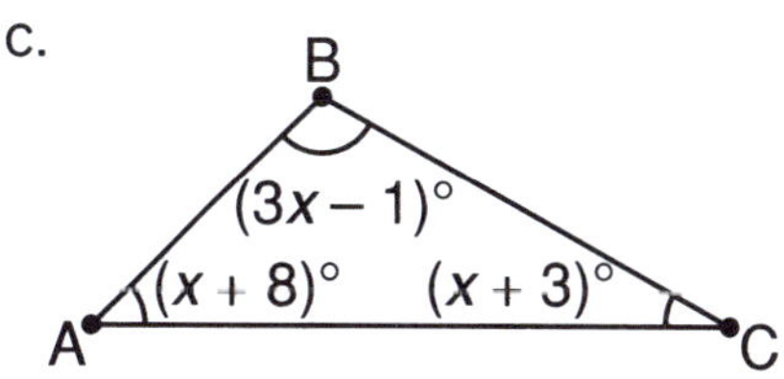

6. Find the interior angles of a triangle if they are in the ratios given below.

a. 1 : 3 : 1 b. 1 : 1 : 2 c. 2 : 2 : 2 d. 2 : 3 : 4

Construction of Triangles

Constructing a Triangle When Three Sides Are Given (SSS Construction)

With the help of an example, let us see how to construct a triangle using a ruler and a compass when the lengths of the three sides are known.

Example 5: Construct a triangle whose side lengths are 6 cm, 4 cm and 3 cm.

Hints and Tips

In SSS construction, it is convenient to start the construction by drawing the longest side first.

Step 1: Draw a rough sketch of the triangle.

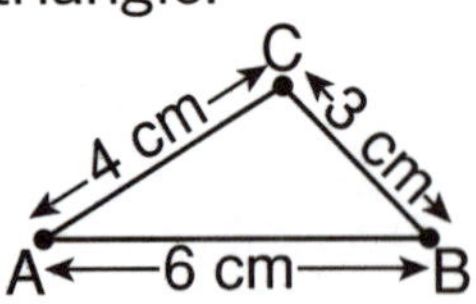

Step 2: Draw a line segment AB of length 6 cm.

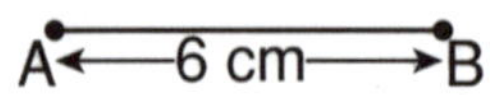

Step 3: With A as centre and 4 cm as radius, draw an arc on one side of AB.

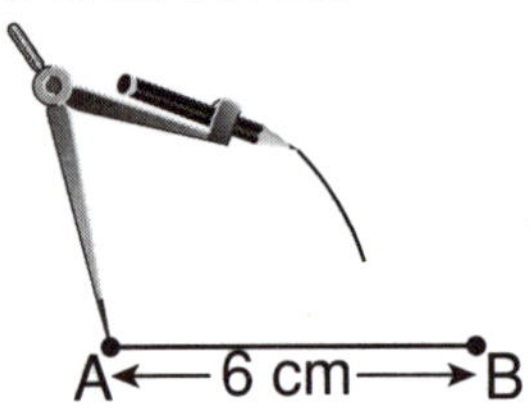

Step 4: With B as centre and 3 cm as radius, draw another arc cutting the previous arc at C.

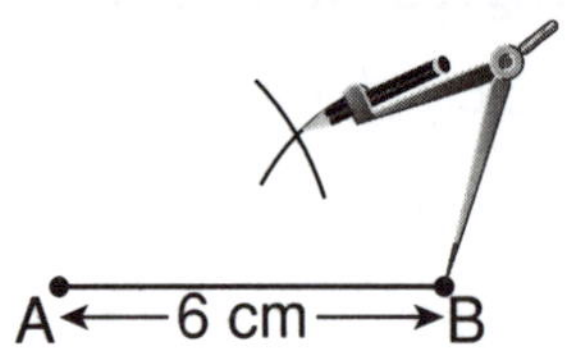

Step 5: Join A and C, and B and C to get the required triangle ABC.

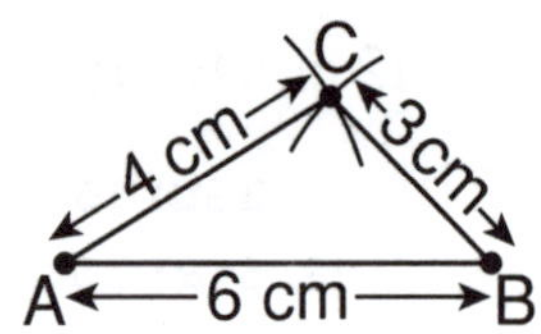

Constructing a Triangle When Two Sides and the Included Angle Are Given SAS Construction

Let us learn how to construct a triangle when the lengths of two of its sides and the angle between them are known.

Example 6: Construct a triangle ABC with AB = 5 cm, AC = 3 cm and ∠BAC = 60°.

Step 1: Draw a rough sketch of the triangle.

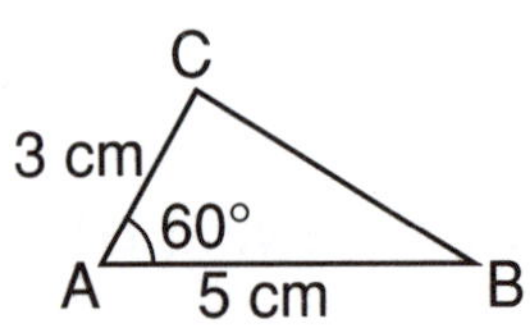

Step 2: Draw a line segment AB of length 5 cm.

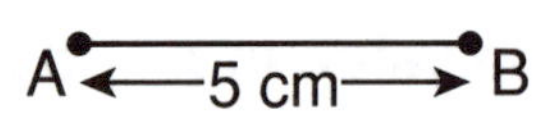

Step 3: Using a compass, draw a ray AX such that ∠XAB = 60°.

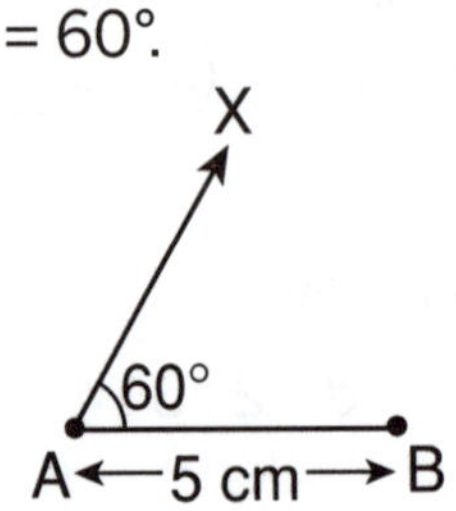

Step 4: With A as centre and 3 cm radius, draw an arc cutting ray AX at C.

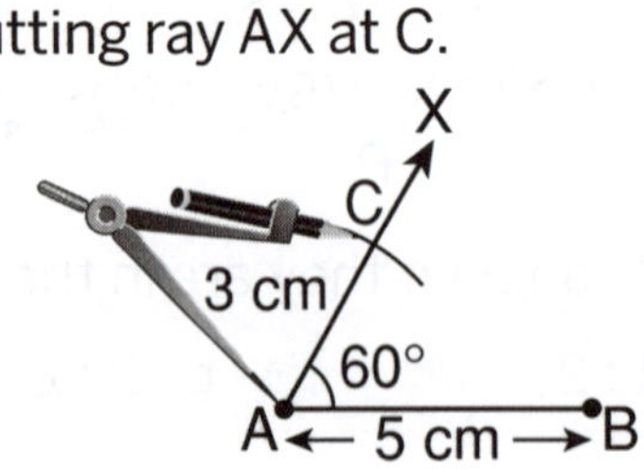

Step 5: Join B and C to get the required triangle ABC.

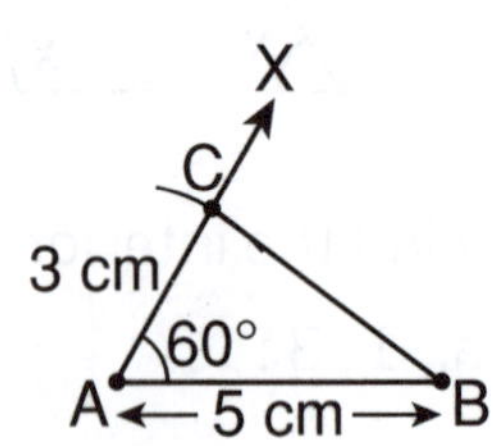

Note: Now, consider the following situation. A teacher asked the students to construct a triangle ABC with AB = 5 cm, AC = 4 cm and ∠B = 50°. Shrija and Latha have constructed their triangles as given below. Both of their constructions are correct even though their triangles are different. Two different triangles are possible with the same given measurements. Hence, if the angle given is not the included angle, then the triangles constructed will not be unique.

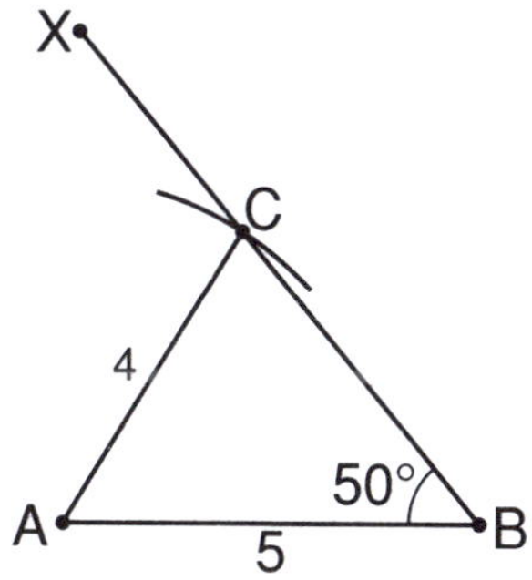

Shrija's Triangle

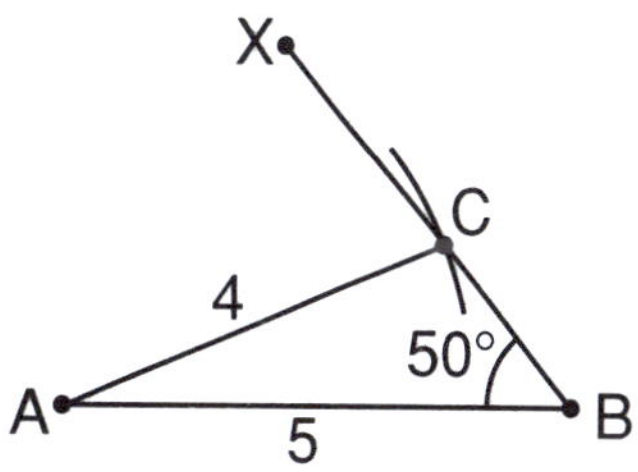

Latha's Triangle

Constructing a Triangle When Two Angles and the Included Side Are Given ASA Construction

Let us learn how to construct a triangle when the measure of two of its angles and the length of the side between them are known.

Example 7: Construct a triangle PQR with QR = 4 cm, ∠Q = 60° and ∠R = 70°.

Step 1: Draw a rough sketch of the triangle.

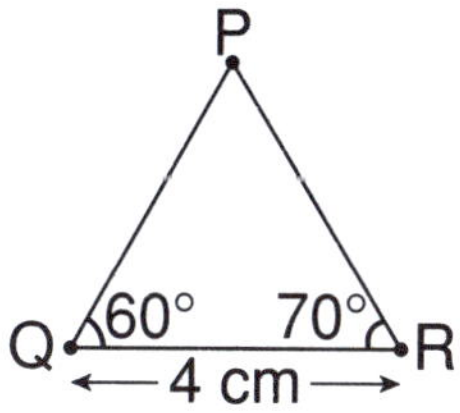

Step 2: Draw the line segment QR of length 4 cm.

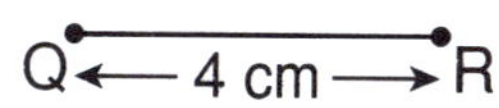

Step 3: Using a protractor, construct ∠Q of measure 60° at point Q.

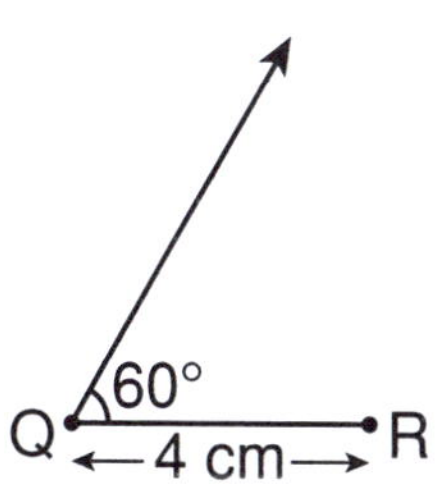

Step 4: Using a protractor, construct ∠R of measure 70° at point R.

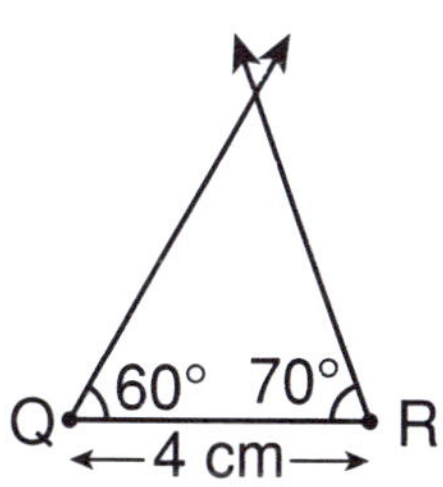

Step 5: The point of intersection is P. ΔPQR is the required triangle.

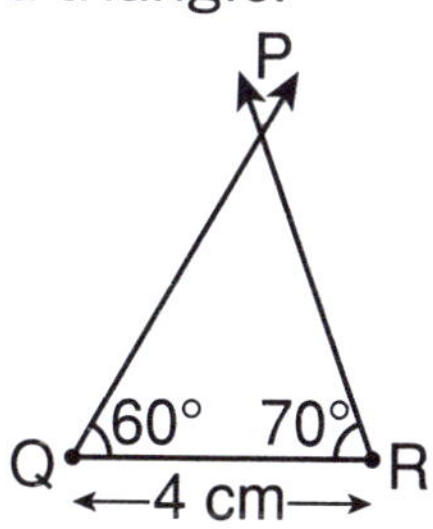

Note: We have seen that while constructing a triangle with two sides and one angle, the angle known must be an included angle, otherwise, the triangle constructed will not be unique. Is it true in case of ASA also? Should the known side be the included side? Can you draw a unique triangle with the following measurements? Try drawing it in your notebook.

Construct a ΔABC with AB = 5 cm, ∠A = 55° and ∠C = 45°. (Hint: Use angle sum property and find the third angle.)

Constructing an Isosceles Triangle

To construct an isosceles triangle, we require only two independent measurements since two sides and two opposite angles of an isosceles triangle are already equal.

Constructing an Equilateral Triangle

To construct an equilateral triangle, it is enough if we know the length of only one side of the triangle because all the sides are of equal length and all the angles are 60°.

Exercise 20.2

1. Construct a triangle DEF with DE = 6.3 cm, EF = 8.5 cm and DF = 9.8 cm.
2. Construct a triangle PQR with PQ = 5 cm, QR = 4 cm and $\angle Q = 110°$.
3. **Find whether unique triangles can be constructed with each of the following measurements. If yes, identify the criterion to be used and construct them in your notebooks.**
   a. AB = 7.5 cm, BC = 4.4 cm and CA = 2.8 cm
   b. Isosceles triangle with equal sides as 4 cm and included angle as 44°
   c. LM = 3.4 cm, MN = 4.2 cm and $\angle N = 50°$
4. **In triangle ABC, AB = 8 cm and BC = 7 cm. Construct the triangle if possible with each of the angles given below and Justify your answer?**
   a. $\angle A = 90°$ b. $\angle A = 61°$ c. $\angle B = 55°$
5. Construct ΔWIN with WI = 6.4 cm, $\angle W = 40°$ and $\angle I = 100°$. Classify this triangle based on its sides.

Summary

1. A triangle is a simple closed figure made up of three line segments.
2. The interior region of a triangle along with the boundary is known as the triangular region.
3.

Classification of Triangles

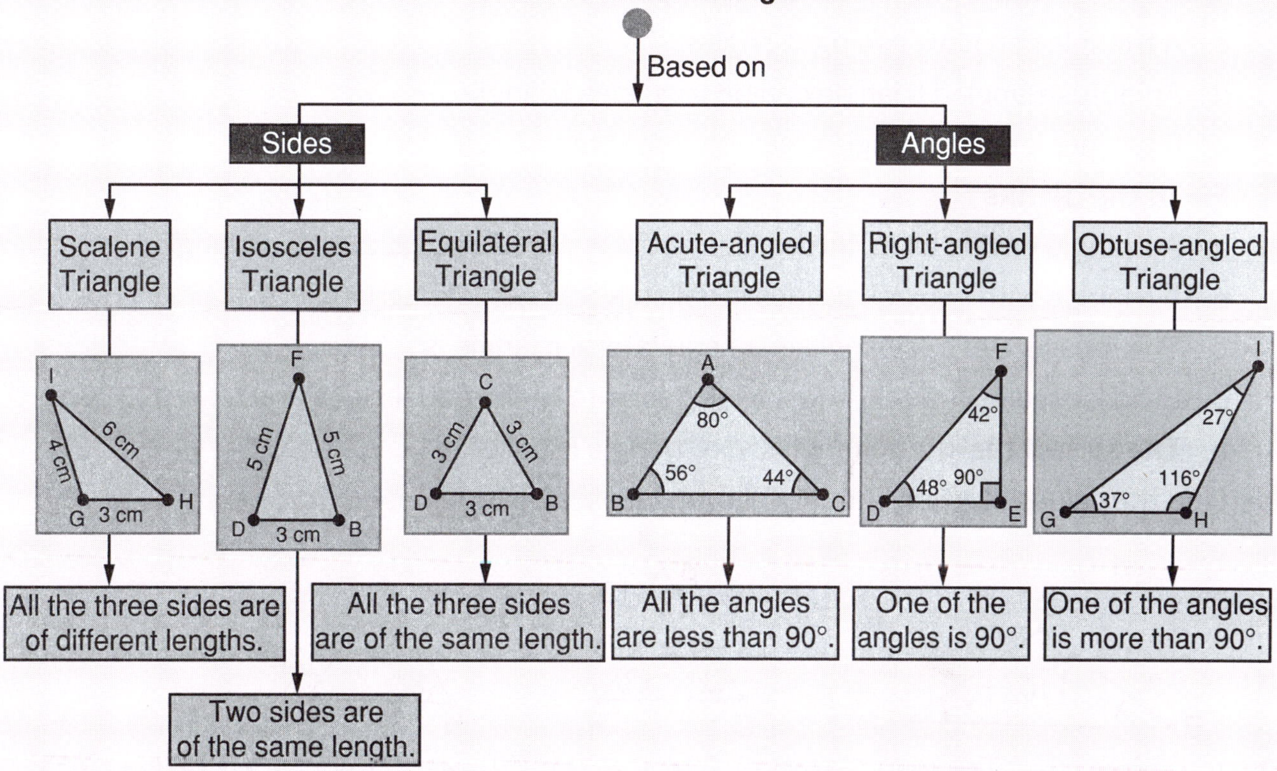

4. In an equilateral triangle, all the angles are equal to 60°. In an isosceles triangle, the angles opposite to the equal sides are equal. In a scalene triangle, none of the angles are equal.
5. An exterior angle of a triangle is an angle that forms a linear pair with one of the interior angles of the triangle.
6. The exterior angle of a triangle is equal to the sum of its opposite interior angles. This is known as exterior angle property of a triangle.
7. The sum of the interior angles of a triangle is 180°. This is called the angle sum property of a triangle.

Revision Exercise

1 **State whether the following statements are true or false. Justify your answers.**

a. Every equilateral triangle is an acute-angled triangle.

b. A triangle must have three acute angles.

c. A triangle can have two right angles.

d. An obtuse-angled triangle can be isosceles triangle.

e. If two angles of a triangle are complementary, it is a right triangle.

2 **Fill in the blanks**

a. A triangle having all its three sides equal is called an __________ triangle.

b. A triangle with two equal sides is called an __________ triangle.

c. The measure of each angle in an equilateral triangle is __________.

d. In an isosceles triangle, the angles opposite to the equal sides are __________.

e. The sum of the interior angles in a triangle is equal to __________.

3 Find the values of x and y in the following isosceles triangles.

a.

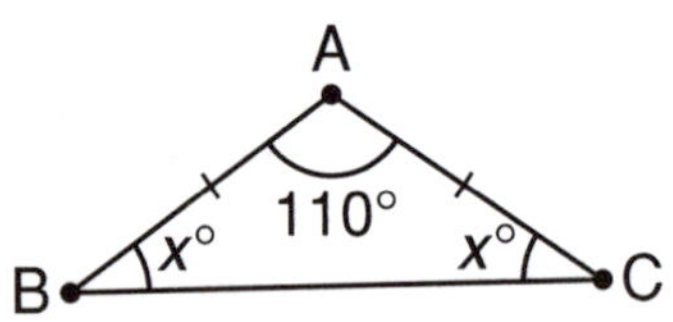

b.

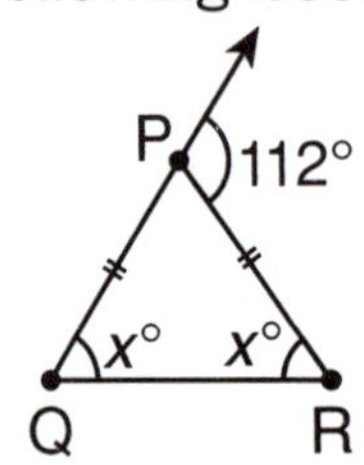

c.

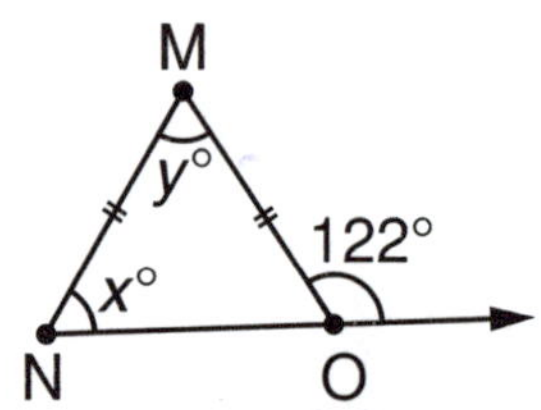

4 If the measures of the interior angles of a triangles are $(3x - 5)°$, $(x + 4)°$ and $(4x + 5)°$, find the angles.

5 Construct ΔABC with AB = 6 cm, AC = 8 cm and BC = 10 cm. Classify this triangle based on its angles.

6 Construct ΔPQR with PQ = 6.5 cm, QR = 6.5 cm and $\angle Q = 60°$. Classify this triangle based on its sides.

7 Construct ΔXYZ with YZ = 5 cm, $\angle X = 90°$ and $\angle Y = 45°$. Measure the other angle and the other sides of the triangle.

For the Curious Mind

Find x, y, z, $\angle CAD$ and $\angle A$ in the given figure.

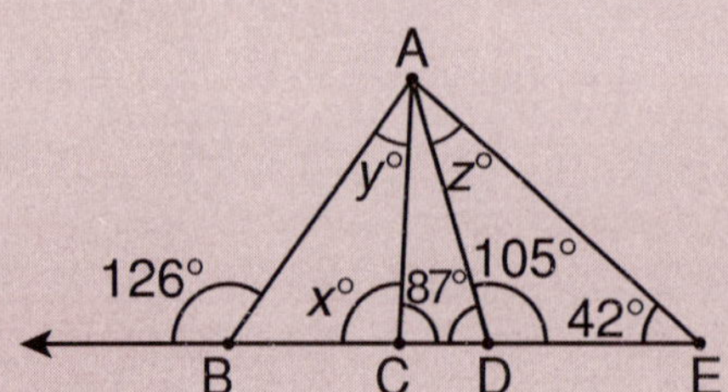

UNIT 4

Circles

21

Let's Get Started

Take a bangle, coin or lid of a jar and trace its boundary on a plain paper using a pencil. What do you observe?

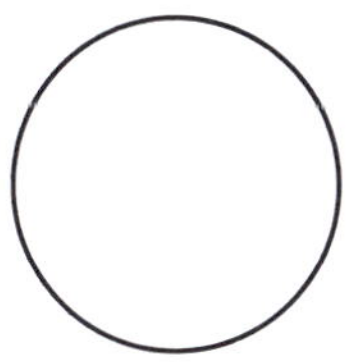

What I shall learn

- To learn about circle and terms related to it
- To learn about concentric circles

You will observe a closed curve as shown here. Such a curve is called a circle.

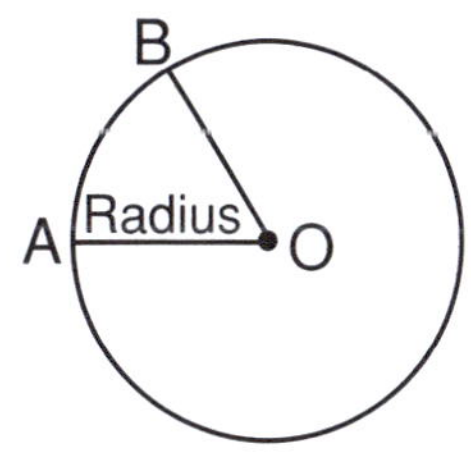

A **circle** is a simple closed curve formed on a plane by points that are at the same distance from a fixed point.

In the adjacent circle, the fixed point is O, which is the **centre** of the circle.

All points on the circle are equidistant from the centre and this distance is called the **radius** of the circle. Here, OA and OB are radii of the given circle.

Note

Among all shapes with the same perimeter, a circle has the maximum area.

The length of the curved line of a circle is called its **circumference**.

Interior and Exterior of a Circle

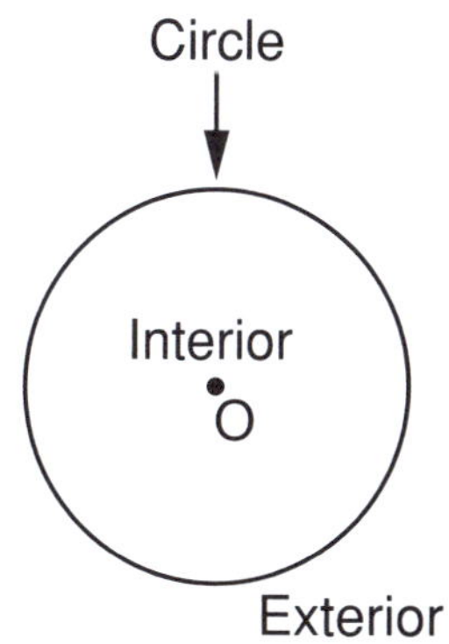

Let us consider a circle with centre O. The circle divides the plane into three parts.

1. The set of all the points that lie inside the circle is called the **interior** of the circle.
2. The set of all the points that lie on the circle form the circle itself.
3. The set of all the points that lie outside the circle is called the **exterior** of the circle.

Activity

Aim: To understand the interior and exterior of a circle

Materials required: Circles with different radii on white paper, ruler and pen/pencil (*Each paper should have minimum 3 circles*)

Activity:

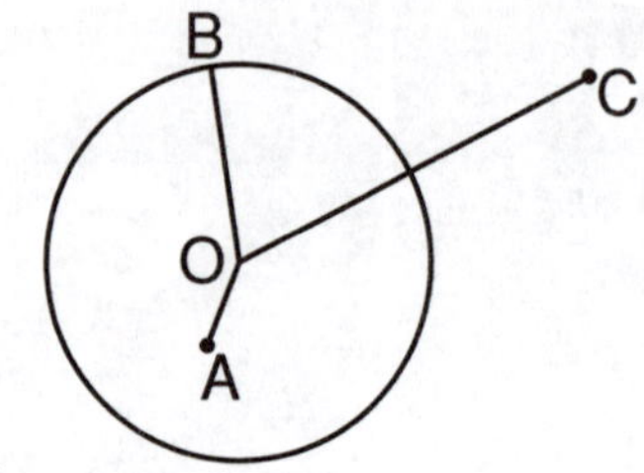

a. Arrange the students in groups and distribute the papers among them.
b. Each group should mark points in the interior, exterior and on the circle.
c. Ask them to measure the radius of the circle with the help of a ruler.
d. Also let them measure the distance from the centre to the points that are in the interior and those in the exterior of the circle.
e. Record the observations in the given table.

Radius = 5 cm
OA = 2 cm
OB = 5 cm
OC = 12 cm

For example, consider the circle given above.

Circle	Radius (cm)	Distance from the centre to the point on the circle (cm)	Distance from the centre to the point lying on the interior of the circle (cm)	Distance from the centre to the point lying on the exterior of the circle (cm)
1	5	5	2	12
2				
3				

Note

The set of points which lie either inside the circle or on the circle is known as the **circular region**.

Observations:

a. Distance from the centre to each point on the circle is always equal. This distance is the radius of the circle.
b. Distance from the centre to each point lying in the interior of the circle is less than the radius.
c. Distance from the centre to each point lying in the exterior of the circle is greater than the radius.

Example 1: Identify the points that lie in the interior, exterior and on the circle in the given figure.

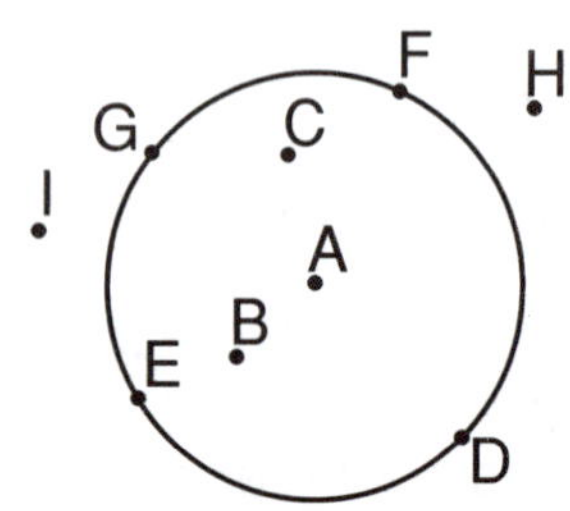

a. Points A, B and C lie in the interior of the circle.
b. Points D, E, F and G lie on the circle.
c. Points H and I lie in the exterior of the circle.

Terms Related to a Circle

Activity

Aim: To understand some terms related to a circle

Materials required: A circle with its centre drawn on a white paper, ruler and pen/pencil

Activity:

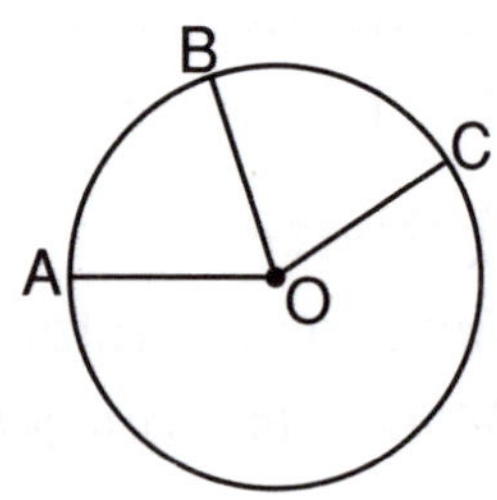

a. Draw 3–4 radii and measure them with a ruler.
b. Extend each radius to other end of the circle as shown. Each of these lines with its endpoints on the circumference of the circle is called a diameter.

c. Measure the lengths of all the radii drawn in the circle.

d. Note down the observations in the following table.

Radius (cm)	Diameter (cm)

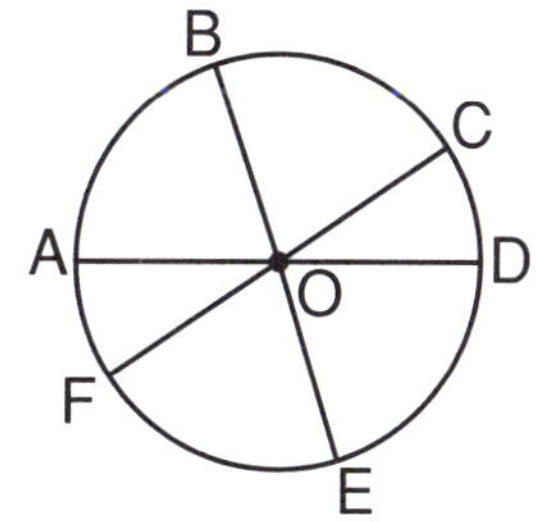

Observation: Diameter is always twice the radius.

Diameter

A line segment passing through the centre of a circle and having its endpoints on the circumference of the circle is called a **diameter** of the circle. It is always twice the radius of the given circle.

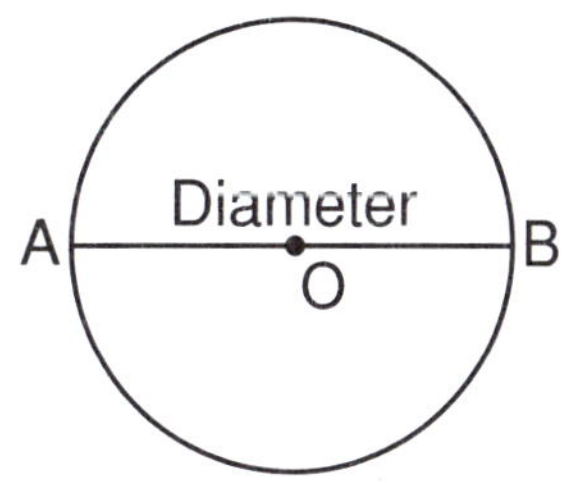

Diameter = 2 × Radius

Note

- An infinite number of diameters can be drawn in a circle.
- The intersection of two diameters is always at the centre of the circle.

AB is the diameter, and AO and OB are the radii of the given circle.

AB = AO + OB = AO + AO = 2AO = 2OB ($\because$ AO = OB)

Chord and Secant

Any line segment that has its endpoints on the circumeference of a circle is called a **chord**. AB is a chord in the adjacent circle.

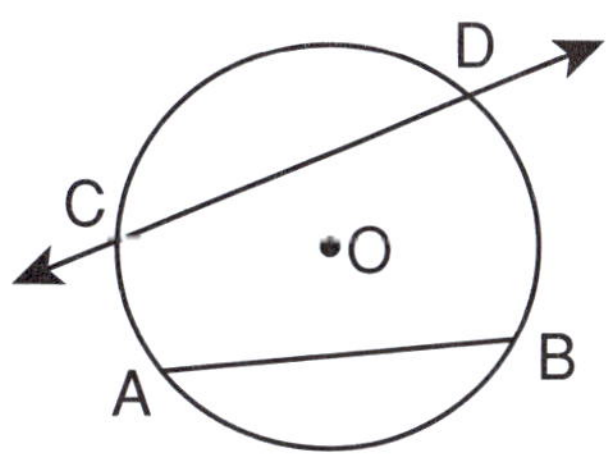

Note

Diameter is the largest chord of a circle.

A line passing through a circle and intersecting the circle at two points is called a **secant**. CD is a secant in the given circle.

Tangent

A line that touches a circle only at one point is known as a **tangent** of the circle. In the adjacent circle, *l* and *m* are the tangents touching the circle at points P and Q respectively.

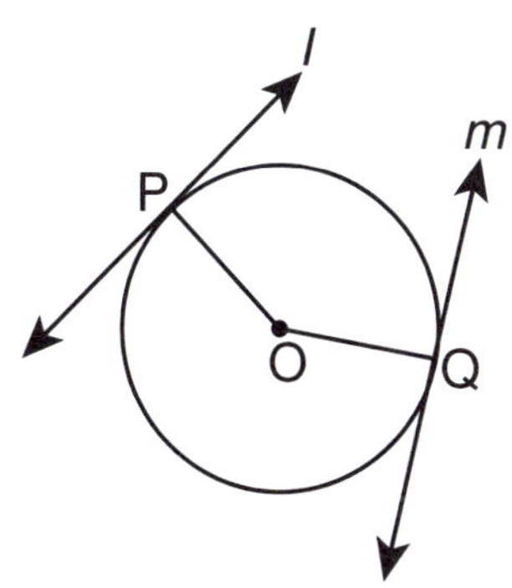

The point where a tangent touches a circle is called the **point of contact**. Here, P and Q are the points of contact of tangents *l* and *m* respectively.

Now, draw radii OP and OQ. What do you observe?

We observe that a tangent to a circle is always perpendicular to the radius drawn to the point of contact.

Arc

An **arc** of a circle is a portion of its circumference. It can also be defined as the boundary that lies between two points on the circumference of a circle.

In the given circle, arc is the portion of the circle between the two points A and B. The shorter arc is called the **minor arc** and the longer one is called the **major arc**. Here, APB is the minor arc and AQB is the major arc.

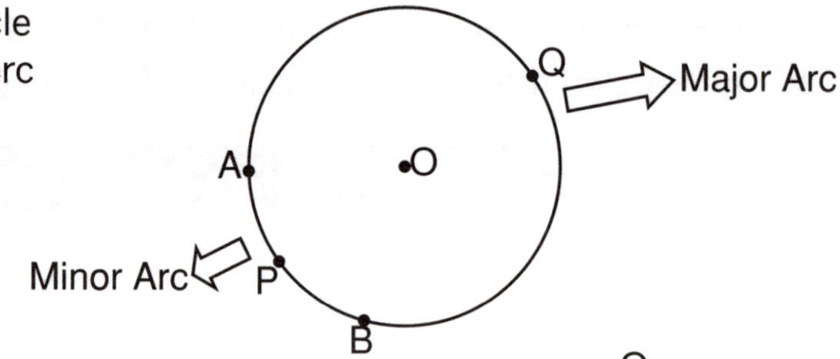

> **Note**
> All minor arcs in any circle measure less than the semicircle and all major arcs measure more than the semicircle.

Semicircle

A diameter of a circle divides it into two equal arcs that are known as **semicircles**. In the given figure, diameter AB divides the circle into two semicircles, APB and AQB.

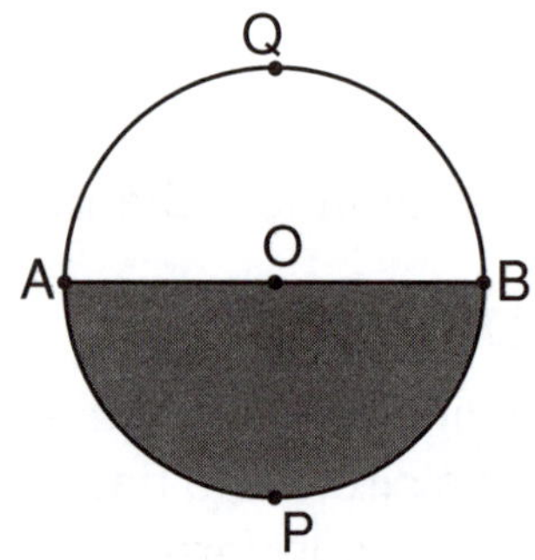

Segment

Segment of a circle is the region enclosed by a chord and an arc of the circle.

> **Note**
> Only the major segment contains the centre of the circle.

In the adjacent circle, AB is a chord that divides the circle into two regions.

The region enclosed by chord AB and minor arc AQB is the **minor segment**.

The region enclosed by chord AB and major arc APB is the **major segment**.

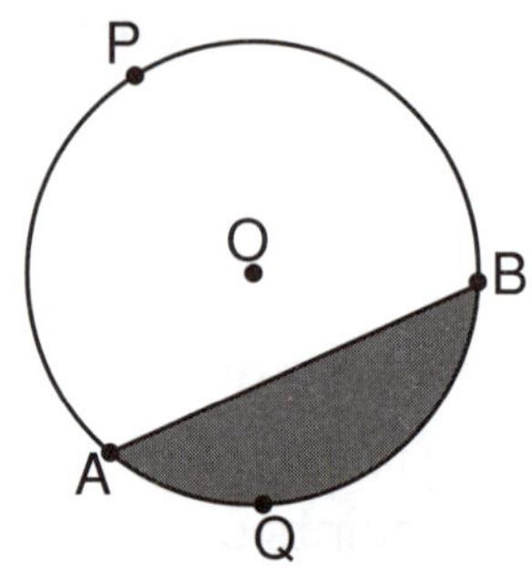

Sector

Sector of a circle is the region enclosed by two radii and an arc.

Sector with the minor arc is considered as the **minor sector** and sector with the major arc is considered as the **major sector**.

In the given circle, the region enclosed by minor arc AQB and radii OA and OB is the minor sector OAQB. Similarly, the region enclosed by major arc APB and radii OA and OB is the major sector OAPB.

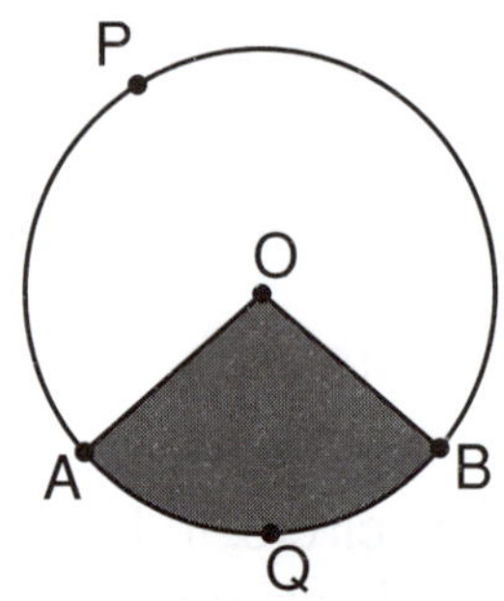

Quadrant

The **quadrant** of a circle is one-fourth of the circle. It is also defined as the minor sector formed by two perpendicular radii. A circle has four quadrants.

In the figure given below, AOB (shaded) is a quadrant.

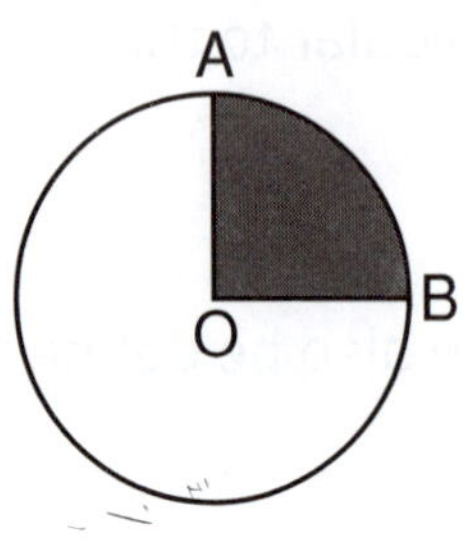

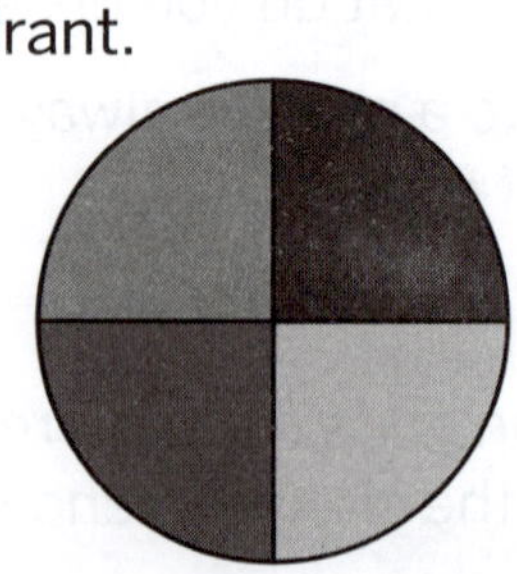

Circle with 4 quadrants

Concentric Circles

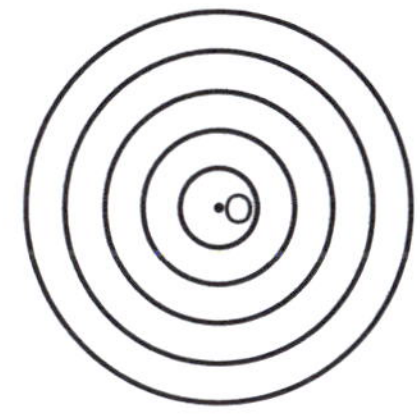

Two or more circles having the same centre are known as **concentric circles**.

The area between two concentric circles is called **annulus**.

Circumference

We have learned that the length of the curved line of the circle is called the **circumference**. The circumference of a circle can be found if the diameter or the radius of the circle is given.

Circumference and diameter are directly proportional to each other. So, circumference can be found using the formula

Circumference = $\pi \times$Diameter = $\pi \times 2 \times$Radius (As diameter is always twice the radius)

$\therefore$ **Circumference of a circle = 2πr**, where r is the radius of a circle

For any given circle, the value of its circumference divided by its diameter is always a constant. This constant is denoted by the Greek letter π (pi). The value of π is approximately ($\cong$) $\frac{22}{7}$.

That is, $\frac{\text{circumference}}{\text{diameter}} = \pi \cong \frac{22}{7}$.

Example 2: Find the circumference of a circle with radius 56 cm.

Given: $r = 56$ cm

$\therefore$ Circumference = $2 \times \frac{22}{7} \times 56 = 2 \times 22 \times 8 = 352$ cm

Example 3: Find the radius of the circle with circumference 308 cm.

Given: Circumference of circle = 308 cm

Circumference = $2 \times \frac{22}{7} \times r = 308$

$r = \frac{308 \times 7}{2 \times 22} = \frac{2156}{44} = 49$ cm

$\therefore$ Radius of the given circle = 49 cm

Summary

1. A circle is a simple closed curve formed on a plane by points that are at a fixed distance from a fixed point. The fixed point is called the centre of the circle and the fixed distance is called the radius.
2. A line segment passing through the centre of a circle and having its endpoints on the circumference of the circle is called a diameter of the circle.
3. Diameter is always twice the radius of a circle.

4. A line segment that has its endpoints on a circle is called a chord.
5. A line that intersects the circle at two points is called a secant.
6. A line that touches the circle at exactly one point is called a tangent.
7. Arc of a circle is a portion of the circumference of the circle.
8. Diameter of a circle divides it into two equal arcs known as semicircles.
9. An arc that is less than a semicircle is a minor arc and an arc that is greater than a semicircle is a major arc.
10. The region between a chord and an arc is called a segment.
11. The region formed by two radii and an arc is called a sector.
12. The quadrant of a circle is one-fourth of a circle.
13. Circumference of a circle = $2\pi r$, where r is the radius of a circle and π is a constant (taken as $\frac{22}{7}$).
14. Concentric circles are circles having a common centre.

For the Curious Mind

1. What should be the radius of a wheel such that each time it turns, it travels 44 feet?
2. Draw a circle using a bangle/coin on a paper and locate its centre exactly by folding it.

Revision Exercise

1. **Fill in the blanks.**
   a. All the radii of a circle are ________.
   b. A chord that passes through the centre of a circle is called its ________.
   c. The midpoint of the diameter is the ________ of the circle.
2. If the circumference of a circle is 440 cm, what is the radius of the circle?
3. **State whether the following are true or false.**
   a. A circle is made up of two semicircles.
   b. A circle has infinite radii.
   c. A circle has infinite chords.
   d. Tangent is a line that intersects a circle at two points.
   e. Quadrant is one half of a circle.
   f. Semicircle is an arc.
4. **Study the given figure and fill in the blanks.**
   a. OA is the ________ of the circle.
   b. AC is the ________ of the circle.
   c. Line m is the ________ of the circle.
   d. Line l is the ________ of the circle.
   e. The shaded area is a ________ of the circle.
   f. The dotted area is a ________ of the circle.

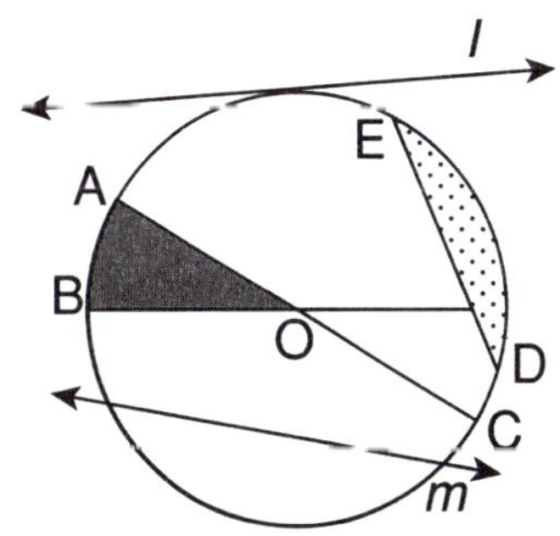

5. How many diameters can be drawn for a given circle?
6. What is the relation between the radius and the diameter of a circle?
7. Which is the biggest chord of a circle?
8. Identify the points that lie in the interior, exterior and on the circumference of the circle given alongside.

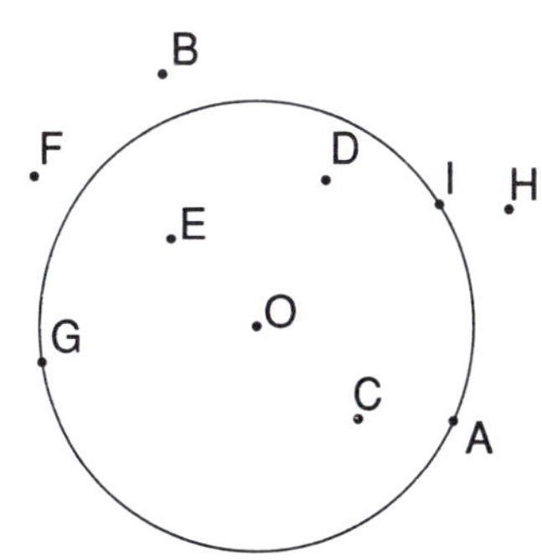

9. What is the relationship between the circumference and the diameter of a circle?
10. Find the circumference of a circle if its radius is 4.2 cm.
11. Find the diameter of a circle if its circumference is 176 cm.
12. How many quadrants does a circle have?
13. What is the difference between a secant and a tangent of a circle?

Linear Symmetry 22

What I shall learn

- To identify lines of symmetry in different figures
- To identify symmetric points
- To construct a point symmetric to a given point with respect to a given line of symmetry
- To draw a line of symmetry for two given points

Let's Get Started

Have you ever observed symmetry in nature? Symmetry exists in many things such as animals, flowers and trees. Artists, manufacturers, designers, architects, etc. also make use of the idea of symmetry in their works.

There are different kinds of symmetry. Look at the following images. Each of them has a line symmetry.

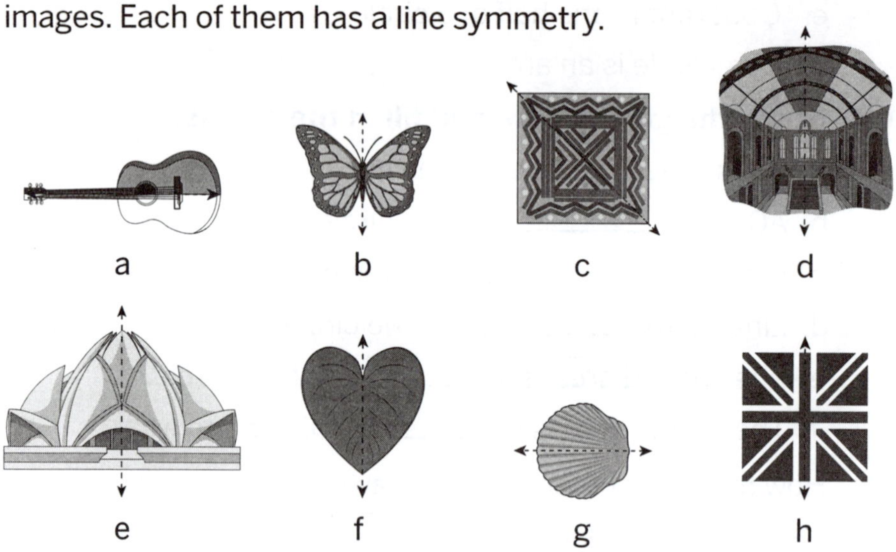

Line Symmetry

A figure is said to have line symmetry if one part of it exactly matches with the other part when it is folded along a line.

Line of Symmetry

A figure has **linear symmetry** if there exists a line that divides the figure into coinciding halves. Such a line is known as **the line of symmetry**. One half will be the mirror image of the other. The line of symmetry is also called the 'mirror line'.

The dotted line in each of the above images is a line of symmetry of that image. The line of symmetry can be horizontal, vertical or slanting. In the above images, the lines drawn for figures (a) and (g) are horizontal lines of symmetry; the ones drawn for figures (b), (d), (e), (f) and (h) are vertical lines of symmetry; and the line drawn for figure (c) is a slanting line of symmetry.

Lines of Symmetry in Regular Polygons

Do you remember what polygons are? A polygon is a simple closed figure made up of line segments.

Observe the following regular polygons (all sides and angles are equal) and their lines of symmetry.

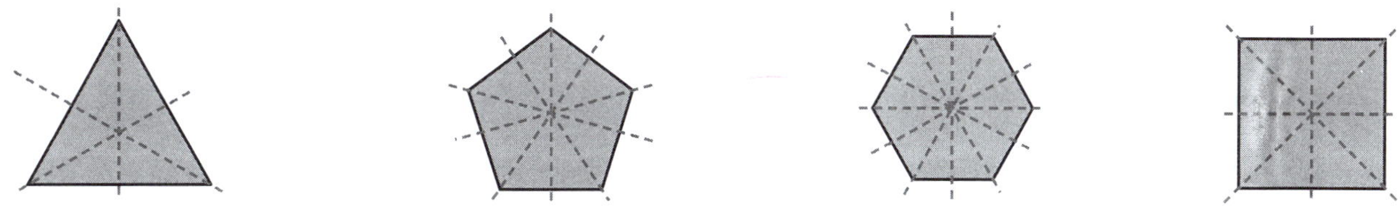

Equilateral triangle | Regular pentagon | Regular hexagon | Square

Count the number of lines of symmetry and find whether there is any relation between the number of sides of a regular polygon and the number of lines of symmetry.

Remember

A regular polygon of *n* sides has *n* number of lines of symmetry.

Can you draw the lines of symmetry for the following shapes?

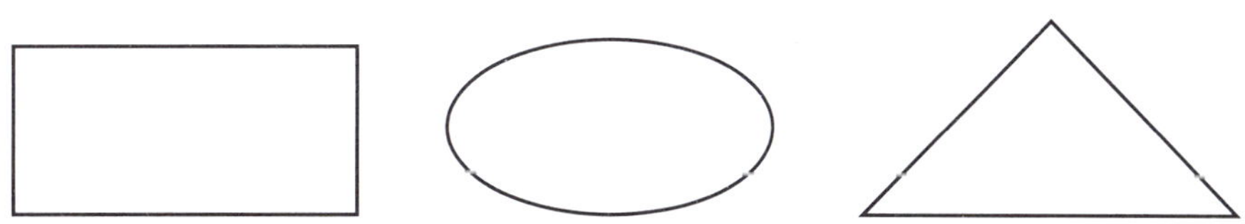

Some More Examples of Lines of Symmetry

1. Circle

Draw a circle on a patty paper and fold it along the diameter. Observe that any diameter of a circle is a line of symmetry. Since a circle has infinite diameters, it has infinite number of lines of symmetry.

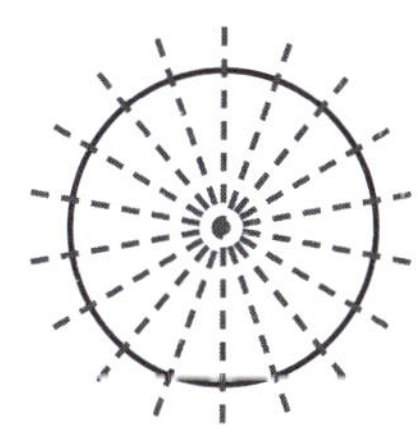

2. Line Segment

The perpendicular bisector of a line segment is the line of symmetry for the line segment. Any point on the perpendicular bisector is equidistant from the two endpoints. In the given figure, let us take any point C on the perpendicular bisector. We observe that this point is equidistant from the endpoints of $\overline{AB}$.

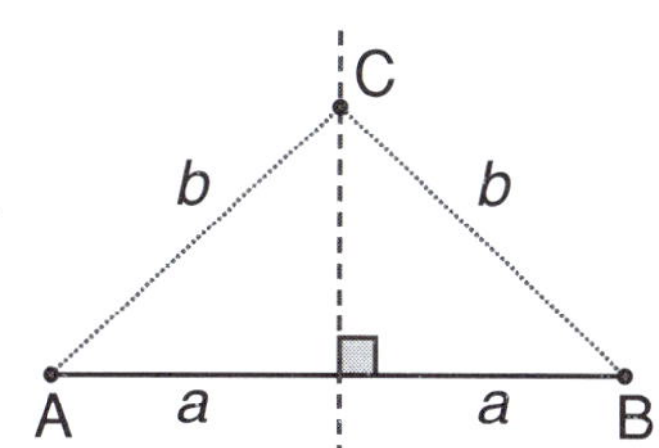

3. Angle

The bisector of an angle is the line of symmetry for the angle. It divides the angle into two equal parts. In the given figure, $\angle ABD = \angle DBC$.

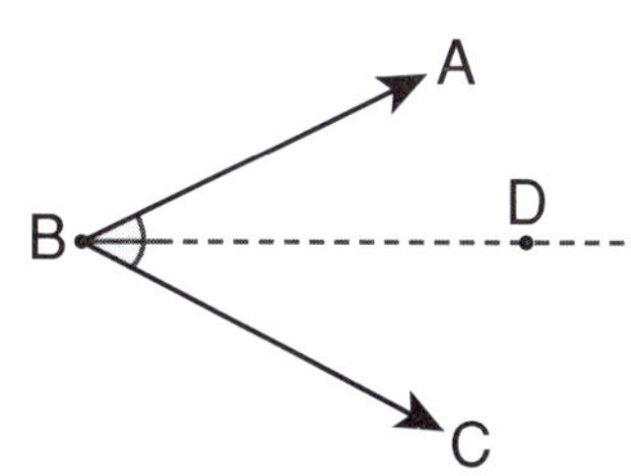

Lines of Symmetry in Letters of the English Alphabet

Letters with one line of symmetry

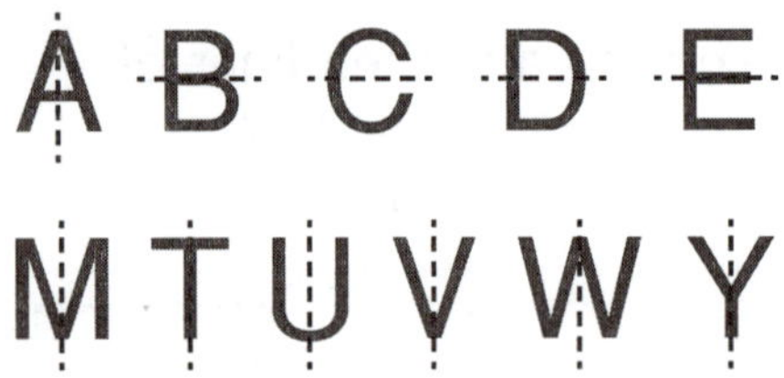

Letters with two lines of symmetry

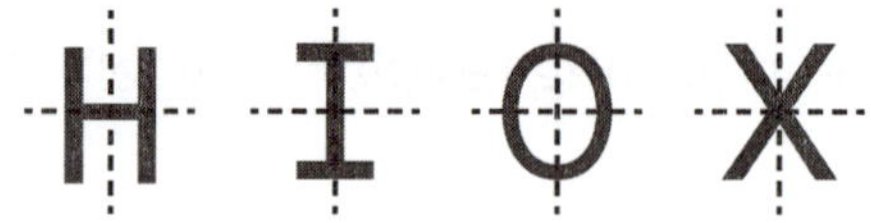

Lines of Symmetry in Rangoli Patterns

You might have seen beautiful rangoli during festivals. Have you ever observed the symmetry in them? Look at a few rangoli patterns with their lines of symmetry.

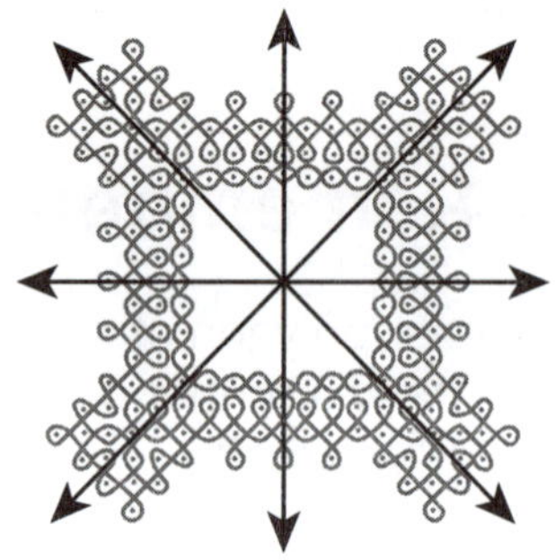

Lines of Symmetry in Equilateral, Isosceles and Scalene Triangles

The following table shows the lines of symmetry in different triangles.

Type of triangle	Figure	Number of lines of symmetry
Scalene triangle	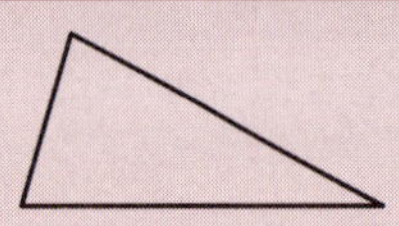	0
Isosceles triangle	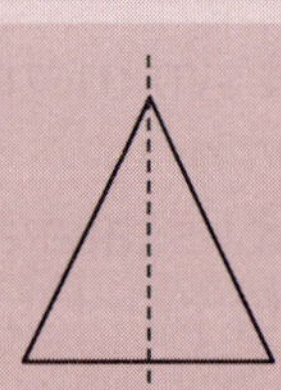	1
Equilateral triangle	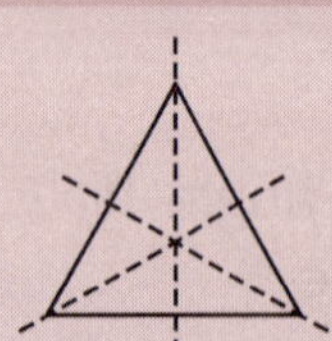	3

Note

The lines of symmetry in an equilateral triangle are also the angle bisectors of the triangle. And the line of symmetry in an isosceles triangle is the bisector of the angle contained by the two equal sides.

From the above table, we can conclude that a scalene triangle has no lines of symmetry, an isosceles triangle has 1 line of symmetry and an equilateral triangle has 3 lines of symmetry.

Exercise 22.1

Draw all the lines of symmetry for the following figures.

Symmetric Point

Let *m* be a line and R be a point (not on the line). Draw a perpendicular from point R to line *m* touching the line at point O. Extend RO to point S such that RO = OS. Here, point S is symmetric to point R about line *m*.

Points R and S are symmetric about line *m*. Therefore, line *m* is called the line of symmetry.

Observe that line *m* is the perpendicular bisector of $\overline{RS}$.

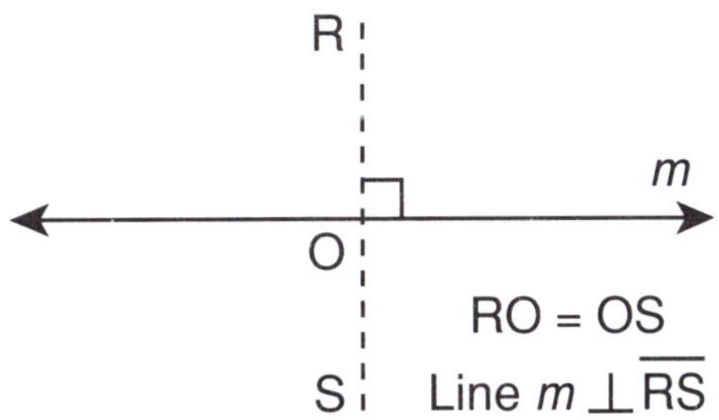

Constructions

Constructing a Point Symmetric to a Given Point With Respect to a Given Line of Symmetry

Let XY be a line and P be a point outside this line. Now, let us find a point Q opposite P, whose distance from XY is equal to the distance of P from XY.

The steps followed in the construction are given below.

Note

To check if Q is symmetrical to P with respect to XY, fold the figure along the line of symmetry XY. If P coincides with Q, then P and Q are symmetrical.

Step 1: Construct PO ⊥ XY and extend PO below XY.

Step 2: With O as centre and radius equal to PO, cut an arc on line PO at Q.

Every point on XY will be equidistant from points P and Q.

Hence, Q is symmetric to P with respect to XY.

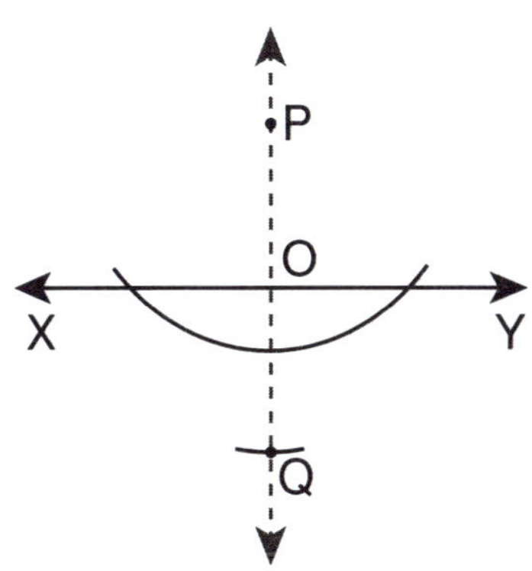

Constructing a Line of Symmetry About Which Two Given Points Are Symmetrical

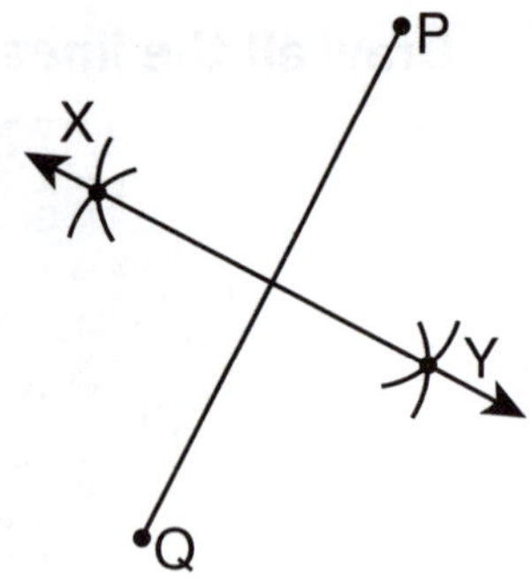

Let P and Q be two points.

We follow the given steps to construct a line XY about which P and Q are symmetrical to each other.

Step 1: Join P and Q.

Step 2: Construct the perpendicular bisector XY of line segment PQ.

Points P and Q will be equidistant from any point on line XY.

Therefore, the given points P and Q are symmetrical to each other about line XY.

Exercise 22.2

1. PQ is a line segment of length 6 cm. Construct a line of symmetry AB about which the endpoints P and Q are symmetrical to each other.
2. Construct a triangle ABC with AB = 6 cm, AC = 4 cm and BC = 3 cm. Construct a point D symmetrical to the point C with respect to AB.

Summary

1. A figure is said to have line symmetry if one part of it exactly matches with the other part when it is folded along a line.
2. A regular polygon of n sides has n number of lines of symmetry.
3. A scalene triangle has no lines of symmetry, an isosceles triangle has 1 line of symmetry and an equilateral triangle has 3 lines of symmetry.

Project

Collect and cut pictures of rangoli patterns from different newspapers/magazines. Paste them on your scrapbook and draw their line(s) of symmetry.

Revision Exercise

1 **Which of the following figures are symmetrical? Draw the line(s) of symmetry for the figures, if any.**

2 **Fill in the blanks.**

a. A parallelogram has __________ lines of symmetry.

b. The number of lines of symmetry for an isosceles trapezium is __________.

c. The letter X has __________ lines of symmetry. One is __________ and the other is __________.

d. A rhombus has __________ lines of symmetry.

e. A regular polygon of *n* sides has __________ number of lines of symmetry.

3 AB is a line segment of length 8 cm. Construct a line of symmetry PQ about which the endpoints A and B are symmetrical to each other.

4 Draw a triangle ABC. Let AB = 7 cm and BC = AC = 6 cm. Draw a line of symmetry about which the points B and C are symmetrical to each other.

For the Curious Mind

1. Draw all the possible symmetric designs by applying the same colour to any three triangles in the following figure.

2. Complete the following diagram and make it symmetrical about OA, OB and OC.

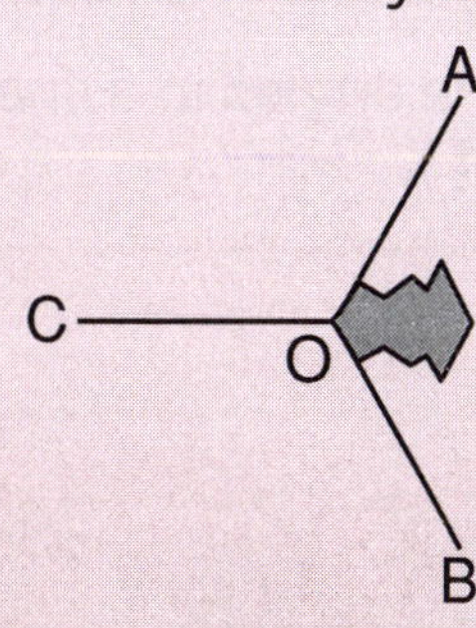

Unit Worksheet 4

1 Complete the flow chart.

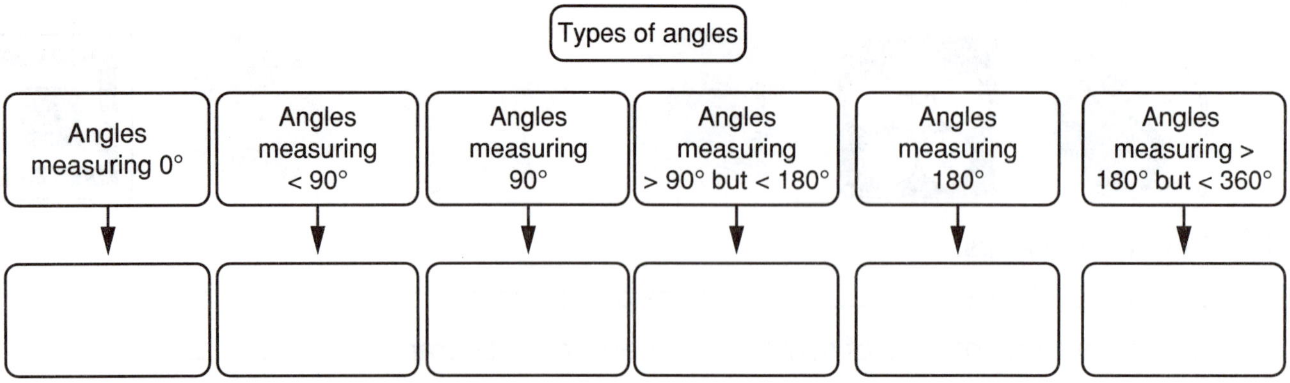

2 Observe the given picture and answer the questions that follow.

a. Name the type of angles marked in the given picture.

i. A ________________

ii. B ________________

iii. C ________________

iv. D ________________

v. E ________________

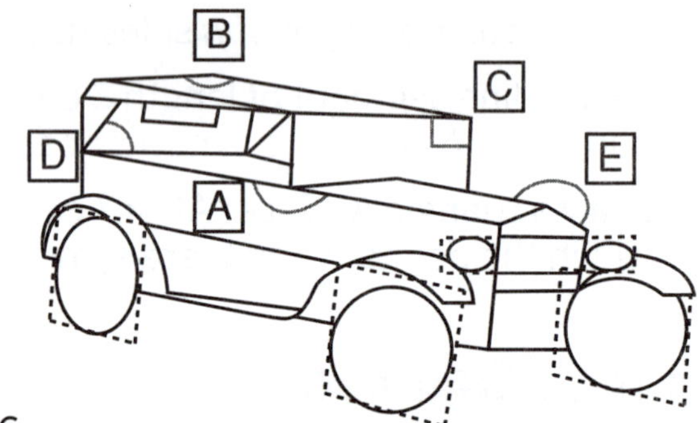

b. Find the radius of the tyre if the diameter is 36 cm.

Mental Maths

1. What is the complement of 55°? ________
2. What is the supplement of 125°? ________
3. If $r = 4.5$ cm, find d in a circle. ________
4. What is the measurement of each angle of an equilateral triangle? ________
5. What are the measurements of the angles in a linear pair if both the angles are equal? ________

UNIT 5

Perimeter and Area

23

Let's Get Started

Let us recall the concepts of perimeter and area which we have learned in the previous classes.

Perimeter: The word perimeter is derived from the Greek words 'peri', meaning around, and 'meter', meaning measure. So, perimeter is the distance covered along the boundary of a closed shape.

Area: Area is the amount of space enclosed within a closed shape.

The concepts of perimeter and area are used in many real-life situations. Some examples are given below.

What I shall learn

- To understand the concepts of perimeter and area
- To find the perimeter of a triangle, a square and a rectangle
- To find the area of a square, a right isosceles triangle and a rectangle

In preparing the layout for a house and for building a fence around it

In preparing the running track in a stadium

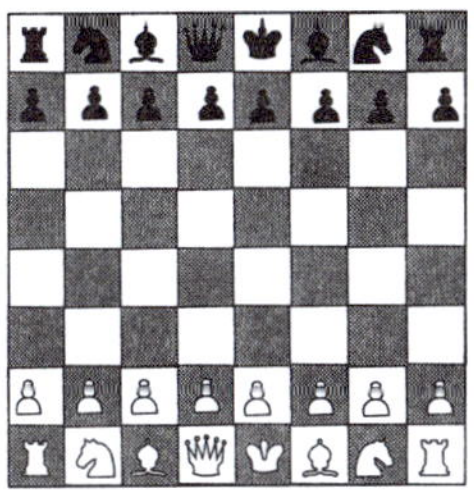

In designing play tools like chessboard

Perimeter

Perimeter can be calculated by adding the lengths of all the sides of a closed figure.

Units of Perimeter

Perimeter is measured in units of length because we add the lengths of different sides to calculate the perimeter of a figure. The most common units of length are:

- millimetre
- centimetre
- metre
- kilometre

The table given below shows the units of measurement of length and their conversions.

Units	Conversions
Millimetre (mm)	
Centimetre (cm)	1 cm = 10 mm and 1 mm = 0.1 cm
Metre (m)	1 m = 100 cm = 1000 mm
Kilometre (km)	1 km = 1000 m

Remember

1 km = 1000 m

1 m = 100 cm

1 cm = 10 mm

Millimetre —×10→ Centimetre —×100→ Metre —×1000→ Kilometre

Example 1: Convert 100 mm to m.

$$100 \text{ mm} = \frac{100}{1000} \text{ m}$$

$$= \frac{1}{10} \text{ m} = 0.1 \text{ m}$$

Example 2: Convert 5 km to cm.

$$5 \text{ km} = 5 \times 100000 \text{ cm}$$

$$= 5{,}00{,}000 \text{ cm}$$

In some countries, the standard units of measuring length are:

- inches
- feet
- yards
- miles

The table given below shows the conversions of these units of length.

Units	Conversions
Inch (in)	
Foot (ft)	1 foot = 12 inches
Yard (yd)	1 yard = 3 feet = 36 inches
Mile (mi)	1 mile = 1760 yards = 5280 feet = 63,360 inches

Try These!

Convert the following.

a. 10 mm to cm

d. 0.01 km to mm

b. 15 m to mm

e. 0.05 m to cm

c. 25 cm to km

f. 25 m to km

Note

1 inch = 25.4 mm
= 2.54 cm = 0.0254 m

Let us calculate the perimeters of some familiar closed shapes like triangle, square and rectangle.

Perimeter of a Triangle

A triangle is a three-sided closed figure. If the lengths of the sides of a triangle are *a*, *b* and *c*, then the perimeter of the triangle will be the sum of the lengths of these three sides.

The perimeter (P) of the given triangle is the sum of the lengths of all the three sides, that is, $a + b + c$.

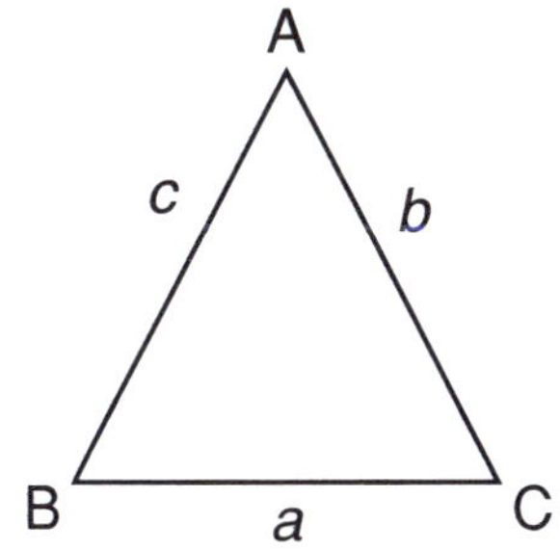

For an equilateral triangle,
$P = a + b + c = a + a + a = 3a$. That is, for an equilateral triangle of side a, $P = 3a$.

Example 3: The perimeter of an equilateral triangle is 6 cm. What is the length of each side?

Since an equilateral triangle has three equal sides, let the side of the triangle be x.

Perimeter of a triangle with equal sides of length x is $3x$.

The given perimeter is 6 cm.

$\therefore 3x = 6 \; x = 2$ cm

Perimeter of a Square

A square is a four-sided closed figure with equal sides.

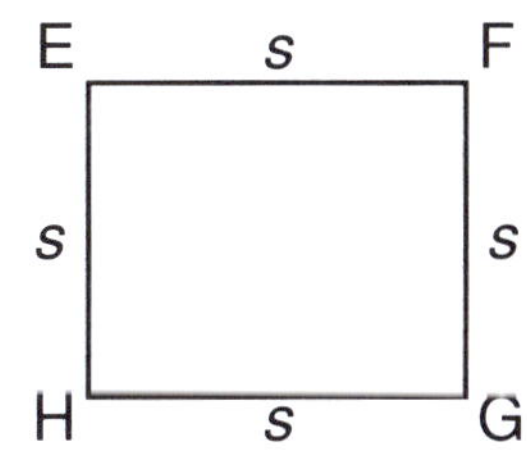

The perimeter of a square with side s is calculated as:

Perimeter of a square EFGH = EF + FG + GH + HE

$= s + s + s + s = 4s$

Perimeter of a Rectangle

A rectangle is a four-sided closed figure with opposite sides equal.

If l is the length and b is the breadth of a rectangle, the perimeter can be calculated as:

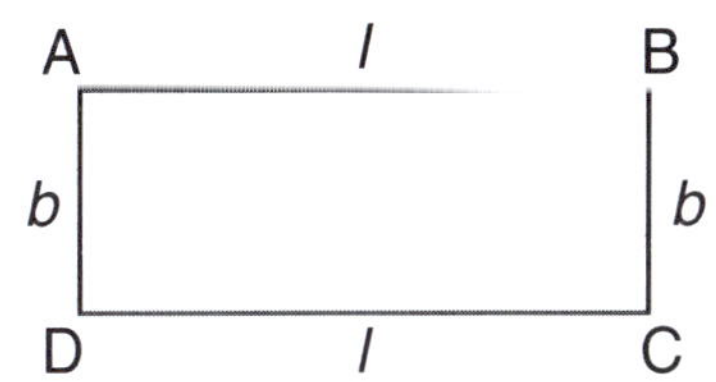

Perimeter of a rectangle ABCD = AB + BC + CD + DA

$= l + b + l + b = 2(l + b)$

Example 4: Mahesh is decorating a photo frame of Mahatma Gandhi on the occasion of Gandhi Jayanti. The length and breadth of the frame are 10 cm and 6 cm respectively. He needs to decorate the borders of the photo frame with a ribbon. What is the length of the ribbon required to do so?

Length of the ribbon would be the perimeter of the photo frame.

Length of the frame = 10 cm

Breadth of the frame = 6 cm

Perimeter of the frame = $2(l + b)$

$= 2(10 + 6) = 2(16) = 32$ cm

Therefore, Mahesh needs 32 cm of ribbon to decorate the borders of the photo frame.

Example 5: Find the cost of fencing a square field of length 60 m at the rate of ₹15 per metre.

Length of the field = s = 60 m

Perimeter of the field = $4s = 4 \times 60 = 240$ m

Cost of fencing per metre = ₹15

$\therefore$ Cost of fencing the field = Perimeter of the field × Cost per metre = 240×15 = ₹3600

Therefore, the cost of fencing a square field would be ₹3600.

Exercise 23.1

1. What is the length of the third side of a triangle if one side measures 10 cm, the second measures 15 cm and the perimeter is 45 cm?
2. A rectangular field has dimensions 30 m by 40 m. How much fencing is needed to enclose the field?
3. If the perimeter of a square is 60 cm, what is the length of each side of the square?
4. The length of a rectangle is twice its breadth. If its perimeter is 144 feet, find the dimensions of the rectangle.
5. A square table cloth is 2.5 cm long. Find the cost of the lace required to stitch along its border if the lace is charged at ₹5 per cm.

Area

The amount of surface enclosed by a closed figure is called its **area**. The shaded portion in each of the following figures represents the area.

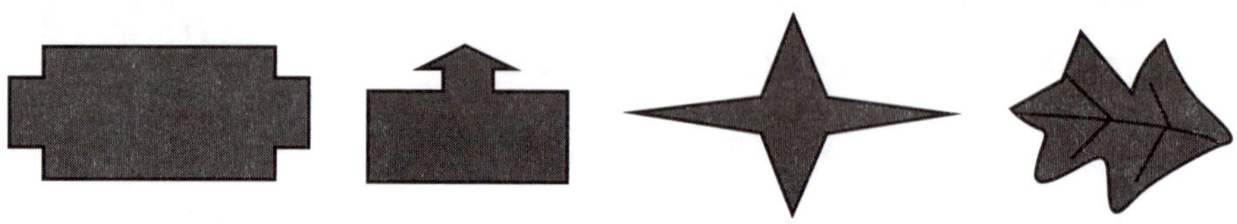

Units of Area

Area is measured in square units. So, for smaller figures, we use square millimetres or square centimetres and for bigger figures, we use square metres and square kilometres.

The following table shows the conversions of different units of area.

Units of length	Units of area	Conversions
1 mm	1 mm² = One square millimetre (sq. mm)	
1 cm	1 cm² = One square centimetre (sq. cm)	1 cm² = 1 cm × 1 cm = 10 mm × 10 mm = 100 mm²

1 m	1 m² = Square metre (sq. m)	$1\ m^2 = 1\ m \times 1\ m = 100\ cm \times 100\ cm = 10{,}000\ cm^2$
1 km	1 km² = Square kilometre (sq. km)	$1\ km^2 = 1\ km \times 1\ km = 1000\ m \times 1000\ m = 10{,}00{,}000\ m^2$

Example 6: Convert 10 km² to m².

We know $1\ km^2 = 10{,}00{,}000\ m^2$

$\therefore 10\ km^2 = 10 \times 10{,}00{,}000\ m^2 = 10 \times 10^6 = 10^7\ m^2$

Example 7: Convert 500 mm² to m².

We know $1\ cm^2 = 100\ mm^2 \Rightarrow 1\ mm^2 = 0.01\ cm^2$

$\therefore 500\ mm^2 = 500 \times 0.01\ cm^2 = 5\ cm^2$

We know $1\ m^2 = 10{,}000\ cm^2 \Rightarrow 1\ cm^2 = 0.0001\ m^2$

$\therefore 5\ cm^2 = 5 \times 0.0001\ m^2 = 0.0005\ m^2$

Hence, $500\ mm^2 = 0.0005\ m^2$

Note

1 cm² is pronounced as 'one square centimetre', whereas pronouncing it as 'one centimetre square' means a square of length 1 cm. Similar is the case with any other unit.

Areas of Rectangle and Square

Consider a rectangular hall of dimensions 11 feet by 10 feet. The floor of this hall is to be covered with tiles of size 1 ft × 1 ft.

To find the number of tiles required to cover the floor, we have to find the area of the hall.

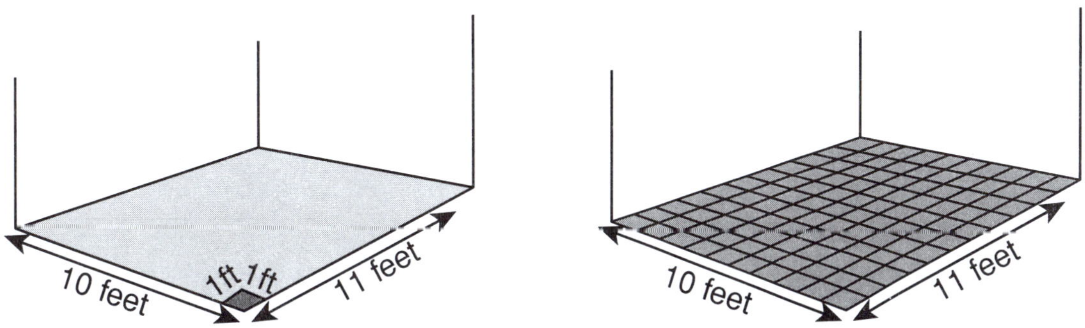

After paving the floor, we find that 110 tiles were required to cover the whole floor. Therefore, the area of the rectangular hall is 110 sq. ft.

What do you observe? We observe that length × breadth is always equal to the number of 1 × 1 tiles required to fill a shape.

∴ Area of rectangle = Length × Breadth

Therefore, the **area of a rectangle whose length is *l* and breadth is *b* is given by $A = l \times b$. This means its length, $l = \frac{A}{b}$ and breadth, $b = \frac{A}{l}$.**

Remember

For rectangle, $A = l \times b$
For square, $A = S \times S$

As the square is a special case of a rectangle whose length and breadth are equal, its area is given by **$A = s \times s = s^2$, where s is its side length, i.e. its side, $s = \sqrt{A}$.**

> **Note**
>
> Among all rectangles having equal perimeter, a rectangle whose all sides are equal (i.e. a square) has the greatest area.

Example 8: A classroom has a length of 10 feet and a width of 18 feet. The principal decides to cover the floor of entire class with tiles. If each tile has a length of 3 feet and a width of 2 feet, how many tiles are needed to cover the classroom?

Area of the classroom = Length $\times$ Width = $10 \times 18 = 180$ ft^2

Area of each tile = Length $\times$ Width = $3 \times 2 = 6$ ft^2

Number of tiles required to cover 180 ft^2 = $\dfrac{180}{6} = 30$

Therefore, 30 tiles are required to fill the classroom.

Example 9: A square garden with side 100 m has a square swimming pool at the very centre of it with side 20 m. Calculate the area of the garden.

Since the swimming pool is at the centre of the garden,

Area of the garden = Area of the total space – Area of the swimming pool

$= (100 \times 100) - (20 \times 20)$

$= 10000 - 400$

$= 9600$ sq. m

Therefore, the area of the garden is 9600 sq. m.

Area of Triangle

Activity

Aim: To find the area of a triangle

Materials required: Plain paper, ruler and pen/pencil

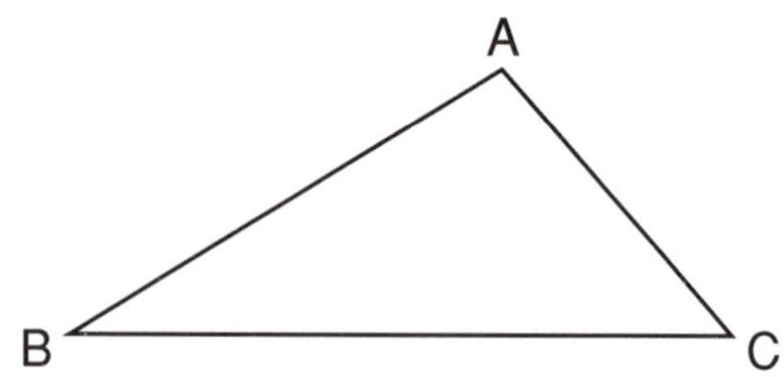

Procedure:

1. Draw a scalene triangle ABC on a paper.
2. Draw a perpendicular line from A to the opposite side so that it meets BC at D.
3. Form a rectangle FECB so that the rectangle covers all the vertices of the triangle.
4. Fold along AB and note the observation.
5. Fold along AC and note the observation.

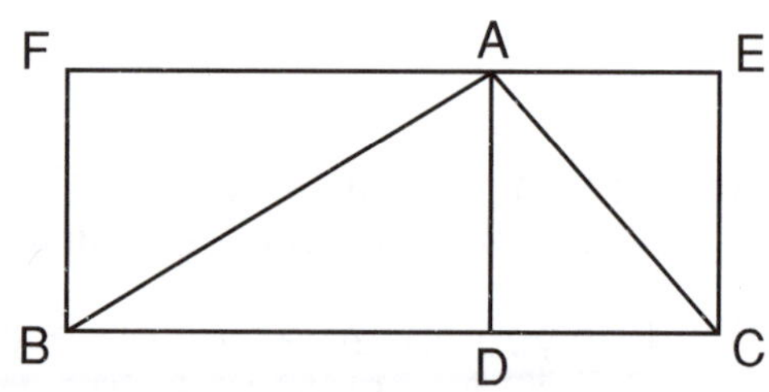

Observations:

1. Triangle AFB coincides exactly with triangle ADB.
2. Triangle AEC coincides exactly with triangle ADC.

So, the area of triangle ABC is half the area of rectangle BFEC.

Area of rectangle = Length × Breadth

Area of triangle = $\frac{1}{2}$(Area of rectangle) = $\frac{1}{2}$(Length × Breadth)

Area of triangle = $\frac{1}{2}(l \times b)$ sq. units

Area of Right Isosceles Triangle

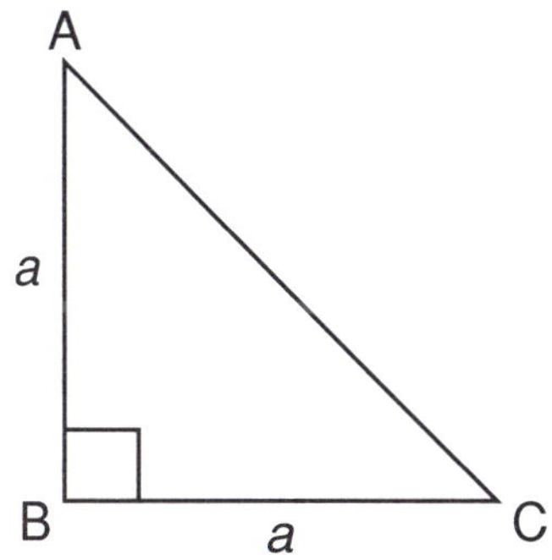

Right isosceles triangle is a right triangle with two equal sides.

In the given triangle, AB and BC are equal sides. BC is the base and AB is the height.

Let BC = AB = a cm

Area of triangle ABC = $\frac{1}{2}(BC \times AB) = \frac{1}{2}(a \times a)$

$= \frac{1}{2}a^2$, where a is the length of one of the equal sides

Example 10: An engineer is surveying a plot of land that is in the shape of a right triangle. The area of the land is 25,000 sq. m. If the base of the triangular plot is 100 m long, what is the height of the plot?

Area of the plot = 25,000 sq. m

Base of the plot = 100 m

Let the height of the plot be h.

Area of the triangle = $\frac{1}{2}$(Base × Height)

$$25000 = \frac{1}{2}(100 \times h)$$

$$25000 = 50h$$

$$h = \frac{2500}{50} = 50$$

Hence, the height of the plot is 50 m.

Example 11: Find the area of a right isosceles triangle having a base of 20 feet.

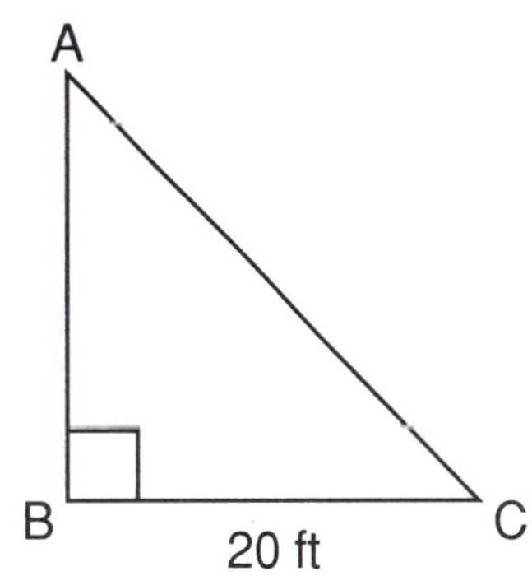

Area of an isosceles right triangle $= \frac{1}{2}a^2$, where a is the length of each side.

Area $= \frac{1}{2}(20)^2 = \frac{1}{2} \times 20 \times 20 = 200$ sq. ft

Hence, the area of the right isosceles triangle is 200 sq. ft.

Exercise 23.2

1. Find the area of a rectangle whose length and breadth are 30 cm and 16 cm respectively. Also, find the perimeter of the rectangle.
2. Find the cost of cultivating a square field of side 42 m at ₹15 per sq. m.
3. A room is 15 m long and 8 m wide. A square carpet of side 6 m is laid on its floor. Find the area of the floor that is not carpeted.
4. What will happen to the area of a square if the lengths of its sides are halved?
5. The floor of a room is 90 cm by 120 cm. Find the number of tiles needed to cover the floor if the length and breadth of one tile are 9 cm and 4 cm respectively.
6. If the area of a right isosceles triangle is 128 sq. m, what will be the length of the identical sides of the triangle?

Summary

1. Perimeter is the distance covered along the boundary of a closed shape.
2. Perimeter of triangle = $a + b + c$, where a, b and c are the lengths of the sides of the triangle.
3. Perimeter of a rectangle = 2(Length + Breadth) = $2(l + b)$
4. Perimeter of a square = 4 × Side = $4a$
5. Area is the amount of space enclosed within a closed shape.
6. Area of a rectangle = Length × Breadth = $l \times b$
7. Area of a square = Side^2 = a^2
8. Area of an isosceles right triangle = $\frac{1}{2}a^2$, where a is the length of one of the equal sides

Revision Exercise

1. If the perimeter of an equilateral triangle is 36 cm, find the measurement of each side of the triangle.
2. Equal sides of an isosceles triangle are given as 30 cm each. If the perimeter of the triangle is 67 cm, find the third side.
3. Find the cost of fencing a triangular park with each side equal to 235 m at the rate of ₹15 per metre.
4. Which of the following has the greater area—a square with side 95 cm or a rectangle with length 150 cm and breadth 60 cm?
5. Find the cost of dyeing a square piece of cloth at the rate of ₹120 per sq. m if the length of one side is 30 m.

For the Curious Mind

1. A four-sided closed figure has ninety-degree angle at its four corners. The sides of the figure are given as 100 cm, 0.001 km, 1 m and 1000 mm.
   a. Name the shape of the figure
   b. Find the perimeter of the figure
2. For a square QRSO, area = A cm^2 and perimeter = P cm. Show that $P \times P = 16A$.

UNIT 5

Surface Area and Volume

24

What I shall learn

- To understand the concepts of surface area and volume
- To find the surface area and volume of cubes and cuboids
- To learn about prism and pyramid
- To understand the units of volume and their conversion

Let's Get Started

In the previous classes, we have learned about 2D (two dimensional) and 3D (three dimensional) shapes.

2D shapes are plane shapes, which can only be measured in two dimensions, length and breadth.

Most of the things we see around us have length, breadth as well as height or depth. Such things have 3D shapes.

Pencil box

Book

2-Dimesnional shapes	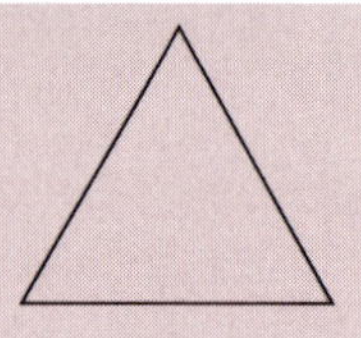 Triangle	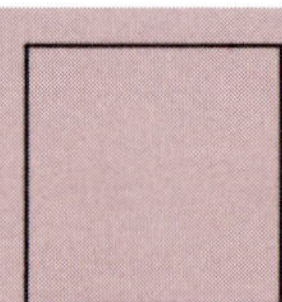 Square	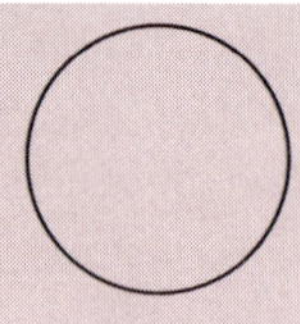 Circle
3-Dimensional shapes	 Dice (cube)	 Cellphone (cuboid)	 Paper weight (prism)

Solid figures have faces, edges and vertices.

- Face is the flat surface of a solid shape/figure.
- Edge is the line formed by the intersection of two faces.
- Vertex is the intersection of two edges.

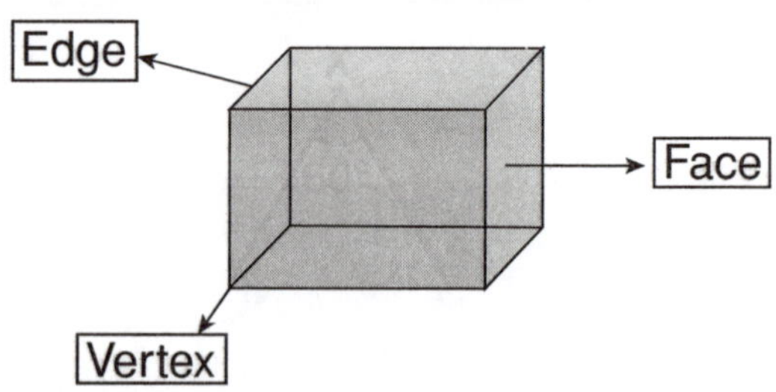

Cube

You must have played many games like ludo using a dice. A dice has 6 equal or congruent sides or faces.

Such a solid in which all 6 faces are squares is known as a **cube**. Thus, a cube is a solid 3D object with 6 equal square faces.

If any of the faces is considered as the base, the remaining faces that meet the base are known as the lateral faces.

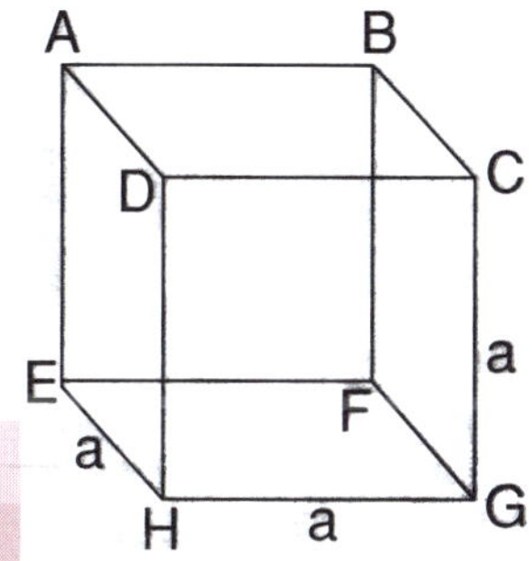

A cube has 8 vertices, 6 faces and 12 edges.

In the given cube:

Vertices	A, B, C, D, E, F, G and H
Faces	ABCD, DCGH, ADHE, BCGF, AEFB and EFGH
Lateral faces (if EFGH is considered as the base)	AEFB, ADHE, BCGF and DCGH
Edges	AB, AD, AE, BC, BF, CD, CG, DH, EF, EH, FG and GH

Dimensions of a Cube

Let the length of the side of a cube be a units.

Since the cube has 6 square faces, its surface area will be the sum of the areas of the 6 faces.

Area of any face of a cube = Area of the square with side length $a = a^2$ sq. units

Lateral surface area of a cube is the sum of the areas of the four faces meeting the base.

Lateral surface area of a cube = Area of lateral faces

= Area of AEFB + Area of ADHE + Area of BCGF + Area of DCGH

$= a^2 + a^2 + a^2 + a^2 = 4a^2$ sq. units

Total surface area of a cube = Lateral surface area + Area of the top + Area of the base

$= 4a^2$ + Area of ABCD + Area of EFGH sq. units

$= 4a^2 + a^2 + a^2 – 6a^2$ sq. units

Example 1: Find the lateral and the total surface areas of a cube if the length of one side is 7 cm.

Length of one side of the cube (a) = 7 cm

Lateral surface area of the cube $= 4a^2 = 4 \times 7 \times 7 = 196$ sq. cm

Total surface area of cube $= 6a^2 = 6 \times 7 \times 7 = 294$ sq. cm

Remember

For a cube of side a:

Area of one face $= a^2$

Lateral surface area $4a^2$

Total surface area $= 6a^2$

Cuboid

A **cuboid** is a solid 3D object with 6 rectangular faces. If any one of the faces is considered as the base, the remaining faces that meet the base are known as the lateral faces.

A cuboid has 8 vertices, 6 rectangular faces and 12 edges.

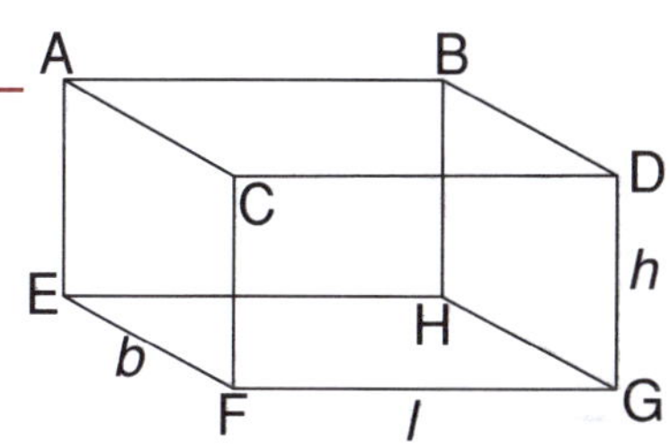

In the given cuboid:

Vertices	A, B, C, D, E, F, G and H
Faces	ABCD, AEFC, AEHB, CDGF, EFGH and BDGH
Lateral faces (If EFGH is considered as the base)	AEFC, AEHB, BDGH and CDGF
Edges	AB, AC, AE, BD, BH, CD, CF, DG, EF, EH, FG and GH

Dimensions of a Cuboid

Let the length of the cuboid be l, the breadth be b and the height be h.

Since the opposite sides of a cuboid are equal,

AB = CD = FG = EH = Length of each rectangular face = l units

AC = EF = BD = GH = Breadth of each rectangular face = b units

AE = CF = BH = DG = Height or depth of the cuboid = h units

Lateral surface area of the cuboid = Areas of the lateral faces

= Area of AEFC + Area of AEHB + Area of BDGH + Area of CDGF

$= b \times h + l \times h + b \times h + l \times h$

$= bh + lh + bh + lh = 2bh + 2lh$ sq. units

$= 2h\,(l + b)$ sq. units $= 2(l + b) \times h$

= Perimeter of the base $\times\ h$

Total surface area of the cuboid = Lateral Surface Area + Area of the top + Area of the base

$= 2h(l + b) + l \times b + l \times b$

$= 2lh + 2bh + 2lb$

$= 2\,(lb + bh + lh)$ sq. units

Example 2: Find the lateral and the total surface areas of a cuboid that is 12 m long, 10 m wide and 8 m high.

Length of the cuboid (l) = 12 m   Breadth of the cuboid (b) = 10 m

Height of the cuboid (h) = 8 m

Lateral surface area of the cuboid = $2h\,(l + b) = 2 \times 8\,(12 + 10) = 16 \times 22 = 352$ sq. m

Total surface area of the cuboid = $2\,(lb + bh + lh) = 2\,(12 \times 10 + 10 \times 8 + 12 \times 8)$

$= 2\,(120 + 80 + 96)$

$= 2\,(296) = 592$ sq. m

Example 3: Priya needs to wrap a gift in a box for her friend. The dimensions of the box are given below.

- The top and bottom of the box are 7×4 cm.
- The sides are both 4×2 cm.
- The front and the back are 7×2 cm.

How much wrapping paper would Priya need to wrap the box?

[Hint: The wrapping paper will cover all the surfaces of the box.]

Let us draw the box of the given dimensions.

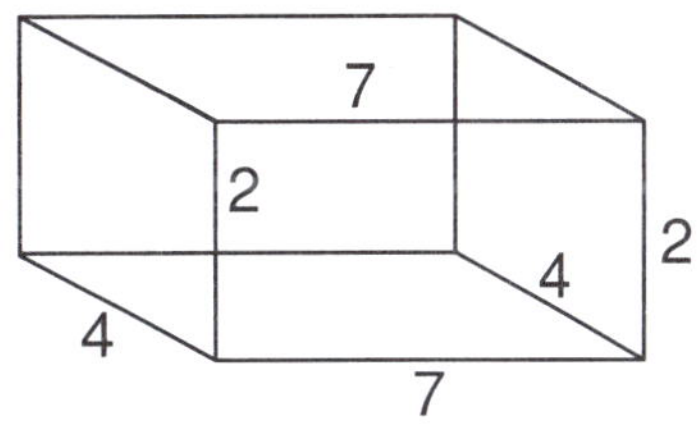

Length of the cuboid (l) = 7 cm

Breadth of the cuboid (b) = 4 cm

Height of the cuboid (h) = 2 cm

So, the wrapping paper needed to wrap the box will be total surface area of the cuboid.

Total surface area of the cuboid $= 2\,(lb + bh + lh) = 2\,(7 \times 4 + 4 \times 2 + 7 \times 2)$

$= 2(28 + 8 + 14) = 2(50) = 100$ sq. cm

Therefore, Priya would require 100 sq. cm of wrapping paper to wrap the box.

Exercise 24.1

1. **Find the lateral and the total surface areas of cubes with the given side lengths.**

   a. 8 cm b. 12.5 cm c. 25 m d. 16.5 m

2. **Find the lateral and the total surface areas of cuboids for each of the following dimensions.**

   a. $l = 6$ cm, $b = 3$ cm, $h = 2$cm

   b. $l = 13.5$ m, $b = 10$ m, $h - 2.5$ m

   c. $l = 4.5$ cm, $b = 3.5$ cm, $h = 1.5$ cm

3. What is the lateral surface area of a box that is in the shape of a cuboid with base area 250 sq. m and total surface area 1750 sq. m?

4. How much material is required to wrap a cubical box of side 13.5 m?

5. How much would it cost to paint an auditorium that is 15 m long, 12 m wide and 7 m high if the cost of painting 1 sq. m is ₹12.50?

6. Neha needs to prepare a carton of 50 cm length, 35 cm breadth and 16 cm height. What will be the cost of the carton if the rate of 1 sq. cm is 10 paisa?

7. Srishti decided to paint 4 walls of her room that is 15 m long, 6 m wide and 3 m high. Find the area of the four walls and the cost of painting at the rate of ₹50 per square metre.

Prism

A **prism** is a solid 3D object with identical and parallel base and top, and rectangular lateral faces.

Prisms are named according to the shape of their base.

Shape	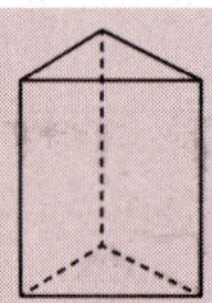	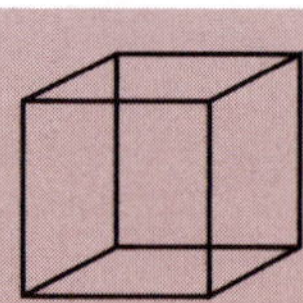	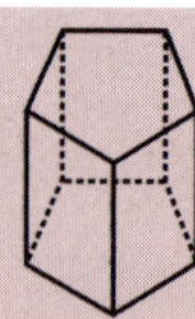	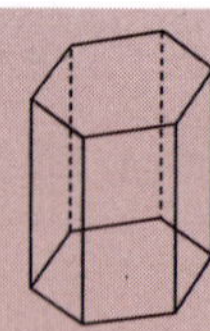
Base	Triangle	Square	Pentagon	Hexagon
Name	Triangular prism	Square prism (Cube)	Pentagonal prism	Hexagonal prism

Remember

Cubes and cuboids are also prisms.

Pyramid

A **pyramid** is a solid 3D object having a base and three or more sides. The lateral faces are triangles that meet at a common point called the **apex**. The apex is the vertex opposite to the base.

Pyramids are also named according to the shape of their base.

Shape	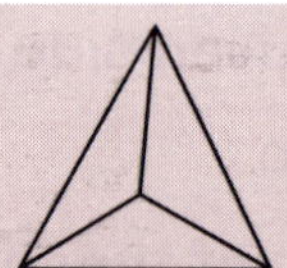	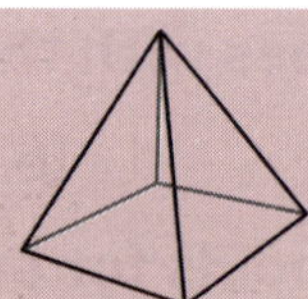	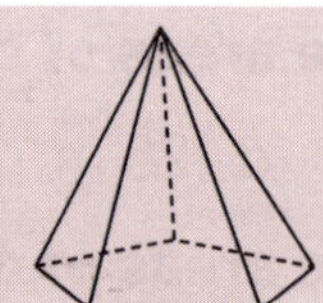	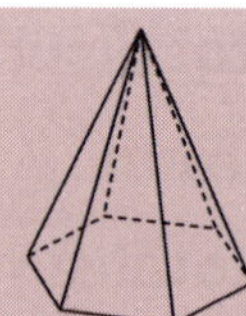
Base	Triangle	Square	Pentagon	Hexagon
Name	Triangular pyramid	Square pyramid	Pentagonal pyramid	Hexagonal pyramid

Note

The Great Pyramids of Egypt are square pyramids as their base are square-shaped.

Activity

Identify the shapes given below and complete the table.

Shape	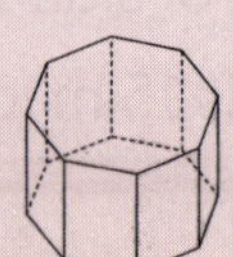	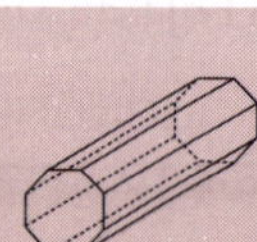	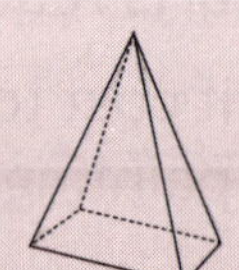	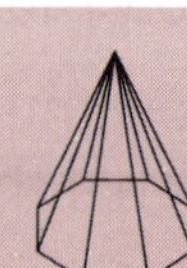
Shape of the base				
Name of the solid				

Volume

Volume is the space occupied by a solid figure. The volume of a solid is the number of unit cubes that it can hold.

The volume of a cube having side of length 1 cm is:

$1\text{ cm} \times 1\text{ cm} \times 1\text{ cm} = 1\text{ cm}^3 = 1$ cubic centimetre

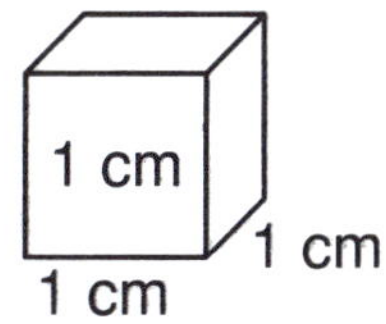

Volume of a Cuboid

Consider the given box which is in the shape of a cuboid.

Let us fill unit cubes until the whole box is filled.

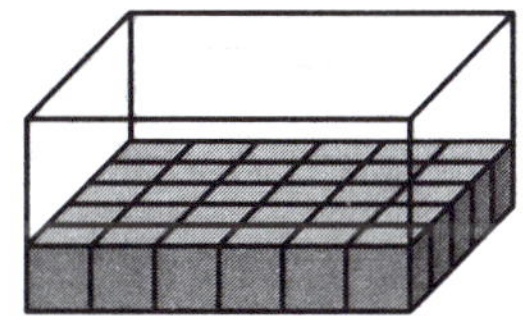

Observe that in one layer, there are 5 rows and in each row, there are 6 cubes.

Therefore, the number of cubes in one layer is $6 \times 5 = 30$.

Let us fill the box completely with unit cubes and count the number of layers.

There are 3 layers. Thus, the total number of unit cubes used to fill the box is $(6 \times 5) \times 3 = 90$.

Therefore, the volume of this empty box is 90 cu. cm or 90 cm³.

This means this box can hold exactly 90 unit cubes.

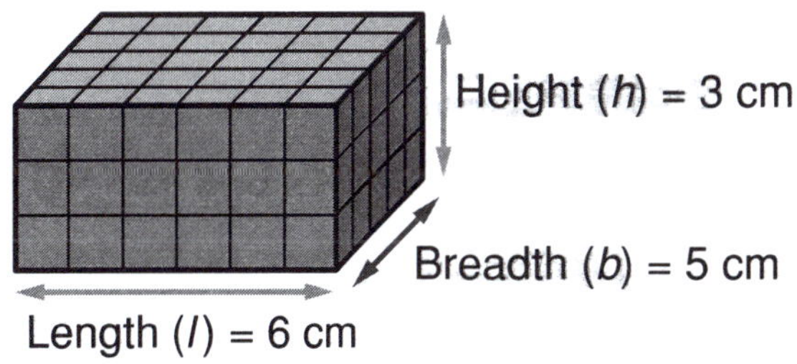

We know that the volume of any cuboidal box is given by

Number of cubes per layer × Number of layers

Number of cubes in each row × Number of rows × Number of layers

Length (l) × **Breadth (b)** × **Height (h)**

Therefore, the volume of a cuboid whose length is l, breadth is b and height is h is given by:

Volume = Length × Breadth × Height

$V = l \times b \times h$ cubic units = Area of the base × Height

Remember

For a cuboid:
$V = l \times b \times h$ cubic units

For a cube:
$V = s^3$ cubic units,
where s = side

Volume of a Cube

We have learned that all sides of a cube are equal.

That is, for a cube, length = breadth = height.

If **s** is considered to be the length of a side of a cube, its volume will be **s** × **s** × **s** cubic units, that is, $\mathbf{s^3}$ cubic units.

Remember

$1\ m\ell = 1\ cm^3$

$1\ \ell = 1000\ cm^3$

$1\ m^3 = 1000\ \ell$

$1\ \ell = 1000\ m\ell$

Units of Volume

For solids, the units of volume are cubic centimetre (cm^3), cubic decimetre (dm^3), cubic metre (m^3), etc.

If a container is filled with liquid or gas, the units of volume are millilitres ($m\ell$), litres (ℓ), kilolitres ($k\ell$), etc.

Unit	Conversion
$1\ cm^3$	$1\ cm \times 1\ cm \times 1\ cm = 10\ mm \times 10\ mm \times 10\ mm = 1000\ mm^3$
$1\ dm^3$	$1\ dm \times 1\ dm \times 1\ dm = 10\ cm \times 10\ cm \times 10\ cm = 1000\ cm^3 = 1\ \ell$
$1\ m^3$	$1\ m \times 1\ m \times 1\ m = 100\ cm \times 100\ cm \times 100\ cm = 1000000\ cm^3 = 1\ k\ell$

Example 4: A water tank is in the shape of a cube with side 5.5 m. What is the volume of the tank?

Length of the tank = 5.5 m

Volume of the tank = $(\text{Side})^3 = 5.5 \times 5.5 \times 5.5 = 166.375\ m^3$

We know $1\ m^3 = 1000\ \ell$

$\therefore 166.375\ m^3 = 166.375 \times 1000\ \ell = 166375\ \ell$

So, the volume of the tank is 1,66,375 ℓ.

Example 5: If the volume of a room, which is in the shape of a cuboid, is 270 cm^3 and the area of its floor is 45 cm^2, find its height.

Volume of the room = 270 cm^3

Length $\times$ Breadth $\times$ Height = 270 cm^3 ...(1)

Area of the floor = 45 cm^2

Length $\times$ Breadth = 45 cm^2 ...(2)

From (1) and (2),

Area of the floor $\times$ Height = 270

$45 \times \text{Height} = 270$

$$\text{Height} = \frac{270}{45} = 6\ cm$$

Therefore, the height of the given room is 6 cm.

Exercise 24.2

1. **Find the volume of a cube with sides of the following lengths.**

   a. 13 cm b. 5.5 m c. 9.5 m d. 1.5 m

2. **Find the volume of a cuboid with each of the following dimensions.**

   a. $l = 13$ cm, $b = 9$ cm and $h = 6$ cm b. $l = 2.5$ m, $b = 2$ m and $h = 1.2$ m

3. If the volume of a cube is 216 cm^3, find its lateral and total surface areas.
4. A restaurant has an aquarium in the shape of a cuboid. The base of the aquarium is 5 m by 3.5 m. If its height is 4 m, how much water would be needed to fill the aquarium?
5. A cuboid-shaped water tank with length 2.5 m, breadth 2 m and height 1.5 m is filled with water. If 1000 ℓ of the water is drained from the tank, how much water would remain in it?
6. A swimming pool is 7 m long, 5 m wide and 2.5 m deep. The owner decided to paint the interior surfaces of the pool with water resistant paint. How much will it cost if ₹60 is charged per sq. m. How many litres of water would be needed to fill the pool? (Hint: 1 m^3 = 1000 ℓ)

Summary

1. A cube is a solid 3D object with 8 vertices, 6 faces and 12 edges.
2.

Cube (side *a* units)	
Lateral surface area	$4a^2$ sq. units
Total surface area	$6a^2$ sq. units
Volume	a^3 cubic units

3. A cuboid is a solid 3D object with 8 vertices, 6 faces and 12 edges.
4.

Cuboid (length *l*, breadth *b* and height *h*)	
Lateral surface area	$2h(l + b)$ sq. units
Total surface area	$2(lb + bh + lh)$ sq. units
Volume	$l \times b \times h$ cubic units

5. A prism is a solid 3D object with identical and parallel base and top, and rectangular lateral faces.
6. A pyramid is a solid 3D object with base having three or more sides. The lateral faces are triangles that meet at a common point called the apex.

Revision Exercise

1. How many litres of water can a cubical tank of side 5.5 m hold?
2. A pit is 7 m long, 4.5 m wide and 75 cm deep. What is the volume of mud taken out of it?
3. Find the cost of the cardboard needed to prepare a box that is 32 cm by 26 cm by 12 cm if the rate is 60 paise per sq. cm.
4. Find the surface area of a cube if its volume is 512 cm^3.
5. Three cubes each of edge 7 cm are placed end to end. Find the volume and the surface area of the cuboid formed.

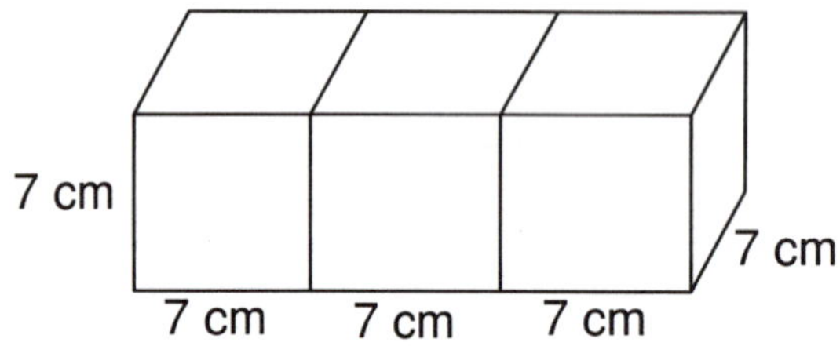

For the Curious Mind

1. If the lateral surface area of a cuboid is 54 sq. cm, what is the value of x in the given figure?

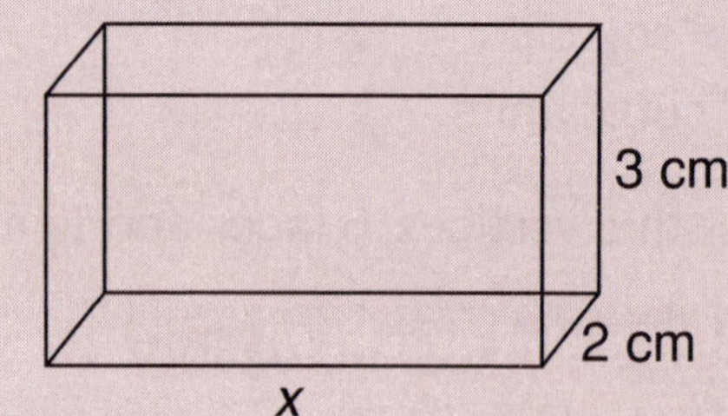

2. If 1 cm^3 of iron has a mass of 8.25 g, what is the mass of an iron bar of rectangular cross section with the dimensions shown in the given figure?

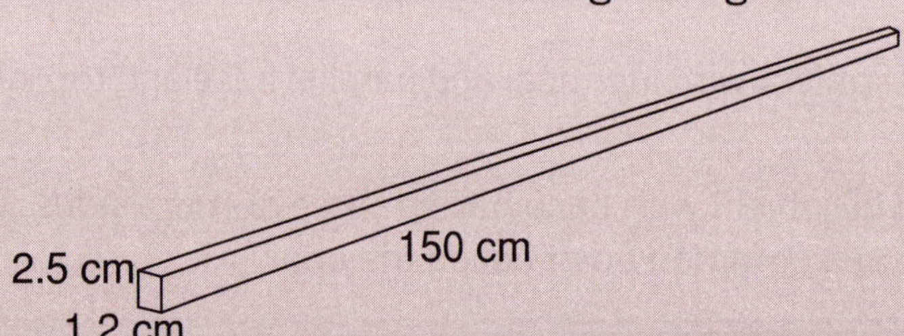

Unit Worksheet 5

Look at the plan of a house given below and answer the questions that follow.

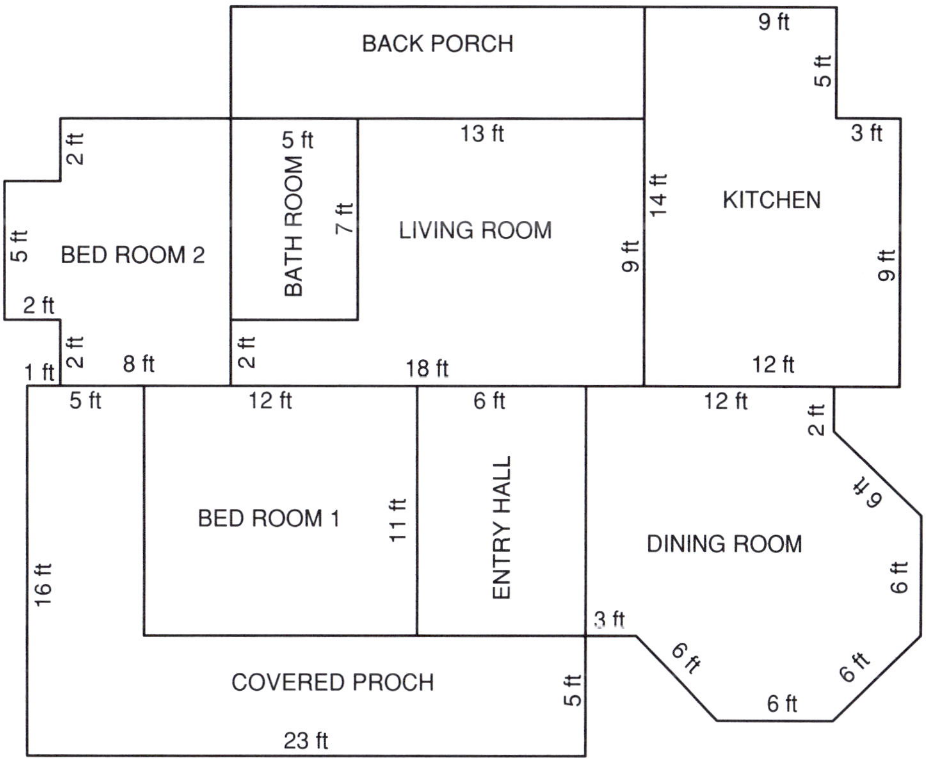

1 Complete the following.

a. Perimeter of the house = ________________

b. Area of Bedroom 1 = ________________

c. Area of Bedroom 2 = ________________

d. Perimeter of Dining Room = ________________

2 Compare the perimeters and the areas of the living room and the kitchen.

a. Greater perimeter = ________________ b. Bigger area = ________________

Mental Maths

1. How many mm are there in 3 cm? ____________
2. What is the measure of the side of a square if its perimeter is 36 cm? ____________
3. What is area of a table whose width is 3 ft and length is 2 ft more than the width? ____________
4. How many litres of juice can a cubical container hold if its edge is 10 cm? ____________
5. What is the area of a right isosceles triangle, if each equal side measures 8 cm? ____________

UNIT 6

Graphical Representation of Data

25

What I shall learn

- To interpret data given in column graphs, pie graphs and line graphs
- To construct column graphs and pie graphs

Let's Get Started

In our day-to-day lives, we come across variety of information in the form of words or numbers. Such information which is used to take meaningful decisions is called **data**. For example, to buy a mobile phone, we collect information on different features (price, camera, memory, etc.) of various models and then decide upon which one to buy.

Statistics is a branch of mathematics that deals with the collection, organization, presentation and interpretation of numerical data.

The data collected can be represented in different ways - pictorial, tabular and graphical.

Let us learn in detail about the different ways of representing data graphically.

Know the Mathematician – Ronald Aylmer Fisher

Sir Ronald Aylmer Fisher (1890–1962) was an English statistician who laid the foundations for modern statistical science. Some people call him the 'Father of Statistics' for his contributions to experimental design, analysis of variance and statistical inference.

Column Graph

A **column graph** is a graphical representation of numerical data in the form of rectangles. A column graph is also known as a **bar graph**.

Constructing Column Graph

Let us learn how to construct column graphs with the help of an example.

Example 1: Swapanjeet collected information on the distances (in kilometres) the students of his school cover to reach school, and prepared the following table.

Construct a column graph for the above data and answer the following questions.

Distance	Number of students
2	30
5	55
8	60
10	30
15	20

a. How many students live at a distance of 8 km from the school?

b. What is the smallest distance that the students cover to come to school?

c. What is the distance covered by the least number of students and how many students are they?

d. Identify the two distances that the same number of students cover.

We can construct the column graph for the given data by following the steps given below.

Step 1: Draw two perpendicular lines OX and OY, that is, the X-axis and the Y-axis respectively.

Note

x-axis and y-axis are also called abscissa and ordinate respectively.

Step 2: Label the axes. The X-axis represents the quantities and the Y-axis represents the frequency of the quantities. In this case, the X-axis represents the distance and the Y-axis represents the number of students. Hence, write 'Distance (in km)' along the X-axis and 'Number of students' along the y-axis as shown in the figure below.

Step 3: Choose a suitable scale on the Y-axis. The scale should be chosen such that all the values given for 'Number of students' can be easily represented on the graph. For the above data, let us choose a scale of 1 unit = 10 students.

Step 4: Starting from O, mark a point after every unit and label them as 10, 20, 30, ... 70. We mark the Y-axis up to 70 because the maximum number of students we have to represent is 60.

Step 5: Calculate the heights of the rectangles using the above mentioned scale. For the given data, the heights of the rectangles are calculated as follows.

Distance (in km)	Number of students	Height of the rectangle
2	30	30 ÷ 10 = **3 units**
5	55	55 ÷ 10 = **5.5 units**
8	60	60 ÷ 10 = **6 units**
10	30	30 ÷ 10 = **3 units**
15	20	20 ÷ 10 = **2 units**

Step 6: Draw rectangles of the same width on X-axis with heights as calculated above and label the graph.

Remember

In a column graph, the rectangles drawn are of equal width with equal spacing between them. The heights of the rectangles represent the values of the data items.

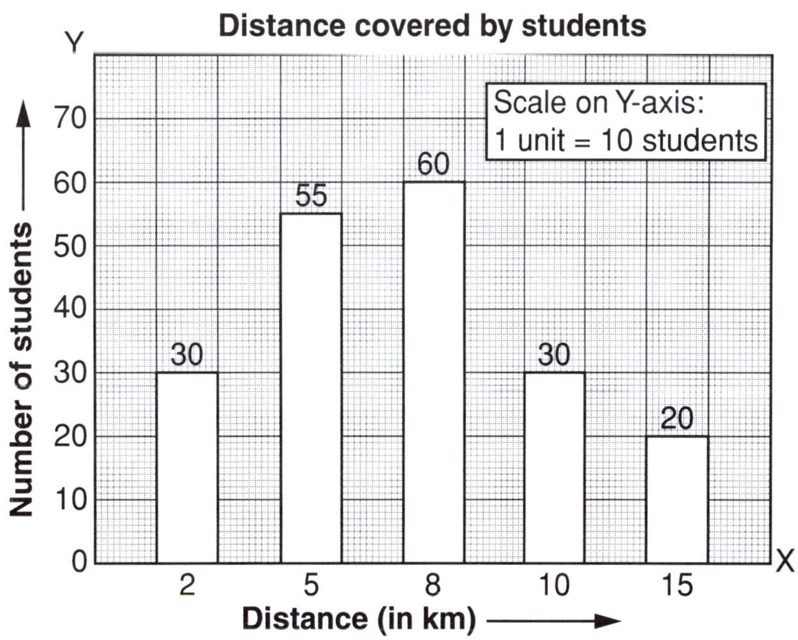

Let us now answer the questions with the help of the column graph.

a. 60 students live at a distance of 8 km from the school.

b. The nearest distance is 2 km and 30 students come from this distance.

c. The least number of students come from a distance of 15 km. They are 20 in number.

d. The same number of students, that is, 30 students each, come from distances 2 km and 10 km.

Note

To read the values in a column graph, draw a perpendicular line from the top of the rectangle to the Y-axis.

Exercise 25.1

1 **The following column graph shows the heights of some mountain peaks in metres.**

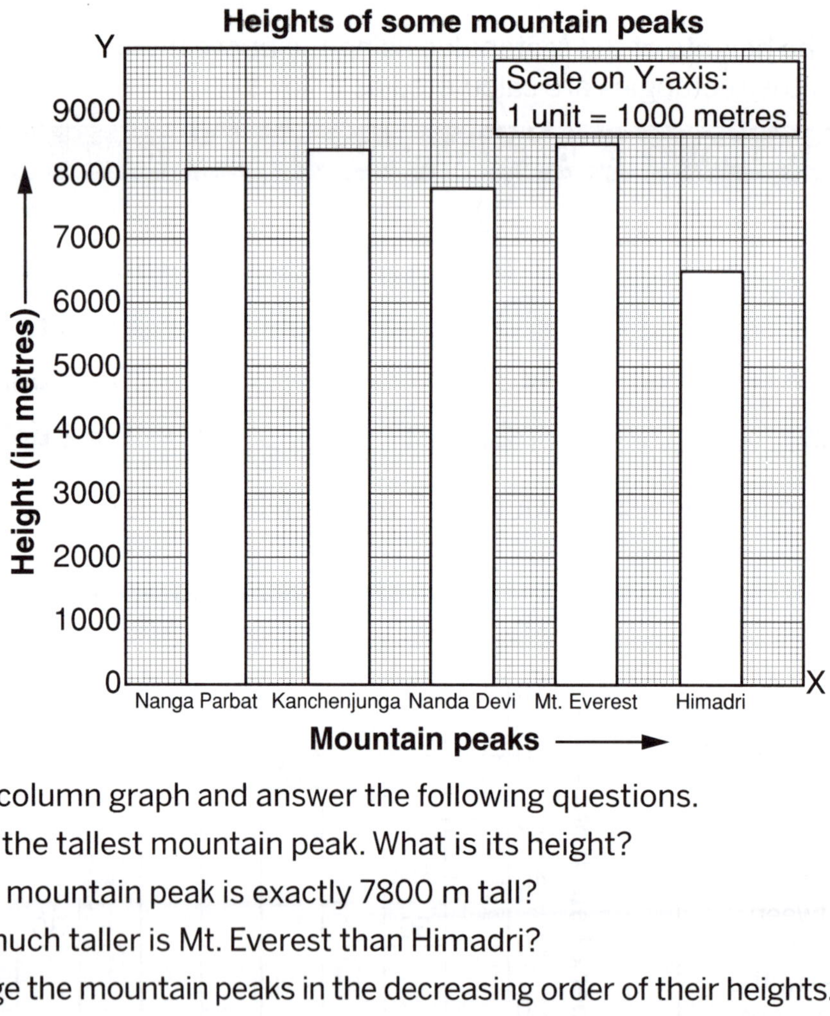

Read the column graph and answer the following questions.

a. Name the tallest mountain peak. What is its height?

b. Which mountain peak is exactly 7800 m tall?

c. How much taller is Mt. Everest than Himadri?

d. Arrange the mountain peaks in the decreasing order of their heights.

2 **The lifespans of some animals are given below. Present the data in a tabular form and then draw a column graph to represent the data.**

Bull – 28 years, Bat – 24 years, Cat – 25 years, Crocodile – 45 years, Fox – 14 years, Chicken – 14 years, Goat – 15 years, Rabbit – 9 years, Tiger – 22 years

Pie Graph

A **pie graph** is a circle that is divided into different sectors to represent some specific data.

Look at the following diagrams. What do you observe? In each of the above diagrams, a circle is divided into different sectors to represent some specific data. Such a diagram representing data is known as a **pie graph**. It is called so because it looks like a pie (a round dessert) that has been cut into slices. Let us learn how to read and interpret pie graphs.

A pie graph shows the relationship of the parts to the whole by comparing the sizes of the sectors. They are widely used to illustrate differences in categories.

Modes of travel used by students

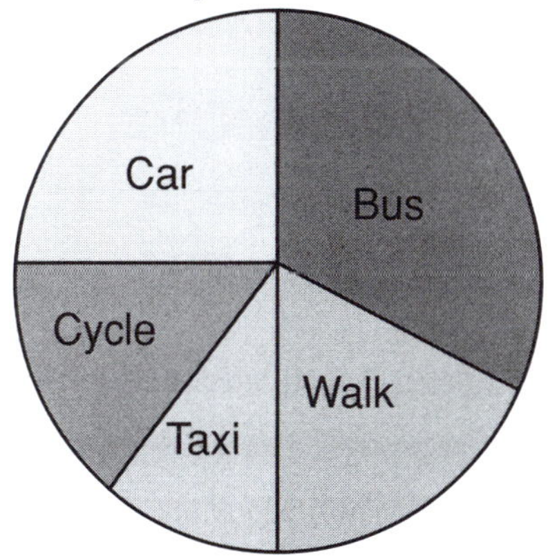

The pie graph given here provides information on the different modes of transportation used by students to travel to school. You can observe that the size of the sector representing 'Bus' is the greatest. Hence, we can infer that most of the students come to school by bus. Similarly, the size of the sector representing 'Taxi' is the smallest. Hence, we can say that only a small number of students come to school by taxi.

By reading the pie graph, we can arrange the different modes of travel used by the students from the most common to the least common as follows:

Bus, Car, Walk, Cycle, Taxi

Example 2: A vehicle showroom conducted a survey among a few people about their likings in terms of the colour of vehicles. The results of this survey is given in the pie graph shown here. Observe the pie graph and answer the following questions.

a. Half of the number of people who like silver-coloured vehicles like white vehicles. What is the number of people who like white vehicles?

Colours of vehicles liked by people

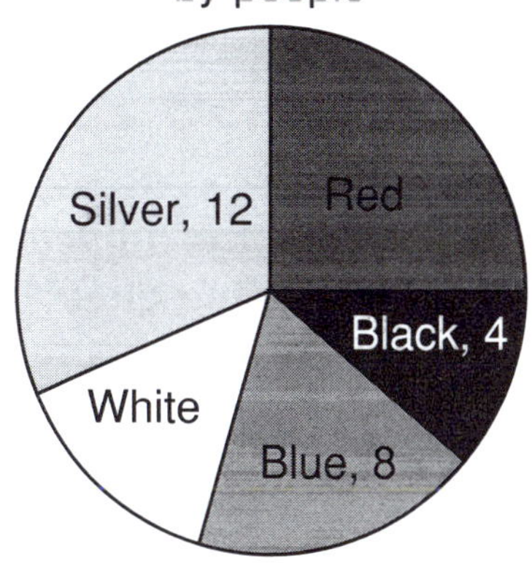

b. The number of people who like red vehicles is equal to the sum of the people who like white and the people who like black vehicles. What is the number of people who like red vehicles?

c. What is the total number of people who are surveyed?

Solution:

a. Number of people who like silver-coloured vehicles = 12

$\therefore$ Number of people who like white vehicles = $\frac{1}{2}(12) = 6$

b. Number of people who like red vehicles

= People who like white vehicles + People who like black vehicles

= 6 + 4 = 10

c. Total number of people surveyed = 12 + 10 + 4 + 8 + 6 = 40

Constructing Pie Graph

To construct a pie graph, we need to find the angles subtended by the sectors representing the quantities at the centre of the circle. Let us learn how to construct a pie graph using the following example.

Example 3: The following table shows the favourite fruit juices of Class 6 students. Represent this data using a pie graph.

Fruit juice	% of students who like it
Orange	15
Grape	15
Apple	25
Pineapple	10
Mango	35

Note

Angles around the centre of a circle always add up to 360°.

Let us calculate the central angles subtended by the sectors representing each fruit juice.

Fruit juice	% of students who like it	Central angle
Orange	15	15% of 360° = 54°
Mango	35	35% of 360° = 126°
Apple	25	25% of 360° = 90°
Pineapple	10	10% of 360° = 36°
Grape	15	15% of 360° = 54°

Favourite fruit juice

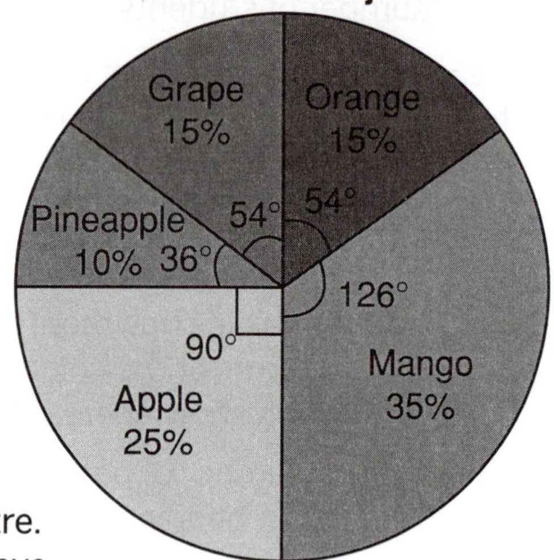

Draw a circle of any convenient radius and mark its centre. Construct the sectors with central angles calculated above.

Exercise 25.2

1 Read the adjacent pie graph and answer the following questions.

a. What information is provided in the pie graph?

b. Which sport has the highest number of participants?

c. Which sport has the least number of participants?

d. Which sports have the same number of participants?

e. How many participants are there in total?

Number of participants in different sports

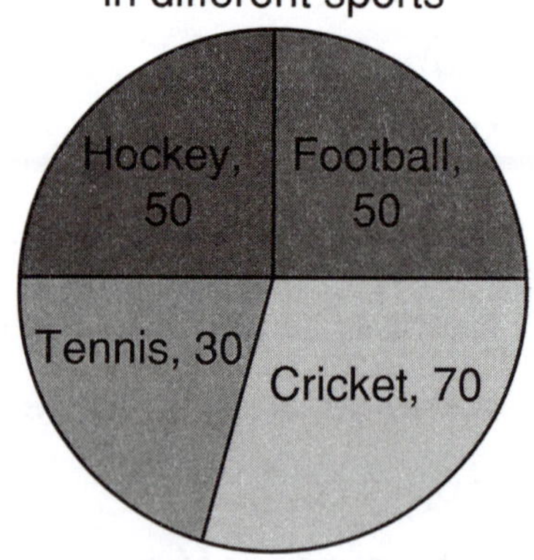

2. **The number of restaurants that serve different kinds of food in a mall is shown in the given pie graph.**

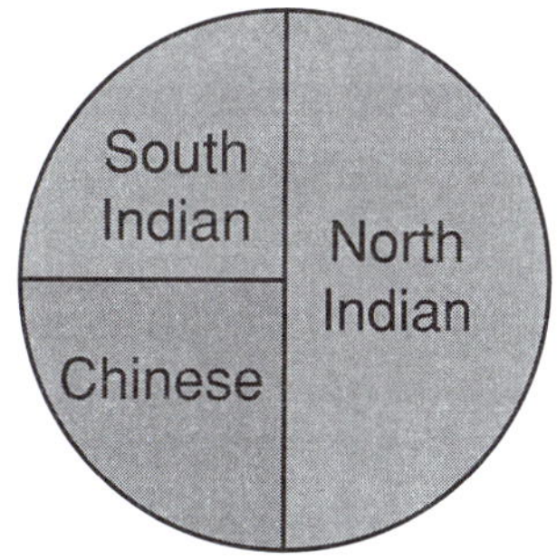

   a. Fill in the blanks by choosing the correct options.

      i. ________ $\left(\frac{1}{2}, \frac{1}{4}\right)$ of the restaurants serve Chinese food.

      ii. ________ $\left(\frac{1}{2}, \frac{1}{4}\right)$ of the restaurants serve North Indian food.

   b. If the circle represents 12 restaurants, how many of them serve South Indian food?

   c. If the circle represents 12 restaurants, how many of them serve North Indian food?

3. **The following data shows the favourite leisure activities of students. Construct the pie graph for this data.**

   Watching TV – 40%, Listening to music – 25%, Playing games – 20%, Dancing – 10%, Painting – 5%

Line Graph

Look at the graph given below. It has been drawn by placing the points and connecting them with straight lines. Such type of representation of data is known as **line graph**. These graphs are used to represent data that varies over a period of time.

Let us learn how to read and interpret line graphs.

To interpret the data in line graphs, follow these steps.

1. Read the X-axis and the y-axis.
2. Choose any point on the line graph and draw perpendicular lines from that point to the axes.
3. Read the value on the Y-axis corresponding to the value on the X-axis.

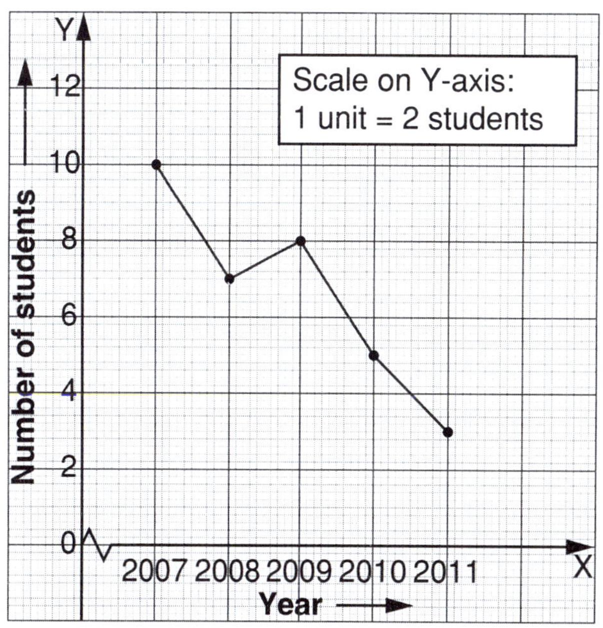

The given graph represents the number of students who took Transfer Certificates in a school during a period of 5 years. Study the graph and answer the following questions.

a. How many students took the transfer certificate in the year 2008?

In 2008, transfer certificate was taken by 7 students.

b. How many students took the transfer certificate from 2007 to 2011?

33 students have taken the transfer certificate from the year 2007 to 2011.

c. What is the difference between the number of students who took the transfer certificate in the year 2007 and 2011 respectively?

The difference between the number of students who took the transfer certificate in the year 2007 and 2011 is 7.

Note

There is a kink (^) before 2007 on the horizontal axis. It means that the full distance from 0 to 2007 is not shown.

Exercise 25.3

1 **The number of students in different years since the school was established in 2007 is shown in the given line graph.**

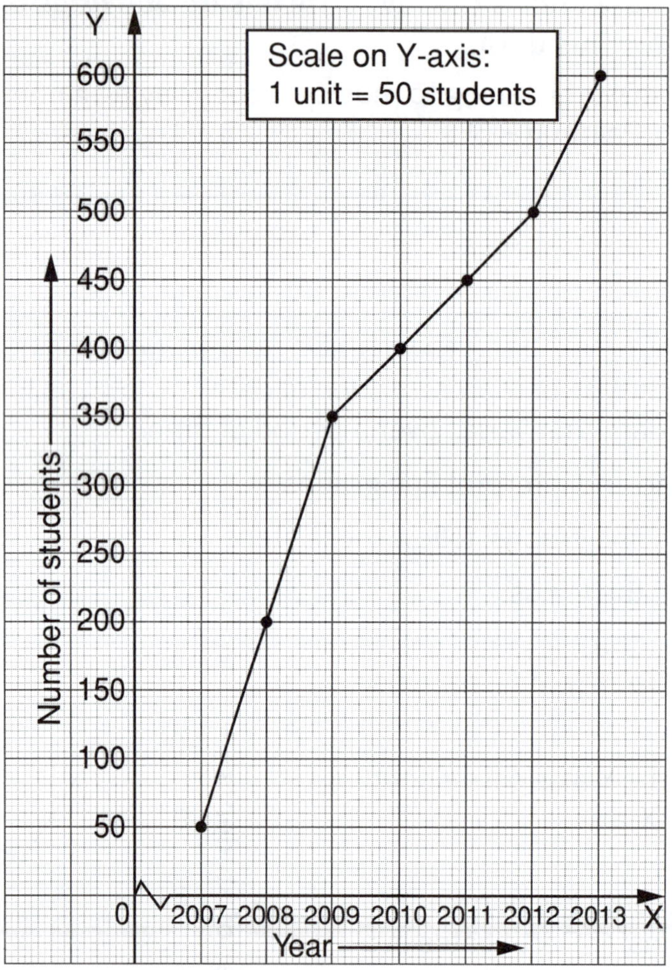

Read the graph and answer the following questions.

a. How many students were there when the school was established?
b. How many students were there in the year 2013?
c. How many students joined in the year 2011?
d. In which particular year, 150 students got admitted?
e. Which year had the maximum number of students?

2 **The given line graph shows the variation of Mary's weight over a span of four years. Interpret the graph and answer the following questions.**

a. How much did Mary weigh in the year 2007?

b. During which years did Mary maintain the same weight?

c. Was there any drop in Mary's weight? If so, in which year?

d. Mary's weight varied between _______ kg and _______ kg.

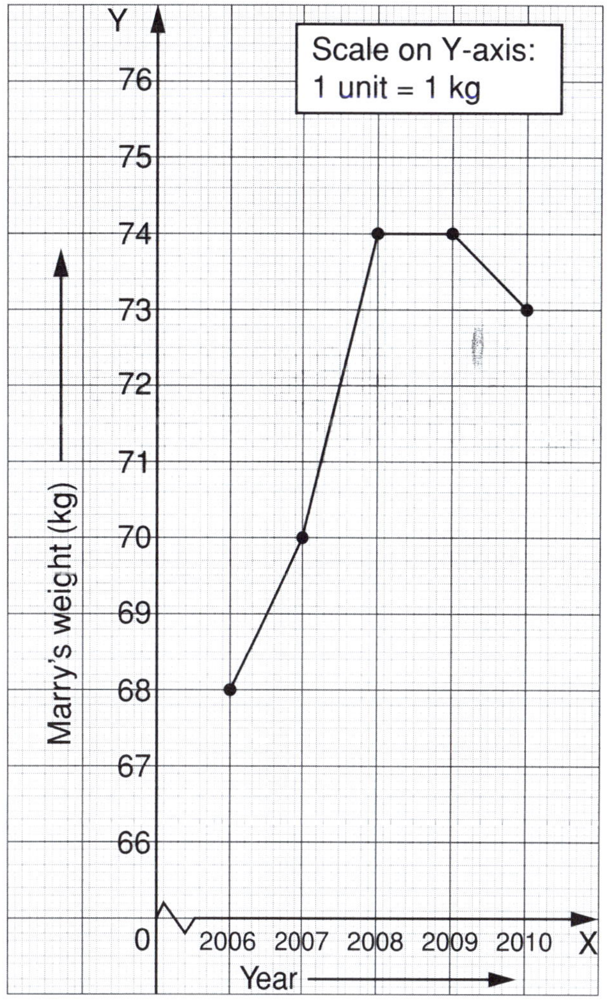

Summary

1. Information collected in the form of words or numbers to take meaningful decisions is called data.
2. A column graph is a graphical representation of numerical data in the form of rectangles of equal width and different heights that represent the frequency of the data items.
3. A pie graph is a graphical representation of numerical data in which data is represented by dividing a circle into different sectors.
4. A line graph is a graphical representation of numerical data in which data is represented by placing points and joining them by straight lines.

Project

Collect data from your classmates on the following and then create column graphs for each of them.

- Favourite subject
- Favourite drink

Choose appropriate scale depending on the data and draw rectangles of equal width and at equal distances from one another. Write the scales chosen on the graphs.

Revision Exercise

1 Read the column graph and answer the questions that follow.

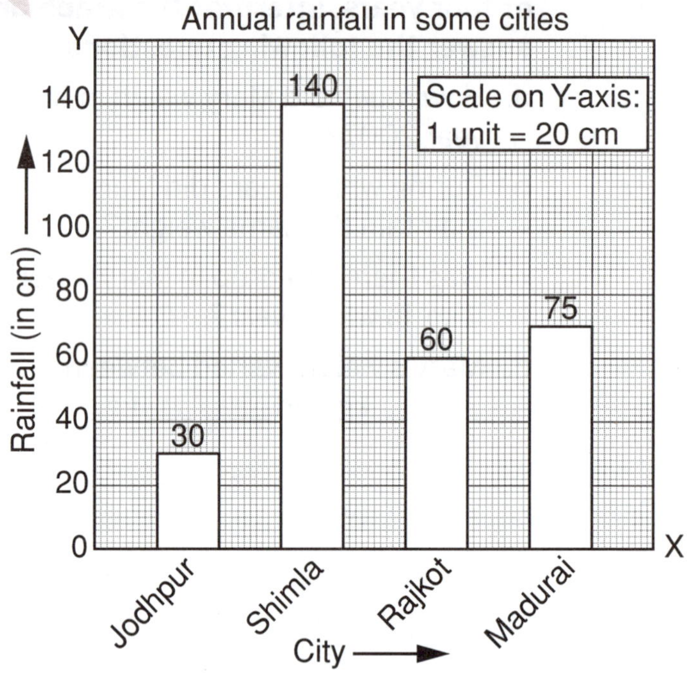

a. What information is provided in the column graph?

b. How much more rainfall did Madurai record as compared to Rajkot?

c. Name the cities that recorded the maximum rainfall and the minimum rainfall. What was the difference between the maximum and the minimum rainfall?

d. Arrange the cities in the increasing order of rainfall they received.

e. What is the ratio of rainfall in Jodhpur to that in Rajkot?

2 Complete the column graph and answer the questions that follow.

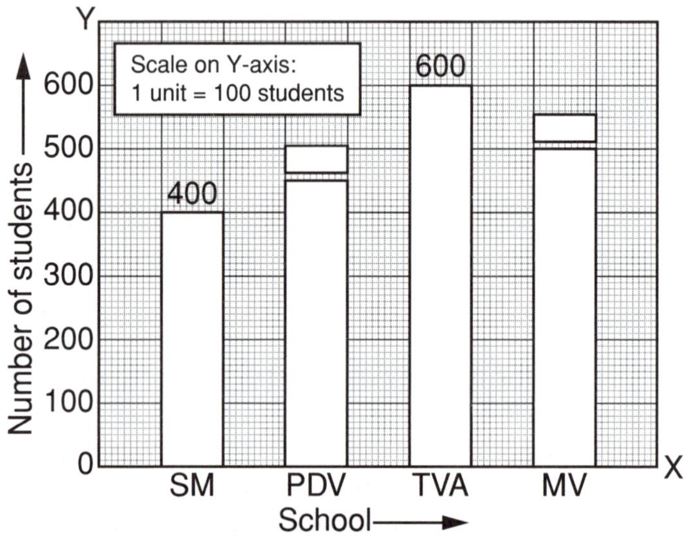

a. What information does the column graph convey?

b. How many students are there in TVA School?

c. How many more students should PDV School admit so that the number of students is same as that in TVA School?

d. How many more students are there in MV School as compared to PDV School?

e. What is the total number of students in all the schools?

3 A survey of 250 students was conducted in a school on the favourite tourist place in India and the data was recorded in the following table.

Construct a column graph for the above data and answer the following questions.

Tourist place in India	Number of students who liked this tourist place
Agra	45
Kanyakumari	40
Kashmir	50
Jaipur	10
Mysore	30
Goa	15
Delhi	20
Kerala	40

a. Which is the most favourite tourist place among the students?

b. Which is the least favourite tourist place among the students?

c. Which tourist places are equally liked by the students?

d. How many more students like Kashmir than Kerala?

4 **Read the pie graph and answer the questions that follow.**

a. What information is provided in the pie graph?

b. How many kilograms of oranges were sold?

c. If the quantity of bananas sold was 4 kg less than that of oranges, then how many kilograms of bananas were sold?

d. Which fruit was sold the maximum?

e. How many kilograms of fruits were sold in total?

Fruits sold (in kg)

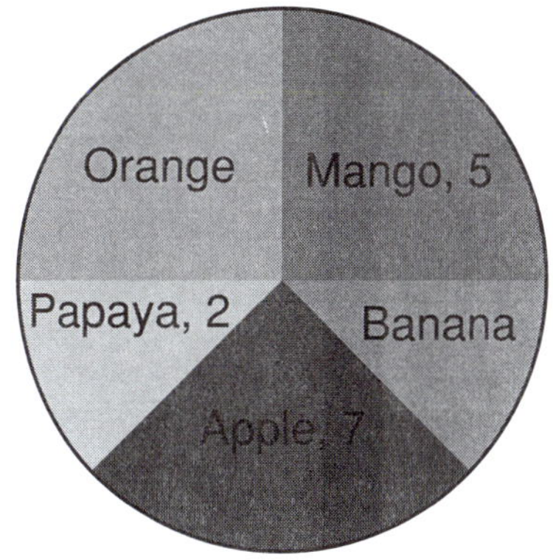

5 **Ashok and his friends went to a village fair. The different types of shops in the fair are shown in the given pie graph. If there were 32 shops in the fair, answer the following questions by referring to the pie graph.**

a. How many food stalls were there?

b. How many toy stalls were there?

c. State whether the following statements are true or false.

i. The number of joy rides is same as that of cloth stalls.

ii. The numbers of game stalls and clothes stalls taken together are more than that of bangle stalls.

Types of shops in a village fair

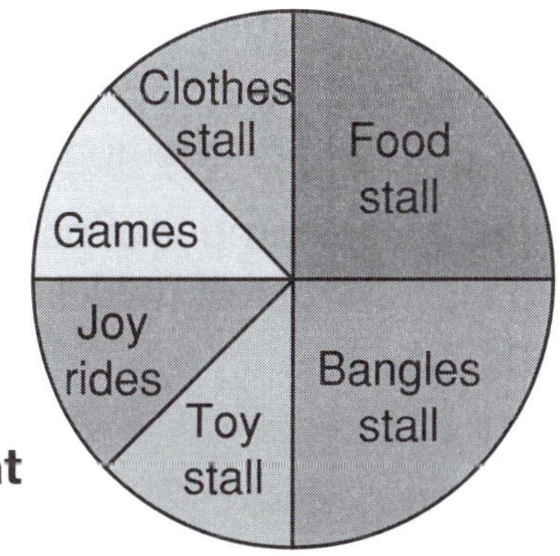

6 **The line graph given below shows the number of people that visited a store at various times during a day.**

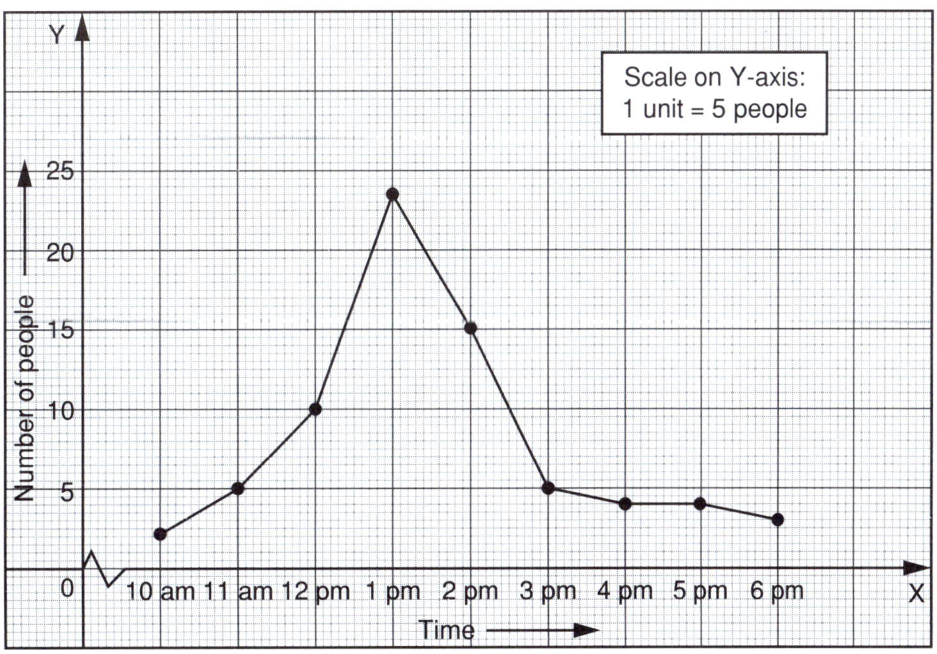

Read the above line graph and answer the following questions.

a. What is the line graph about?

b. At what time did the store attract the highest number of people? How many were they?

c. How many people were in the store when it opened?

d. How many people were in the store at 2 pm?

e. At what time did the store attract the least number of people? How many were they?

f. How many people visited the store in total?

Unit Worksheet 6

1 **A librarian recorded the data of the books borrowed by the students of classes 1–6 as given below. Interpret the data and create a table with class and number of books borrowed. Construct a column graph for the data by choosing a suitable scale.**

- Students of Class 1 borrowed 10 books.
- Students of Class 2 borrowed thrice the number of books borrowed by students of Class 1.
- Students of Class 3 borrowed the same number of books as that by Class 2.
- Students of Class 4 borrowed the same number of books as that by Class 6.
- The number of books borrowed by students of Class 5 is equal to the difference between the number of books borrowed by those of Class 4 and Class 1.
- The number of books borrowed by Class 6 is equal to the difference between the number of books borrowed by the students of Class 2 and Class 1.

2 **Ranjith got some money on his birthday. The given pie graph shows how he spent the money on different things.**

If he gave ₹50 to his sister, how much money did he get and how much did he spend on each of the things mentioned?

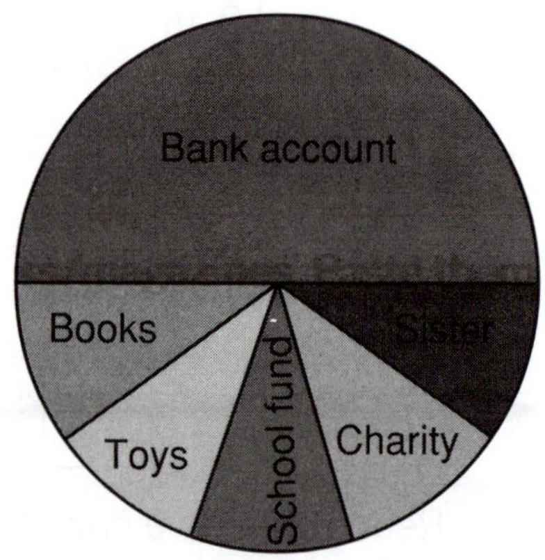

UNIT 7

Introduction to Sets

26

Let's Get Started

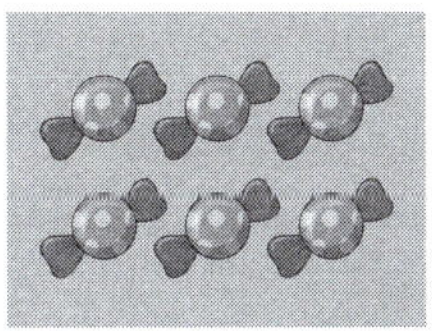

What do the pictures shown above represent?

They represent a collection or group of some specific objects or people. Such a collection is known as a set.

What I shall learn

- To understand the concept of sets
- To represent sets in roster and set-builder forms
- To identify different types of sets

Set

A **set** is a collection of well-defined objects. We usually denote sets by capital letters.

Well-defined Objects

The term 'well-defined' means that there is a definite criteria to determine whether an object belongs to the given set or not.

Example: The collection of months in the year = {January, February, March, April, May, June, July, August, September, October, November, December}

Here, we can say that all the objects belong to the mentioned set.

Can we say that the collection of good students in a class is well-defined?

No, as we cannot define a distinct criteria to select good students in a class. Students considered good by some teachers may not be considered good by others.

We can identify sets in our day-to-day lives, for example, the collection of books written by A. P. J. Abdul Kalam is well-defined and hence forms a set.

Some more examples of sets are given below.

1. The collection of currency notes of different denominations
2. The collection of flags of different countries
3. The collection of lions in India
4. The collection of multiples of 2 less than 10

Know the Mathematician – Georg Cantor

The German Georg Cantor created a theory of abstract sets of entities. This theory grew out of his investigations of some concrete problems regarding certain types of infinite sets of real numbers. A set, written by Cantor, is a collection of definite, distinguishable objects of perception or thought conceived as a whole.

Elements of a Set

The objects in a set are called **elements** or **members** of the set.

Consider the set of the first 5 whole numbers. In this set, the elements are 0, 1, 2, 3 and 4.

The elements of a set are written within a pair of curly braces { }. They are separated using commas.

Therefore, the set of the first 5 whole numbers can be written as A = {0, 1, 2, 3, 4}.

Example 1: Write the set of all even numbers between 9 and 15.

The even numbers between 9 and 15 are 10, 12 and 14.

Let the set be named as A.

Then, A = {10, 12, 14}

Here, 10 is an element of set A, that is, 10 belongs to A. This is written as $10 \in A$. 13 is not an element of this set, so it is written as $13 \notin A$.

In this example, it is possible to identify clearly whether an element belongs to A or not. Therefore, A is a collection of well-defined objects.

Note

We usually denote sets by capital letters and their elements by small letters of the English alphabet.

Example 2: State whether the following collections are sets.

a. Collection of all the schools in Kolkata

Clearly, the given collection will contain the names of all the schools in Kolkata, which may be known. Hence, the given collection is a set.

b. Collection of intelligent girls in a school

The term 'intelligent' can be interpreted differently by different people, so the elements are not well-defined. Hence, the given collection is not a set.

Exercise 26.1

State which of the following collections are sets. Justify your answer.

1. Collection of beautiful birds in India
2. Collection of all the students in a school
3. Collection of all the letters in your name
4. Collection of all whole numbers
5. Collection of roses in a basket
6. Collection of polygons having three sides

Representation of Sets

There are two ways of representing a set—the roster form and the set-builder form.

Roster Form

In the given image, A = {Sunday, Monday, Tuesday, Wednesday, Thursday, Friday, Saturday}. Here, we have listed all the elements of the set. This form of representing sets is known as the **roster form**. It is also called the **listing method**.

Example 3: Write the following sets in roster form.

a. The collection of integers between −10 and 10 that are divisible by 3

$D = \{-9, -6, -3, 0, 3, 6, 9\}$

b. The collection of even numbers between 10 and 100

$E = \{12, 14, 16, \ldots, 96, 98\}$

Note

The symbol '|' is read as 'such that'. We can also use the symbol ':' in its place.

Set-Builder Form

Look at the image given above once again. In set $B = \{x \mid x \text{ is a day in the week}\}$, we have listed the property or character of the set. This method in which we list the property or properties satisfied by the elements of the set is called the **set-builder form or rule method**.

Example 4: Represent S as the collection of all the integers between 10 and 20 in the set-builder form.

$S = \{x \mid x \text{ is an integer}, 10 < x < 20\}$

Example 5: Represent set $A = \{3, 6, 9, 12, 15, 18, 21\}$ in the set-builder form.

$A = \{x \mid x \text{ is a multiple of } 3, x < 24\}$

Example 6: Represent set $F = \{1, 3, 5, 15\}$ in the set-builder form.

$F = \{x \mid x \text{ is a natural number and a factor of } 15\}$

Standard Sets of Numbers

1. The set of natural numbers is denoted by N, that is, $N = \{1, 2, 3, 4, \ldots\}$.
2. The set of whole numbers is denoted by W, that is, $W = \{0, 1, 2, 3, 4, 5, \ldots\}$.
3. The set of integers is denoted by I or Z, that is, $Z/I = \{\ldots, -3, -2, -1, 0, 1, 2, 3, 4, \ldots\}$.

Example 7: Identify the methods by which the following sets have been represented.

a. $A = \{2, 4, 6, 8, 10, 12\}$

Roster form

b. $B = \{x \mid x \text{ is a desk in your classroom}\}$

Set-builder form

Example 8: Represent the following sets in the roster form.

a. $A = \{x \mid x \text{ is a letter in the English alphabet which comes after the letter u}\}$

$A = \{v, w, x, y, z\}$

b. $B = \{x \mid x \text{ is a month of the year having 31 days}\}$

B = {January, March, May, July, August, October, December}

Note

While counting the distinct elements of a set to find its cardinal number, we consider the repeated elements only once.

Cardinal Number of a Set

The number of distinct elements of a set A is called the **cardinal number** of A, which is denoted by $n(A)$.

Consider the following examples.

a. Set $X = \{a, b, c, d, e, f, g\}$ has 7 distinct elements.

b. Set $Y = \{1, 1, 2, 3, 4, 4, 5, 6\}$ has 6 distinct elements although it has 8 elements.

Example 9: What is the cardinal number of the set C = $\{m, n, o, m, p, q, r, s, p, t, u, v, w, x, y, z\}$?

Set C has 14 distinct elements. Therefore, its cardinal number is 14. This is written as $n(C) = 14$.

Example 10: Write the cardinal number of Set E = { }.

Set E has no element. Therefore, its cardinal number is 0. This is written as $n(E) = 0$.

Exercise 26.2

1 Express the following sets in roster form.

a. Set of all integers between −20 and −5

b. Set of all 2-digit numbers greater than 79

c. Set of all the multiples of 8 that are less than 80

d. Set of the first 5 odd numbers that are divisible by 7

e. Set of all consonants in the word KARNATAKA

f. Collection of colours in a rainbow

2 Represent the following sets in set-builder form.

a. D = {52, 54, 56, 58, 60, 62, 64, 66}

b. P = {101, 103, 107, 109, 113, 127, 131, 137, 139, 149}

c. M = {September, October, November, December}

d. F = {2, 3, 5, 7, 11}

e. S = {Mercury, Venus, Earth, Mars}

f. G = {1}

3 Write the cardinal numbers of the following sets.

a. A = $\{p, q, r, s, t\}$

b. B = {2, 2, 3, 5, 15, 15, 16, 17}

c. C = $\{x \mid x - 3 = 2\}$

d. D = $\{x \mid x$ is prime factor of 20$\}$

e. E = $\{x \mid x$ is a 1-digit prime number$\}$

f. F = {100, 101, 102, 103, 104}

Types of Sets

Let us learn about different types of sets.

Equivalent sets

If two sets have equal number of elements, then those sets are called **equivalent sets**.

Consider the following two sets.

A = $\{a, b, c, d\}$ B = {3, 6, 9, 12}

What can you say about the number of elements in each set?

We notice that both the sets have equal number of elements. So, they are equivalent sets.

Thus, set A $\leftrightarrow$ set B if $n(A) = n(B)$.

Example 11: Identify if the given pairs of sets are equivalent sets.

a. A ={x | x is a multiple of 4, $x < 24$} and B = {x | x is a multiple of 5, $x < 30$}

A = {4, 8, 12, 16, 20} and B = {5, 10, 15, 20, 25}

As n(A) = 5 = n(B), the sets A and B are equivalent sets.

b. S = {1, 2, 3, 6} and T = {1, 2, 3, 4, 6, 12}

As n(S) = 4 and n(T) = 6, the sets S and T are not equivalent sets.

Equal Sets

If each element of one set is also an element of another set, then the sets are called **equal sets**.

Consider the following sets.

P = {x | x is an even natural number, $x < 20$} Q = {x | x is a multiple of 2, $x < 20$}

Here, P = {2, 4, 6, 8, 10, 12, 14, 16, 18} and Q = {2, 4, 6, 8, 10, 12, 14, 16, 18}

Here, both the sets have the same elements. So, they are equal sets.

Example 12: Identify if the given pairs of sets are equal.

a. A = {x | x is a multiple of 3, $x < 15$} and B = {x | x is an odd number, $x < 8$}

A = {3, 6, 9, 12} and B = {1, 3, 5, 7}

Here, all the elements of set A are not elements of set B, so the sets are not equal.

b. C = {x | x is a natural number, $x < 8$} and D = {x | x is an integer, $0 < x < 8$}

C = {1, 2, 3, 4, 5, 6, 7} and D = {1, 2, 3, 4, 5, 6, 7}

Here, the sets C and D have the same elements. Therefore, they are equal sets.

Finite Sets

If the elements of a set can be counted, then the set is a **finite set**.

Consider the set A = {x | x is multiple of 10, $0 < x < 100$}.

Here, n(A) = 9. So, it is a finite set.

Infinite Set

If the number of elements of a set cannot be counted, then the set is an **infinite set**.

Consider the set, N = {1, 2, 3, 4, 5, 6, ...}

Here, the counting does not stop and the number of elements is not finite. Therefore, N is an infinite set.

Example 13: Classify the following as finite and infinite sets.

a. A = {10, 20, 30, 40, 50, ...}

Infinite set

b. B = {x | x is a factor of 35}

Finite set

Singleton Sets

A set that contains only one element is known as a **singleton set**.

Consider the set A = {2}.

This set has only one element in it, so it is a singleton set.

Similarly, set F = {x | x is the smallest even number} is a singleton set.

Example 14: Identify if the following are singleton sets.

a. A = {100000}

It is a singleton set.

b. C = {x | x is a month of the year}

It is not a singleton set.

Empty Sets

A set that contains no elements is called an **empty or null or void set**.

Consider the set E = { }. This set has no element, so it is an empty set.

For example, consider the set W of negative whole numbers.

Set W = { }

This is an empty set since there are no negative whole numbers.

Example 15: Identify if the following are empty sets.

a. A = {x | x is an even prime number}

It is not an empty set.

b. B = {x | x is a month having 33 days}

It is an empty set.

Disjoint Sets

Consider the sets A = {1, 3, 5, 7} and B = {2, 4, 6, 8}.

Do they have any elements in common? No.

Such sets that have no common elements between them are known as **disjoint sets**.

Overlapping Sets or Intersecting Sets

Consider the sets A = {2, 4, 6, 8, 10} and B = {4, 8, 12, 16, 20}.

The elements 4 and 8 are common to both the sets.

Such sets that have at least one common element are called **overlapping or intersecting sets**.

Properties of a Set

1. The elements of a set can be written in any order, that is, change in the order of the elements does not change the set.

   For example, sets A = {1, 2, 3, 4, 5} and B = {4, 5, 3, 1, 2} are the same as they contain the same elements.

2. If one or many elements of a set are repeated, the set remains the same.

   For example, sets A = {1, 2, 3, 4, 5, 5, 5, 6, 7, 8} and B = {1, 2, 3, 4, 5, 6, 7, 8} are the same. This is because in a set, even if an element is repeated, we consider it once.

Exercise 26.3

1. **Identify if the following pairs of sets are equivalent.**
   a. A = {11, 13, 15, 17, 19} and B = {10, 12, 14, 16}
   b. C = {p, q, r, s, t} and D = {d, e, f, g}
   c. E = {x | x is a prime factor of 20} and F = {x | x is a multiple of 5, $x < 40$}
   d. G = {x | x is a letter in the word SOCIAL} and H = {x | x is a letter in the word SCIENCE}
   e. I = {2, 3, 5, 7} and J = {2, 4, 6, 8}
2. **Identify if the following pairs of sets are equal.**
   a. A = {a, b, c, d, e} and B = {e, d, c, b, a}
   b. C = {x | x is a vowel in the word COUNT} and D = {x | x is a vowel in the word WRITE}
   c. E = {x | x is an odd number, $5 < x < 15$} and F = {x | x is an even number, $5 < x < 15$}
   d. G = {1, 2, 3, 4, 5} and H = {0, 1, 2, 3, 4, 5}
   e. The set of the first 5 positive integers and the set of the first 5 negative integers
3. **Classify the following sets as singleton and empty sets.**
   a. The set of all negative natural numbers
   b. The set of all whole numbers less than 1
   c. A = {n}
   d. B = {x | x is a month having 27 days}
   e. C = {x | x is a natural number, $10 < x < 11$}
4. **Classify the following as finite and infinite sets.**
   a. The set of all the factors of 100
   b. The set of all the multiples of 4
   c. The set of all the integers between −1000 and 1000
   d. The set of all the points on a given line
   e. The set of the states of India

Summary

1. A set is a collection of well-defined objects.
2. Roster form and set-builder form are the two ways of representing sets.
3. The number of distinct elements of a set A is called the cardinal number of A.
4. There are different types of sets, namely, equivalent sets, equal sets, finite sets, infinite sets, singleton sets and empty sets.

Revision Exercise

1 State which of the following are sets. Justify your answer.

a. The collection of tigers in India
b. The set of prime numbers
c. The set of beautiful flowers in a garden
d. The set of fast-flying birds
e. The collection of computers in the computer lab of a school

2 Represent the following sets in roster form and write the cardinal number of each set.

a. A = {x | x is a prime factor of 48}
b. B = Set of all the letters in the word COURAGE
c. C = {x | x is a multiple of 6, $x < 40$}
d. D = {x | x is a composite number, $10 < x < 12$}
e. E = {x | x is an odd prime number, $x < 20$}

3 Match the following.

a. Set of all integers	i. Empty set
b. A = {x | x is a vowel} and B = {x | x is a whole number, $x < 5$}	ii. Finite set
c. Set of all the prime factors of 20	iii. Infinite set
d. C = { }	iv. Singleton set
e. Y = {x | x is the largest 5-digit number}	v. Equal sets
	vi. Equivalent sets

4 State whether the following statements are true or false.

a. {2, 4, 6, 8, 10, 12} = {6, 4, 2, 10, 12, 8}
b. Two equivalent sets are always equal.
c. If A = {x | x is an integer, $-1 < x < 2$}, then $-2 \in$ A.
d. The collection of all 2-digit numbers is a finite set.
e. If B = {x | x is a factor of 28}, then n(B) = 6.

For the Curious Mind

Rahul says the set A = {x | x is a fraction, $\frac{1}{3} < x < \frac{2}{3}$} is an infinite set, but Shreya said it is an empty set. Who is correct? Justify your answer.

UNIT 7

Operations on Sets

27

Let's Get Started

Addition, subtraction, multiplication and division are the fundamental operations on numbers. Similarly, union and intersection are the basic operations on sets. Let us learn about these two operations in some detail.

What I shall learn

- To understand the concepts of union and intersection of two sets
- To find the cardinal number of union and intersection of two sets

Operations on Sets

Union of Sets

Consider the sets A = {2, 3, 5, 7, 13} and B = {7, 11, 13, 17}.

The union of sets A and B is the set that contains all those elements that are either in A or in B, or in both A and B.

Therefore, C = {2, 3, 5, 7, 11, 13, 17} is the union of A and B, and it is represented by $A \cup B$.

Example 1: Let A = {*a*, *b*, *f*, *s*, *r*, *t*} and B = {*e*, *d*, *f*, *s*, *r*, *c*}. Find $A \cup B$ and $B \cup A$.

$A \cup B = \{a, b, f, s, r, t\} \cup \{e, d, f, s, r, c\}$

$= \{a, b, c, d, e, f, s, r, t\}$ [Although *f* and *r* are present in both the sets, we consider them only once.]

$B \cup A = \{e, d, f, s, r, c\} \cup \{a, b, f, s, r, t\}$

$= \{a, b, c, d, e, f, s, r, t\}$

Properties of Union of Sets

1. The union of sets is commutative. That is, $A \cup B = B \cup A$.

   Example: Let A = {1, 2, 3, 4, 5} and B = {2, 4, 5, 6, 7} be two sets.

   Then, $A \cup B = \{1, 2, 3, 4, 5, 6, 7\}$ and $B \cup A = \{1, 2, 3, 4, 5, 6, 7\}$.

   $\therefore A \cup B = B \cup A$

2. As the elements in a set are distinct, the union of a set and the set itself is the set itself. That is, $A \cup A = A$.

   Example: Let A = {*a*, *b*, *c*, *d*, *e*, *f*} be a set

   Then, $A \cup A = \{a, b, c, d, e, f\} \cup \{a, b, c, d, e, f\} = \{a, b, c, d, e, f\} = A$

3. The union of a set and an empty set is the set itself. That is, $A \cup \phi = A$.

   Example: If A = {2, 4, 6, 8, 10} and ϕ = { }, then $A \cup \phi = \{2, 4, 6, 8, 10\}$.

Intersection of Sets

Observe the sets A = {1, 2, 3, 4, 5} and B = {2, 5, 7, 8}.

The intersection of sets A and B is the set that contains all those elements that are in both A and B.

Therefore, C = {2, 5} is the intersection of sets A and B and is denoted by $A \cap B$.

Example 2: If A = {5, 10, 15, 20, 25, 30, 35} and B = {10, 20, 30, 40, 50, 60}, find $A \cap B$ and $B \cap A$.

$A \cap B$ = {5, 10, 15, 20, 25, 30, 35} $\cap$ {10, 20, 30, 40, 50, 60} = {10, 20, 30}

$B \cap A$ = {10, 20, 30, 40, 50, 60} $\cap$ {5, 10, 15, 20, 25, 30, 35} = {10, 20, 30}

Properties of Intersection of Sets

1. The intersection of sets is commutative. That is, $A \cap B = B \cap A$.

   Example: Let A = {1, 2, 3, 4, 5} and B = {2, 4, 5, 6, 7} be two sets.

   Then, $A \cap B$ = {2, 4, 5} and $B \cap A$ = {2, 4, 5}.

   $\therefore A \cap B = B \cap A$

2. As the elements in a set are distinct, the intersection of a set and the set itself is the set itself. That is, $A \cap A = A$.

   Example: Let A = {*a*, *b*, *c*, *d*, *e*, *f*} be a set.

   Then, $A \cap A$ = {*a*, *b*, *c*, *d*, *e*, *f*} $\cap$ {*a*, *b*, *c*, *d*, *e*, *f*} = {*a*, *b*, *c*, *d*, *e*, *f*} = A

3. The intersection of a set and an empty set is the empty set. That is, $A \cap \phi = \phi$.

   Example: If A = {2, 4, 6, 8, 10} and ϕ = { }, then $A \cap \phi = \phi$.

   Can you verify the above properties by taking some other examples?

Exercise 27.1

1 Write the sets that represent $A \cup B$ and $A \cap B$ in each of the following.

a. A = {*a*, *b*, *c*, *d*, *f*, *g*, *k*} and B = {*j*, *l*, *d*, *f*, *c*, *e*, *h*}

b. A = {2, 4, 6, 8, 10, 12} and B = {4, 8, 12, 16, 20}

c. A = {2, 4, 6, 8, 10, 12} and B = {1, 3, 5, 7, 9, 11}

d. A = {*x*, *y*, *z*, *a*, *c*, *d*} and B = {*b*, *e*, *f*, *i*, *j*}

e. P = {10, 20, 30, 40, 50} and B = {20, 40, 60, 80}

2 Write the sets that represent $A \cup B$ and $A \cap B$ in each of the following.

a. A = {x | x is a letter in the word SUPER} and B = {x | x is a letter in the word POWER}

b. A = {x | x is a prime number, $15 < x < 35$} and B = {x | x is an odd number, $15 < x < 30$}

c. A = {x | x is a factor of 20} and B = {x | x is a factor of 24}

d. A = {x | x is a multiple of 5, $x < 30$} and B = {x | x is a multiple of 40, $x < 200$}

e. P = {x | $x + 5 = 2$} and B = {x | x is a an integer $-9 < x < -1$}

Cardinal Number of the Union and Intersection of Two Sets

Consider the sets A = {5, 10, 15, 20, 25, 30, 35} and B = {10, 20, 30, 40, 50, 60}.

Here, $n(A) = 7$ and $n(B) = 6$.

Now, $A \cup B = \{5, 10, 15, 20, 25, 30, 35, 40, 50, 60\}$

$\therefore n(A \cup B) = 10$

And $A \cap B = \{10, 20, 30\}$

$\therefore n(A \cap B) = 3$

Observe that $n(A \cup B) = [n(A) + n(B)] - n(A \cap B)$.

That is, $10 = (7 + 6) - 3$

Thus, we can conclude that the number of elements (cardinal number) in the union of two sets is the sum of the cardinal numbers of the sets minus the cardinal number of the intersection of the two sets.

That is, $n(A \cup B) = [n(A) + n(B)] - n(A \cap B)$

Example 3: If set $A = \{x \mid x$ is a factor of 12$\}$ and set $B = \{x \mid x$ is a factor of 18$\}$, then find $n(A \cap B)$ and $n(A \cup B)$.

In roster form, set A = {1, 2, 3, 4, 6, 12} and set B = {1, 2, 3, 6, 9, 18}.

$A \cap B = \{1, 2, 3, 6\}$

$\therefore n(A \cap B) = 4$

And, $(A \cup B) = \{1, 2, 3, 4, 6, 9, 12, 18\}$

$\therefore n(A \cup B) = 8$

Also, $8 = [6 + 6] - 4$

Remember

1. The cardinal number of the union of set A and ϕ is the cardinal number of set A itself.
2. The cardinal number of the intersection of set A and ϕ is 0.

Exercise 27.2

1. If $A = \{x \mid x = 2m, m < 4$ and $m \leftrightarrow N\}$, $B = \{x \mid x$ is a multiple of 6, $x < 60\}$ and $C = \{x \mid x$ is a factor of 90$\}$, then write the sets that represent the following.
   a. $\Lambda \cup B$
   b. $\Lambda \cap B$
   c. $B \cap C$
   d. $A \cup C$
   e. $A \cup C \cap B \cap C$
2. If $n(A) = 6$, $n(B) = 4$ and $n(A \cup B) = 8$, find $n(A \cap B)$.

Summary

1. The union of sets A and B is the set that contains all those elements that are either in A or in B, or in both A and B.
2. (a) $A \cup B = B \cup A$ (b) $A \cup A = A$ (c) $A \cup \phi = A$.
3. The intersection of sets A and B is the set that contains all those elements that are in both A and B.
4. (a) $A \cap B = B \cap A$ (b) $A \cap A = A$ (c) $A \cap \phi = \phi$
5. $n(A \cup B) = [n(A) + n(B)] - n(A \cap B)$.

Revision Exercise

1. **Write the sets A ∪ B and A ∩ B for the following pairs of sets.**
   a. A = {1, 3, 5, 7, 9} and B = {1, 2, 3, 4, 5, 6}
   b. A = {*s*, *l*, *e*, *e*, *p*} and B = {*r*, *e*, *l*, *a*, *x*}
   c. A = {5, 10, 15, 20, 25, 30} and B = {2, 4, 6, 8, 12}
   d. A = {*x* | *x* is a prime factor of 8} and B = {*x* | *x* is a factor of 4}

2. **Find *n*(A ∪ B) and *n*(A ∩ B) for the following pairs of sets.**
   a. A = {10, 12, 14, 16, 18, 20} and B = {10, 13, 15, 16, 18, 19, 20}
   b. A = {*a*, *b*, *c*, *d*, *e*, *i*} and B = {*a*, *e*, *i*, *o*, *u*}
   c. A = {*x* | *x* is a whole number, *x* < 8} and B = {*x* | *x* is an integer between −5 and 5}
   d. A = {*x* | *x* is a letter in the word GAME} and B = {*x* | *x* is a letter in the word SPORTS}

3. **State whether the following statements are true or false.**
   a. If A = {8, 16, 24} and B = {16, 32, 48}, then *n*(A ∩ B) = 6.
   b. If A = {*q*, *w*, *e*, *r*} and B = {*p*, *q*, *r*, *s*}, then (A ∩ B) = {*q*, *r*}.
   c. If A = {7, 14, 21, 28} and B = {14, 28, 52}, then *n*(A ∪ B) = 5.
   d. If A = {*x* | *x* is a vowel in the word REAL} and B = {*x* | *x* is a vowel in the word IMAGE}, then, (A ∪ B) = {E, A, I, R, L, M, G}.

4. **Match the following.**

a. A ∪ B	i. ϕ
b. A ∩ B	ii. A
c. A ∩ ϕ	iii. B ∩ A
d. A ∪ A	iv. B ∪ A

5. If A = {1, 2, 3, 4, 5}, B = {3, 4, 5, 6, 7}, C = {5, 6, 7, 8, 9} and D = {7, 8, 9, 10, 11}, then find the following.
   a. A ∪ B   b. A ∪ C   c. B ∩ C   d. C ∩ D

For the Curious Mind

If A = {*x* | *x* is a letter in the word OFFICE}, B = {*x* | *x* is a letter in the word WORKERS} and C = {*x* | *x* is a letter in the word SALARY}, then write the sets representing the following.

a. A ∪ B ∩ C   b. (A ∪ B) ∩ (B ∪ C)

UNIT 7

Venn Diagrams 28

Set Representation

What I shall learn

- To represent sets using Venn diagram

Venn diagrams, a concept of graphical method of representation of sets and its operations, were introduced by a British Mathematician John Venn.

A circle or an ellipse is usually used to represent a set. Inside the circle or ellipse, we write the elements of the set.

Example 1: Represent set A = {0, 1, 2, 3, 4, 5} by Venn diagram.

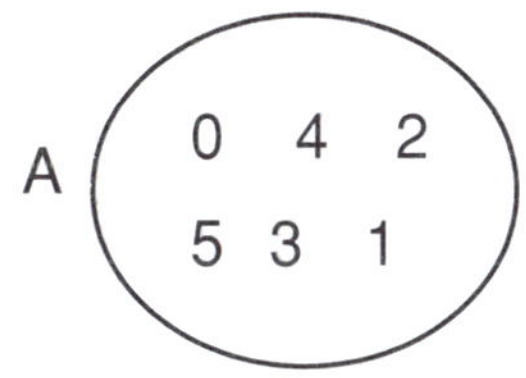

Example 2: Represent set B = {x | x is a consonant in the word DIAGRAMS} by Venn diagram.

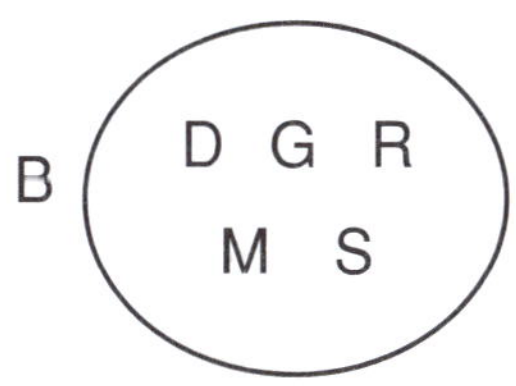

In roster form, set B = {D, G, R, M, S}

Now, let us see how we represent a set that contains infinite elements.

Look at the following example.

Example 3: Represent set N = {Set of natural numbers} and set W = {Set of whole numbers} by Venn diagram.

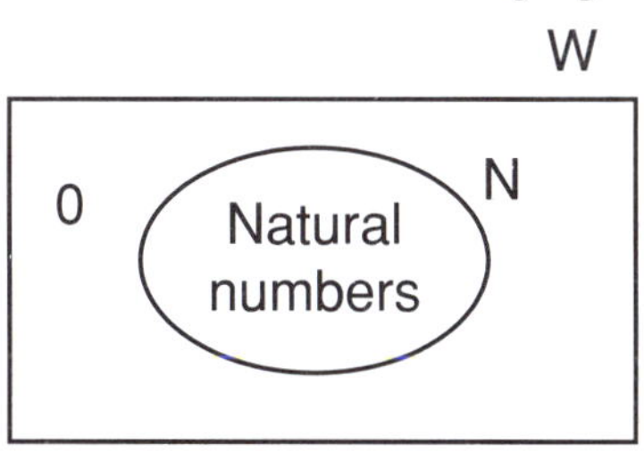

Know the Mathematician – John Venn

John Venn was a British mathematician and philosopher born on August 4, 1834 in Hull, Yorkshire. He was considered an expert in the branch of mathematics called 'logic'. He took up the concept of Venn Diagrams in the year 1881. These diagrams were a representation of the relationships between sets using circles within circles.

Set Operations and Venn Diagrams

Case 1: Where There Are Two Disjoint Sets

We represent two disjoint sets A and B by two separate closed, bounded figures as they do not contain any common elements. So, in this case, $A \cap B = \phi$.

Example 4: Represent the following sets by Venn diagram.

a. A = {5, 6, 7, 8, 9} and B = {−5, −6, −7, −8, −9}

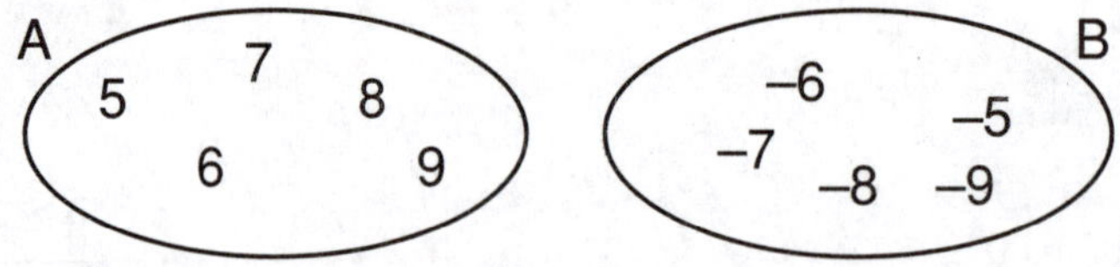

b. A = {x | x is a prime number, $x < 10$} and B = {x | x is a composite number, $x < 10$}

In roster form, A = {2, 3, 5, 7} and B = {4, 6, 8, 9}.

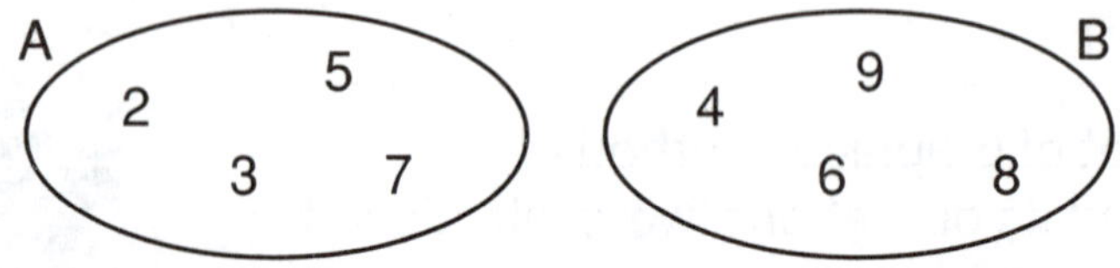

Case 2: When There Are Two Intersecting or Overlapping Sets

In this case, we draw two intersecting closed, bounded figures and list the common elements in the common part.

Example 5: Represent the following sets by Venn diagram.

a. A = {10, 20, 30, 40, 50} and B = {20, 40, 60, 80, 100}

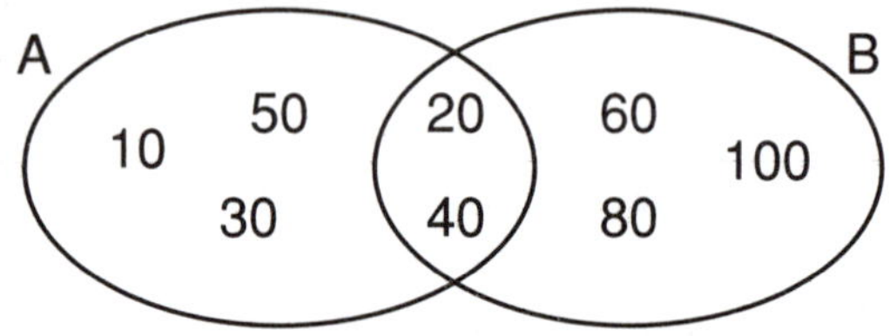

b. A = {x | x is a factor of 10} and B = {x | x is a factor of 15}

In roster form, A = {1, 2, 5, 10} and B = {1, 3, 5, 15}.

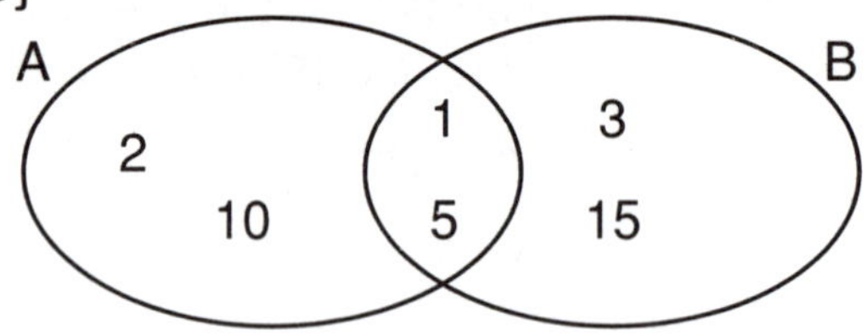

Case 3: When All the Elements of One Set Are Contained in Another Set

In this case, one closed figure is drawn inside the other to represent the given sets.

Example 6: Represent set A = {0, 1, 2, 3} and set B = {0, 1, 2, 3, 4, 5, 6, 7} by Venn diagram.

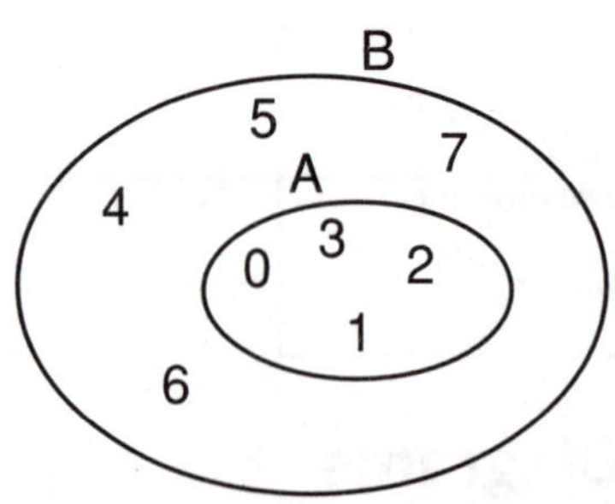

Example 7: Observe the given Venn diagram and represent the following sets in roster form.

a. Set A   b. Set B   c. $A \cup B$ d. $A \cap B$

a. Set A = {6, 12, 18, 24, 30}

b. Set B = {12, 24, 36, 48}

c. $A \cup B$ contains all the elements that are in set A and set B. The elements common to both the sets are written only once.

That is, $A \cup B$ = {6, 18, 30, 12, 24, 36, 48}

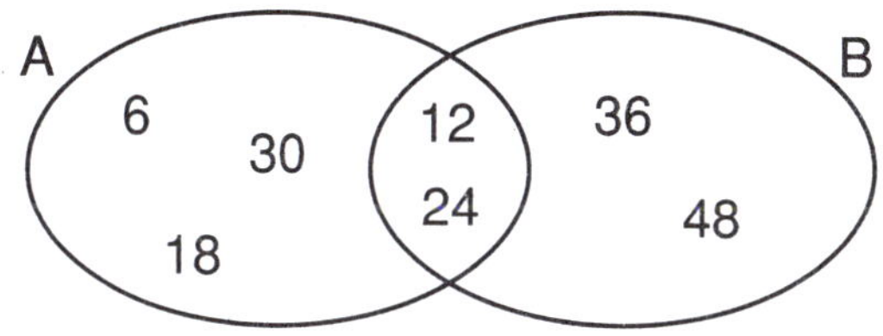

d. $A \cap B$ contains only those elements that are common to both the sets.

That is, $A \cap B$ = {12, 24}

Exercise 28.1

1 **Represent the following pairs of sets by Venn diagram.**

a. A = {5, 10, 15, 20} and B = {2, 4, 6, 8}

b. A = {*c*, *o*, *u*, *r*, *a*, *g*, *e*} and B = {*b*, *r*, *a*, *v*, *e*, *r*, *y*}

c. A = {x | x is a multiple of 4, $x < 15$} and B = {x | x is a factor of 24}

d. A = {x | x is a letter in the word SMILE} and B = {x | x is a vowel in the word IMAGINE}

e. A = Set of the first 6 negative integers and B = Set of the first 6 whole numbers

2 **Observe the given Venn diagrams and write the following sets in the set-builder form for each of the Venn diagrams.**

i. A   ii. B   iii. $A \cup B$ iv. $A \cap B$

a.

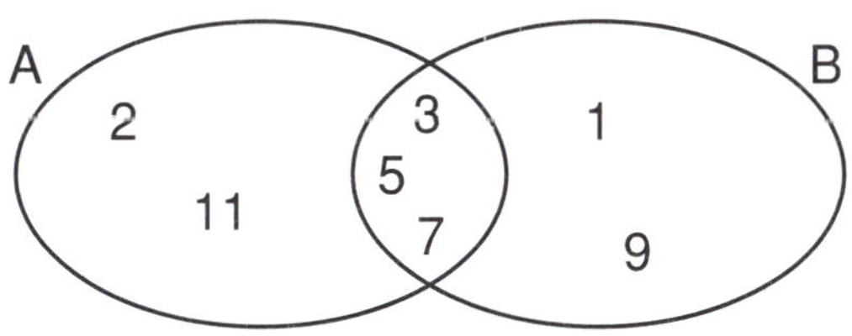

b.

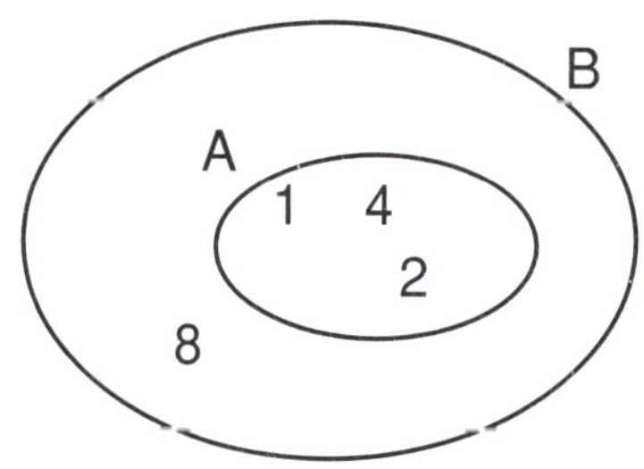

Summary

1. A circle or an ellipse is usually used to represent a set and the elements of the set are written inside the circle or ellipse.
2. Two disjoint sets are represented by two separate closed, bounded figures.
3. In case of two intersecting or overlapping sets, two intersecting closed, bounded figures are drawn and the common elements are listed in the common section.
4. When all the elements of one set are contained in the other, a closed figure is drawn inside another closed figure to represent the given sets.

Revision Exercise

1 **Represent the following pairs of sets by Venn diagram.**

a. A = {50, 100, 150, 200} and B = {20, 40, 60, 80}

b. A = {*c*, *h*, *a*, *l*, *e*, *n*, *g*} and B = {*s*, *u*, *c*, *e*, *f*, *l*}

c. A = {x | x is a multiple of 3, $x < 15$} and B = {x | x is a factor of 15}

d. A = {x | x is a consonant in the word THANKS} and B = {x | x is a letter in the word WELCOME}

e. A = Set of the first 5 prime numbers and B = Set of the first 5 positive integers

2 **Observe the given Venn diagrams and write the following sets in the set-builder form for each of the Venn diagram.**

i. A ii. B iii. $A \cup B$ iv. $A \cap B$

a.

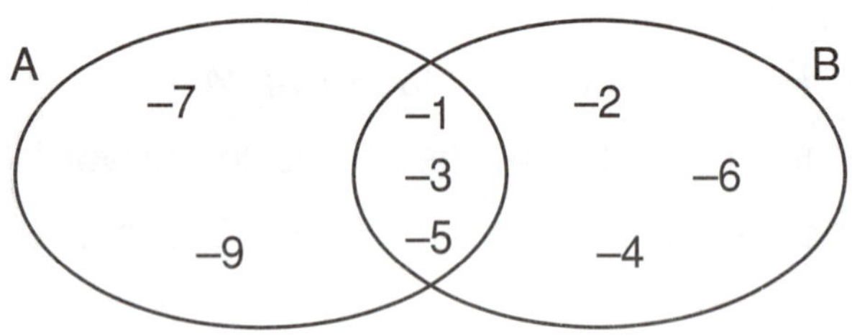

b.

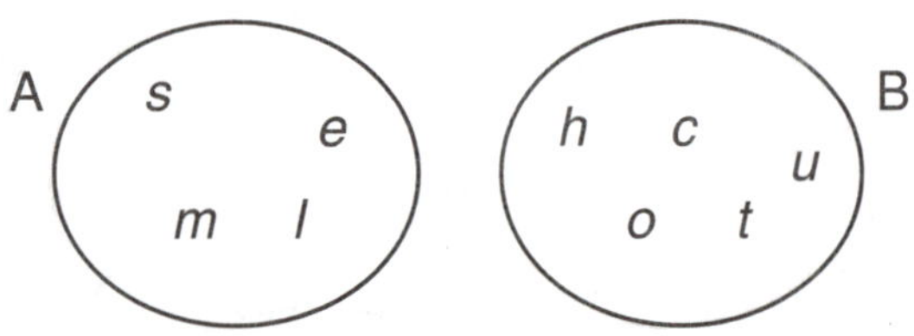

c.

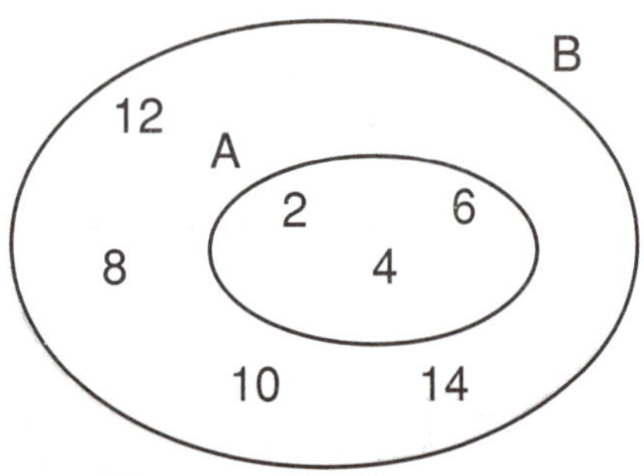

For the Curious Mind

Represent set A = {1, 2, 3, 4, 5}, set B = {x | x is a whole number, $x < 6$} and set C = {−3, −2, −1, 0, 1, 2, 3} by Venn diagram. Find $A \cup (B \cap C)$.

Unit Worksheet 7

I. Choose the correct option for each of the following.

1. **The method/s in which we list the elements of a given set is/are called** [ ]
   a. Roster form b. Listing method
   c. Set-builder form d. Both a and b

2. **An example for an empty set is** [ ]
   a. A = {set of even prime numbers} b. B = {0}
   c. C = { } d. D = {a, b, c, d}

3. **The cardinal number of the intersection of set A and ϕ is ______.** [ ]
   a. Roster form b. Listing method
   c. Set-builder form d. Both a and b

4. **For two disjoint sets A and B, $A \cap B$ = ____.** [ ]
   a. 0 b. Set A c. ϕ d. Set B

5. **The Venn diagram representation of the sets A = {a, b, c, d} and B = {c, d, b, a, e, f, g, h} Is** [ ]

a.

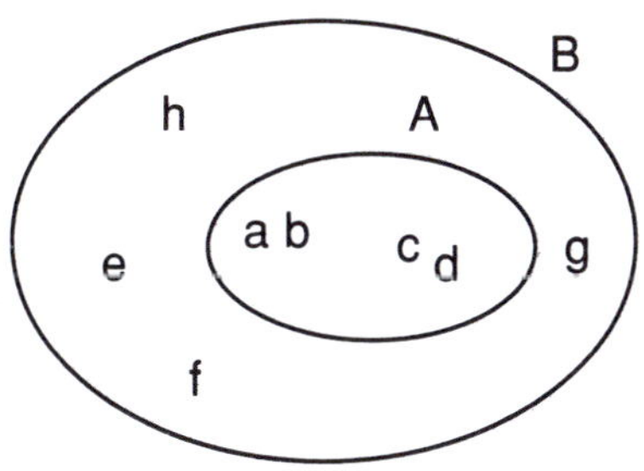

b.

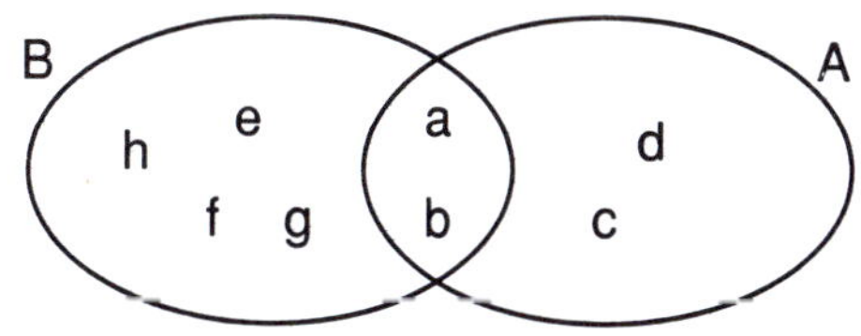

c.

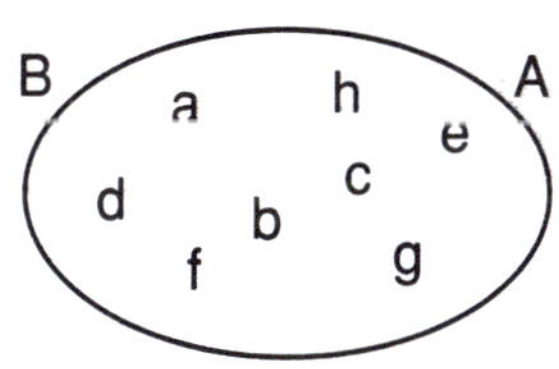

d.

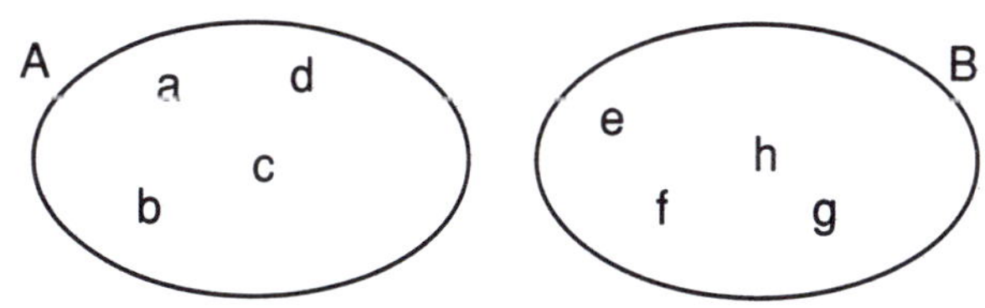

II. State whether the following statements are True (T) or False (F).

1. **If A = {a, c, e, g, i} and B = {b, c, d, e, f}, then $(A \cap B)$ = {c, e}.** [ ]
2. **If A = {18, 15, 26, 25} and B = {26, 32, 78}, then n $(A \cap B)$ = 3.** [ ]
3. **If A = {107, 204, 301, 308} and B = {104, 308, 602}, then n $(A \cup B)$ = 4.** [ ]
4. **If A = {x | x is a letter in the word 'learn'} and B = {x | x is a letter in the 'earn'}, then, $(A \cup B)$ = {l, e, a, r, n}.** [ ]

Test 1

Chapters 1–3 **Maximum marks: 25**

1 Choose the correct options. **(5 × 1 = 5)**

a. The natural numbers along with 0 are called ______. [ ]

i. whole number ii. integers

iii. prime numbers iv. factors

b. A natural number with more than two factors is a ______. [ ]

i. prime number ii. composite number

iii. factor iv. multiple

c. What should be added to (−26) to get 17? [ ]

i. 53 ii. 63 iii. 43 iv. 9

d. The difference in the place values of the two fives in 157850 is ______. [ ]

i. 4950 ii. 49950 iii. 49500 iv. 500

e. The LCM of 48 and 72 is ______. [ ]

i. 144 ii. 154 iii. 164 iv. 72

2 Fill in the blanks. **(5 × 1 = 5)**

a. The product of an integer and zero is ____________.

b. A number one more than another number is called its ____________.

c. Two natural numbers which do not have a common prime factor are called __________.

d. (−64) + (+49) = ____________

e. The number corresponding to thirty-two lakh six thousand five hundred sixty-eight is ______________.

3 Write T for True and F for False. **(5 × 1 = 5)**

a. 35672109 > 35672209 [ ]

b. The product of two negative integers is always a positive integer. [ ]

c. Every whole number is an integer. [ ]

d. 24 is a multiple of 7. [ ]

e. The HCF of 36 and 60 is 12. [ ]

4 Answer the following questions briefly. **(2 × 2 = 4)**

a. How many four-digit numbers are there?

b. The sum of two integers is −32. If one of them is −12, find the other.

5 Answer the following questions. **(2 × 3 = 6)**

a. Write the greatest 8-digit number using the digits 0, 1, 5, 4, 3, 9, 8 and 7 only once. Also, write the number in both Indian and International place value systems.

b. Find the highest common factor (HCF) of 184, 230 and 276 using the long division method.

Test 2

Chapters 4–6 **Maximum marks: 25**

1 Choose the correct options. **(5 × 1 = 5)**

a. $a^m \times a^n =$ ________ [ ]

i. a^{m+n} ii. a^{m-n} iii. $a^{m/n}$ iv. $\left(a^m\right)^n$

b. Which of the following shaded figures represents the fraction $\frac{3}{4}$? [ ]

i. 

ii. 

iii. 

iv. 

c. Which of the following pairs of fractions is not equivalent? [ ]

i. $\frac{5}{9}, \frac{30}{54}$ ii. $\frac{3}{10}, \frac{12}{40}$

iii. $\frac{7}{13}, \frac{21}{52}$ iv. $\frac{8}{7}, \frac{72}{63}$

d. What is the place value of 4 in the decimal number 18.543? [ ]

i. $\frac{4}{1000}$ ii. $\frac{4}{100}$ iii. $\frac{4}{10}$ iv. 4

e. $\sqrt[3]{9261} =$ ________ [ ]

i. 21 ii. 31 iii. 41 iv. 11

2 Fill in the blanks. **(5 × 1 = 5)**

a. Fractions with different denominators are called ____________.

b. The fractions in which the denominators are 10, 100, 1000, etc. are called ____________.

c. $(-1)^{353} =$ ____________

d. $0.8613 \div 9 =$ ____________

e. $21\frac{3}{5} \div 3\frac{11}{15} =$ ____________

3 Write T for True and F for False. **(5 × 1 = 5)**

a. Two fractions are unlike if their numerators are different. [ ]

b. $0.07 < 0.02$ [ ]

c. Square of an integer is always positive [ ]

d. $(-1)^{42} \times (-1)^{21} \times (-1)^{2} \times (-1)^{567} = 1$ [ ]

e. $3\frac{4}{5} + 1\frac{2}{3} = 4\frac{7}{15}$ [ ]

4 **Answer the following questions briefly.** **(2 × 2 = 4)**

a. Simplify $\left(3\frac{1}{5}+1\frac{3}{8}\right)\div\left(2\frac{3}{4}-2\frac{1}{2}\right)$.

b. The cost of a book is ₹19.85. Find the cost of 55 such books.

5 **Answer the following questions.** **(2 × 3 = 6)**

a. Simplify $\frac{\sqrt[3]{8000}+\sqrt[3]{343}}{\sqrt[3]{1000}-\sqrt[3]{729}}$.

b. Mahesh gave $\frac{7}{12}$ of his money to a friend, $\frac{3}{5}$ of remaining amount to his son and the remaining to his wife. If his wife got ₹3500, what was the total amount?

Test 3

Chapters 7–9 **Maximum marks: 25**

1 **Choose the correct options.** **(5 × 1 = 5)**

a. If $p:q::r:s$, then _________. [ ]

i. $ps = qr$ ii. $pr = qs$ iii. $pq = rs$ iv. $pqr = s$

b. A ratio $a:b$ is in simplest form if HCF of a and b is _________. [ ]

i. 0 ii. 1 iii. 2 iv. 3

c. The average of the first three odd numbers is _________. [ ]

i. 5 ii. 4 iii. 3 iv. 2

d. 36% as a fraction in its lowest terms is _________. [ ]

i. $\frac{36}{10}$ ii. $\frac{9}{25}$ iii. $\frac{36}{100}$ iv. $\frac{3}{5}$

e. 15% of 1600 is _________. [ ]

a. 1000 b. 240 c. 340 iv. 740

2 **Fill in the blanks.** **(5 × 1 = 5)**

a. The value of x in $3:4::x:20$ is ____________.

b. The average of the numbers 4, 5, 6 and 17 is ____________.

c. In a proportion, the first and the last terms are called ________________.

d. The number whose 16% is 800 is ________________.

e. The average of $\frac{1}{10}, \frac{3}{10}, \frac{1}{5}, \frac{3}{5}$. and $\frac{2}{5}$ is ______________.

3 **Write T for True and F for False.** **(5 × 1 = 5)**

a. Two quantities can be measured only if they have the same unit. [ ]

b. The first and the fourth terms of a proportion are called means. [ ]

c. 8% as a fraction is $\frac{2}{25}$. [ ]

d. All fractions can be converted into decimals. [ ]

e. Average can be calculated even if the readings are in different units. [ ]

4 Answer the following questions briefly. **(2 × 2 = 4)**

a. The marks obtained by a student in three unit tests are 18, 20 and 22. What is his average mark?

b. Find the ratio of ₹5.75 to 50 p in its simplest form.

5 Answer the following questions. **(2 × 3 = 6)**

a. The ratio of the number of apples to that of oranges in a fruit basket is 9 : 5. If the total number of oranges in the basket is 1560, find the number of apples and the total number of fruits in the basket.

b. The price of a pair of trousers is reduced from ₹10,500 to ₹8925. Find the reduced percentage.

Test 4

Chapters 10–12 **Maximum marks: 25**

1 Choose the correct options. **(5 × 1 = 5)**

a. Amount (A) to be repaid in terms of principal (P) and Interest (I) is ________. [ ]

i. P − I ii. P + I iii. P × I iv. P ÷ I

b. Time (T) taken in terms of speed (S) and distance covered (D) is ________. [ ]

i. D ÷ S ii. D + S iii. D × S iv. D − S

c. 7.5 km = ________ m [ ]

i. 7500 ii. 0.75 iii. 750 iv. 75

d. If a bike travels 200 km with 5 litres of petrol, then the mileage per litre is ________. [ ]

i. 1000 km ii. 40 km iii. 80 km iv. 45 km

e. Simple interest is directly proportional to ________. [ ]

i. principal ii. rate of interest

iii. time period iv. All the above

2 Fill in the blanks. **(5 × 1 = 5)**

a. Rate of interest (R) in terms of simple interest (S), principal (P) and time period (T) is ________.

b. Profit (P) in terms of cost price (CP) and selling price (SP) is ________.

c. If an athlete covers 100 m in 10 s, then the speed of the athlete is ________.

d. If an object is bought for ₹100 and sold for ₹190, then the profit percentage is ________.

e. If the cost of 25 kg of rice is ₹1025, then the cost of 1.5 kg of rice is ________.

3 Write T for True and F for False. **(5 × 1 = 5)**

a. Distance travelled = Speed ÷ Time taken [ ]

b. Profit is earned when the selling price is less than the cost price. [ ]

c. If the rate of interest is 25 paise for 2 months per rupee, then the interest per year per rupee is ₹1.50. [ ]

d. Simple interest on ₹500 for 2 years at 5% per annum is ₹50. [ ]

e. Loss percentage can be calculated if loss and selling price are known. [ ]

4 Answer the following questions briefly. **(2 × 2 = 4)**

a. The cost of 15 m cloth is ₹1537.50. Find the cost of 10 m cloth.

b. If the speed of a car is 32.4 km/h, find its speed in metres per second.

5 Answer the following questions. **(2 × 3 = 6)**

a. Neha purchased a microwave oven for ₹20,100 and sold it for a loss of 9%. At what price did she sell the oven?

b. If ₹10,000 is invested at the rate of 6% per annum simple interest, how long will it take for this amount to become ₹12,400?

Test 5

Chapters 13–16 **Maximum marks: 35**

1 Choose the correct options. **(5 × 1 = 5)**

a. In $7xy$, the numerical factor (part) is _________. [ ]

i. x ii. y iii. xy iv. 7

b. In the expression $3x - 6y + 5$, the constant term is _________. [ ]

i. 3 ii. 6 iii. 5 iv. y

c. The degree of the polynomial $5x^3 + 3x^2 - 6$ is _________. [ ]

i. 3 ii. 2 iii. 1 iv. 0

d. What is the formula for 'If 8 is added to four times a number, the result is 9'? [ ]

i. $8 + x^4 = 9$ ii. $8 + 4x = 9$ iii. $4x - 8 = 9$ iv. $8 + x = 9$

e. What is the length of the side of a square whose area is 64 cm^2? [ ]

i. 16 cm ii. 14 cm iii. 8 cm iv. 32 cm

2 Fill in the blanks. **(5 × 1 = 5)**

a. The literal coefficient of the term $12pq^2$ is ___________.

b. An algebraic expression having two terms is called a ___________.

c. The degree of the polynomial $a^3b^3 + a^2b^2 + ab + 5$ is ___________.

d. The value of $7a^2 + 12ab$ when $a = 4$ and $b = 5$ is ___________.

e. The formula for 'the square of a number multiplied to the sum of three times the number and 12 gives 49' is ___________.

3 Write T for True and F for False. **(5 × 1 = 5)**

a. The expression $5x$ has 2 terms. [ ]

b. $6xy, -4yx, 5xy$ are unlike terms. [ ]

c. When $m = 3$, m^3 and 3m have equal values. [ ]

d. The nth term of an odd number pattern is given by the formula $2n + 1$. [ ]

e. $4x^2 - 3x + \frac{5}{x} + 8$ is a polynomial. [ ]

4 Answer the following questions briefly. **(4 × 2 = 8)**

a. Write the following in mathematical form using symbols and signs.

i. Five-sixth of p multiplied by the sum of q and 15

ii. Quotient of x by 5 multiplied by y decreased by 12

b. Write the formula for the following to find the number.

i. A number reduced by 25 divided by the number reduced by 10 gives 15.

ii. The sum of the square of a number and 8 multiplied by 5 gives 21.

c. Solve $\frac{x}{3} + \frac{7}{3} = 7$ using the method of balancing.

d. If $X = 4x^2 + 5y^2 - z^2$, $Y = z^2 - 5x^2 + 16y^2$ and $Z = 4z^2 + 13x^2 - 4y^2$, find the value of $X + Y - Z$.

5 Answer the following questions. **(4 × 3 = 12)**

a. Find the degree of each of the polynomials given below.

i. $4x^3 + 3x^2y^2 + 5x^4 + 9$ ii. $3x^5y^3z + 4xy^3 + 5x^2yz^2 + 3$

iii. $p^2q^2r^4 + p^3r^2 + 12p^2q^3r^5 + q^4r$

b. Find the value of $\frac{a^2 + b^3 - c^2}{ab - bc + ac}$, when $a = 4$, $b = 5$ and $c = 3$.

c. The sum of three consecutive odd numbers is 51. Find the numbers.

d. Multiply $(10\,ab - 8b)$ and $(4ab + 3b)$. Divide the result by $2b$.

Test 6

Chapters 17–19 **Maximum marks: 25**

1 Choose the correct options. **(5 × 1 = 5)**

a. The number of lines that can be drawn through a given point is ______. [ ]

i. 1 ii. 3 iii. 0 iv. infinite

b. An angle whose measure is more than 180° but less than 360° is called ______. [ ]

i. acute angle ii. reflex angle iii. obtuse angle iv. complete angle

c. If the sum of two angles is 180°, they are called ________ angles. [ ]

i. complementary ii. adjacent iii. supplementary iv. congruent

d. The complement angle of 32° is __________. [ ]

i. 158° ii. 58° iii. 48° iv. 148°

e. Which of the following is used to construct a circle? [ ]

i. Compass ii. Ruler iii. Divider iv. Set square

2 Fill in the blanks. **($5 \times 1 = 5$)**

a. A line segment has __________ endpoints.

b. If an angle measures exactly 180°, then it is known as a __________.

c. If three or more lines intersect each other at a common point, they are known as __________.

d. $50°27'30'' - 40°17'32'' =$ __________

e. If a line is perpendicular to another line, the angle formed is __________.

3 Write T for True and F for False. **($5 \times 1 = 5$)**

a. Angle equal to its complement is 45°. [ ]

b. A ray AB is represented as $\overleftrightarrow{AB}$. [ ]

c. Parallel lines meet each other at a definite point. [ ]

d. The supplementary angle of 98°43' is 81°17'. [ ]

e. Divider is used to compare lengths. [ ]

4 Answer the following questions briefly. **($2 \times 2 = 4$)**

a. Find the measure of an angle which is 46° less than its supplement.

b. Construct 120° using protractor. Bisect the constructed angle.

5 Answer the following questions. **($2 \times 3 = 6$)**

a. Draw a line segment of length 12 cm using a ruler and construct a perpendicular bisector using compass. Write the steps of construction.

b. In the given figure, find the value of x and state whether it is acute angle or obtuse angle.

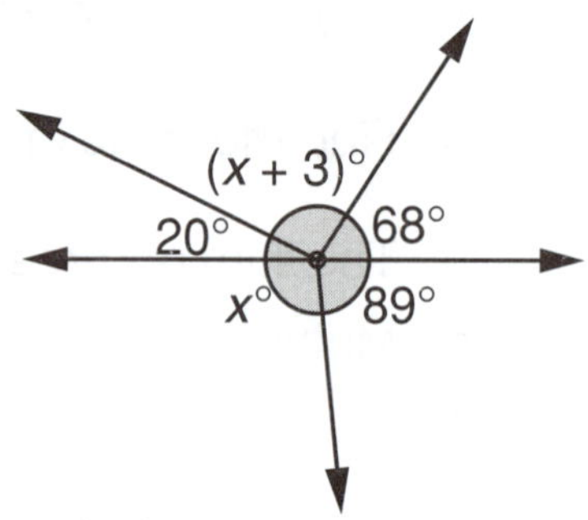

Test 7

Chapters 20–22 **Maximum marks: 25**

1 Choose the correct options. **($5 \times 1 = 5$)**

a. In a triangle ABC, if ∠A = 45° and ∠B = 45°, then ∠C is a/an _____. [ ]

i. acute angle ii. obtuse angle iii. right angle iv. straight angle

b. The largest chord of the circle is the _____ of the circle. [ ]

i. diameter ii. radius iii. tangent iv. secant

c. A scalene triangle has _____ line(s) of symmetry. [ ]

i. 1 ii. 2 iii. 3 iv. 0

d. The measure of each angle in an equilateral triangle is ______. [ ]

i. 45° ii. 90° iii. 50° iv. 60°

e. A regular heptagon has ______ lines of symmetry. [ ]

i. 7 ii. 6 iii. 3 iv. 4

2 Fill in the blanks. **(5 × 1 = 5)**

a. A right triangle cannot have ____________ angle.

b. In an isosceles triangle, if the unequal angle is 110°, then the other two angles are ____________.

c. A rhombus has ____________ lines of symmetry.

d. The quadrant is ____________ of a circle.

e. If the circumference of a circle is 198 m, then its diameter is ____________.

3 Write T for True and F for False. **(5 × 1 = 5)**

a. A circle has three quadrants. [ ]

b. The line of symmetry of a semicircle is the perpendicular bisector of its diameter. [ ]

c. An infinite number of chords can be drawn for a circle. [ ]

d. A triangle can have two right angles. [ ]

e. The two acute angles are equal in a right-angled isosceles triangle. [ ]

4 Answer the following questions briefly. **(2 × 2 = 4)**

a. Find the unknown values in the triangles given below.

i.

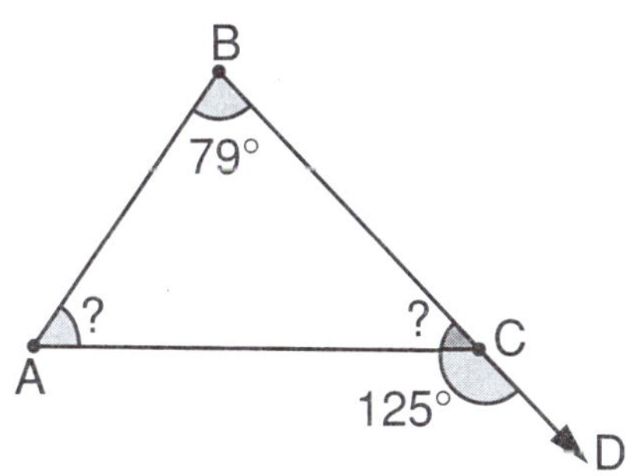

ii.

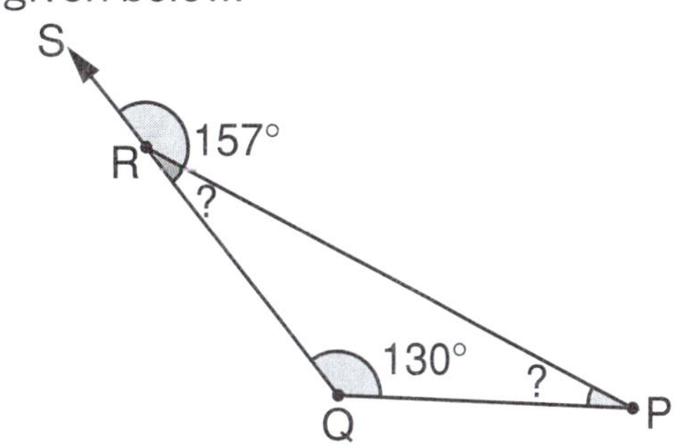

b. Complete the following figures such that they are symmetrical along the green line.

i.

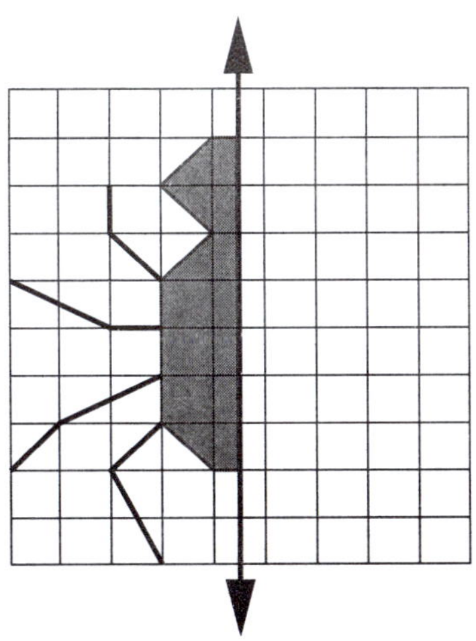

ii.

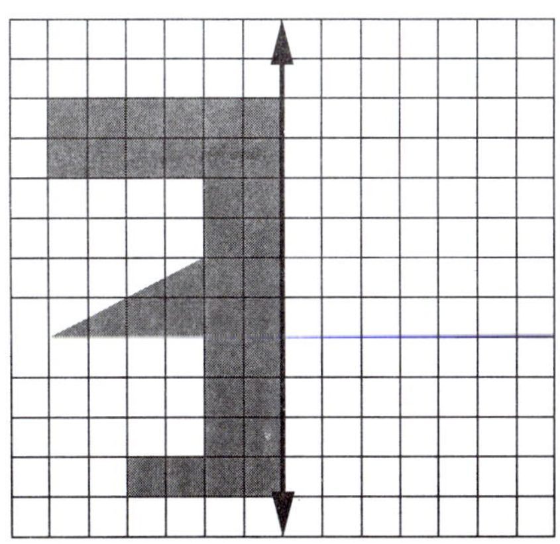

5 **Answer the following questions.** **(2 × 3 = 6)**

a. Construct the incircle for the triangle of dimensions given below. Also, write the steps of construction.

AB = 11 cm, BC = 7 cm and AC = 8 cm

b. In the given figure, find the measure of the following angles.

i. ∠ACB ii. ∠DCE iii. ∠CED iv. ∠BED

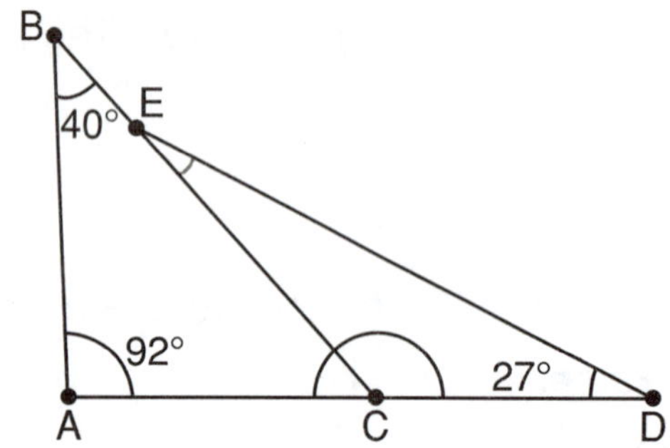

Test 8

Chapters 23–24 **Maximum marks: 25**

1 **Choose the correct options.** **(5 × 1 = 5)**

a. $1\ m^2$ = __________ cm^2 [ ]

i. 100 ii. 1000 iii. 10000 iv. 10

b. The area of a square of side 6 cm is __________. [ ]

i. 36 mm^2 ii. 360 mm^2 iii. 3600 mm^2 iv. 3.6 mm^2

c. The area of a right isosceles triangle whose equal sides are 34 cm each is __________. [ ]

i. 578 cm^2 ii. 1156 cm^2 iii. 68 cm^2 iv. 408 cm^2

d. The lateral surface area of a cube whose side is 6 m is __________. [ ]

i. 144 m^2 ii. 216 m^2 iii. 36 m^2 iv. 216 m^2

e. A wire which is in the shape of a square of side 15 cm is re-bent into a rectangle of breadth 10 cm. What is the length of the rectangle formed? [ ]

i. 20 cm ii. 30 cm iii. 40 cm iv. 50 cm

2 **Fill in the blanks.** **(5 × 1 = 5)**

a. The perimeter of a regular pentagon of side length 10 cm 12 mm is __________ cm.

b. The total cost of flooring a room at ₹15 per sq. m is ₹1335. If the breadth of the room is 5 m, then the length of the room is __________.

c. 10 km = __________ cm

d. The area of a square increases by __________ times if all the sides are doubled.

e. A cuboid has __________ vertices, __________ faces and __________ edges.

3 **Write T for True and F for False.** **(5 × 1 = 5)**

a. Volume is always expressed in cubic units. [ ]

b. The height of a cuboid is the ratio of the volume to the product of length and breadth. [ ]

c. The total surface area of a cube having side length p cm is $4p^2$ sq. units. [ ]

d. Cubes and cuboids are prisms. [ ]

e. The volume of a cube whose side is 12 cm is 1728 cu. cm. [ ]

4 **Answer the following questions briefly.** **(2 × 2 = 4)**

a. The ratio of the perimeter of Square A to the perimeter of Square B is 4 : 6. If the perimeter of Square B is 60 cm, then what is the difference between the perimeters of the two squares?

b. How many 3 cm cubes can be obtained from a cube of side 15 cm?

5 **Answer the following questions.** **(2 × 3 = 6)**

a. The length of each side of an octagonal garden is 24 m 70 cm. If it costs ₹ 50 per metre to fence it once, then how much does it cost to fence four rounds?

b. Three cubes of side length 9 cm are placed end to end. Find the volume and total surface area of the cuboid formed.

Test 9

Chapter 25 **Maximum marks: 25**

1 **Study the column graph and fill in the blanks.** **(4 × 1 = 4)**

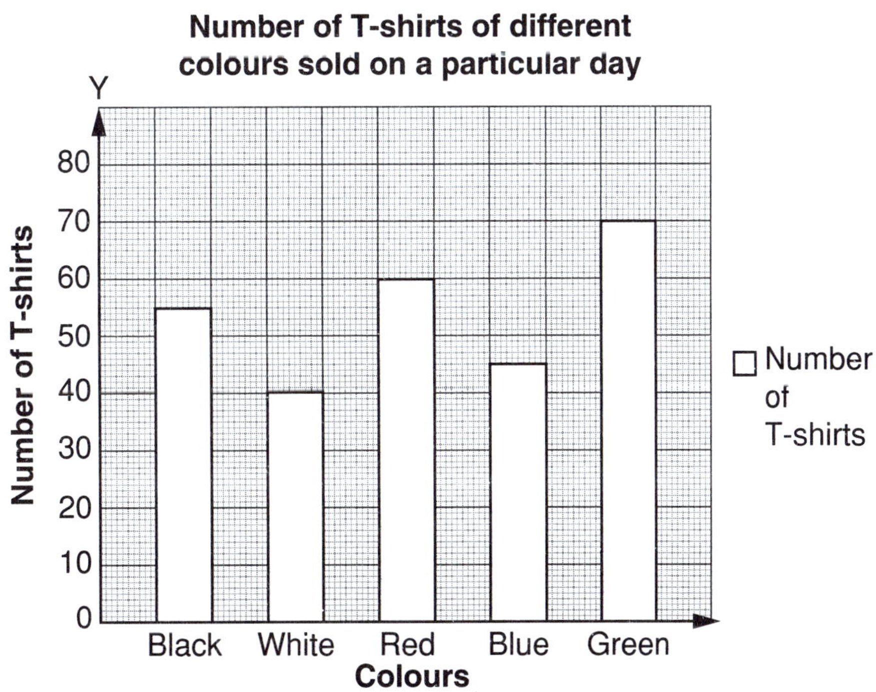

a. The number of green T-shirts sold is ________ more than the number of blue T-shirts.

b. __________ T-shirts are sold in least number.

c. The total number of T-shirts sold on that day is ____________.

d. The highest demand was for _________ T-shirts.

2 Study the pie graph and choose the correct options. **(4 × 1 = 4)**

Amount earned by Suresh in different professions

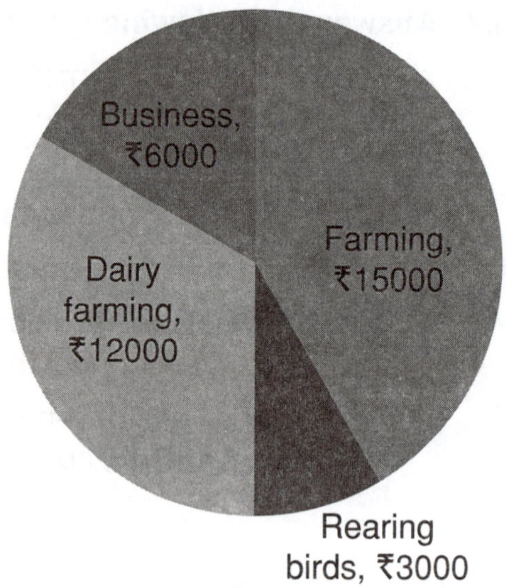

a. The amount earned by Suresh from the dairy farming is _________.

   i. ₹3000 ii. ₹15000

   iii. ₹12000 iv. ₹6000

b. He earned ₹6000 from ____________.

   i. rearing birds ii. farming

   iii. dairy farming iv. business

c. He earned ₹___________ more from farming than from his business.

   i. ₹9000 ii. ₹10000

   iii. ₹15000 iv. ₹6000

d. He earned the least amount from _______________.

   i. business ii. farming

   iii. fairy farming iv rearing birds

3 Study the given line graph and write T for True and F for False. **(5 × 1 = 5)**

Quantity of tomatoes sold (in kg)

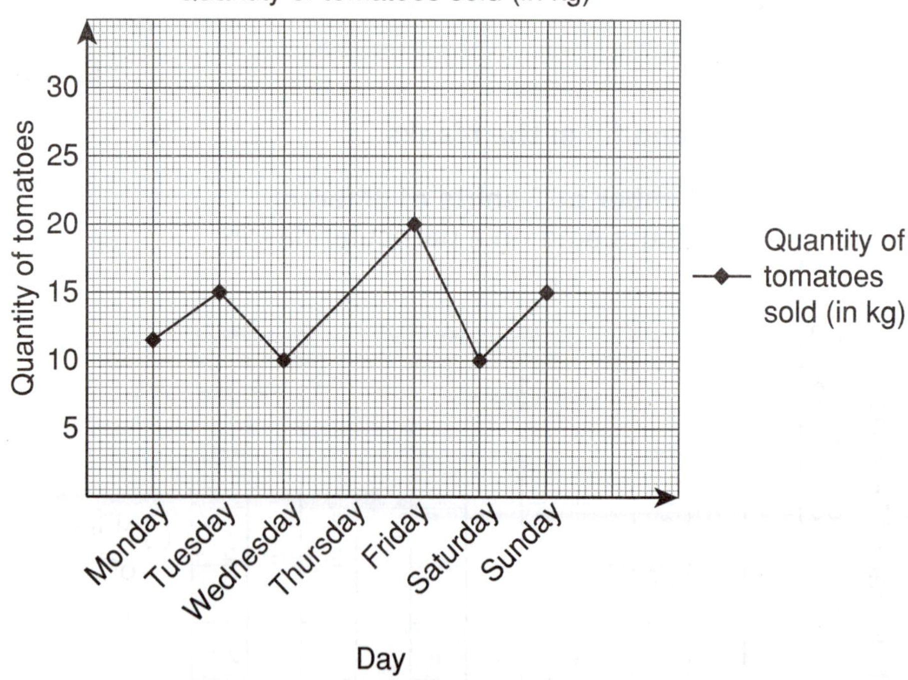

a. On Monday, 12 kg of tomatoes were sold. [ ]

b. The highest quantity of tomatoes was sold on Sunday. [ ]

c. The quantity of tomatoes sold on Friday was 10 kg more than the quantity sold on Tuesday. [ ]

d. The least quantity of tomatoes was sold on Wednesday and Saturday. [ ]

e. The total quantity of tomatoes sold was 96 kg. [ ]

4 Answer the following questions. **(2 × 6 = 12)**

a. Number of students who like different types of music is given in the following table. Construct the column graph for the data.

Type of Music	Folk	Rock	Pop	Jazz	Melody
Number of Students	14	13	10	8	15

Using the graph, answer the following.

i. Which is the favourite type of music among the students?

ii. How many fewer students like jazz than folk music?

b. The details of expenditure of the program in a school are given in the following table. Construct the pie graph for the following data.

Category	Stage	Guest hospitality	Sweets	Costumes	Others
Expenditure (in ₹)	8000	4000	3000	2000	1000

Using the graph answer the following.

i. For which activity did they spend more money?

ii. What was the total cost for the program?

Test 10

Chapters 26-28 **Maximum marks: 30**

1 Choose the correct options. **(5 × 1 = 5)**

a. Which of the following is a set? [ ]

i. Collection of birds in India
ii. Collection of students in a university
iii. Collection of first ten even numbers
iv. Both a and b

b. The sets A = {10, 30, 50, 70} and B = {20, 40, 60, 80} are ________. [ ]

i. disjoint sets
ii. overlapping sets
iii. intersecting sets
iv. equal sets

2 Write T for True and F for False. **(5 × 1 = 5)**

a. The set of all the whole numbers between 125 and 126 is an empty set. [ ]

b. The sets of prime factors of 6 and 13 are examples of overlapping sets. [ ]

c. Set A = {x, y, z, p, q} and set B = {p, q, x, y, z} are equal sets. [ ]

3 Answer the following questions briefly. **(4 × 2 = 8)**

a. Write the cardinal numbers of the following sets.

i. A = {x | x is multiple of 7, $x < 100$}
ii. B = {a, b, c, d, e, a, b, f, g, d}

b. Identify the disjoint and overlapping sets in the following pairs of sets.

i. P = {x | x is letter in the word 'Savitri'} and Q = {x | x is letter in the word 'Chetna'}

ii. R = {12, 24, 36, 48, 60, 72} and S = {13, 26, 39, 52, 65, 78}

c. Write the sets A ∪ B and A ∩ B for the following pairs of sets.

i. A = {101, 301, 501, 701, 901} and B = {101, 201, 301, 401, 501, 601}

ii. A = {w, r, o, k} and B = {e, n, g, r, y}

d. Represent the following sets using Venn diagram.

i. A = {25, 26, 27, 28,29} and B = {−25, −26, −27, −28, −29}

ii. Set A = {50, 51, 52, 53} and set B = {50, 51, 52, 53, 54, 55, 56}

4 Answer the following questions. **(4 × 3 = 12)**

a. Represent the following sets in the set-builder form.

i. A = {99, 88, 77, 66, 55, 44, 33}

ii. B = {1, 4, 9, 16, 25, 36, 49, 64, 81, 100}

iii. C = {i, l, o, v, e, m, y, n, d, i, a}

b. Give an example for each of the following types of sets.

i. Equivalent sets

ii. An infinite set

iii. A null set

c. Find n(A ∪ B) and n(A ∩ B) for the following pairs of sets in the set-builder form.

i. P = {−10, −12, −14, −16, −18, −20} and Q = {−10, −13, −15, −16, −18, −19, −20}

ii. A = {m, n, o, p, r} and B = {o, p, q, r, s, t}

iii. A = {x | x is an integer, $-5 < x < 7$} and B = {x | x is an integer between 10 and −10}

d. Write the sets represented by following Venn diagrams in the set-builder form.

i.

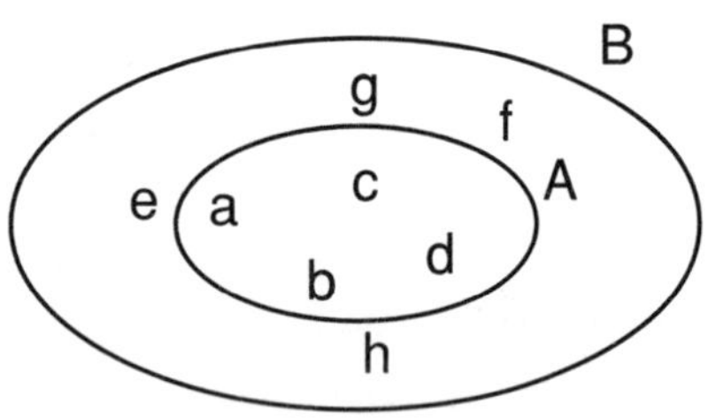

ii.

iii.

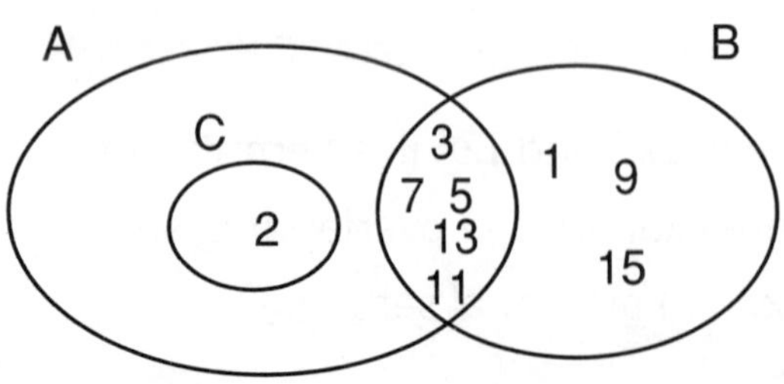

Answers

Chapter – 1

Exercise 1.1

1. a. Predecessor = 2 and Successor = 3
   b. Predecessor = 24,529 and Successor = 24,531
   c. Predecessor = 78,90,213 and Successor = 78,90,215
   d. Predecessor = 85,12,045 and Successor = 85,12,047

2.

	Indian place value system	International place value system
a.	One lakh thirty-five thousand two hundred four	One hundred thirty-five thousand two hundred four
b.	Ninety lakh fifty-two thousand twenty	Nine million fifty-two thousand twenty
c.	Five crore twenty-one lakh forty-seven thousand six hundred and eighty-three	Fifty-two million one hundred forty-seven thousand six hundred eighty-three
d.	Five crore four lakh twelve thousand five hundred sixty-five	Fifty million four hundred twelve thousand five hundred sixty-five
e.	Two crore fifty-three lakh eighty-six thousand one hundred twenty-five	Twenty-five million three hundred eighty-six thousand one hundred twenty-five
F.	Five crore two lakh sixty-three thousand fifty	Fifty million two hundred sixty-three thousand fifty
g.	Five crore twenty lakh ten thousand five hundred nine	Fifty-two million ten thousand five hundred nine
h.	Two crore forty-five lakh two thousand twelve	Twenty-four million five hundred two thousand twelve

3. a. Face value(FV) of 7 = 7, Place value(PV) of 7 = 7,000,000, Face value(FV) of 9 = 9 and Place value(PV) of 9 = 90, 000
   b. FV of 7 = 7, PV 7 = 70,00,000, FV of 5 = 5 and PV of 5 = 50, 000
   c. FV of 1 = 1, PV of 1 = 100,000,000, FV of 4 = 4 and PV of 4 = 40, 000
   d. FV of 5 = 5, PV of 5 = 5,00,000, FV of 9 = 9 and PV of 9 = 90, 000
   e. FV of 7 = 7, PV of 7 = 7,000,000, FV of 3 = 3 and PV of 3 = 3, 000
   f. FV of 2 = 2, PV of 2 = 20, 00,000, FV of 8 = 8 and PV of 8 = 800
   g. FV of 8 = 8, PV of 8 = 80,00,000, FV of 3 = 3 and PV of 3 = 30, 000
   h. FV of 3 = 3, PV of 3 = 30,00,000, FV of 8 = 8 and PV of 8 = 800
4. a. 23,70,40,205 b. 9,01,33,807
   c. 99,41,590 d. 67,000,004
5. a. 237,050,205 b. 34,700,006 c. 5,000,004

Exercise 1.2

1. a. > b. < c. < d. > e. <
   f. < g. < h. <
2. a. 3052608, 3350720, 4345608, 21007891, 724562187
   b. 1112222, 2000123, 9999901, 10200123, 20607812, 204500123
   c. 1243015, 102067891, 120102141, 120430156, 230156701
   d. 1000245, 10024005, 78045123, 700502369, 705223690, 790505100
3. a. 7856824, 5067891, 5026078, 1262187, 1205679
   b. 81110203, 28902823, 22102183, 20801503, 20450023, 20104712
   c. 701306002, 701301145, 701301145, 701301142, 701301102
   d. 43551012, 31278451, 31251236, 312502024, 310102301, 25020245

Exercise 1.3

1. a. Greatest = 765321, smallest = 123567
   b. Greatest = 98654321, smallest = 12345689
2. Greatest = 9763210, smallest = 1023679
3. Greatest = 98654320, smallest = 20345689
4. Four 3-digit; 803, 830, 308, 380

Exercise 1.4

1. a. 3049 b. 90,333 c. 0 d. 6031

Exercise 1.5

1. a. 604 b. 0 c. 1
   d. 806 e. (205 + 705)
2. a. Commutative property under multiplication
   b. Associative property under multiplication
   c. Multiplicative property of zero d. Multiplicative identity
3. a. 1633674000 b. 43093050000 c. 50410840000
   d. 162745272900 e. 1446000000 f. 164000000000
4. a. 41025 b. 1025104 c. 8965324 d. 1021501
5. a. Q = 2640, R = 22 b. Q = 4955, R = 50
   c. Q = 2339, R = 73 d. Q = 2853, R = 286
   e. Q = 9755, R = 519 f. Q = 38436, R = 142
6. The other number is 201
7. a. 12 b. 6728 c. 3 d. 10102

Exercise 1.6

1. a. DXXXII b. MXXV c. DCXX d. DCCCL
   e. DIV f. MMLIV g. CMXCIX h. CCCLVIII
   i. DCCLXXXII j. DCCCLXXXVIII
2. a. 3991 b. 2910 c. 2722
   d. 2548 e. 1904 f. 1799

Revision Exercise

	Indian place value system	International place value system
a.	60,45,896 = Sixty lakh forty five thousand eight hundred and ninety six	6,045,896 = Six million forty five thousand eight hundred and ninety six
b.	2,04,56,087 = Two crore four lakh fifty six thousand and eighty-seven	20,456,087 = Twenty million four hundred fifty six thousand and eighty-seven
c.	2,08,50,135 = Two crore eight lakh fifty thousand one hundred and thirty-five	20,850,135 = Twenty million eight hundred fifty thousand one hundred and thirty-five
d.	50,21,369 = Fifty lakh twenty one thousand three hundred and sixty-nine	5,021,369 = Five million twenty one thousand three hundred and sixty-nine
e.	789,45,62,154 = Seven hundred eighty-nine crore forty five lakh sixty two thousand one hundred and fifty-four	7,894,562,154 = Seven billion eight hundred ninety four million five hundred sixty two thousand one hundred and fifty-four
f.	20,85,00,140 = Twenty crore eighty five lakh one hundred and forty	208,500,140 = Two hundred eight million five hundred thousand one hundred and forty
g.	9,00,01,009 = Nine crore one thousand and nine	90,001,009 = Ninety million one thousand and nine
h.	41,03,02,410 = Forty one crore three lakh two thousand four hundred and ten	410,302,410 = Four hundred ten million three hundred two thousand four hundred and ten

i.	10,23,80,014 = Ten crore twenty three lakh eighty thousand and fourteen	102,380,014 = One hundred two million three hundred eighty thousand and fourteen
	Largest number = 7894562154	smallest number = 6045896

2. a. 49,92,04,206 b. 5,019,004,211
   c. 7,13,24,909 d. 2,092,004,150
   e. 78,75,40,150 f. 2,794,014,905
   Ascending order: 7,13,24,909; 49,92,04,206; 78,75,40,150; 2,092,004,150; 2,794,014,905; 5,019,004,211
3. a. 185297, 1089201, 1825790, 1825901, 1825970
   b. 7852015, 7852016, 9985214, 78543012, 78596541
   c. 98562001, 98562104, 98562140, 98562875, 98568025
   d. 98752149, 900856029, 900856092, 900856379, 900860012
4. a. 516 b. 674 c. 1227
   d. 1388 e. 3127 f. 3990
5. a. > b. > c. < d. > e. < f. >
6. a. Greatest = 543210 and Smallest = 102345
   b. Greatest = 98765430 and Smallest = 30456789
   c. Greatest = 9754320 and Smallest = 2034579
7. a. 39133 b. 54570
   c. 4059000 d. 1593243600
8. a. 557220 b. 590254
   c. 6781536 d. 88765000

For the Curious Mind

18 four-digit numbers can be formed

Chapter – 2

Exercise 2.1

1. a. +25 meters b. −36°C c. −2 kg
   d. 0°C e. −10 meters f. +₹1000
2. Any six integers less than −2 (−3, −4, −5,.....)
3. 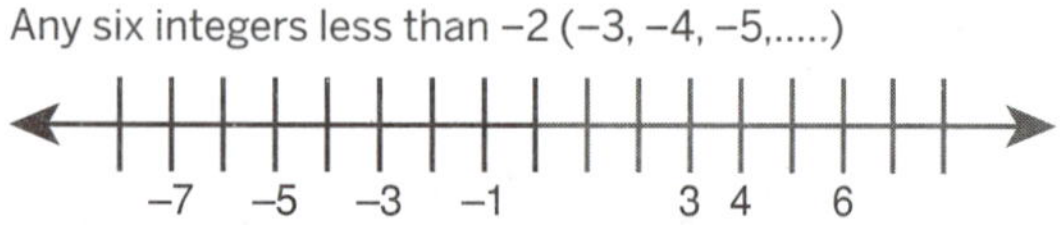

4. a. < b. > c. > d. > e. < f. >
5. a. −10, −4, −2, 0, 1, 4, 5 b. −24, −11, −9, −5, −2, 3, 8
6. a. 10, 7, 4, −3, −5, −10, −13 b. 8, 3, 0, −2, −9, −11, −24
7. a. −4, −3, −2, −1, 0, 1, 2 b. −10, −9, −8, −7, −6, −5, −4
   c. −3, −2, −1
8. a. 3 b. 232 c. 0 d. −3 e. −3 f. 0
9. a. Integers b. 0 c. −1 d. Loss
10. a. True b. False c. True d. False e. True
    f. True g. True h. False i. False j. False

Exercise 2.2

1. a. 11 b. −3 c. 3 d. −11
2. a. 144 b. 47 c. −100 d. −5
3. a. −4 b. −10 c. 5 d. 5
4. a. −40 b. 53 c. −32 d. −120
5. a. < b. = c. < d. =
6. a. 0 b. +20 c. 14 d. −5
7. −54 8. 136 9. 16°C 10. 322 km

Exercise 2.3

1. a. −144 b. −1400 c. 625 d. 104
   e. 0 f. −1029 g. −643 h. 243
2. a. −7 b. −8 c. 25 d. 32
   e. 756 f. 1 g. 0 h. not defined
3. a. −6 b. −7 c. −8 d. −12 e. −1
   f. −1 g. −31 h. not defined i. 0
5. −8
6. a. −54 b. 18 c. 32 d. −5
   e. −6 f. −49 g. −10 h. 13

Revision Exercise

1. a. Negative sign b. Positive sign c. Positive sign
   d. Negative sign e. Positive\negative sign
2. a. −5 b. −3 c. 3 d. 7 e. 5
3. a. True b. False c. True d. False e. True
   f. False g. True h. True i. False j. False
4. a. < b. > c. > d. < e. < f. >
5. −1, 0, 1, 2,.... 6. −22, −21, −21, −20,.....
7. a. −5, −4, −3, −2, −1, 0 b. −3, −2, −1, 0, 1, 2, 3
   c. 3, 4, 5, 6, d. −8, −7, −6, −5, −4, −3
8. 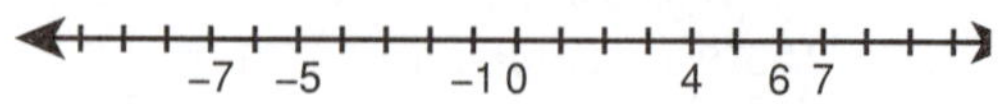

9. (+5) +(−5); 8 + (−5)
10. a. −7 b. −142 c. −65 d. −29
11. a. 45 b. 72 c. 50 d. −43
12. a. 0 b. 5 c. 7 d. 7
13. a. −120 b. −108 c. −7000 d. 0
14. a. −11 b. −16 c. Not defined d. 1

For The Curious Mind

One possible solution.

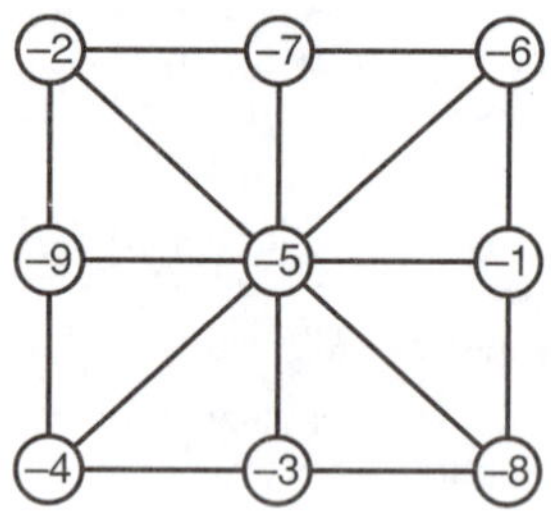

They are called Magic squares. One possible magic square with positive and negative numbers:

9	−5	5
−1	3	7
1	11	−3

Chapter – 3

Exercise 3.1

1. a. T b. T c. F d. F
2. a. 1, 2, 4, 5, 8, 10, 20, 40 b. 1, 5, 13, 65
   c. 1, 2, 3, 5, 6, 9, 10, 15, 18, 30, 45, 90
   d. 1, 2, 3, 5, 6, 10, 15, 25, 30, 50, 75, 150
3. a. 3, 6, 9, 12, 15, 18 b. 11, 22, 33, 44, 55, 66
   c. 8, 16, 24, 32, 40, 48 d. 4, 8, 12, 16, 20, 24
4. a. 5 b. 10 c. 45

Exercise 3.2

1. a. A prime number has only two factors, that is, 1 and the number itself.
      Example: 2, 3, 5, 7, 11 etc
   b. A composite number has more than two factors; it has factors other than 1 and the number itself.
      Example: 4, 6, 9, 10, 12.
   c. Two numbers are said to be co-prime/relatively prime if their common factor is only 1.
      Example: 2 and 5
   d. If the difference between two prime numbers is 2 then they are said to be twin primes.
      Example: 3 and 5
2. 15 and 91
3. a. 3, 5, 7, 11, 13, 17, 19
   b. 17, 19, 23, 29, 31, 37, 41, 43, 47
   c. 67, 71, 73, 79, 83
   d. 23, 29, 31, 37, 41, 43, 47, 53, 59, 61, 67, 71, 73, 79
4. a. No. Odd numbers can be composite numbers.
   b. No. 2 is the only prime number
   c. No not always.
   d. yes
   e. No co prime numbers may not be prime numbers.
5. 74 composite numbers and 33, 63, 93 are composite numbers with digit 3 in the ones place.
6. 90, 91, 92, 93, 94, 95, 96

Exercise 3.3

1.

Number	Divisible by									
	2	3	4	5	6	7	8	9	10	11
7,020	Yes	Yes	Yes	Yes	Yes	No	No	Yes	Yes	No
11,456	Yes	No	Yes	No	No	No	Yes	No	No	No
7,31,541	No	Yes	No	No	No	No	No	No	No	No
97,240	Yes	No	Yes	Yes	No	No	Yes	No	Yes	Yes
7,89,430	Yes	No	No	Yes	No	No	No	No	Yes	No

2. a. No b. Yes c. No d. No e. No

Exercise 3.4

1. $2\times2\times2\times17$
2. $2\times2\times3\times3\times7$
3. $7\times11\times11\times11$
4. $5\times9\times23$
5. $5\times11\times11\times23$

Exercise 3.5

1. a. 4 b. 6 c. 24 d. 9
2. a. 4 b. 8 c. 12 d. 8
3. a. 13 b. 40 c. 48 d. 70
4. 4 m 5. 96

Exercise 3.6

1. a. 6 b. 28 c. 15 d. 50
2. a. 72 b. 240 c. 2250 d. 2080
3. a. 720 b. 540 c. 4200 d. 4900
4. 180 days 5. 261

Revision Exercise

1.

Number	Divisible by									
	2	3	4	5	6	7	8	9	10	11
12,453	No	Yes	No	No	No	Yes	No	No	No	No
34,512	Yes	Yes	Yes	No	No	No	Yes	No	No	No
78,145	No	No	No	No	No	No	No	No	No	No
8,45,746	Yes	No	No	No	No	No	No	No	No	Yes

2. a. No b. Yes c. No d. No
3. a. 13 b. 28 c. 52 d. 77
4. a. 126 b. 450 c. 468 d. 432
5. The largest square tile is 40 cm. 9 tiles along width and 49 tiles along length can be tiled.
6. 24

For the Curious Mind

The composite numbers are 64 and 37.

Chapter – 4

Exercise 4.1

1.

Proper fractions	Improper fractions	Mixed fractions
$\frac{1}{4}, \frac{9}{11}, \frac{7}{10}, \frac{1}{8}$	$\frac{7}{3}, \frac{13}{7}, \frac{14}{5}, \frac{12}{11}$	$1\frac{8}{9}, 2\frac{3}{5}, 2\frac{4}{7}, 5\frac{1}{7}$

2.

Like fractions	Unlike fractions
$\frac{1}{2}$ and $\frac{5}{2}$	$\frac{7}{8}$ and $\frac{8}{7}$
$\frac{5}{6}$ and $\frac{1}{6}$	$\frac{4}{9}$ and $\frac{4}{7}$
$\frac{6}{10}$ and $\frac{7}{10}$	

3. a. $1\frac{5}{6}$ b. $4\frac{1}{2}$ c. $1\frac{7}{10}$ d. $2\frac{2}{3}$ e. $1\frac{10}{11}$
4. a. $\frac{12}{5}$ b. $\frac{14}{3}$ c. $\frac{12}{7}$ d. $\frac{11}{4}$ e. $\frac{36}{10}$

Exercise 4.2

1. a. $\frac{4}{5}=\frac{8}{10}=\frac{12}{15}=\frac{16}{20}=\frac{20}{25}$ b. $\frac{6}{7}=\frac{12}{14}=\frac{18}{21}=\frac{24}{28}=\frac{30}{35}$
   c. $\frac{3}{4}=\frac{6}{8}=\frac{9}{12}=\frac{12}{16}=\frac{15}{20}$ d. $\frac{5}{8}=\frac{10}{16}=\frac{15}{24}=\frac{20}{32}=\frac{25}{40}$
2. a. $\frac{5}{8}\neq\frac{8}{12}$ b. $\frac{1}{8}\neq\frac{6}{10}$ c. $\frac{4}{9}\neq\frac{12}{27}$ d. $\frac{5}{13}\neq\frac{6}{14}$
3. a. $\frac{2}{3}$ b. $\frac{1}{5}$ c. $\frac{1}{4}$ d. $\frac{2}{3}$

Exercise 4.3

1. a. < b. > c. < d. > e. > f. <
2. a. $\frac{3}{11}<\frac{3}{10}<\frac{3}{7}<\frac{3}{5}<\frac{3}{4}$ b. $\frac{3}{14}<\frac{3}{7}<\frac{4}{7}<\frac{9}{14}<\frac{6}{7}$
   c. $\frac{1}{5}<\frac{2}{5}<\frac{3}{5}<\frac{4}{5}<\frac{5}{5}$ d. $\frac{1}{6}<\frac{1}{3}<\frac{1}{2}<\frac{2}{3}<\frac{5}{6}$
3. a. $\frac{4}{5}>\frac{4}{7}>\frac{4}{8}>\frac{4}{9}>\frac{4}{10}$ b. $\frac{4}{5}>\frac{2}{3}>\frac{2}{5}>\frac{1}{3}>\frac{1}{5}$
   c. $\frac{9}{10}>\frac{8}{10}>\frac{7}{10}>\frac{4}{10}>\frac{3}{10}$ d. $\frac{3}{4}>\frac{5}{8}>\frac{1}{2}>\frac{1}{4}>\frac{1}{8}$

Exercise 4.4

1. a. $\frac{5}{9}$ b. $\frac{5}{6}$ c. $1\frac{2}{15}$ d. $6\frac{11}{14}$
2. a. $\frac{3}{9}$ b. $\frac{1}{2}$ c. $\frac{1}{12}$ d. $\frac{9}{20}$
3. $3\frac{7}{15}$ 4. $4\frac{9}{28}$

Exercise 4.5

1. a. 9 b. $\frac{35}{66}$ c. $8\frac{2}{5}$ d. $3\frac{1}{5}$ e. $37\frac{1}{2}$ f. $\frac{5}{32}$

Exercise 4.6

1. a. $13\frac{1}{2}$ b. $\frac{2}{45}$ c. $\frac{2}{3}$ d. $\frac{4}{5}$ e. $1\frac{11}{16}$ f. $3\frac{2}{3}$

Exercise 4.7

1. a. $2\frac{5}{8}$ b. $\frac{32}{93}$ c. $2\frac{8}{27}$ d. $1\frac{1}{2}$ e. $1\frac{2}{3}$ f. 2

Exercise 4.8

1. 510 boys.
2. Total amount = ₹7875 and Anil's share amount = ₹4375
3. The capacity of drum is 120 litres and 80 litres of water was filled when it was $\frac{2}{3}$ ful.
4. Sketch pen cost ₹$4\frac{1}{4}$ more than pen. 5. 11 m

Revision Exercise

1. a. iii. b. iii. c. ii. d. i. e. iii.
2. a. $1\frac{1}{5}$ b. $1\frac{23}{90}$ c. $11\frac{3}{20}$ d. $18\frac{1}{24}$ e. $1\frac{5}{18}$
3. a. $\frac{2}{9}$ b. $\frac{1}{12}$ c. $\frac{3}{10}$ d. $\frac{13}{77}$ e. $\frac{11}{12}$
4. a. 12 b. $\frac{5}{24}$ c. $\frac{8}{15}$ d. $1\frac{1}{3}$ e. $6\frac{3}{4}$

5. a. $\frac{1}{40}$ b. $\frac{5}{6}$ c. $\frac{2}{3}$ d. $1\frac{2}{25}$ e. 3

6. a. $3\frac{4}{7}$ b. $\frac{9}{14}$ c. $3\frac{3}{20}$ d. $1\frac{3}{4}$ e. 0 f. 2/21

7. a. Megha bought $3\frac{19}{20}$ kg fruits.
   b. $3\frac{23}{32}$ litres of petrol is left in the bike.
   c. 4 CD's are classical music.
   d. 219 days (1 year is considered as 365 days)
   e. 28 days.

For The Curious Mind

32 students did not participate in sports from Class VI.

Chapter – 5

Exercise 5.1

1. a. 5.5 b. 83.17 c. 267.003 d. 14.203 e. 10.087
2. a. $\frac{7}{10}$ b. 7 c. 70 d. $\frac{7}{1000}$
   e. $\frac{7}{100}$ f. 700
3. a. 400 + 90 + 5 + 0.6 b. 20 + 3 + 0.1 + 0.8
   c. 10 + 4 + 0.08 + 0.007
   d. 3000 + 500 + 20 + 7 + 0.1 + 0.07
   e. 500 + 5 + 0.5 + 0.005
   f. 7000 + 600 + 50 + 4 + 0.3 + 0.02 + 0.001
4. a. Like decimals b. Unlike decimals c. Like decimals
   d. Unlike decimals e. Unlike decimals f. Unlike decimals
5. a. $<$ b. $<$ c. $>$ d. $>$ e. $=$ f. $>$
6. a. 0.003, 0.03, 0.3, 0.33, 3.03, 3.3
   b. 1.463, 4.346, 4.364, 4.436, 4.643
   c. −4.25, −3.05, −1, 0, 0.13, 2.05, 2.45, 3.92
   d. 1.4576, 1.5467, 1.7564, 1.8927
7. a. 55.5, 50.5, 5.05, 0.55, 0.505
   b. 3.999, 3.712, 3.617, 3.434, 3.279
   c. 6.75, 1.78, 0.404, −0.415, −1.75, −2, −3.45
   d. 0.9366, 0.63121, 0.6312, −0.936, −0.93661
8. a. 0.07 b. 6.18 c. 65.076
   d. 0.4 e. 1.3 f. 0.128
9. a. $\frac{29}{50}$ d. $\frac{7}{10}$ b. $\frac{327}{250}$ e. $\frac{1}{50}$ c. $\frac{6021}{500}$ f. $\frac{5}{8}$

Exercise 5.2

1. a. 99.01 b. 72.05 c. 149.115
   d. 116.767 e. 131.383 f. 688.509
2. a. 36.73 b. 69.31 c. 21.577
   d. 99.999 e. 308.093 f. 42.173
3. a. 24.08 b. 0.98 c. 1.973
   d. 34.79 e. 12.77 f. 65.415
4. 3.751 5. 8.534 6. ₹356 7. 16.1 km

Exercise 5.3

1. a. 865 b. 347.54 c. 7634
   d. 3964.1 e. 7800 f. 8590
2. a. 110.6 b. 1142.46 c. 320.625
   d. 21.28 e. 636.116 f. 83.856
3. a. 0.08 b. 2.475 c. 2.06
   d. 2.154 e. 2.036 f. 0.3185
4. a. 1.12 b. 0.143 c. 1.2 d. 3.02 e. 3.25 f. 1.28
5. a. 1.3125 b. 17.685 c. −21.62 d. 49.359 e. 0 f. 0.1
6. 0.273 7. 5657.5 km 8. ₹5.25 9. 25

Revision Exercise

1. a. 0.513, zero point five one three
   b. tenths; tens c. $\frac{29}{25}$
   d. decimal point e. decreases; ten
2. i. d ii. e iii. b iv. c v. a
3. a. 10 + 2 +0.3; 30 + 2 + 0.4 + 0.04; 600 + 40 + 4 + 0.3 + 0.06 + 0.008
   b. i. 4.3 ii. 32.78 iii. 121.104
   c. i. $\frac{4}{100}$ ii. $\frac{5}{10}$ iii. $\frac{7}{1000}$
4. a. 0.6 b. 0.5 c. 4 d. 0.64
5. a. $\frac{1}{2}$ b. $\frac{3}{2}$ c. $\frac{123}{1000}$ d. $\frac{1223}{100}$
6. a. $>$ b. $>$ c. $<$ d. $<$
7. a. 152.6 b. 76.04 c. 158.446 d. 221.691
8. a. 55.26 b. 9.17 c. 4.002 d. 1.969
9. a. 2629.83 b. 49.227 c. 0.762
   d. 84.6 e. 1634 f. 9500
10. a. 0.9645 b. 4.856 c. 5.8
    d. 680 e. 0.17 f. 0.7635

For The Curious Mind

400.509

Chapter – 6

Exercise 6.1

1. a. Base = 8 Exponent = 7
   b. Base = 5 Exponent = 6
   c. Base = 2 Exponent = 7
   d. Base = 9 Exponent = 4
   e. Base = 6 Exponent = 3
2. a. 8^6 b. 6^7 c. $(-7)^4$ d. $(-1)^6$ e. p^8
3. a. $7^2 \times 5^3$ b. 2^9 c. 3^6 d. 7^4 e. $2 \times 3 \times 5 \times 7 \times 11$
4. a. 1296 b. 576 c. 2401 d. −1000 e. −6561
5. a. 3^8 b. 6^2 c. $(-2)^{29}$ d. 5^2 e. 5 f. 1

Exercise 6.2

1. a. 16 b. 18 c. 6 d. 12 e. 13
2. a. 80 b. 90 c. 6 d. $\frac{1}{2}$ e. 20

Revision Exercise

1. a. ii b. i c. iii d. i e. iii
2. a. 5^8 b. 1 c. 60 d. 6^3 e. 100
3. a. iv b. iii c. v d. ii e. i
4. a. 26 b. 48 c. 15 d. 6 e. $\frac{10}{3}$

For the Curious Mind

Least number to be multiplied is 5 and number is 3375 and the cube root of 3375 is 15

Unit Worksheet

Crossword

[1] −1	6	■	[2] −1	5	■
1	■	[3] 1	4	■	[4] −1
■	[5] −1	3	■	[6] 1	9
[7] 1	6	■	[8] 1	8	■
7	■	[9] 1	0	■	[10] 1
■	[11] 1	1	■	1	[12] 4

Mental Maths

1. 10 million 2. MCMXLVII 3. 4
4. $\frac{1}{7}$ 5. 0.001

Chapter – 7

Exercise 7.1

1. a. 6.8 ℓ b. $\frac{11}{12}$ c. 5.5 d. 4.25

2. 139 3. 1.408 kg 4. ₹1200
5. 32.3°C 6. 37 7. 33 sq. cm

Revision Exercise

1. a. ₹76611 b. 1062.536 cm c. 54.125 d. 6619.75
   e. 11 f. 21 g. 5.6 h. 6
2. 81 3. 74 4. 30 5. 5
6. 270 kg 7. 36.2 8. 95 9. 6 10. 42 kg

For The Curious Mind

99

Chapter – 8

Exercise 8.1

1. a. 9% b. 38% c. 63%
2. a. $\frac{1}{20}$ b. $\frac{3}{4}$ c. $\frac{5}{8}$ d. $\frac{11}{400}$
3. a. $12\frac{1}{2}\%$ b. 65% c. $41\frac{2}{3}\%$ d. $162\frac{1}{2}\%$
4. a. 0.07 b. 0.44 c. 33.2 d. 0.164
5. a. 60% b. 7% c. 105% d. 162.5%
6. a. 1:50 b. 7:10 c. 13:200 d. 8:1000
7. a. 10% b. 5% c. 25% d. $62\frac{1}{2}\%$

Exercise 8.2

1. a. 40% b. $31\frac{1}{4}\%$ c. 1% d. $6\frac{1}{4}\%$ e. 30% f. 10%
2. a. ₹15 b. 1 m 26 cm c. 312.5 m
   d. 9 litres e. 400 g f. 9.6 cm
3. 36% 4. $25\frac{175}{186}\%$ 5. 48%, 32%, 20% 6. ₹5000

Revision Exercise

1. a. decimal fractions
   b. per hundred/for every hundred c. %
2. 30%, 12%, 20%, 16%, 22% 3. $8\frac{1}{3}\%$ 4. 782
5. 9.25 interests for ₹10500 6. ₹50000 7. ₹934.8
8. 300000 9. $7\frac{1}{7}\%$ 10. Physics 11. 100000
12. 1080 13. 99.995%; 0.005% 14. 5%

For The Curious Mind

School-1: 75%; School-2: 80%; School-2 is the best school in the village

Chapter – 9

Exercise 9.1

1. a. 1:3 b. 5:7 c. 13:16 d. 629:407
2. a. 4:1 b. 10:3 c. 36:11 d. 48:5
3. a. 7:6 b. 7:24 c. 9:10 d. 3:2
4. a. yes b. no c. no d. yes
5. a. (6:7) > (5:6) b. (19:25) > (37:50)
   c. (24:13) > (12:7) d. (43:100) > (21:50)
6. a. yes b. yes c. no d. no
7. a. 12 b. 12 c. 40 d. $5\frac{1}{4}$
8. a. 3 b. 20 c. 30 d. 9
9. 1:8 10. 54 cm, 60 cm 11. 2.52 litres 12. 30°, 60° and 90°
13. i. 7 : 8 ii. 7 : 15 14. i. 3 : 2 ii. 3 : 5

Exercise 9.2

1. a. Direct b. Inverse c. Direct d. Inverse e. Direct
2. b = $\frac{1}{4}$ and a = 5 3. 200 kg 4. $6\frac{2}{5}$ week 5. 5 litres

Revision Exercise

1. a. 1:2 b. 37:47 c. 5:6 d. 17:30
2. a. yes b. no c. yes d. no
3.

Ratio	Simplified ratio
50:100	1:2
750:1000	3:4
60:30	2:1
500:125	4:1
300:5	60:1
30:10	3:1

4. ₹40000; ₹64000 5. 15 kg 6. 380.29 cm (approx)
7. $32\frac{8}{11}$ 8. a = 19; b = 15 9. ₹33750 10. $17\frac{1}{3}$ days

For The Curious Mind

400 sq. cm

Chapter – 10

Exercise 10.1

1.

Quantity	Value in ₹	Required quantity	Value of required quantity in ₹
3 pen sets	180	5 pen sets	300
5 kg flour	165	12 kg flour	396
15 m ribbon	105	8 m ribbon	56
2 dozen eggs	144	46 eggs	276

2. 105 3. 12 km/ℓ 4. 2 kg 5. 1645 bricks

Revision Exercise

1.

Ingredients	Quantity for 10 people	Quantity for 4 people	Quantity for 25 people
Flour	400 g	160 g	1000 g
Oil	350 g	140 g	875 g
Essences	10 drops	4 drops	25 drops
Eggs	5	2 eggs	12–13 eggs
Baking Powder	15 g	6 g	37.5 g
Almonds	100 g	40 g	100 g

2. ₹2310 3. 2364 bricks 4. ₹750 5. 18
6. 135 books weigh 9 kg and 75 books weigh 5 kg.
7. 22 days 8. 540 cm

For The Curious Mind

1. Onions are cheaper at Sharma's shop by ₹0.5
2. 75 litres of oil is required for a month.

Chapter – 11

Exercise 11.1

1. Profit – ₹22.50 2. Profit – ₹40 3. ₹7750
4. ₹913 5. i. ₹2 profit ii. ₹12 profit

Exercise 11.2

1. 24% profit 2. 5% loss 3. 15% profit 4. 20% loss

Exercise 11.3

1. a. ₹825 b. ₹546 c. ₹980 d. ₹460
2. ₹16800
3. ₹470000 if sold at loss of 6%. ₹530000 if sold at a profit of 6%

Exercise 11.4

1. ₹64/- 2. ₹3700; discount% = 20%
3. ₹6 of discount amount at 24%
4. ₹90000/- of discount amount at 20%
5. ₹15000; ₹6500 profit 6. ₹52,200; ₹12,200
7. ₹2400 at 4% discount. 8. ₹700; 20% 9. ₹3200; 8%

For The Curious Mind

1. Expected profit percentage = 20% and actual profit percentage = 12%
2. ₹900

Revision Exercise

1. a. ₹100 b. ₹200 c. ₹310 d. ₹945
2. a. Profit – 20% b. Profit – 6.66%
   c. Loss – 8% d. Loss – 3%
3. a. True b. True c. False d. False
4. a. Loss 20% b. ₹38150 c. ₹42500
   d. Profit 5% e. 150% f. 4%
   g. 25% h. ₹3520 and at 12% discount

Chapter – 12

Exercise 12.1

1. a. 12 paise b. ₹12 c. 12%
2. a. ₹36 b. ₹3 c. 3 paise
3. ₹13.50
4. i. ₹$3333\frac{1}{3}$ b. ₹200
5. i. ₹25625 b. ₹102000
6. i. ₹1762.2; ₹21762.2 b. ₹1952.9; ₹16952.9
7. ₹35000
8. $2\frac{1}{2}$ years
9. $7\frac{1}{2}$ years
10. 8% p.a.

Revision Exercise

1. a. Rate per cent b. Interest c. Principal
   d. Interest e. Rate of interest
2. a. ₹2 b. ₹24 c. 24%
3. ₹590
4. ₹103500
5. ₹37600
6. ₹1346.4 ₹6786.4
7. ₹420000
8. ₹38000
9. $7\frac{1}{2}$ years
10. 16 years
11. ₹336
12. 22.592592...

For The Curious Mind

₹20856.8

Unit Worksheet

1.

1 year	3 years	5 years
₹4500	₹14,250	₹25,000

2.

1 year	3 years	5 years
9%	9.5%	10%

3. a. 6 : 19 b. 9 : 50 c. 5.7 : 10
4. ₹11,250

Mental Maths

1. 250 g
2. 2
3. $\frac{1}{8}$
4. 3600
5. 10%

Chapter – 13

Exercise 13.1

1. a. N b. N c. A d. N 5 e. A f. A
2. a. 15 b. –14 c. 2 d. 57
3. a. 27816 + 14908 = 42724 b. 8,75,134 – 7,89,052 = 86082
   c. 584 × 160 = ₹93440 d. 975 ÷ 13 = 75 kg
4. a. 25 b. –35 c. 115

Exercise 13.2

1. a. 5 – 6*x*: Variable: *x*, Constant: 5
   b. 2 + *m*: Variable: *m*; Constant: 2
   c. 3*p* + 10: Variable: p; Constant: 10
   d. 56*l* : Variable: l; Constant: 0
   e. 39: No Variable; Constant: 39
2. a. C b. V c. C d. C e. V
3. a. i. y^6 – *y* raised to the power of six
   ii. z^2 – *z* raised to the power of two or *z*-squared
   iii. p^4 – *p* raised to the power of four
   iv. 6^9 – 6 raised to the power of nine
   b. i. 7^2 ii. 16^p iii. m^4 iv. x^y

Exercise 13.3

1. a. $5x + 7$ b. $4x + 13$ c. $7 - 10x$ d. $\frac{1}{2}(2x + 2y)$ e. $t - 3$ f. $\frac{4}{a}$
   g. $3q - (w + 20)$ h. $\frac{14x}{7} = 10$ i. $6 \times 2 - 2x$ j. $2 + x^6 = 20$
2. a. 10 added to the product of 25 and *p* gives 60
   b. The quotient when the product of 16 and *m* divided by 2 gives 24
   c. 15 subtracted from the sum of 10*x* and 7*y*
   d. The product of 15 and *y* taken away from 100
3. a. $500p$ b. $\frac{10000}{k}$
   c. Age of elder brother = *x* + 5 (Any consecutive even integers differs by 2.)
   d. Tom's Age = *x* – 4, where *x* – Steve's Age

Exercise 13.4

Algebraic Expression	Terms	Numerical Coefficient	Power of the variable
$-25x^3 + 2x^2 + x$	$-25x^3$	–25	3
	$2x^2$	2	2
	x	1	1
$4a^3b^2 - 2b^2 + 3a - 4$	$4a^3b^2$	4	3, 2
	$-2b^2$	– 2	2
	3a	3	1
	– 4	Constant term	
$52z^2 + 19zx$	$52z^2$	52	2
	19*zx*	19	1, 1
$6x^4 + 4x^5 + 20x^3 - 6x^2 + 2$	$6x^4$	6	4
	$4x^5$	4	5
	$20x^3$	20	3
	$-6x^2$	– 6	2
	2	Constant term	
$2l^3 + 24$	$2l^3$	2	3
	24	Constant term	
$(a + 4b + 5) \div 2$	$\frac{a}{2}$	$\frac{1}{2}$	1
	2b	2	1
	$\frac{5}{2}$	Constant term	

2. a. $10p^2q, -6qp^2; -4pq^2, 12q^2p$ b. $12a^2, -10a^2; 5a, -8a, 9a$
   c. $2x^2y^3, -3x^2y^3; 5x^3y^2, -10x^3y^2$ d. $24y^{10}, -4y^{10}; y^6, -26y^6; 4y^2, 7y^2$
3. a. The powers of the variables are different
   b. The variables are different
   c. Variables and the powers of the variables are different
   d. The powers of the variables are different
   e. The variables are different
4. Monomials – *a*, *b* and *f* ; Binomials –*c* and *g*; Trinomials – *d*; Polynomials –e

Exercise 13.5

1. a. –37 b. 87 c. –28 d. –56
2. a. –1002 b. 582 c. 2294 d. 15
3.

X	2	4	8	10
Value of the expression	38	38	59	70.64

Revision Exercise

1. a. A b. N c. A d. N

2. A variable in an expression is the quantity that varies. It can take different values.
A constant in an expression is the quantity that is fixed.It cannot take any other value.
3. a. Constant b. Variable c. Constant d. Variable
4. a. x raised to the power of ten b. z raised to the power of three
c. p raised to the power of six
5. a. $x + x + 1 + x + 2 = 3x + 3$ or $x - 1 + x + x + 1 = 3x$ b. $\frac{4}{x} - 2$
c. d − 3 d. $\frac{3x}{2}$ e. $2x - 2$
f. Rajesh's age = $x - 10$, where x – Rajesh's mother's age
6. a. Terms: $15x, 6y, z$ b. Terms: $16, 6a$
c. Terms: $4x^2, 16x, -16$ d. Terms: $a^3, 4b, -3c$
e. Terms: $\frac{6}{2}, \frac{12x}{2}$
7. Like terms: $14x^3, -11x^3$; $-26y^2, 49y^2$; $100x^2y, 30x^2y$; $36a^3, 23a^3$; $42x^2, -12x^2$; $-19a^2b^2, 13a^2b^2$
8. a. −1 b. 42 c. 7
9. $r = d + 8$ 10. $3x + 4$

For The Curious Mind

Total number of pearls is $\frac{x}{3} + \frac{x}{5} + \frac{x}{6} + \frac{x}{10} + 6 = x$, where x is the number of pearls in the necklace

Chapter – 14

Exercise 14.1

1. a. $-11ab^2$ b. $100xyz$ c. $23y^2$ d. $-14x + 4y$
e. $5x^2 + 2x - 2$ f. $7p^2 + 8p - 6$
2. a. $-38b^3$ b. $-19abc$ c. $-8l^6$ d. $2p^2 - 6q + 8pq + 10p$
e. $6x^3 - 24y^3$ f. $-13ab + 24bc - 25ca$
3. a. $30x^2 - 9y^2 - 16xy$ b. $-2x^2 - 13y^2 + 14xy$
c. $12x^2 + 5y^2 - 10xy$ d. $-20x^2 + y^2 + 20xy$
4. $76p^4 - 66p^3 + 38p^2 + 27p + 23$
5. $33x^5 - 10x^4 + 10x^3 - 22x^2 + 8x - 9$
6. a. $19ab + 8a + 28a^2b - 26b - 7$
b. $x^2yz + 3xy^2z + 13xz^2 - 226$
c. $19pq^2 + 11p^2q^2 - 15pq - 26p^2q + 9p - 10$

Exercise 14.2

1. a. $12ap^2$ b. $15d^{15}$ c. $12y^{10}$
d. $63a^3b^{12}$ e. $-15x^3y^5$ f. $16k^5r^3$
2. a. $30e^7 - 90e^5 + 60e^2 + 45e + 15$ b. $-14k^9 + 35k^5 - 63$
c. $-10x^{11} - 40x^5 + 250x - 60x$ d. $105b^5 - 28b^{16} + 84b^2 + 49b^3$
e. $-12d^8 + 42d^6 - 12d^4 - 21d^2 - 24d$ f. $-27x^2 + 6x + 5$
g. $12m^2 - 14mn - 20n^2$ h. $3a^6 + 15a^3b^5 - 6a^3b^2 - 30b^7$
i. $15k^4 - 19k^3 - 8k^2$ j. $x^2 - \frac{19}{3}xy + 2y^2$

Exercise 14.3

1. a. $3m^2$ b. $8p^6$ c. $36a^5b^3$ d. $64x^6z^{-2}$
2. a. $4b^3 + 2b^5 + 8b$ b. $4z^3 - 6z + 9z^{-1}$
c. $3t^8 - 2t^6 + 4t^3$ d. $-36j^{13} + 10j^9 - 6j^6$

Revision Exercise

1. a. $3x^2 + 3x - 9$ b. $x^3 + 8x^2 - 6x + 11$ c. $-4y^2 - 2y - 1$
d. $8a^5 + 10a^3 - 3a^2 + 7a - 15$ e. $-8p^2 - 7p - 2$
2. a. $36ab$ b. $-37m^2n$ c. $-7p^3 + 3p^2 + 17p$
d. $13xz + x - 6z^2$ e. $-7lx + 10x^2 - 18l^2$
3. a. $36d^6$ b. $88p^5q^3r^7$ c. $63k^5l^3m^6$ d. $8a^3b^3$
4. a. $-5k^3 + 15k^2 - 100k$ b. $12r^4v - 30r^5$
c. $-32q^4 - 8q^3 + 60q^2$ d. $5s^{16} - 15s^{13} + 20s^6$
5. a. $12z^2 + 22z - 20$ b. $10p^2 - 35pq + 30q^2$ c. $8k^4 - 32l^2k^2 - 18l^4$
6. a. $6g^2$ b. $-5i^6$ c. $-4uv^{-1}w^2$ d. $9c^2d^2$
7. a. $2s^4tv^{-3} - 5tv^{-2}$ b. $-6q^2 - 7p^3q^2$ c. $8f^{10} - 9f^7 + 10f^3 + 1$

For the Curious Mind

$(55x + 42y + 15z)(30 - a) = 1650x - 55xa + 1260y - 42ya + 450z - 15za$

Chapter – 15

Exercise 15.1

1. a. $3x - 12 = 3$ b. $4x + 15 = 55$ c. $\frac{3x - 18}{2}$
d. $x^2 + 5(x + 6) = 24$ e. $3x + 3 = 9$ or $3x = 9$
2. Number of balls = $\frac{2500}{50}$
3. $x - 20 = 26$, where x is Ramesh's mother's age
4. $2(2x + x) = 192$ 5. Number of Rows = $\frac{120}{8}$ 6. $C = 2\pi k$
7. $\frac{20}{100}x = 450$ 8. $y = \frac{100x}{105}$
9. Volume of the globe = $\frac{4}{3}\pi y^3$ cm³

For The Curious Mind

Area of the shaded region = $a \times a) + (a \times b) - [(a - 2) \times (b - 3)]$
$= a^2 + 2b + 3a - 6$

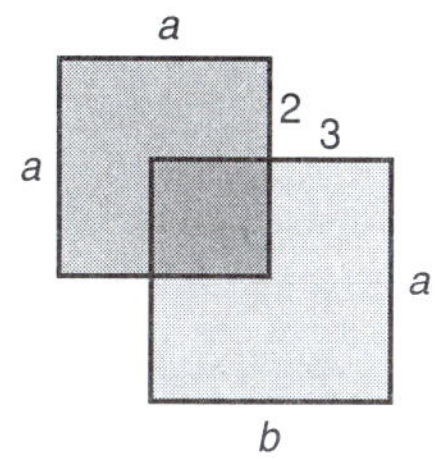

Chapter – 16

Exercise 16.1

1. a. Algebraic Expression b. Algebraic Equation
c. Algebraic Equation d. Algebraic Expression
2. a. LHS = $x - 8$, RHS = 11 b. LHS = $10z + 2$, RHS = 18
c. LHS = $5p - 7$, RHS = 23 d. LHS = $15a^2 - 5b$, RHS = 25
3. a. $3x = 36$ b. $9 - 5x = -11$
4. The number of boys in the class = 50 − 22.
5. Let x be the amount spent by Sudeshna. Money spent by Sukanya is $x - 5 = 15$

Exercise 16.2

1. a. $r = -1$ b. $b = 4$ c. $p = 6$ d. $k = 8$ e. $y = 6$
f. $x = 10$ g. $m = 5$ h. $x = 6$
2. a. $x = 15$ b. $j = -10$ c. $t = -15$ d. $x = 18$ e. $g = 42$
f. $r = 12$ g. $p = 40$ h. $y = 9$ i. $k = 56$ j. $u = 9$
k. $e = -6$ l. $a = \frac{3}{2}$

Exercise 16.3

1. $x = 4$ 2. $t = 20$ 3. $y = 4$ 4. $k = 9$ 5. $r = 7$
6. $p = 10$ 7. $d = 6$ 8. $r = 11$ 9. $l = 8$ 10. $g = \frac{42}{5}$
11. $x = 9$ 12. $x = 15$ 13. $z = 2$ 14. $p = 26$ 15. $w = 204$

Exercise 16.4

1. 9 2. 11 3. 9 4. 24
5. The three consecutive odd numbers are 33, 35 and 37
6. Length of the rectangle is 64 m and its breadth is 32 m.
7. Rakesh's father's age is 37 years.
8. The number of boys is 30 and number of girls is 20.
9. The number of giraffes in the zoo is 80 and the number of elephants is 220.
10. Therefore, the number of days Arya worked is 15.

Revision Exercise

1. a. $y = 12$ b. $t = 3$ c. $r = 1$ d. $x = -2$
2. a. $k = 4$ b. $n = 3$ c. $p = 7$ d. $x = 4$ e. $f = 6$ f. $d = 8$
g. $j = 11$ h. $t = 36$ i. $x = \frac{8}{5}$ j. $h = \frac{3}{2}$ k. $a = 1$ l. $b = 2$

3. 11 4. 6.8 5. 320

6. Shashank's age = 16 years, his younger brother's age = 4 years

7. 100 chocolates

For the Curious Mind

16	2	3	13
5	11	10	8
9	7	6	12
4	14	15	1

Unit Worksheet

1. +2 2. −6 3. +10 4. −120 5. −18

Mental Maths

1. 10 2. 2 3. −7 4. 3 5. 20

Chapter – 17

Revision Exercise

1. Points: P , Q , R , S , E , F, G, H, D , M, N,K, L, J, I, A, B, O, C.

   Line segments: $\overline{PQ}$, $\overline{QR}$, $\overline{RS}$, $\overline{EF}$, $\overline{EG}$, $\overline{FH}$, $\overline{FD}$, $\overline{KL}$, $\overline{IJ}$, $\overline{MN}$, $\overline{NO}$, $\overline{BO}$,$\overline{MB}$, $\overline{DC}$, $\overline{AB}$, $\overline{GH}$, $\overline{HD}$, $\overline{GA}$, $\overline{AO}$, $\overline{OC}$, $\overline{LJ}$, $\overline{JB}$, $\overline{KI}$, $\overline{AI}$

   Angles: ∠FHD, ∠FEG, ∠FDH, ∠DFH, ∠GAI, ∠MBJ, ∠NOB, ∠MBO, ∠MNO, ∠BMN, ∠DCO, ∠DHM

   Parallel lines: $\overleftrightarrow{EF} \parallel \overleftrightarrow{GH}$, $\overleftrightarrow{EF} \parallel \overleftrightarrow{AB}$, $\overleftrightarrow{KL} \parallel \overleftrightarrow{IJ}$, $\overleftrightarrow{HD} \parallel \overleftrightarrow{MN} \parallel \overleftrightarrow{BO}$, $\overleftrightarrow{KI} \parallel \overleftrightarrow{LJ}$

   Perpendicular lines: $\overleftrightarrow{GA} \perp \overleftrightarrow{AI}$, $\overleftrightarrow{MB} \perp \overleftrightarrow{JO}$, $\overleftrightarrow{NO} \perp \overleftrightarrow{BC}$, $\overleftrightarrow{DC} \perp \overleftrightarrow{OC}$, $\overleftrightarrow{LJ} \perp \overleftrightarrow{IB}$, $\overleftrightarrow{KI} \perp \overleftrightarrow{AJ}$

   Collinear points: P, Q, R and S, G, H and D, A, I, J, B, O and C

   Plane surfaces :

2. a. False b. True c. True d. True e. True
   f. False g. False h. False i. True

3. a. Parallel b. Perpendicular c. Perpendicular
   d. Parallel

4. a.

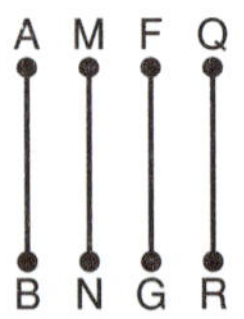

b.

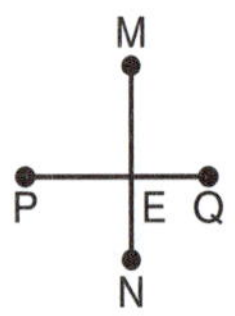

c.

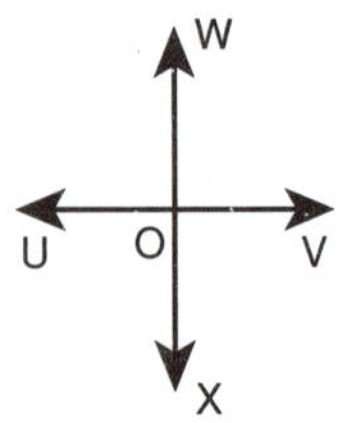

d.

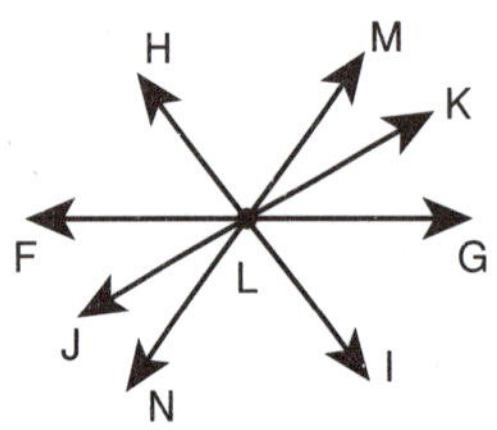

5. a. One b. No c. 90 d. Line

6.

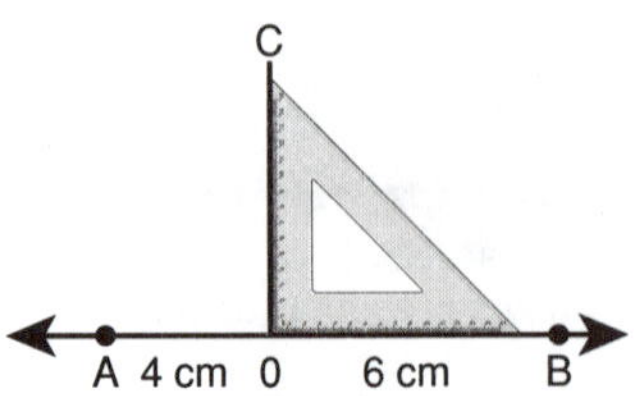

7.

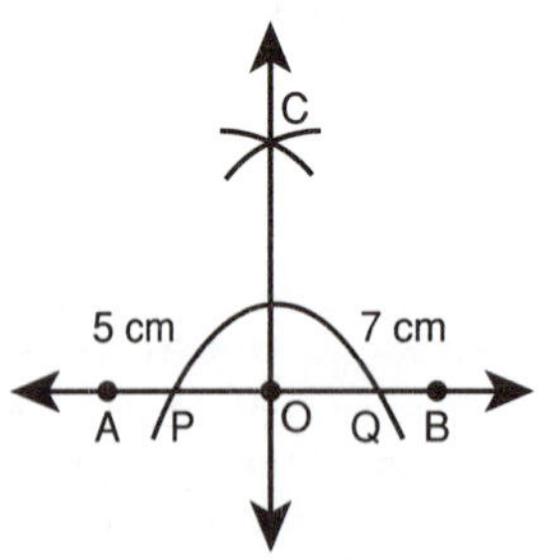

8.

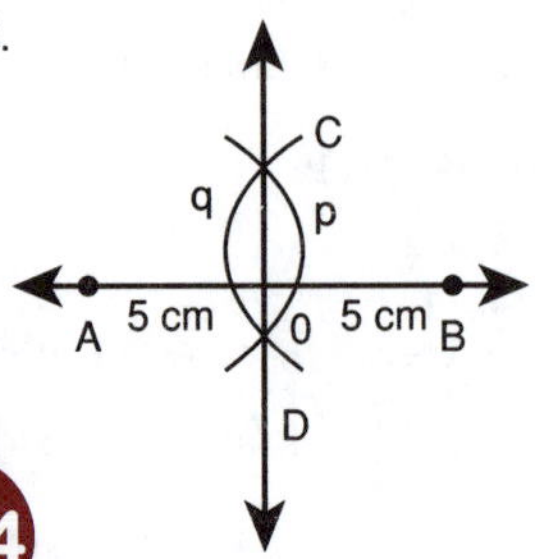

For The Curious Mind

1. No, this can be justified by folding the paper such that the points A and B coincide
2. **Step 1**: Use a ruler to draw a line AB

   Step 2: Mark point X outside line AB

   Step 3: Place one side of the set square so that the tip where reading starts should lie on the line AB

   Step 4: Slide the set square along AB till the vertical side of the set square meets the point X

   Step 5: Use a pencil along the vertical side of the set square to draw the perpendicular to line AB

   Step 6: Mark point O at the intersection of the perpendicular and line AB

   Step 7: We have OX ⊥ AB

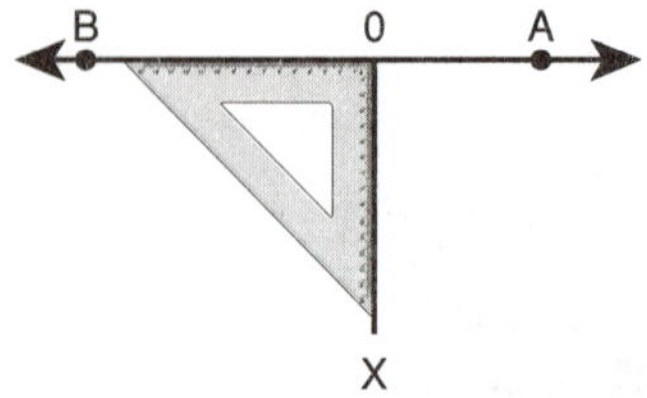

Chapter – 18

Exercise 18.1

1. a. Interior points = A,B,C,D On the boundary line = H,I,P,J,K,Q Exterior points = X,Y,Z

   b. Interior points = I,J,K On the boundary line = C,A,P, R Exterior points = Q,H

2. 2.24°11′50″

3. a. acute angle b. acute angle c. acute angle
   d. obtuse angle e. reflex angle

Exercise 18.2

1.
   a. Adjacent angles on the straight line adds up to 180°& x = 50

   b. All the angles adds up to 360°. Hence, x = 22.5, 2x = 45, 4x = 90, 9x = 202.5

   c. Adjacent angles on the straight line adds up to 180°. Therefore, $x + x + 20 = 180°$ $x = 80°$, $x + 20 = 100°$. Then, ∠AOQ = 100° & ∠QOC = 80°

   d. ∠URC = ∠VCB = x = 110° – Corresponding angles are equal
   ∠VCB + ∠BCQ = 180° – Adjacent angles on the straight line adds up to 180°. Therefore, ∠BCQ = 70°
   ∠URC = ∠RCQ =110° – Alternate interior angles
   ∠BCQ = ∠RCV =70° – vertically opposite angles
   ∠VCR = ∠PRC = 70° – Alternate interior angles
   ∠PRC = ∠ARU = 70° – vertically opposite angles
   ∠URC = ∠ARP = 110° – vertically opposite angles

2. a. 42°, 132° b. 17°,107° c. (90 – x)°, (180 – x)°
   d. (70 – x)°, (160 – x)° e. 67°, 157° f. 0°, 90°
   g. 45°, 135° h. 3°, 93°

3. 15° and 75° 4. 54° and 126°

Revision exercise

1. a. Corresponding angles are equal. ∠AUR = ∠PVU = 60°
   ∠AUV + ∠AUR = 180° – Adjacent angles on the straight line adds up to 180°. Therefore, ∠AUV = 120°
   ∠AUV = ∠PVC = x = 120° – Corresponding angles are equal
   ∠AUV = ∠UVQ = 120° – Alternate interior angles
   ∠PVU = ∠CVQ = 60° – vertically opposite angles
   ∠AUR = ∠VUB = 60° – vertically opposite angles
   ∠AUV = ∠RUB = 120° – vertically opposite angles

   b. ∠RUB = ∠AUV=130° – Vertically opposite angles
   ∠RUB + ∠BUV = 180° – Angles on a straight line. Therefore, ∠BUV = 50°
   ∠RUB = ∠UVQ = 130° – Corresponding angles are equal
   ∠BUV = ∠QVC = 50° – Corresponding angles are equal
   ∠UVQ = ∠PVC = 130° – vertically opposite angles
   ∠QVC = ∠PVU = 50° – vertically opposite angles
   ∠BUV = ∠AUR = 50° – vertically opposite angles

2. a. 78° b. 50° c. 34° d. 15° e. 11° f. 57°
g. 40° h. 22° 04′ 38″ i. 76° j. 0°
3. a. 145° b. 123° c. 88° d. 180° e. 0° f. 30°
g. 90° h. 57° i. 60° j. 21° 53′ 27″
4. a. False b. True c. False d. True
e. False f. True g. False h. False
5. a. complementary b. supplementary c. congruent
d. complementary e. supplementary f. supplementary
g. supplementary h. congruent

Chapter – 19

Revision Exercise

6. a. (ii) Ruler b. (iii) 2

For the Curious Mind

Yes

Chapter – 20

Exercise 20.1

1. a. Isosceles triangle b. Equilateral triangle
c. Scalene triangle
2. a. Right angled triangle b. acute angled triangle
c. Obtuse angled triangle
3. a. Yes b. No c. Yes d. No
4. a. 116° b. 57° c. 137°
5. a. $55\frac{1}{2}$ b. 7 c. 34
6. a. 36°, 108°, 36° b. 45°, 45°, 90°
c. 60°, 60°, 60° d. 40°, 60°, 80°

Revision Exercise

1. a. Yes, All the angles in a equilateral triangle measures 60°
b. No, In right-angled and Obtuse-angled triangle we do not have three acute angles
c. No, Then the third angle measures 0°, which is impossible
d. Yes, We may have two equal sides included by an obtuse angled triangle
e. Yes, If two angles are complementary then the third angle is 90°
2. a. Equilateral triangle b. Isosceles triangle
c. 60° d. Equal e. 180°
3. a. $x = 35°$ b. $x = 56°$ c. $x = 58°, y = 64°$
4. 61°, 26°, 93°

For the Curious Mind

1. $x° = 93°, y° = 33°, z° = 33°$, $\angle CAD = 6°$ and $\angle A = 72°$

Chapter – 21

Exercise 21.1

1. a. Radius b. Diameter c. Secant
d. Tangent e. Sector f. Segment
2. Infinite
3. Diameter is always twice the radius of circle
4. Diameter
5. Interior and Exterior:
a. Points D,E,O and C lie in the interior of the circle
b. Points A,I and G lie on the circumference of the circle
c. Points B,F and H lie on the exterior of the circle.
6. Circumference and diameter are directly proportional to each other.
Circumference of a circle = $\pi \times$ diameter
7. 26.4 cm 8. 56 cm 9. Four
10. Secant is a line that intersects the circle exactly at 2 points, whereas tangent is the line that touches the circle exactly at one point.

Revision Exercise

1. a. Equal b. Diameter c. Centre 2. 70 cm
3. True or False
a. True b. True c. True
d. False e. False f. True

For The Curious Mind

1. 7 feet

Chapter – 22

Revision Exercise

2. a. No b. One c. Two, vertical, horizontal
d. Two e. n

Unit Worksheet

1.

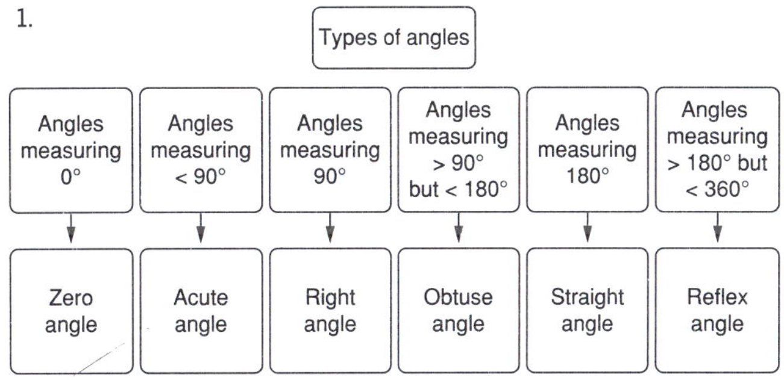

2. a. i. Straight angle ii. Obtuse angle iii. Right angle
iv. Acute angle v. Reflex angle b. 18 cm

Mental Maths

1. 35° 2. 55° 3. 9 cm 4. 60° 5. 90° each

Chapter – 23

Exercise 23.1

1. 20 cm 2. 140 m 3. 15 cm
4. Length = 48 feet, breadth = 24 feet 5. ₹50

Exercise 23.2

1. Area = 480 sq. cm , perimeter = 92 cm 2. ₹26460
3. 84 sq. m 4. Area will be reduced by $\frac{1}{4}$th of original area.
5. 300 tiles 6. Length of identical sides = 16 m

Revision Exercise

1. 12 cm 2. 7 cm 3. ₹10575
4. A square of side 95 cm 5. ₹1,08,000.

For the Curious Mind

1. a. Geometrical shape is Square.
b. Perimeter of a square is 4 × Side length = 4 × 1 m = 4 m.
2. In square QRSO, let the side be "a" cm; P × P = 4a × 4 a = 16 (a × a) = 16 A

Chapter – 24

Exercise 24.1

1. a. LSA = 256 sq.cm; TSA = 384 sq.cm
b. 625 sq.cm; 937.5 sq.cm
c. 2500 sq.cm; 3750 sq.cm
d. 1089 sq.cm; 1633.5 sq.cm
2. a. LSA = 36 sq.cm, TSA = 72 sq.cm
b. 117.5 sq.cm ; 387.5 sq.cm
c. 24 sq.cm; 55.5 sq.cm
3. LSA of tin = 1250 sq.cm 4. 1093.5 sq. m
5. ₹6795 6. ₹20.20 7. 126 sq.m; ₹6300

Exercise 24.2

1. a. 2197 cm^3 b. 166.375 m^2
c. 857.375 m^2 d. 3.375 m^2
2. a. 702 cm^3 b. 6 m^3
3. LSA of cube = 144 sq. cm, TSA of cube = 216 sq. cm
4. Volume of water required = 70,000 litres
5. 6500 litres
6. a. ₹5700 b. 87,500 litres

Revision Exercise

1. 1,66,375 litres 2. 23.625 m^3 3. ₹1833.60 4. 8 cm
5. Surface area = 686 cm^2
Volume = 1029 cm^3

For the Curious Mind

1. X = 7cm
2. Mass of given iron bar = 3712.5 g

Unit Worksheet

1. a. 143 ft b. 132 ft^2 c. 82 ft^2 d. 58 ft
2. a. Kitchen (52 ft) b. Kitchen (153 ft^2)

Mental Maths

1. 30 mm 2. 9 cm 3. 15 ft^2 4. 1ℓ 5. 32 cm^2

Chapter – 25

Exercise 25.1

1. a. Mt. Everest, 8750 m b. Nanda Devi c. 2250 m
   d. Mt. Everest, Kanchenjunga, Nanga Parbat, Nanda Devi, Himadri
2.

Animal	Life Span (years)
Bull	28
Bat	24
Cat	25
Crocodile	45
Chicken	14
Fox	14
Goat	15
Rabbit	9
Tiger	22

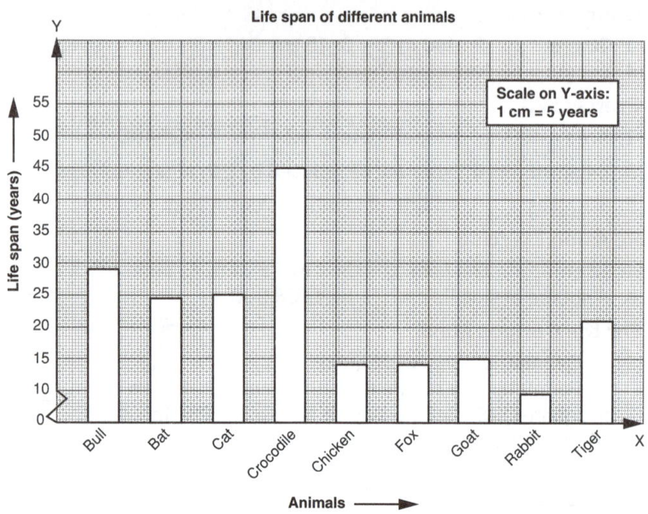

Exercise 25.2

1. a. Number of participants in different sports b. Cricket
   c. Tennis d. Hockey and football e. 200
2. a. i. $\frac{1}{4}$ ii. $\frac{1}{2}$ b. 3 c. 6
3.

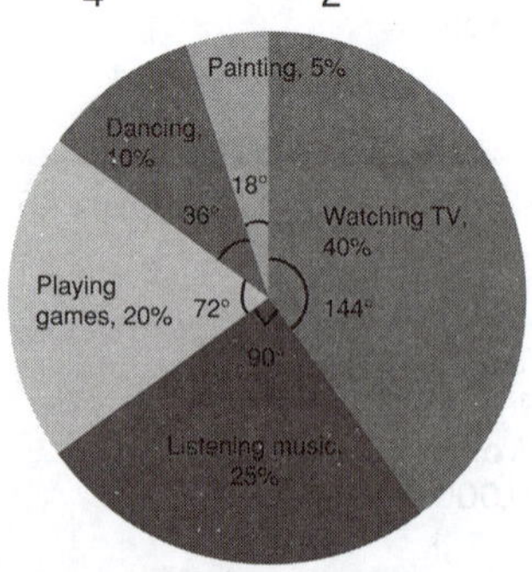

Exercise 25.3

1. a. 50 b. 600 c. 50 d. 2009 e. 2013
2. a. 70 b. 2008–2009 c. Yes, in 2010
   d. 68 kg and 74 kg

Revision Exercise

1. a. Annual rainfall recorded in some cities
   b. Madurai recorded 15 cm more than Rajkot
   c. Max: Shimla, min: Jodhpur, difference: 110 cm
   d. Jodhpur, Rajkot, Madurai, Shimla e. 1:2
2. a. Students' strength in different schools b. 600
   c. 150 d. 50 e. 1950
3.

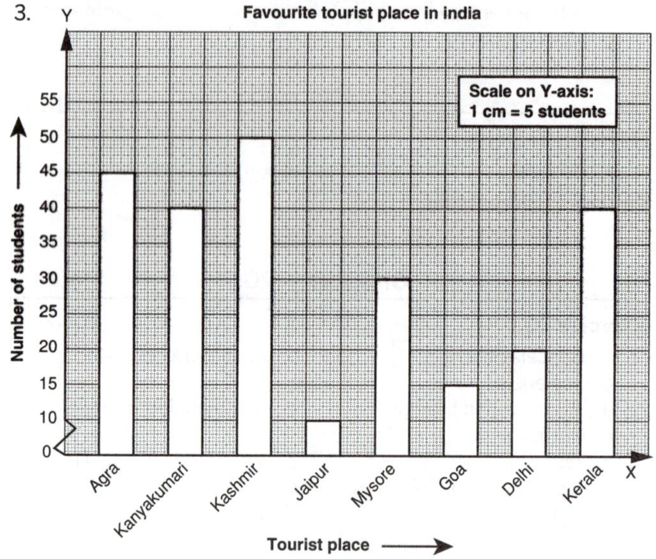

   a. Kashmir b. Jaipur c. Kerala and Kanyakumari
   d. 10
4. a. Number of kilograms of different fruits sold at a shop
   b. 5 kg c. 1 kg d. apple e. 20 kg
5. a. 8 b. 4 c. i. True ii. False
6. a. Number of customers visited the store at different times of the day
   b. At 1 pm and the number is 22. c. 2 d. 15
   e. At 10 am; 2 people. f. 70

Unit Worksheet

1. Class I – 10, Class II – 30, Class III – 30, Class IV – 20, Class V – 10 and Class VI – 20
2. ₹50 × 5 = ₹250, Bank account = ₹250, Total = ₹500

Chapter – 26

Exercise 26.1

1. Not a set as it not a well defined 2. It is a set
3. It is a set 4. It is a set 5. It is a set 6. It is a set

Exercise 26.2

1. a. I = {–19, –18, –17, –16, –15, –14, –13, –12, –11, –10, –9, –8, –7, –6}
   b. A = {80, 81, 82, 83, 84, 85, 86, 87, 88, 89, 90, 91, 92, 93, 94, 95, 96, 97, 98, 99}
   c. M = {8, 16, 24, 32, 40, 48, 56, 64, 72}
   d. O = {7, 21, 35, 49, 63}
   e. C = {k, r, n, t}
   f. R = {red, orange, yellow, green, blue, indigo, violet}
2. a. D = {x: x is an even number, $50 < x < 68$}
   b. P = {x: x is prime number, $100 < x < 150$}
   c. M = {Set of last four months of a year}
   d. F = {Set of first 5 prime numbers}
   e. S = {Set of first 4 inner planets of the Solar System}
   f. G = {x: x is neither a prime number nor a composite number}
3. a. n(A) = 5 b. n(B) = 6 c. n(C) = 1
   d. n(D) = 2 e. n(E) = 4 f. n(F) = 5

Exercise 26.3

1. e 2. a
3. a. Empty set b. Singleton set c. Singleton set
   d. Empty set e. Empty set
4. a. Finite set b. Infinite set c. Finite set
   d. Infinite set e. Finite set

Revision Exercise

1. a. It is set as it contains well defined objects
   b. It is a set as it contains well defined objects
   c. It is not a set as we can not exactly find the beautiful flowers in the garden
   d. It is not a set as the word 'fast' is not well defined
   e. It is a set as it contains well defined objects
2. a. A = {2, 3} and n (A) = 2
   b. B = {c, o, u, r, a, g, e} and n (B) = 7
   c. C = {6, 12, 18, 24, 30, 36} and n (C) = 6
   d. D = ϕ and n (D) = 0
   e. E = {3, 5, 7, 11, 13, 17, 19} and n (E) = 7
3. a. iii b. vi c. ii d. i e. iv
4. a. True b. False c. False d. True e. True

For the Curious Mind

Rahul is correct as there are infinitely many fraction are there between $\frac{1}{3}$ and $\frac{2}{3}$

Chapter – 27

Exercise 27.1

1. a. $A \cup B = \{a, b, c, d, e, f, g, h, j, k, l\}$ and $A \cap B = \{d, c, f\}$
   b. $A \cup B = \{2, 4, 6, 8, 10, 12, 16, 20\}$ and $A \cap B = \{4, 8, 12\}$
   c. $A \cup B = \{1, 2, 3, 4, 5, 6, 7, 8, 9, 10, 11, 12\}$ and $A \cap B = \phi$
   d. $A \cup B = \{x, y, z, a, c, d, b, e, f, i, j\}$ and $A \cap B = \phi$
   e. $A \cup B = \{10, 20, 30, 40, 50, 60, 80\}$ and $A \cap B = \{20, 40\}$
2. a. $A \cup B = \{s, u, p, o, w, e, r\}$ and $A \cap B = \{e, r\}$
   b. $A \cup B = \{17, 19, 23, 29, 31, 21, 25, 27\}$ and $A \cap B = \{17, 19, 23, 29\}$
   c. $A \cup B = \{1, 2, 3, 4, 5, 6, 8, 10, 12, 20, 24\}$ and $A \cap B = \{1, 2, 4\}$
   d. $A \cup B = \{5, 10, 15, 20, 25, 40, 80, 120, 160\}$ and $A \cap B = \phi$
   e. $A \cup B = \{-8, -7, -6, -5, -4, -3, -2\}$ and $A \cap B = \{-3\}$

Exercise 27.2

1. A = {2, 4, 6}, B = {6, 12, 18, 24, 30, 36, 42, 48, 54} and C = {1, 2, 3, 5, 6, 9, 10, 15, 18, 30, 45, 90}
   a. $A \cup B = \{2, 4, 6, 12, 18, 24, 30, 36, 42, 48, 54\}$
   b. $A \cap B = \{6\}$
   c. $B \cap C = \{6, 30\}$
   d. $A \cup C = \{1, 2, 3, 4, 5, 6, 9, 10, 15, 18, 30, 45, 90\}$
   e. $(A \cup C) \cap (B \cap C) = \{1, 2, 3, 4, 5, 6, 9, 10, 15, 18, 30, 45, 90\} \cap \{6, 30\} = \{6, 30\}$
2. n($A \cap B$) = 2

Revision Exercise

1. a. $A \cup B = \{1, 3, 7, 9, 2, 4, 5, 6\}$ and $A \cap B = \{1, 3, 5\}$
   b. $A \cup B = \{s, e, p, r, l, a, x\}$ and $A \cap B = \{e, l\}$
   c. $A \cup B = \{5, 10, 15, 20, 25, 30, 2, 4, 6, 8, 12\}$ and $A \cap B = \phi$
   d. A = {2} and B = {2}, then $A \cup B = \{2\}$ and $A \cap B = \{2\}$
2. a. n ($A \cup B$) = 9 and n ($A \cap B$) = 4
   b. n ($A \cup B$) = 9 and n ($A \cap B$) = 2
   c. n ($A \cup B$) = 12 and n ($A \cap B$) = 5
   d. n ($A \cup B$) = 9 and n ($A \cap B$) = 0
3. a. False b. True c. True d. True
4. a. iv b. iii c. i d. ii
5. a. $A \cup B = \{1, 2, 3, 4, 5, 6, 7\}$ b. $A \cup C = \{1, 2, 3, 4, 5, 6, 7, 8, 9\}$
   c. $B \cap C = \{7\}$ d. $C \cap D = \{7, 8, 9\}$

For the Curious Mind

a. $A \cup (B \cap C) = \{o, f, i, c, e, r, s\}$
b. $(A \cup B) \cap (B \cup C) = \{o, r, k, w, e, s\}$

Chapter – 28

Exercise 28.1

1. a.

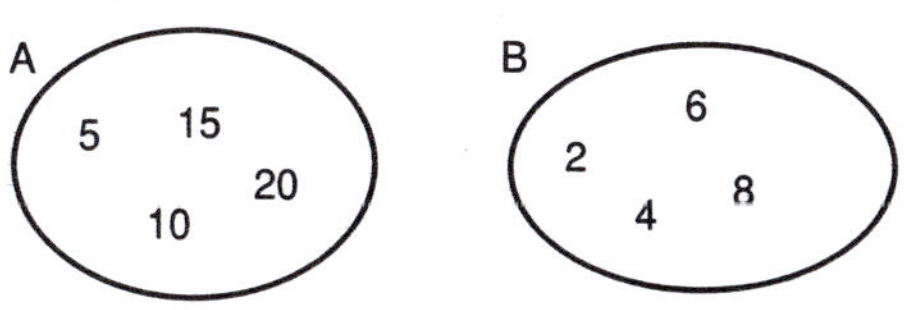

b.

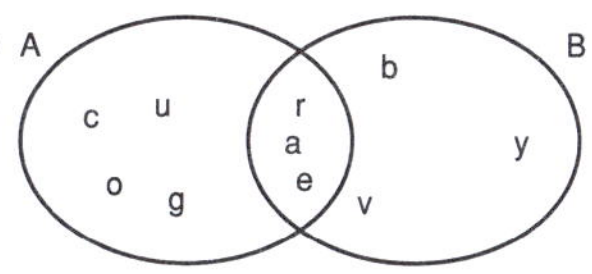

c.

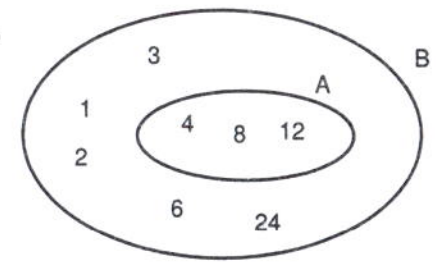

d.

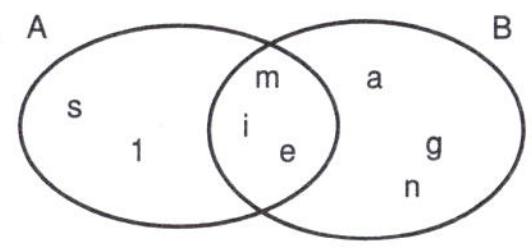

e.

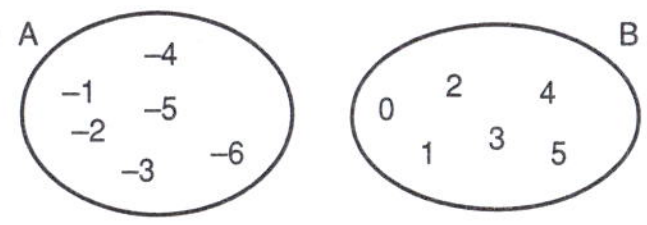

2. a. i. Se t A = {2, 3, 5, 7, 11} ii. Set B = {1, 3, 5, 7, 9}
   iii. Set $A \cup B = \{1, 2, 3, 5, 7, 9, 11\}$ iv. Set $A \cap B = \{3, 5, 7\}$
   b. i. Set A = {1, 2, 4} ii. Set B = {1, 2, 4, 8}
   iii. Set $A \cup B = \{1, 2, 4, 8\}$ iv. Set $A \cap B = \{1, 2, 4\}$

Revision Exercise

1. a.

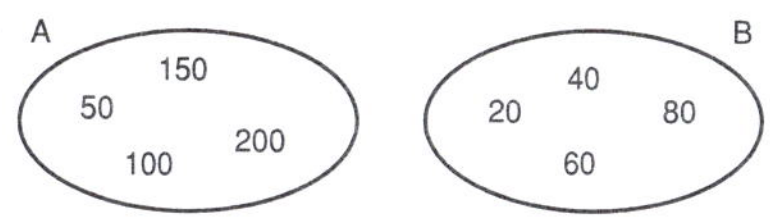

b.

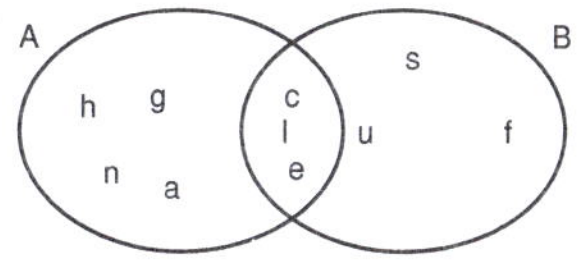

c.

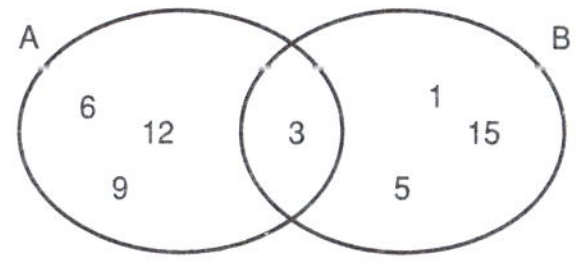

d.

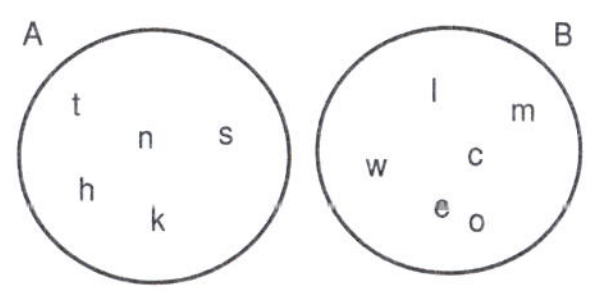

Unit Worksheet

1. a. iv b. iv c. iii d. i e. iii f. i
2. a. singleton b. cardinal number c. finite
   d. 3 e. equivalent
3. a. T b. F c. F d. T e. F

Test Paper 1

1. a. i b. ii c. iii d. ii e. i
2. a. zero b. successor c. co-primes
   d. −15 e. 32,06,568
3. a. F b. T c. T d. F e. T
4. a. 8997 b. −20
5. a. 98754310; Indian place value system: 9,87,54,310; International place value system: 98,754,310
   b. 46

Test Paper 2

1. a. i b. iii c. iii d. ii e. i
2. a. unlike fractions b. decimal fractions c. −1
   d. 0.0957 e. $5\frac{11}{14}$
3. a. F b. F c. T d. T e. F
4. a. $18\frac{3}{10}$ b. ₹1091.75
5. a. 27 b. ₹81,000

Test Paper 3

1. a. ii b. ii c. iv d. ii e. ii
2. a. 15 b. 8 c. extremes d. 5000 e. $\frac{8}{25}$

3. a. T b. F c. T d. T e. F
4. a. 20 b. 23 : 2
5. a. Number of apples = 2808; Total number of fruits = 4368
b. 15%

Test Paper 4

1. a. ii b. i c. i d. ii e. iv
2. a. $R = \frac{SI \times 100}{P \times T}$ b. SP − CP c. 10 m/s
d. 90% e. ₹61.50
3. a. F b. F c. T d. T e. T
4. a. ₹1025 b. 9 m/s
5. a. ₹18,291 b. 4 years

Test Paper 5

1. a. iv b. iii c. i d. ii e. iii
2. a. pq^2 b. binomial c. 6
d. 352 e. $x^2(3x + 12) = 49$
3. a. F b. F c. T d. T e. F
4. a. i. $\frac{5}{6}p(q+15)$ ii. $\frac{x}{5}(y-12)$
b. i. $\frac{x-25}{x-10} = 15$ ii. $5x(x^2+8) = 21$
c. $x = 14$ d. $-14x^2 + 25y^2 - 4z^2$
5. b. i. 4 ii. 5 iii. 10 b. $\frac{132}{17}$
c. 15, 17 and 19 d. $20a^2b - ab - 12b$

Test Paper 6

1. a. iv b. ii c. iii d. ii e. i
2. a. two b. straight angle c. concurrent lines
d. 10°9'58'' e. 90°
3. a. T b. F c. F d. T e. T
4. a. 67° 5. b. $x = 110°$; Obtuse angle

Test Paper 7

1. a. iii b. i c. iv d. iv e. i
2. a. obtuse b. 35° c. two d. one-fourth
e. 63 m
3. a. F b. T c. T d. F e. T
4. a. i. ∠ACB = 55°, ∠CAB = 46° ii. ∠QPR = 27°, ∠QRP = 23°
5. b. i. 48° ii. 132° iii. 21° iv. 159°

Test Paper 8

1. a. iii b. iii c. i d. i e. i
2. a. 56 b. 17.8 m c. 10,00,000
d. four e. 8, 6, 12
3. a. F b. T c. T d. F e. T
4. a. 20 cm b. 125
5. a. ₹39,520 d. Volume of the cuboid = 2187 cu. cm; Total surface area = 1134 sq. cm

Test Paper 9

1. a. 25 b. White c. 270 d. Green
2. a. iii b. iv c. i d. iv
3. a. T b. F c. F d. T e. T
4.

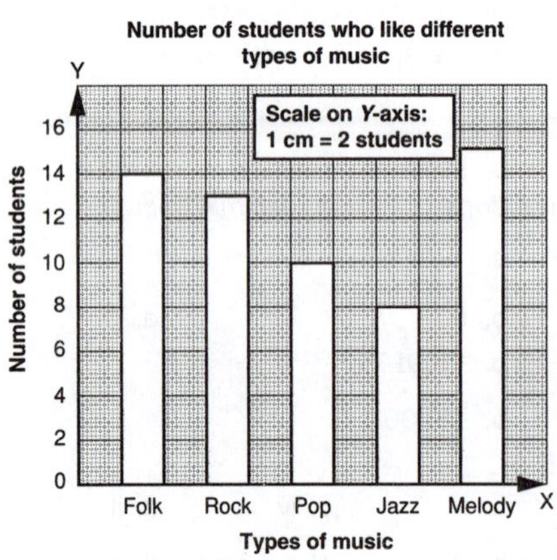

i. Melody ii. 6

b. The details of expenditure of the program in a school

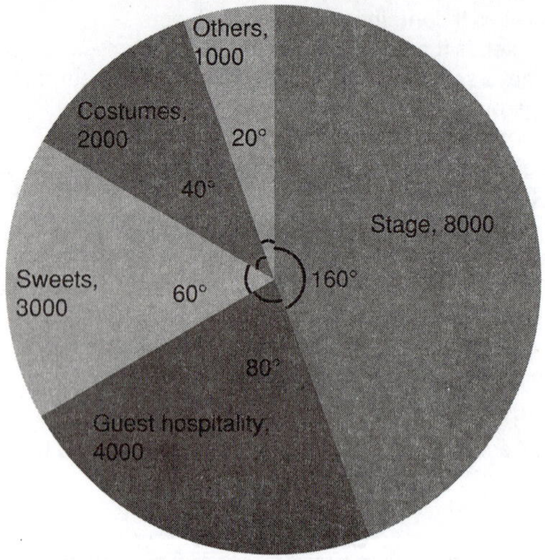

i. Stage ii. ₹18,000

Test Paper 10

1. a. iv b. i
2. a. T b. F c. T
3. a. i. $n(A) = 14$ ii. $n(B) = 7$
b. i. Overlapping sets ii. Disjoint sets
c. i. A ∪ B = {101, 201, 301, 401, 501, 601, 701, 901}; A ∩ B = {101, 301, 501}
ii. A ∪ B = {w, r, o, k, e, n, g, y}; A ∩ B = {r}
d. i.

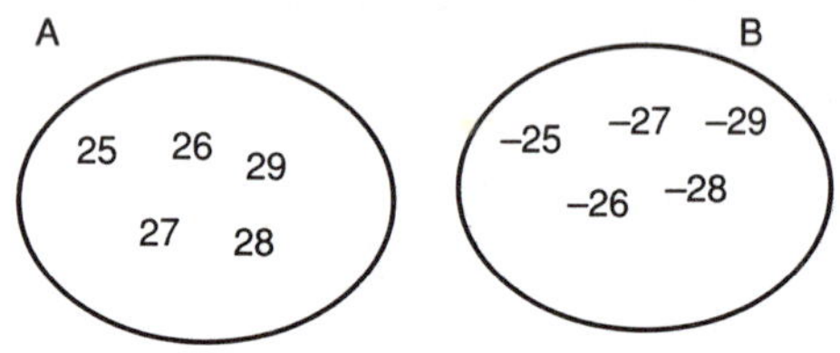

ii.

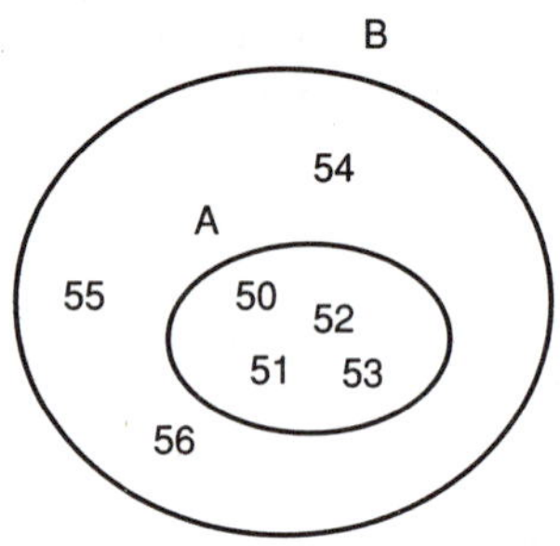

4. a. i. A = {x | x is a multiple of 11, $22 < x < 110$}
ii. B = {x | x is a square number $x < 121$}
iii. C = {x | x is a letter in the sentence 'I love my India'}
b. (Sample answer) i. A = {2, 4, 6, 8} and B = {1, 3, 5, 7}
ii. W = {x | x is a multiple of 25}
iii. N = {x | x is a natural square number, $5 < x < 8$}
c. i. $n(A \cup B) = 9$ and $n(A \cap B) = 4$
ii. $n(A \cup B) = 8$ and $n(A \cap B) = 3$
iii. $n(A \cup B) = 19$ and $n(A \cap B) = 11$
d. i. A = {x | x is a letter in the English alphabet from a to d} and B = {x | x is a letter in the English alphabet from a to h}
ii. A = {x | x is a multiple of 11, $x < 77$} and B = {x | x is a multiple of 12, $x < 84$}
iii. A = {x | x is a prime number, $x < 17$}, B = {x | x is a odd number, $x < 17$} and C = {x | x is an even prime number}